Comprehensive Handbook
of
Christian Doctrine

Comprehensive Handbook

of

Christian Doctrine

John Lawson

Candler School of Theology
Emory University

Prentice-Hall, Inc., *Englewood Cliffs, New Jersey*

Library of Congress Catalog Card Number: 67–10011

Printed in the United States of America: 16552–C

Current printing (last digit):

10 9 8 7 6 5 4 3 2

PRENTICE-HALL INTERNATIONAL., INC., *London*
PRENTICE-HALL OF AUSTRALIA, PTY. LTD., *Sydney*
PRENTICE-HALL OF CANADA, LTD., *Toronto*
PRENTICE-HALL OF INDIA (PRIVATE) LTD., *New Delhi*
PRENTICE-HALL OF JAPAN, INC., *Tokyo*

*to my friends
Claude and Sue Thompson,
faithful witnesses to the Gospel*

Preface

This textbook is designed as introductory reading for students in college and seminary and for the thoughtful Christian laity. It is written for all who wish to make a careful attempt to learn more about the beliefs of the Christian faith and for those who seek guidance in how they may start in the most helpful way.

There are already many handbooks of Christian doctrine for beginners, written with the primary aim of being as simple as possible. Certainly there is a place for these. Yet there are multitudes of thoughtful people who wish to understand their faith in an adult manner and to read a book that goes systematically and comprehensively into all important issues, shirking no difficulty.

There are likewise many standard textbooks of Christian doctrine that do give a careful and complete treatment. However, these are commonly written for professed students of theology and presuppose familiarity with a considerable variety of sometimes difficult technical terms, which become even more obscure when the reader approaches the study of outstanding modern theological writers. There is need, therefore, for an introductory study, which will enable the reader to familiarize himself with the general ground of this subject. In the present book a serious attempt has been made to give a considered treatment to the whole system of Christian theology, such as will provide a secure foundation for further and more detailed study. Yet so far as is possible the work has been written in simple and nontechnical language.

It is anticipated that the use of this textbook will by no means be limited to seminary students. Many colleges give courses in the Bible, and some knowledge of the system of Christian doctrine is a necessary partner in the intelligent study of the Scriptures. It is a well-established position that Christian theology is founded upon the Bible. Accordingly, every care has been taken in this book to provide comprehensive Scripture proofs for the articles of Christian belief. Furthermore, if the Bible is to be understood correctly for the establishment of doctrine it requires interpretation, so that the various parts of Scripture may be given the right order, proportion, and emphasis. And the canon of Biblical interpretation is the system of Christian doctrine, as it has commended itself to the mature and balanced wisdom of the Church.

There are also other classes of careful Christian readers, with less formal purposes in mind. Within the university community there are discussion groups and community lectures. Many churches run Christian workers' schools and adult Sunday-school classes, and there is the private Christian reader. It is hoped that all these may find this book suited to their various interests.

It is impossible to write any essay in theology without adopting, consciously or unconsciously, some particular point of view. Therefore it is well for the Christian writer candidly to state his own conviction. It will be found that the main substance of this book is a treatment of the system of Christian thought as it has been accepted by the historic Church. There are indeed some critics who will declare that there is no such thing as an "accepted" Christian position. These will argue that a large part of what has been taught as the Christian faith is simply a reflection of the general secular thought of the time, as it has evolved in successive periods. This is virtually to deny that the Christian religion is a continuous historic faith. If this proposition is pressed to an extreme, as some modern writers do, the effect at the beginning of the process is to explain away the Gospel portrait of Christ as largely the imaginative construction of the early Church. The effect at the end is for the modern theologian to affirm that he has the right to reconstruct the Christian religion into something radically different from what it has been through the centuries. The present writer must make his testimony that he cannot follow this way of thinking.

It is to be admitted, we judge, that the intellectual robes which have been used in successive ages to display Christ to the world are borrowed from the thought forms natural to the period. Candid allowance is certainly to be made for this factor, both in the reading of the New Testament and in the understanding of later Christian doctrine. Nevertheless, we venture upon the basic affirmation that it is only possible to make a rational understanding of the great historical phenomenon of Christianity by allowing that the Christian faith is a historic faith, as indeed it has always claimed to be. It is not a system of human ideas accepted as wise and good, but a witness to an act performed by God in history. Here, we believe, is the continuous element. Although the intellectual robes have been modified many times, the Christ within remains recognizably the same.

Thus in successive doctrinal controversies and restatements there have commonly been expressed extreme views, which have displayed one authentic aspect of the Christian truth at the expense of other and complementary truths. An unbalanced pronouncement of truth is always in error. Furthermore, there have been minglings of Christian and non-Christian elements, whenever the attempt to improve the robes of Christ has changed the very Christ Himself. Nevertheless, we believe that in each age there has also been discovered a central, comprehensive, and balanced position of Christian interpretation, and that all through the ages a long line of development recognizably connects those central positions, from the first preaching of Christ to the present. Thus, though it has no simply defined "sharp edges," there is in fact an "accepted" Christian position, which comes to the modern seeker as the authoritative divine counsel of the ages.

We submit that the historic Christian theological tradition is an intellectual and spiritual system so spacious, so well balanced and well articulated, and so tested by experience, that it well merits the deep respect even of those moderns who do not personally accept every part of it. Thus the teacher of theology, no matter how zealous he be to introduce his students to the findings of the distinctive modern writers, has not really done justice to his great subject unless he has first brought his hearers to appreciate something of the majesty of the traditional system. And the student likewise, no matter how radical be his findings at the end, has not truly and honestly exercised his mind if he has never exercised it upon this great Christian system. Therefore the main structure of this textbook is a comprehensive outline of historic Christian theology.

Nevertheless, the Christian writer must seek to be comprehensive in a further way. There is, as we have argued, a recognizable Christian tradition that unites the apparently separated parts of the church. The denominational confessions are largely in accord with regard to their main structure. Nevertheless, these confessions are not at one at every point. Therefore it is necessary that at these certain points we punctuate our system with a "Summary of Divergence." One or two of these summaries answer important disputes in the ancient church. Many more, and the more important, concern differences that emerged between Roman Catholicism and the main body of Protestantism at the Reformation and between various schools of Protestant thought after the Reformation. Some other of these summaries have to do with issues that arose particularly in the nineteenth century, in connection with the relation of natural science to the authority of the Bible. Others belong to the modern period, and are chiefly concerned with the effort of certain theologians to restate the doctrine of God and His relation to the world, and also with the challenge of radical criticism to the historical character of the Gospel narrative. In all these cases a sincere attempt will be made to place the leading views alongside one another as fairly and dispassionately as possible, so that the reader may make his thoughtful judgment.

It is hoped that in this way the book will be found comprehensive of the doctrinal standpoint of the chief historic Christian denominations, and will illuminate alike the extent to which they are agreed in doctrine and the precise nature of their divergences. The elimination of misunderstanding on both these scores is important in a period when the Ecumenical movement attracts so much attention. It is also hoped that the book may prove comprehensive of both conservative and radical views, and so serve as an introduction to the modern dialogue. The writer must, however, plead for the indulgence of those who feel themselves committed to the advocacy of particular views. It is not possible in the space available to do full justice to all the competing schools of thought, with full citation of supporting authorities. The most one can hope for is a brief summary which, if not complete, will at least not be found misleading.

One of the happiest tasks of an author is to pay that tribute of thanks which is justly due to friends who have helped in his work. I am deeply in debt to the dean, the faculty, and the students of the Candler School of Theology for providing that fellowship of Christian devotion, study, and discussion which alone provides the occasion for the writing of Christian theology. In particular are my thanks due to one of the best of friends, Dr. Claude H. Thompson, Professor of Systematic Theology, who has rendered invaluable help by his constant encouragement and by the painstaking reading and criticism of the whole manuscript. I would also like to thank a number of successive faculty secretaries for cheerful and efficient aid in typing and retyping the work. In particular I am grateful to Mrs. Virginia Boland, who has helped me so splendidly in the final revision.

J. L.

Contents

Comprehensive Handbook

of

Christian Doctrine

Chapter One

Belief in God

I believe in God the Father Almighty,
maker of heaven and earth

I. I Believe

A. Definition of Faith

The word "faith" is commonly used in two different senses, which must be carefully distinguished.

1. There is the body of teaching about God, Christ, man, and salvation, which is the intellectual substratum to religious devotion and obedience. This is "The Faith," as in Galatians 1:23; Ephesians 4:5; Jude 3.

2. There is the human experience of being confronted immediately by God in the secret place of the heart, of being held by Him, and of holding on to Him in trust, depending upon Him in all things. At its deepest this is the experience of union in loving personal trust with the God who has made Himself known in His crucified and risen incarnate Son. This is "faith": Christian saving faith (see pp. 221–22).

To bring out something of the importance of this distinction of usage it will suffice to say that the teacher who claims, quite rightly, that true religion is founded upon objective facts and sound reason, is arguing in terms of (1). The teacher who maintains, equally rightly, that mere orthodoxy does not make a man into a Christian, but that he must come to a living personal faith, is discussing the matter in terms of (2). Neither side logically needs to deny what the other says about Christian belief, but they

1

may seem to be contrary, on account of differences in usage of the word "believe."

B. The Ground of Faith

The vast majority of Christian believers do not come to their religious faith by being argued into it, either by texts from the Bible or by venerable ecclesiastical authority or by the latest learned book. Commonly they start with the experience of worship, though some would emphasize the place of ethical experience. In some moment of worship, either prayer or the devotional reading of the Bible or the sacrament or song, or in the challenge of awakening preaching, the soul becomes aware of the sense of the presence of God, with a solemn and mysterious awe. Normally the first stages of this divine encounter happen when children are taken to church by their parents, or pray at home, before they have any self-conscious and reasoned thought on the subject. Sometimes there is also in adult life a conscious crisis of divine encounter. This walk of the soul with God is immediate, personal, and mysterious. Like an ear for music or an eye for beauty, this form of "faith" is a gift which some few persons appear to enjoy to an exceptional extent, and which makes them the rightful spiritual leaders of their fellows. Many more possess it to a more moderate extent, though the gift may be developed by training and discipline, while a few sadly and mysteriously appear to enjoy it hardly at all.

Religion, therefore, normally starts with what may be termed "the devotional experience." The thoughtful person, who wishes to bring his whole life to a rational system, then naturally proceeds to reflect about this experience. He will examine it critically to determine whether it is indeed a reasonable and trustworthy form of human experience, or a subjective delusion. He will draw out its logical conclusions, and frame them in terms of the apparatus of thought proper to his time. Thus a *theology* is formed.

C. Religious Authority

We cannot escape the question whether or not it is possible to be certain about religion, and if so, what the organ of this certainty is. In times when the Christian witness has been faced by a searching challenge, those parts of the Church have endured best which have made the most satisfactory appearance of speaking to the people with a reasonable yet confident authority. At the same time, the circumstance that there are competing systems of authority shows that it is not easy to define the proper nature of Christian certainty. The confusion arises because, corresponding naturally to the two uses of the word "faith" which we have noticed, there are two chief aspects of religious authority.

1. There is the authority which can bring to the inquirer a rational degree of certainty that he has a sound grasp of "The Faith," considered as a body

of doctrine. Within this sphere authority is a matter of fact, not of feeling, and the organ of it is largely corporate, rather than purely individual.

   For the Christian, The Faith is based in the first place upon the record of the facts about Christ: namely, the account of the preparation of the world for His coming, His spiritual background, His wonderful birth and life, His character, teaching, death, and resurrection. The only record of these facts is in the Bible, and therefore The Faith is founded on the Bible. Hence is deduced the traditional Christian position that every true Christian doctrine must be in accord with Scripture. However, the Bible was written by men who in the main were more interested in spiritual devotion and moral obedience than in systematic theology. Their doctrine is implicit more often than explicit. Therefore the Bible needs to be interpreted, that one may verify the historical facts about Christ, and understand aright the spiritual and theological implications of what He was and what He did. The doctrine implicit in Scripture requires to be made explicit, and to be focused into carefully framed and unambiguous terms. Simple Christian believers do not necessarily need to understand this technical theology in order to come to God in Christ, and to partake of salvation. The preaching of the gospel is based on the plain facts of The Faith, as recorded in Scripture, not on the theological theories constructed to explain the facts. Nevertheless, a teacher of The Faith must seek to understand this theology, for only so can he give reliable guidance on the way his hearers are to understand the facts recorded in the Bible.

   This interpretative and safeguarding activity of the theologian is an activity of divinely guided reason, and is in the last resort a scholarly activity. It is therefore a corporate activity. Christian truth is rich and various. Some parts of it make a natural appeal to some individuals, and some to others. Therefore there may be an apparent tension between the Christian Faith as it is understood by one historical period or school of thought, and by another. The apprehension of Christian truth proper to men of many different temperaments, casts of mind, walks of life, and social and racial backgrounds, needs to be brought together into a developing world-wide consensus of Christian thought, under the guidance of the Holy Spirit. Theologians supplement one another, correct one another, and discipline one another, by heeding the long experience of the past, and by maintaining intellectual and spiritual fellowship with one another in the present. Purely individualist thought is ever in danger of being found partial, unbalanced, subjective, and erroneous. Corporate thought is well considered, balanced, comprehensive, and reliable. Thus if correct doctrine and morals are to be established from the Bible it requires to be interpreted by the Church. The guide into a rational degree of certainty on points of doctrine is the witness of Scripture, interpreted and understood by the reasoning activity of the living tradition of the whole Church, guided as she is by the

Holy Spirit. That which is accepted as The Faith by the whole of the universal, or Catholic, Church is the reliable and orthodox Faith, that is to say, the Catholic Faith.[1]

Christian teachers who speak of religious authority in terms of the Church and her historic creed, and who uphold religious certainty with the threefold cord of Scripture, tradition, and reason, have in mind chiefly the kind of authority which can assure the inquiring mind regarding "The Faith."

— 2. We then ask what sort of authority can hope to bring to the human soul certainty in "faith," that is, in the experience of the divine encounter, in reverence, trust, love, and obedience. This is a very different matter! A teacher may be thoroughly versed in knowledge of the Bible and of theology, and so have a most authoritative grasp of "The Faith," and yet have in his own life no vivid sense of God, no compelling urge for obedience to God, and no power to communicate the sense of God to others. His religion is a dry academic orthodoxy. What is it, then, which can quicken "The Faith," so that it makes personal appeal in the human heart, and gives birth to "faith"?

The quickening of faith is nothing less than the immediate activity of God Himself upon the human heart. Faith is a gift, and the gift of faith is the work of the Holy Spirit (1 Corinthians 12:3; Ephesians 2:8). The "seeing eye," to which God is the most pressing reality of life, is akin to the artist's view, the musician's ear, or the poet's tongue. It is a wonderful faculty, which can indeed be developed and trained by disciplined human response, but which is itself an implanted "gift." The means which God uses to quicken the gift of faith are very commonly corporate—the Christian family and school, the evangelistic service, or the sacraments of the Church. Nevertheless, though the means to the gift are corporate, the gift itself is essentially individual. Each man meets God in the loneliness of his own heart. No man can go proxy for another in this solemn transaction. The time and the manner in which the gift is bestowed remains a divine mystery (John 3:8).

Those who insist that true spiritual religion is individual and personal,

---

1 The word "Catholic" suffers seriously from confusion, through being used in varying senses. The Roman Catholic calls his own communion "the Catholic Church" to register the claim that his is the only properly ordered and authenticated Church. Though he will acknowledge that his "separated brethren" are in a real sense Christians, and are in some sense a part of the Church, yet he has to maintain that their parts of the Church are not properly ordered and disciplined. Many Protestants, who do not acknowledge this claim, call the Roman Catholic Church "the Catholic Church" as a matter of common but theologically careless parlance. In this book, where the Roman Catholic Church is referred to, it is always spoken of as such. By "the Catholic Church" is meant the whole body of historic and orthodox Christianity, of which the Roman Catholic Church is an important part. "The Catholic Faith" is the faith of the Catholic Church, that is, the fundamental body of orthodox and essential belief which unites all the parts of the Catholic Church, as distinct from particular theological opinions emphasized by particular denominations or schools of thought (see p. 143).

and not just a matter of the Church, with her sacraments, institutions, and creeds; and that certainty in the religious life is founded upon "personal experience," are trying to say just this.

Summary of Divergence: Doctrines of Authority

a. Traditional

The general attitude of the ancient Church was that true doctrine is founded on Scripture, and that the Church, as the guardian of Scripture, is the authoritative interpreter of Scripture. The organ of this authority is particularly the episcopate, and the writings of the authoritative Church fathers of bygone ages. The bishops who are in succession to the apostles, particularly as they meet together in council, reliably interpret Scripture, so as to guard the Church from heresy. In particular, an Ecumenical (universal) or General Council of bishops, speaking for the whole Church, is empowered under the guidance of the Holy Spirit to make a fully authoritative determination of orthodox faith or practice for the universal Church. This is still the attitude of the Eastern, or Orthodox, Churches. They account the first seven General Councils of the Church, which took place before the division of the Eastern and Western (or Latin) Churches, to be true Ecumenical Councils. Since then it has not been possible to hold any councils fully authoritative for the universal Church. Thus continuing ecclesiastical authority is in abeyance. Authority rests on antiquity.

b. Roman Catholic

In western Europe during the Middle Ages the Pope was gradually accorded a greater share of the determining power within the Council of Bishops, until the Papacy became the predominating voice of ecclesiastical authority. A Roman Catholic would affirm that this development was the rightful and necessary outworking of the promise which Christ made to St. Peter (see p. 141). The aftermath of the disputes attendant upon the Protestant Reformation made it necessary for the Roman Catholic Church at the Council of Trent (1546–1563) further to define her doctrine of religious authority. It was there decided, in antithesis to Protestantism, that there is a twofold organ of dogmatic authority in the Church. Written Scripture and the unwritten tradition of the Church are in partnership. The ancient fathers of the Church may also be cited as a true authority. It is not the position of the Roman Catholic Church that ecclesiatical authority can determine doctrine in opposition to Scripture. It is affirmed that all true Christian doctrine is in accord with Scripture. Nevertheless, the tradition of the Church is a true authority in its own right, so that ecclesiastical authority is not limited simply to the power to interpret Scripture.

It is noteworthy that some modern Roman Catholic and Protestant discussion of the relation of Scripture to tradition appears to be moving to a position of greater mutual understanding, and perhaps ultimately to common ground. Thus Protestant New Testament scholarship is familiar with the circumstance that Christian faith was first transmitted in unwritten tradition, and that this was later recorded as the apostolic writings. On the other hand, some Roman Catholic scholars may now be found to restate the position of the Council of Trent in the following way. God's Christian revelation was in the first place the impact of the person and acts of Christ. The single witness to this revelation was in the first place the oral tradition of the Church, and was then recorded in the writings of the New Testament. The tradition of the Church guaranteed these writings and determined the authoritative canon of the New Testament. Furthermore, the New Testament can only be understood in light of the faith and life of the community which gave it birth. It is not the case that some Christian doctrines are supported by Scripture and others by the tradition of the Church. Written tradition, interpreted aright in the necessary context of the unwritten but living tradition of the Church, is the witness to the unified Christian Faith. A salient example of this process in action is the argument stated in relation to our Lord's institution of the Eucharist (see p. 143). The foundation for the Church's belief is our Lord's recorded words of institution, but these precious yet enigmatic words require to be interpreted in light of the evident conviction and usage of the ancient Church.

The growing predominance of the Papacy within the Council of Bishops culminated in the promulgation of the dogma of the Infallibility of the Pope, at the Vatican Council of 1870. This dogma does not involve the claim that all papal pronouncements of every sort are free from error. The doctrine thus defined is that when, after all the authorities within the Church have duly conferred, the Pope as earthly head of the Church determines the considered mind of the Church upon some matter of faith or morals by an authoritative public statement on behalf of the Church, then that pronouncement is final and without error, and is to be accepted by all the faithful as fully authoritative. It is noteworthy that the recent Vatican Council has to some extent balanced and complemented this doctrine by a new affirmation of the ancient position that all bishops are teaching and governing bishops in their own right, by succession from the apostles. Thus their right authoritatively to confer in a General Council is a real one, though the Pope is still the acknowledged infallible head. Furthermore, in scholarly Roman Catholic circles an increasing effort is being made to vindicate the position that ecclesiastical authority is not to be used to silence the new findings of reverent and sober Biblical scholarship. Thus the scriptural element in religious authority is also being reaffirmed within the Roman Catholic Church.

c. Protestant

The classic Protestant doctrine of religious authority is expressed in the phrase *"sola Scriptura"—Scripture alone.* It is not intended by this formula to assert that the meaning of every part of the Bible is self-evident, so that the corporate scholarly activity of interpretation is unnecessary. What is meant is that Christian scholars should not bring their human opinions or prepossessions to the Bible, but should reverently seek to be molded in their thinking by the Bible, which alone is the God-given authority within the Church. It is affirmed that if, under the guidance of the Holy Spirit, the careful student of the Bible seeks to interpret obscure passages of Scripture in the light of plain ones, and texts of secondary import in light of leading texts, that then the whole will fall into place. The Bible will thus constitute a self-sufficient authority on Christian faith and practice.

Note on the above.

It would appear to the present writer that the validity of the classic Protestant doctrine of religious authority is more clearly seen when it is applied to that aspect of authority which has been defined under point (*C2*), that is, the authority which brings "saving faith," rather than "The Faith."

Experience shows that one of the chief means which God uses to bring the experience of the divine encounter is the devotional reading and evangelical preaching of the Bible. The great prophetic and devotional chapters of both the Old Testament and the New are full of a sense that the most pressing reality of life is a God of sovereign majesty and love. As we look on the work of a great and sensitive artist we come to appreciate a beauty in a landscape or a face, which unaided we would never have fully observed. As we look in company with the artist, and through his eyes, we begin to see. In the same way, as we look out on life as it is seen from the viewpoint of the Bible writers we see it as it truly exists under the eye of God. Supremely, it is by seeing Christ in all His beauty and majesty that man meets God (Matthew 11:27; John 1:14, 18). Clearly, the Gospel record is the secure ground for this distinctively Christian form of religious experience. Thus the proverbial "open Bible" in the hand of the humble believer can and does speak with an immediate divine authority. Christ steps out of the page, and makes Himself real to the heart.

It has to be admitted that "the open Bible" in the hand of the simple believer does not of itself suffice to guarantee that he will come to a sound grasp of Christian doctrine. When the great Protestant Reformers speak of the right of the private believer to read the Bible, and of the sufficiency of Scripture for salvation, they tacitly assume that the reader already has an effective grasp of "The Faith." He accepts the Church, and her creed and sacraments, and reads the Bible from this believing point of view. Yet as he reads he is seeking to go on from "The Faith" to *faith,* to the saving "faith which works by love." He is not seeking to establish a purely private and individual authority for Scripture exposition or for doctrine (2 Peter 1:20).

d. Anglican

The doctrine of religious authority developed in the Church of England, following the Reformation period, represents a characteristic effort to find a mediating position between the Roman Catholic and classic Protestant views. In substance it followed the ancient traditional position, but sought to find a clearer vindication for the primary authority of Scripture than was apparent in much current Roman Catholic teaching. It has been held that authority rests upon the threefold foundation of Scripture, tradition, and reason. In matters of doctrine, morals, and Church practice which appear to be securely determined by Scripture, Scripture is affirmed to be the sufficient and final authority. However, there are other matters which are not clearly determined by Scripture, and here tradition, that is, the general usage and consensus of the Church, is of effective authority. It is characteristic of the Anglican position regarding tradition that chief weight is given to the usage and consensus of the first four or five Christian centuries, to the Church fathers of this early period, and to the first four Ecumenical Councils. It has been felt that the ancient Church was more manifestly united, and more free from corrupt accretions, than in later centuries. Ecclesiastical tradition originating only from the Middle Ages has been an object of reserve, or even suspicion, in contradistinction to the Roman Catholic position. The third element of reason finds place in that Scripture is to be expounded always according to competent and honest learning, and that traditional usages and ideas are to be placed under critical scrutiny. That which is ancient is to be followed where possible, but not simply because it is ancient.

Summary of Divergence : Existential Theology

a. Definition

Thinkers and philosophers have usually assumed that "behind" or "above" the world of matter and space and events passing around us, there is an invisible order of universal principles, which are intellectual or spiritual. By careful rational thought, or by the sudden enlightenment which comes in the moment of meditation, it is possible for man to grasp something of these principles, and so come to an understanding of the "meaning" of the world and of human life. The so-called existentialist philosophy is a mode of thought which repudiates this endeavor to rise above our existence in this world to a general intellectual order. It regards as a fruitless task the search for an overarching speculative "meaning." All that man can do is to receive the immediate impact of experience, and to find himself as a human being by resolutely reacting to it. Existentialist theology is a modern attempt to use this philosophy as a thought form for the expression of the essential Christian message.

b. Affirmative Statement

The exponents of this theology affirm that the existentialist philosophy is the mode of thought natural to the modern man in the age of science. Therefore if Christian faith is to be made intelligible to him, so as to win his respect as credible, it must be rendered into the thought forms of this system, in the same way that Christian theology has employed other current philosophies in past periods.

It is also affirmed that this position accords with biblical thought, and with the earliest Christian thought. The Hebrews, unlike the Greeks, were not interested in abstract speculative thought, or in the reflective search for a supposed "higher" order of general intellectual principles. In biblical thinking, God always acts immediately upon the world and upon man, while the concern of the man of God is always with immediate devotional experience and moral obedience, not with speculative doctrine. Thus biblical thought is "existential," as was the thought of the first Church. The first disciples did not first receive a doctrine that their Lord was divine by nature, and then on this account go on to worship Him and trust Him as divine. It was the other way about. They received an immediate experience that in the life of Christ God had met them in His person, His love, and His saving power. Out of this existential experience they confessed Him in trust and worship as their divine Lord, and from this point elaborated the doctrine of His divine nature.

Existential theology strongly emphasizes that it is not possible to "prove" the truth of the Christian religion either by arguments from the probability of historical fact (for example, efforts to demonstrate the fact of Christ's physical resurrection), or by arguments to demonstrate the reasonableness of the system of Christian doctrine (for example, by the traditional "proofs of the existence of God"). The sole and sufficient ground of the Christian Faith is the act of faith, that is, the response in decision, love, and trust, made when God encounters man.

c. Critical Statement

The exponent of the traditional Christian Faith can allow that this case is one aspect of the truth. Thus "Christian existentialism" may in some writers be no more than an exaggerated statement of the traditional Christian position that the essence of Christian faith is not just the acceptance of a body of speculative doctrine, but includes a life of personal trust in, and obedience to, the Saviour. So it is possible for an uneducated believer, who does not understand Christian theology, to be a genuine Christian. However, from the point of view of the established Christian system, the existential scheme, if taken to an extreme, comes dangerously near to an attempt to maintain "faith" (that is, loving and obedient trust in God) apart from its necessary intellectual and rational foundation in "The Faith" (that is, the Church's historic witness to the facts about Christ, and the doctrine formulated to expound and safeguard the meaning of these facts).

Some would question whether modern man is in fact so captivated by the existential philosophy that it is necessary to make a radical reconstruction of the Christian Faith in order to communicate it to him. However, it is to be accepted that Hebrew and biblical thought is concrete rather than abstract, practical and devotional rather than speculative. Furthermore, the faith of the first Church in her divine

Lord did apparently grow up in just this way. The experience of salvation was the cause, and the doctrine to expound this experience the consequence (see pp. 42–43, 47). Again, the Church from the very beginning has been aware that the most compelling demonstration of even so remarkable a fact as Christ's empty tomb will not drive unbelieving men to have faith (Luke 16:31; see pp. 101–2). Nor have the wiser theologians of the Church ever assumed that arguments in support of Christian belief, no matter how cogent, will ever of themselves suffice to constrain men from unbelief.

However, many writers who style themselves as Christian existentialists, finding natural allies in the "demythologizing" exegetes of the New Testament (see pp. 35–36), appear to go much further than this, and to advance upon what the traditional theologian regards as most dangerous ground. For example, arguing from the admitted fact that some heard the message of the empty tomb, yet did not receive faith, it has been affirmed that the supposed fact of the empty tomb is not important for faith, or even, to push the matter to the extreme, that the empty tomb is not a fact. So it has been taught that Christ died on the Cross and moldered in the tomb, while the disciples, reflecting upon His morally victorious life, received an "existential" experience that He had triumphed over death, and constructed the legend of the empty tomb in order vividly to symbolize this conviction of faith, and to communicate it to others. This is a salient example of a general treatment. So the Christ of historical fact more or less withers away, while a "Christ of faith," known chiefly or solely in the heart, remains.

To the traditional Christian this appears an incredible account of the origin of the Christian Faith and the Christian Church, and of the New Testament literature (see pp. 194–200). He feels that apart from the marvelous facts of God's action in history Christian faith would not have come into existence. Apart from continued belief in the historical facts faith will not continue. Furthermore, he will affirm that this is to make the Christian religion into a matter of subjective opinion. It ceases to be a gospel of God's saving power in Christ, actually exerted in the course of the history of this world, in which man can trust. It becomes at best a call to man to follow in his own strength a body of ethical teaching, at worst an invitation that he expose himself to autosuggestion, or even mass hysteria. To knock away the appeal to proved historical fact, and to the rational system of doctrine, in the supposed interests of "faith" is to make the Christian religion into something quite other than it has always been, and entirely to denature it as a religion of grace (see pp. 83–84).

II. God the Father Almighty

A. Definition

God may be defined in the broadest terms as the uncaused cause of all things which exist. He is the ultimate origin and sovereign governing principle of all.

B. Transcendence and Immanence

Christian theology holds that God is transcendent. This means that He is more than the governing principle of all things. He exists in His own right, apart from His creation. Thus there is a great division of existence between God, who from eternity alone is self-existent, and all other things which exist. The universe is His creation, and He is superior to it and in control of it. He existed in full perfection of being before the universe came into existence. This carries the implication that God is a spiritual being. That is to say, He does not have any kind of material body, and does not exist in any manner of place, any more than His being is confined to time.[2]

Christian theology also holds that God is immanent, which means that the transcendent God is not remote from the created universe, as though He cannot have direct contact with it, and act in it and through it. The Christian believes that God is in constant sovereign control of everything which exists, from the vastest galaxies to the most minute atomic particles. The natural laws which all these things obey are not a mere lifeless and careless mechanism. They are an expression of His control.

C. A Personal God

It is a fundamental article of the Christian Faith that God is a personal God. This means that the transcendent God is a thinking and feeling being, who knows Himself to be Himself, a being separate from and superior to His creation, of which He is the intelligent sovereign ruler. The contact and control of the immanent God is an intelligent and thoughtful control, not a bare law of action (Matthew 10:29). God is indeed the principle of existence and of "values," moral, intellectual, and aesthetic. He is (to use the phrase popularized by Tillich) "the ground of being." Yet Christian theology has insisted that language of this kind, though not untrue, should not be used in such a way as to obscure the vitally important truth that God is also a thinking, feeling, living, active being, who is personally interested in us. It is almost superfluous to cite texts to illustrate this doctrine, for it is the presupposition of every part of the Bible. The leading and most striking biblical phrase to express the idea of a personal God is "the living God" (Deuteronomy 5:26; Jeremiah 10:10; Acts 14:15). The most important consequence for religion of the personal nature of God is that it is possible for man to have personal fellowship with Him (Exodus 33:11). Thus worship is not just meditation about God. It is communion with God. It is to express the idea that God is personal that Christian theology speaks of God as "He," not "It."

---

2 The charge has sometimes been leveled by critics against traditional Christianity that it has taught that God exists in a place "above" or "beyond" the universe, which view must now be given up as unscientific. This would appear to be an injustice. Simple and uneducated Christians may indeed often have pictured God as in some sort of remote place, but such a view has never been part of the Christian system, as correctly understood. It is however difficult to do without a *symbolical* use of such terms as above.

D. The Father

The distinctive Christian title for God, as He is known as the creator and governor of the universe, is "the Father." This was the usage Christians learned from our Lord (Matthew 6:9). In the family a father is the source of his child. He is superior to his child, in a position of government over him, and of responsibility for him. He is also a loving and self-sacrificing superior. The word "Father" as applied to God therefore aptly indicates the two contrasting propositions that God is the one who gives to us our being, infinitely superior to us, the governor at whose absolute disposal we are, and also that He loves us and is interested in us with personal and sympathetic care.

E. Almighty

This word, as used in Christian thought, indicates that God is the sovereign ruler of all things. There is no power outside Himself which can frustrate His purpose (Isaiah 43:13). There is no sphere of existence where His law does not fully apply (Psalm 139:7–12). The word does not mean that God is a God of arbitrary might, who is unaccountable in His dealings with man, or that there is no conceivable thing which God cannot do. He is a morally and rationally accountable God, who is never inconsistent with Himself (2 Timothy 2:13). Thus even God cannot make man both morally free and also incapable of sinning. In creating man He has for an entirely good and wise end used His sovereign will to limit somewhat the exercise of His own sovereignty. In consequence, it is possible for events to happen in a world ruled by a sovereign God which are nevertheless not the direct will of God, though they are permitted by Him.

F. The Use of Symbolical Language

The use of the term "Father" introduces the reader to the employment in theology of symbolical language. Symbolism is a form of expression which, superficially at any rate, appears to be alien to the factual and "common-sense" language natural to the modern world. It is therefore often a subject of misunderstanding.

It is clear that to call God "the Father" is to take a word out of human experience, and to make of it a comparison or imaginative mental picture of that which is beyond direct human experience. This is what is meant by saying that the term "Father" as theologically applied to God is a *symbol*. The word "Father" is not a factual description of God, to be taken literally. The nature of God is beyond direct human experience of this world, and therefore He cannot be described in matter-of-fact language. His nature is to be set forth in the medium of imaginative word pictures. This principle of symbolic expression holds true of all those parts of Christian doctrine which concern matters which are outside the sphere of direct human experience, such as the beginning and the end of the creation, the origin of evil, and the destiny of the human soul.

Some critics[3] have argued that in attempting to discuss heavenly things Christian theology is guilty of using words in variable, unreal, and misleading senses, and is entangled in radical intellectual stultification. Thus if the word "Father" is taken seriously it would appear to indicate that the Christian thinks of God as a superior kind of man. God is the comforting "image" of a protective being which the subconscious mind has suggested after the image of man himself. In response the theologian attempts to clarify his case, and, as the critic will claim, conducts a partial forced retreat. He now allows that God is indeed a Father, but not as a human father is a father. God has no body, and has not procreated us. Yet, the theologian argues, he rightly uses the highest aspects of human nature as a symbol.

The critic's attack may then be renewed by speaking of the proverbial innocent child, dying painfully of some horrible disease. How is this consistent with a doctrine of God's fatherly love? So the theologian restates his case yet again, allowing that the word "love" is also a symbol when applied to God. There are indeed dark things in life which one finds hard to understand, yet the believer trusts that God's wisdom is higher than ours. He loves, but he does not love as a human father loves. He loves with a higher, though at times a mysterious, love. Thus the skeptic's charge is that in Christian theology the proper meaning of language has been eroded, inch by inch, in "the death of a thousand cuts." The theologian is seeking to know the unknowable, and to conceal his obscurity of thought by playing fast and loose with words.

In replying to this charge the Christian has first to admit that there is an element of truth in it. The theologian does indeed need at times to use symbolical language. Furthermore, a word drawn from the language of experience, and used as a symbol, does have a special meaning attached to it for this purpose. This meaning must be understood if the symbolism is to convey truth and not error. The symbol must not be taken in its matter-of-fact sense. So much is to be allowed. However, it is a common but serious confusion to speak of "mere" symbolism, as though literal and matter-of-fact language represents secure and rational knowledge, whereas symbolical language represents the fanciful, the unsubstantial, the unimportant. In every branch of knowledge the higher truths have to be expressed in symbolism appropriate to the subject. This is true in science. The initial stages of research are matter-of-fact: weighing, measuring, counting, directly or indirectly. The higher stage is a formula to demonstrate a general principle deduced from the experimental data. A scientific formula is a particular kind of *symbol*. This is the case with religious thought also. By the use of meaningful imaginative symbols the mind can advance from the world of immediate spiritual experience into the realm of spiritual principles. The comparison is never entirely adequate. Symbolism does not give a perfect knowledge of the world of God. Yet we need not feel that it leaves man

---

[3] Logical positivists.

with an illusion. The Christian believes that it gives man the most real knowledge of heavenly things which he can have in this world, and knowledge which will not be discredited when he comes to higher knowledge in heaven.

III. Arguments for the Existence of God

A. Fundamental Assumptions

Around us is the *universe*—the physical universe known to science. It comprises everything which exists physically from galaxies to atomic particles, including all living creatures, and man. It can be assumed by the thinker, as he takes up from the very start the process of thought, either that the universe corresponds to a rational plan, or that it does not. There seem to be no other possible basic assumptions. We may say that there is no prior train of argument which can be used either to prove or to disprove either of these fundamental assumptions. This is where the process of thought arises. The validity of the assumptions can only be tested by considering the final result which issues from proceeding upon them.

1. If it be assumed that the universe corresponds to a rational plan these consequences appear to follow: (a) Objects do not exist, nor events happen, without a sufficient prior cause.[4] (b) The process of rational thought corresponds to the very nature of existence, and if carried out correctly can lead to knowledge of ultimate principles of the truth regarding existence. Careful examination of the physical universe, and correct argument from the data observed, can rise above the universe, and lead to knowledge of the plan to which the universe corresponds. (c) This basic assumption of a rational plan to the universe makes possible the scientific outlook. (d) It also, so the Christian affirms, makes possible religious knowledge.

2. If, on the other hand, it is assumed that the physical universe does not correspond to a rational plan, an alternative set of consequences appears to follow: (a) There is no ground for assuming that objects or events correspond to a sufficient rational cause, so it is a waste of time to inquire why objects exist or events happen. (b) The reasoning human mind does not necessarily correspond to the nature of things. Therefore there is no ground for supposing that thought can lead to the knowledge of general and eternal principles of truth. (c) This reduces philosophy to the mere discussion of what one decides different words shall mean, and how logical argument ought to be arranged. (d) Science is reduced from a way of

---

[4] A critic may observe at this point that strictly speaking it is not possible to prove that event A (commonly called the "cause") *makes* event B (commonly called the "effect") happen. All we can say is that so far as we can observe, when event A happens event B always happens immediately afterwards. There is an observed fixed pattern of behavior. The affirmation that this pattern of behavior *is* fixed is one of the chief principles of physical science. However, we are not arguing this point here, regarding "causation." What we are stating is that the fixed pattern of behavior itself does not exist without a sufficient rational cause to make it happen.

fundamental understanding to a mere description of the universe, and to practical methods of making machines. (e) Religion is reduced to a set of unsubstantial subjective feelings.

Thus alternative (2) yields a radical skepticism regarding abstract thought or eternal spiritual principles. The Christian theologian has to admit that it is not possible by logical argument to drive the radical skeptic off his chosen ground. As we have stated above, it is a basic assumption made before the process of argument starts. Nevertheless, one is confident that this solution to the problems of thought will not permanently hold the allegiance of thinking humanity. It is a solution which chiefly commends itself in a period of strain and disillusionment, when men are inclined to despair of coming to an understanding of human life. However, the thinking mind has a deep implanted desire to see all things reduced to order and rational principles, and demonstrated as the outcome of an intelligible plan. This desire will not permanently be denied by an *a priori* assurance that this cannot be done. In particular, if science itself is not a system for the understanding of exist-ence, the ground is cut away from beneath the feet of the radical skeptic himself, for he claims to base himself upon "the scientific attitude"!

The theologian, then, will take up alternative (1) as for him the truly constructive intellectual attitude. He will assume that the universe corres-ponds to a rational plan. One does not look for a logical proof of this, argued from prior principles. The "proof" of the rightness of this assumption must be provided by experience of where the process of thought leads in the end. It will stand or fall by the degree of justice which it does to the existence of the human mind, and by the satisfaction which it brings to the desire of the mind to see reason and order displayed in all things.

B. General Statement

If the universe corresponds to a rational plan the following train of consequences is to be observed.

1. That which exists in the universe known to experience and to science must have a sufficient cause. Objects do not exist meaninglessly, or by accident.

2. The universe is a unity. The most careful scientific examination appears to indicate that the same coherent reign of law runs through all things, from the heavenly galaxies to the atoms, and throughout all time. Therefore the sufficient source and plan of all must be *one*.

3. The universe appears not to suffer from any kind of limitation or constraint. The power behind it completely suffices for all its needs. The law of its action is constant, unerring, and exact. Therefore the source and plan of all must be unlimited in power, infinite and constant in wisdom.

4. The universe appears to have a purpose or destination. In its develop-ment one stage naturally and fittingly leads to another, which is the climax of all that has gone before. Thus the evolution of stars produced a planet

suited to the existence of organic life, and organic life then duly appeared
to fulfill the development of the planet. The evolution of organic life under
the influence of successive changes of environment on the earth at length
came to its climax in an organism, man. He was adapted in body, nerve, and
sense to be the potential medium of personal, rational, and moral life.
Personal life then duly awoke, and man became man, fulfilling the previous
organic development. The process has continued in the development of man.
If the whole train of development, from beginning to end, corresponds to
a sufficient cause and rational plan, it would appear that the earlier stages
have been undergone in order that the later and higher may arise. Therefore the source and plan of all must have purpose.

5. The crown of the development of the physical universe is apparently
man. He is a *personal* being. That is to say, he is self-conscious, thinking,
feeling, and capable of moral choice. Man is also in part a spiritual being.
These higher and nobler faculties of his, which make him human, are
not merely part of the material body, though they work through it. The
sufficient and rational cause of this effect must be at least as rich in being
as man. Therefore the source of all is a Person, not merely a law of
existence. He is a spiritual being, invisible, not having a material body, and
not confined to time and space. Presumably this originating Person is altogether richer in personality than even the noblest of men, at a higher level
of self-consciousness, more profound in thought, more pure and strong in
feeling. He is not merely the impersonal "soul of the world," but a personal
God who knows Himself as separate in existence from the world which He
has created, and which He rules with sovereign power.

6. In the minds of men there are thoughts of goodness, truth, and beauty,
which are the highest qualities of human life. If existence is a rational thing,
these qualities cannot exist by accident, with no sufficient cause. They
cannot be in the nature of an illusion. Therefore in the mirror of the mind
of man they must form as the imperfect reflection of qualities of perfect
goodness, truth, and beauty which exist in the mind of God.

Summary. We here have formulated in general terms the Christian argument for the existence of God, who is the all-wise and all-powerful spiritual
and personal creator and ruler of the universe, and the ground and source
of all goodness, truth, and beauty.

C. Traditional Statements

This argument has in the Church been traditionally formulated in a
number of so-called "proofs of the existence of God."

1. ONTOLOGICAL ARGUMENT. The word "ontological" is derived from the
Greek verb for "to be," "to exist." This is the argument from the very nature
of existence, and is in fact the traditional statement of the basic assumption
of the rationality of existence. Deeply implanted in the mind of man there
is the idea that God exists, and that He is one and all-sufficient, and good.
It is argued that this demonstrates that such a God actually does exist. We

have the idea of a perfect being, and a necessary part of this perfection is that He should actually exist. This mode of argument was first clearly stated by St. Anselm of Canterbury (1033–1109), in his book *Proslogion,* and this argument was the effective starting point of the great medieval venture of Christian philosophy known as Scholasticism. The ontological argument was later notably restated by the French philosopher and mathematician, Descartes (1596–1650), who argued that because the thoughts of goodness and truth in the mind of man are so distinct and clear they must correspond to reality.

It is easy for the skeptic to object that in thinking of God man may very possibly be the victim of subjective illusion. Thus critics have correctly argued that the idea in one's mind that a proverbial beautiful island exists beyond the farthest seas by no means demonstrates that it is there. However, the Christian will answer that he is not arguing about the existence of mundane objects such as this. He is concerned with the noblest and most profound thoughts which have moved in the minds of the greatest, the most sensitive, and the most rational of men. To affirm that these thoughts do not correspond substantially to the very nature of existence, but are of the nature of a profound illusion, overthrows the integrity of the thinking mind. It seems to presuppose that man himself, considered as a thinking person, is an unworthy illusion. The mind will not finally accept this conclusion, compelling though it may seem to some able and sincere men. Radical skepticism starts by acclaiming the worth of "reason," but ends in overthrowing much of the process of thought itself.

2. COSMOLOGICAL ARGUMENT. The word "cosmological" is derived from *cosmos,* the Greek word for the world, and particularly the world of nature considered as an orderly system. The existence of God is here argued from the evidence of order in the universe. The creation shows too much of majesty, wisdom, and wonder to be the result of an accident. Its existence declares the existence of an all-wise Creator, in the same way that if one discovered a delicately made watch on a desert island one would presume that an intelligent man had left his handiwork there, for a watch could not be the result of chance. This is a natural form of argument, and is repeatedly declared in the Bible (for example, Psalm 19:1–4, 94:9; Acts 14:17; Romans 1:19–20). It was notably restated by St. Thomas Aquinas (1225–1274), the classic figure of Scholasticism, that is, of the philosophical theology of the Schoolmen, or leading teachers of the medieval universities.

The chief thing to be said here is that the impressiveness of this argument largely depends upon what one assumes to be the proper end of existence. The argument from the majesty and order of the heavenly bodies, and of the rule of law in nature, is indeed impressive. Question arises chiefly when one considers sentient animal life, and in particular, self-conscious and sensitive human life. Animal existence is full of the strain and competition of "nature red in tooth and claw," while human experience is darkened by suffering, and by suffering which often cannot well be explained as due to the disordering of God's good order by the sin of man. There is also the fiendish ingenuity of some parasites, which to some would almost seem to speak of an intelligent designer of evil, as well as of good. One does not claim that every hard question can be completely answered, but the chief consideration here is that in his objection the "this-worldly" thinker almost instinctively makes the tacit assumption that the highest good in life is an untroubled existence in comfort, free from anxiety and pain. If this be so, it is then clear that the basic design of life is not completely good, for the order of nature is not as free from strain and pain as it could conceivably be. However, it can be argued that in the highest sense of the word it is good for man to have his bodily existence in a certain state of insecurity, so as to remind him of spiritual values beyond the bodily. Also there may be spiritual good to be gained by the discipline of uncomfortable effort, and by the patient endurance of pain. If this be so, the argument from wise design is much more obvious. It is the Christian, who has seen the wisdom of God revealed in the Cross of Christ, and in the Christian life of "cross-bearing," who is more likely to see things this way.

3. TELEOLOGICAL ARGUMENT. The term "teleological" is derived from the Greek *telos,* the end or aim of a process. The existence of God is argued from the appearance of developing purpose in the universe, because a sense of rational purpose in the development of the world of nature speaks of an origin in an intelligent mind.

In the modern period this argument has been assailed in the name of the scientific doctrine of organic evolution. Most of the traditional teleological arguments were based upon the admittedly wonderful adaptation of living creatures to their habitat, and of organs to their proper use. Thus Newton, to an eminent degree a man of science, could declare: "Was the eye contrived without skill in optics, or the ear without knowledge of sounds?" However, the doctrine of evolution through natural selection seems to show that living creatures adapt themselves automatically to their environment. Some have argued that this abolishes the idea of intelligent design in nature, and speaks of an eye which has designed itself, without recourse to a Designer having knowledge of optics. It is, however, not necessary to draw this conclusion. It can be argued that there is still room in the system for an intelligent original Designer of the whole evolutionary process (see pp. 26–27).

4. MORAL ARGUMENT. It is argued that there is within the heart of man a most majestic voice, which tells him that he must do that which he knows to be right.[5] This is a mark of the existence of a God whose will is the moral

---

[5] Though it need not be supposed that there is a divine voice which immediately informs man what in fact is right. Views of right appear to depend directly on background, the tradition of society, experience, and education, though this process is doubtless ultimately guided by God.

law for mankind. This form of argument is largely associated with the teaching of the German philosopher Kant (1724–1804), who demonstrated the difficulties in the traditional Scholastic arguments for the existence of God, and sought instead to base his system upon the moral argument.

C. Summary and Evaluation

We can see that the cosmological, teleological, and moral arguments rest upon the basic and *a priori* ontological argument. If it be granted that the mind of man is a real spiritual entity, and that the higher flights of the human intellect give some reliable grasp of reality, then the arguments have much force. However, if the mind of man itself is pronounced to be somewhat in the nature of an illusion, then the arguments lose their force. It is not surprising, therefore, that religious skeptics have in the modern situation largely followed those schools of psychological thought which maintain that the mind of man is not a directing spiritual entity, but a passing phenomenon set up by the physical and nervous activity of the body, which alone is "real." In the eyes of the Christian, belief in God is a fundamentally rational belief, and acceptable to the candid mind, because of the rational and humane view of life which it engenders. The religious basic assumption enshrines rationality and goodness as the very principle of existence, and as the purpose of human life.

Arguments for the existence of God will not suffice to constrain the mind of the man who lacks the sense that the spiritual is real. He may bring himself to agree with the logic of the argument, but he cannot take the initial evidence seriously as evidence. To the Christian, however, it is a mark of the goodness and wisdom of God that it is thus impossible to produce an absolutely coercive proof of the religious position, because it is this alone which guarantees that man's faith and love of God shall be free. A man confronted by a theorem in geometry is not free to reject the proof. If he will not agree he proves himself either deficient in understanding or deliberately dishonest. God never drives the unbeliever into a corner like this. However pressing be the arguments in favor of the reasonableness of religion (and they are cogent, and even majestic in their force), there always remains some genuine difficulty to which the skeptic can reasonably cling, and which preserves to him an admitted intellectual right to continue to be a skeptic. It is a Christian view that a good and wise God has allowed this, so that whenever man opens his heart to the Father in faith and love it shall always be freely, for the sake of faith and love. However, the arguments here summarized to appear to be an important part of the foundation of Christian theology. They enable the thoughtful man to assure himself that in practicing the discipline of worship, and in living by trust in God, he is acting in a thoroughly rational manner.

Summary of Divergence: Modern Unbelief and the Doctrine of God

Practical materialism is not new. In the past millions who have professed a belief in the existence of God have found their lives dominated practically by the pursuit of the good things of this world— its comforts, its security, its prestige. Nor in the history of thought is theoretical materialism any new thing. There have always been some to argue that the universe of matter and of physical force is the only thing which really exists. However, it is clear that today practical materialism is much more widespread than it has ever been before, particularly in advanced industrial societies. A majority of the population of many of the world's most advanced countries has ceased to pray or to attend worship with any regularity, without any apparent sense of loss. Most of these people would not positively say that they are unbelievers, but their religion is inhibited from practise. Some other advanced countries, in particular the United States, retain a great deal of popular churchgoing. Yet many critics would affirm that much of this is superficial escapism, and would hold that men who do not possess the intellectual courage to face the testing problems of the modern age seek a spurious emotional release by a spare-time resort to modes of worship which are appropriate only to a bygone and simpler age. Still more significant is the fact that theoretical materialist thought is more widespread than ever before, and enjoys much intellectual prestige. There is not only the influence of avowed materialist philosophies, and in particular the dialectical materialist doctrine of Marxism. Of perhaps even more force is the indirect persuasion of the unspoken materialist assumptions of many prominent literary figures and publicists.

 The general materialist argument is that in the childhood of the race man found himself helpless and frightened in a mysterious and perilous world. It was comforting to suppose that some great "father figure" of superior power and wisdom invisibly supervised and protected the tribe. Therefore the subconscious mind, in search of that which would give emotional security, naturally suggested that this being actually exists. Since then new discoveries have brought into being new ways of earning a living, and these in turn new forms of society. Each of these successive forms of society have required certain rules of thought and action to make them work, and the subconscious mind has naturally suggested that these rules are "right," and "the will of God." Thus religion has gradually accumulated. Yet "the spiritual" does not actually exist, but is only an insubstantial shadow cast in the mind of the race by the physical business of living. In the modern scientific age, it is argued, man is no longer a child, but an adult. He has the power to understand the universe, so that it is no longer mysterious. He has the power to control it, so that he is no longer helpless before the forces of nature. Therefore he no longer needs religion, which may have been relatively beneficial or at least inevitable at one time, but is now outworn.

A practical rejoinder of the religious believer to this materialist argument is that the alleged "adulthood" of the race has not in fact produced emancipation into a more rational and humane form of living. Much popular religion of the past, including some which passed as Christian religion, was in fact degrading superstition which held mankind in bondage to unreason, fear, and cruelty. However, the abolition of these ancient superstitions has only left room for the world to be filled with other superstitions, such as fanatical revolutionary movements, hysterical nationalism, the adulation of popular figures in amusement and sport, and the frantic cult of material "status symbols." These have been found just as fertile as anything in the past to engender cruelty, fear, and unreason.

a. The Doctrine of God: The Call for a Restatement

It is affirmed by some critics that the decline of a vivid sense of the unseen world and of a vital belief in God which is characteristic of the modern age is due in the first place to a mental picture of God which is no longer credible. Traditional theology has spoken of God as though He were a kind of invisible man of great power and knowledge, who dwells in some sphere which is "above" our own, or "beyond" it. The scientist, on the other hand, knows that there is no sphere of existence "above" or "beyond" the universe. He does not take so exalted a view of puny human nature, existing in this tiny world, as to find it fitting to use human comparisons as symbols to set forth the nature of God. If the Christian religion is to be respected, theology must therefore be drastically reconstructed, so as completely to avoid any phrase which may be misunderstood as teaching that a "man-like" God exists in some form of "place." Rather is He to be spoken of as "the ground of being," as "that which gives value to existence."

Furthermore, in the coming adulthood of the race man will find less and less sense of reality in definite acts of prayer, and particularly in traditional communal religious ceremonial. His contact with God must rather be an attempt to express spiritual value in the course of ordinary daily life, and in useful humane social service. This concept of a life of devotion to the principle of value has been described as "religionless Christianity" ("religion" in this phrase being used in the sense of Christianity as expressed in formal speculative dogmatic statements, and in definite clerically organized acts of public worship). In this way alone can the essential spirit of Christ live on in the modern world.

These ideas are particularly associated with the writings of Tillich and Bonhoeffer, and have been widely discussed in relation to the popular book *Honest to God.*

b. Man's Sense of God: A Rejoinder from Christian Tradition

The exponent of the traditional system of Christian theology must first admit that among simple-minded Christians in the past, and to some extent even today, God has been thought of as "like a man," and as dwelling in some sort of glorious "place." However, this is no true or necessary part of Christian theology. The Bible does not, when correctly understood, speak of God as though He had a body, or experienced human emotions. On the contrary, instructed Christians in every age have been perfectly well aware that God is a spiritual being, and is not to be thought of as existing in space or time. Thus the critic is criticizing something which in fact is not part of the Christian system.

However, the idea of God can only be expressed in symbolical language, and the framing of this symbolism is a much more subtle undertaking than the critic is disposed to assume. It is to be allowed that God is "the ground of being," and "that which gives value to existence." What is said under this heading is a part of the Christian system, and is true so far as it goes. However, taken in isolation this language comes dangerously near to reducing the concept of God to that of a bare principle of existence. The idea of the sovereign transcendence of God, and above all, of the personal nature of God, is obscured. This shuts the door upon the most valuable feature of the Christian religion, the sense of personal communion in worship and prayer with the personal Living God of the Bible. God becomes an object of meditation, not of loving and obedient devotion.

Furthermore, it may be argued, whatever may be the case with a small minority of highly gifted intellectuals, who may perhaps be moved to a sense of deep personal release by abstract thought, God must be symbolized in vivid and realistic terms if the thought of Him is to be made real to the mind of man, though admittedly these realistic symbols are not to be misunderstood in a crude and material sense. Thus it is almost inevitable in worship to say "Lift *up* your hearts!" though the throne of God's majesty is not "up" in a place. We cannot avoid saying "Come Lord!," though He does not have to move from another sphere in order to answer the prayer. And it is right to use the noblest aspects of human nature as our highest symbols of God's nature, so as to speak of Him as "Father," and of His "love," though these are only comparisons, not to be taken humanly and literally. If this vivid language is forbidden ordinary people cannot think about God at all.

Furthermore, the exponent of Christian tradition will urge that it is not in fact true that men of the age of science cannot accept the symbolical language of the Christian Faith, as it is reflected in accepted doctrine and traditional modes of worship. Some indeed do not appear to possess the sense of God, and find no sense of reality in acts of prayer and worship. However, it is quite the reverse with many others who are fully attuned to the characteristic modern and scientific method and outlook. They understand, and can with intellectual honesty use, the traditional symbolism. In prayer and Christian worship they do find a sense of personal communion with God. In this way they enjoy the advantage that they are joined in fellowship with other and simpler believers, who perhaps in their own devotional lives take some of the traditional Christian language in a less reflective sense.

Thus, we may argue, the failure to hold some of the modern generation to the Christian Faith is not due to a radical fault in Christian
theology or worship. It is perhaps an accompaniment of the dislocation
of the times, something serious indeed, but passing. Some would argue
that the drift of so many from customary Christian worship is not a
revolt against Christian faith as such, but only against the Church,
considered as ⌐ socio-political group. In many lands the formerly
unprivileged classes have turned against the former "establishment."
The Church appeared in their eyes to be part of this "establishment,"
and so they have simply turned from the Church. Furthermore, the
industrialized masses have had their imagination bemused by the triumph
of the material. The city man works at a machine or a desk. He amuses
himself with a mechanical gadget. Everything in the city street is made
by man, and has its price. Man is hemmed in by the material, so that
by comparison the sense of the unseen has become vague and uncertain,
and therefore worship seems like "talking into the air." Nevertheless,
as man adjusts to his changed surroundings these disorders may pass,
and religion will again win a hearing if the Church maintains her
witness.

IV. Revelation and Inspiration

A. Revelation

The use of the word "revelation" indicates that man only has knowledge
of God because God of His free grace chooses to make it known. The
Christian answer to the question, "Canst thou by searching find out God?"
(Job 11:7) is "No." God belongs to a sphere of existence outside man's this-
worldly experience. He is great and holy, whereas man is frail and sinful,
separated from God by a great gulf both of intellectual and moral blindness
(Isaiah 6:5). Man could discover nothing about God had not God of His
goodness first made Himself known.

The word can be used in two senses. "Revelation" is the process by which
God makes Himself known. "The revelation" is the divine truth thus made
known. Revelation is often classified in two parts.

1. GENERAL REVELATION. This is the divine truth made known through
the general order of nature, including the social, moral, and aesthetic life
of man. It is all that truth which has been considered in relation to the
evidence for the existence of God. This evidence is a revelation. The heavens
only declare the glory of God because God has created them to be an
expression of His mind. The mind of man can only see God's glory in the
heavens because God of His goodness has made the mind capable of doing
so. Thus all is of God, a gift of free grace, a self-disclosure. Yet it is also
a *general* revelation, made to all men. It is the knowledge of God which can
be attained by every honest and candid mind, quite apart from Christ or the
Bible (Romans 1:19–20).

That part of religion which is based on the general revelation is natural religion. This is not specifically Christian, but is "the religion of all reasonable men." Examples of natural theology are a belief in one just and good God, the claims of morality, and the expectation of a future life.

2. SPECIAL REVELATION. This is the self-disclosure of God to man through the Bible, and supremely, in Christ. To the Christian this special and specifically Christian revelation conveys to man a body of truths more sublime than the general revelation. Examples of such truths are the Trinity, the Incarnation, and the Atonement. Indeed, the special revelation is not only a body of truth about God. It is essentially a *personal* disclosure of God in Christ. At the center of divine revelation we meet a Person, though He brings the declaration of a doctrine.

That part of religion which is based on the special revelation is known as revealed religion.

Summary of Divergence: Catholic and Protestant Views of Natural Religion

There is a significant difference of emphasis at this point.

a. Catholic[6] tradition affirms that natural theology, which may be deduced by reason from the character of God's creation, and which may be known outside the specifically biblical revelation known to the Church, is of distinct value to the soul of man. It is, as it were, the due setting, in which the precious jewel of revealed theology is displayed. Intellectual arguments to explain and vindicate natural religion are an important contribution to the understanding of Christian theology, though the higher and distinctively Christian truths of revelation extend beyond the power of human reason.

b. Protestant tradition, seeking to vindicate the primacy of faith, lays less emphasis upon natural religion, and some schools of Protestant thought have looked upon it with suspicion. Thus Protestantism in general gives a smaller place to human reason in the construction of theology. It is allowed that reason can discern evidence for some important truths about God, but it is emphasized that these are not those distinctive Christian truths concerning the gospel of grace, whereby man comes to salvation. Man can only savingly know God by means of the divine gift of faith. An extreme form of this position may be seen in the so-called existential theology (see pp. 8–9).

B. Inspiration

This word indicates the doctrine that God, by His grace through the operation of the Holy Spirit, quickens the human faculties He has given to men, in order that they may more readily understand and accept what He has

---

6 Including Catholic tradition held outside the Roman Catholic Church.

revealed (1 Corinthians 2: 9–11). Sinful man is by nature in a state of partial blindness to spiritual things. Inspiration comes to his assistance. Divine inspiration should not be regarded as the suspension of natural human faculties. It is the stimulation of human faculty by God's action, so that man may come closer to his divinely intended power of understanding. Inspiration makes man more fully human, not less.

It is the usual Christian belief that divine inspiration extends to some extent to all good and wise men who desire to know the truth, including believers in other religions. However, to the Christian the most particular and important work of inspiration was the writing of the Bible, and since that time, the continued guidance of the Church in understanding it.

V. Maker of Heaven and Earth

A. Creation

By "creation" is meant the principle that the universe exists solely because the sovereign God wills that it should exist, and that His will is the sufficient ground for its existence (Genesis 1:1; Psalm 33:6; Revelation 4:11). The main interest of Christian thought has been to symbolize as adequately as possible the absolute sovereignty of God. Thus it is the generally accepted Christian teaching that the creation is not eternal. It had a beginning, and before time began God was alone in glory (Psalm 90:2). He also has the power to bring the creation to an end (Isaiah 51:6; Revelation 20:11). To affirm, with some thinkers, that God is eternally creative borders upon the supposition that He is the Creator by the inward necessity of His being, with the implied conclusion that the creation is in some way necessary to His self-fulfillment. Christian thought rejects the latter suggestion, as it appears to infringe upon God's divine sovereignty and self-sufficient perfection. Nor is divine creation an activity upon previously existing matter. It is creation in the proper sense of the word, that is, creation "from nothing."

Summary of Divergence: Doctrines of Creation

a. The Ancient Church

The interest of the ancient Church in framing the first clause of the Creed, quoted at the beginning of this chapter, was to repel Gnosticism. The Gnostics of the early centuries claimed to illuminate the Christian Faith with "knowledge" (gnosis). Basing their ideas upon presuppositions about the nature of God drawn from contemporary secular, and therefore nonbiblical, thought, they taught that the Supreme God was transcendent, but not immanent (see p. 11). He (or rather, "It") could not have contact with anything so ignoble as the material creation, which must therefore be the handiwork of an intermediary being who proceeded indirectly from the highest God. Thus the bungling god of creation, mentioned in the Old Testament, is not the Christian God the Father. Christianity was cut off from its Jewish roots, and the Jewish Scriptures discarded. The Church firmly denied all this, and her interest was to affirm in the strongest possible manner the biblical doctrine that the Christian Father was "the creator of heaven and earth." However, the ancient Church was quite familiar with the idea that the authoritative Scriptures, including the creation narratives, may rightly be interpreted in a symbolic or allegorical sense.

b. Classic Protestantism

The traditional Protestant position regarding creation has been to emphasize as strongly as possible the full authority and integrity of Scripture. Many have felt that this involves interpreting the Genesis creation narratives in a manner as near to the literal as possible, particularly as and when traditional theology was apparently assailed by evolutionary concepts. However, within the conservative evangelical school there is still a degree of liberty of interpretation as to how far some of the details of the narrative may be taken in a symbolic sense without detracting from the inspiration of Scripture. For example, the "days" of creation may not be periods of twenty-four hours (2 Peter 3:8).

c. Genesis and Evolution

The generally accepted findings of astronomy, geology, and biology affirm that the universe gradually developed into its present form over an immensely long period of time, and furthermore, that the human race, considered as a physical organism, evolved like other organisms from an animal ancestry. It is not possible to reconcile this view of nature with the Genesis creation narrative, interpreted literally. This would appear to involve that the Christian theologian should revive and greatly extend the ancient doctrine that the early chapters of Genesis can rightly be expounded symbolically or allegorically, as divinely inspired and authoritative parables of spiritual principles. They are not to be taken literally, in contradiction to secure scientific findings.

The doctrine of evolution does not of itself exclude the general idea of divine creation. Even if it be allowed to the scientific determinist that the whole process of the development of stars, the world, and organic life upon it, from beginning to end is an unbroken chain of mechanistic necessity, even so the whole process still, it may be argued, requires a sufficient First Cause (see pp. 14–16). Evolution is a method of describing the manner in which God created the universe, but does not abolish the Creator. Nor do the findings of physical science of themselves require a complete mechanistic necessity. This doctrine would appear to be a matter of philosophical assumption rather than of scientific fact, and the Christian may affirm that it is possible to defend the idea that God is in intelligent control of the processes of nature (see pp. 28–29). In particular, it may never be possible to produce scientific evidence which will completely illuminate the change by which man became man. The awakening in a purely animal subman of those distinctively human faculties of personal self-consciousness, morally responsible choice, and the potentiality of communion with God, was not a physical or material change. No fossil evidence of it can ever be discovered! It is perfectly reasonable for the Christian to see in the creation of man (that is, in the raising of the race to the "human" level), a special, significant, and mysterious divine intervention in the evolutionary process.

B. Natural Law

The traditional Christian doctrine of the divine government of the world and of God's immanence within it (see p. 11) has been strongly questioned by some because of the scientific conception of natural law[7] and of the general scientific doctrine of the continuity of nature. We must first define the scientific term "natural law." For example, if one pumps twice the quantity of air into a vessel the pressure on the walls is doubled. If the quantity be increased to three times, the pressure is tripled, and so on. This happens in an orderly way. It happens in reverse when the air is let out. It happens similarly with a container of a different shape, or with a gas other than air. In particular, it happens in the same way in a year's time, or in another country, and however many times the experiment is performed. Such an observation that events happen in a fixed and orderly manner is called a natural law. Each natural law is a particular example of the general scientific principle of the continuity of nature. Scientific investigation has demonstrated fixed laws governing even the most complicated events, and the further the investigation is taken the more fully is the reign of fixed natural law displayed and confirmed.[8]

This scientific conception of the reign of natural law is an idea of great importance to Christian belief. To the believer the continuity of nature is a token of the constancy and rationality of God's own being and purpose. He is shown by His handiwork to be trustworthy and constant. He never performs an unaccountable action. He is never taken by surprise in events, or under the necessity of changing His mind. To the religious skeptic, on the other hand, these same facts may be viewed as a token that the whole universe, throughout its entire course of existence, is a fixed train of cause and effect, for all the causes of events are but the effects of causes which were before them. The universe is, as it were, a great machine, with every action predetermined by an iron law of necessity. The life of man is likewise determined. He may fancy he is free to choose, but this is an illusion. He

---

[7] The phrase "natural law" is here used in its ordinary modern scientific sense. This is to be distinguished from the classical sense of "natural law" as the principles of reason and morality implanted in man's nature.

[8] Strictly speaking it is not the concern of physical science to discuss the ultimate reason *why* natural phenomena occur in this orderly manner. This is the business of philosophy. Science is concerned with revealing and applying patterns of orderly behavior.

acts in terms of his environment and his inherited character, which character is molded by previous environment. Thus the mind, with its sensation of freedom, is by some explained away as the illusory subjective effect of psychological causes. Thus a law of necessity denies human moral freedom. The doctrine of scientific determinism tends towards the notion that the thinking mind and all ideas of "the spiritual" are unreal. Even if the idea of God is not in principle abolished, the doctrine is denied of a God who can care for man and answer prayer.

C. Providence

A Christian answer to this difficulty regarding God's government of the universe and natural law is that if it is once allowed that there is a thinking mind behind the universe, there is then no need to suppose that God is a prisoner of the machine which He has made. It is true that "mind" does not "break" natural law, but it can cooperate with it and work through it to bring about events which would not have happened had not the thinking mind been at work. For example, when a plane flies through the sky an event takes place which would not have happened had nature been left to itself, and which the science of a former day would quite possibly have stated to be contrary to well-known natural laws. Yet the reign of natural law has not been broken. Natural law has been understood and used by the mind of man to produce a new and significant event, which has to a small extent changed the apparently fixed course of nature. If our limited human minds can "work through" the law of nature to a small extent, surely the infinite mind of God can do the same to a much more commanding degree!

The thoughtful Christian will prefer not to say that God "suspends" the law of nature, for that reign of natural law is fixed by Him and is an expression of His being. Yet He can prevailingly work through it to bring things to pass which would not happen were nature left to itself. What physical science says about the exactitude of the machine of nature is to be accepted as true so far as it goes, within the scope of scientific experiment. However, it is the faith of the Christian that there is another sphere of activity by no means contradictory to this, yet interpenetrating it and superior to it. God can work through the natural order of the world in which we live to care for His children, to answer prayer, and to uphold the cause of right with resources of which the men of this world cannot take account. This is the belief in divine *providence* (Psalm 124:1-3; Matthew 6:25-33).

There is indeed an element of mystery in the operation of providence. God does not always guide and bless His own in the way which they themselves desire (2 Corinthians 12:7-10). Yet experience shows that He does guide and bless. It is surely an excess of dogmatism on the part of the skeptic to affirm that a divine action cannot happen in the world because we men cannot fully understand the manner of it! Particularly is this so in

light of the amazing and unforeseen advances of scientific knowledge, which
bring home to us how little we really know about nature. It is significant
that in recent years the more thoughtful scientist is often much less inclined
than formerly to affirm that the universe is a closed system of mechanical
necessity.

D. Miracles

If God can work through the natural order to care for His own and to
accomplish His will, it is surely reasonable to suppose that He can on
occasion work some outstanding act of providence—an act of deep spiritual
significance, completely outside man's understanding and beyond man's
ordinary expectation. Such an exceptional providence may be called a
miracle. A miracle, therefore, is best not described as a "breach" or "suspension" of the natural order, though this phrase has often been used in
theology. Yet it is a wonderful act worked by the God who is in sovereign
control of nature.

It is to be expected that miracles should occur at times of high spiritual
crisis in the life of humanity, when God is especially vindicating His purpose,
and in the lives of especially devoted men and women, who are to an
outstanding degree the instruments of His purpose. The experience of the
Church affirms that this has actually been the case. To the Christian the
chief historical occasion when it will be found fitting for miracles to have
occurred is the life of Christ Himself, for His earthly career was to a unique
degree the divine intervention into this world. This brief discussion of
general principles is inadequate to cover the contentious issue of the attitude
of the thoughtful Christian to the miracles recorded in the Bible. This will
be referred to when we consider the character of the Gospel narrative and
the doctrine of Christ's resurrection (see pp. 105–8).

E. The Natural and the Supernatural

1. THE SUPERNATURAL AND BIBLICAL THOUGHT. The idea of a God
who is able by His power mysteriously to overrule the natural order with
His providential government has traditionally been expressed in theology
by the contrast between the lower order of the natural and the higher of the
supernatural. This notion of a "two-story" universe is derived from Greek
thought, rather than from the Bible. The ancient Hebrews were largely
deficient in the means of expressing the idea of "indirect causation," that is,
the conception that natural events happen according to a self-acting natural
law, so that God is responsible for the event only in the modified and indirect
sense that He has created the world in the way He has. Thus it was hard for
them to say that something "happened" without saying that God caused it.
Many phrases in the Bible which appear strange to us bear the mark of this
difficulty, and it is important for this principle to be kept in mind as one
reads the Bible. Thus the statement "the Lord hardened Pharaoh's heart"

(Exodus 7:13) is not far in intention from "Pharaoh's heart became hardened" (but in a world where every event is overruled by God).

Therefore the biblical writers are not at home with the inquiry "Is this event natural or supernatural?" Thus the standing still of the sun recounted in Joshua 10:12–13 would have been regarded as a wonderful sign from God, but hardly as "supernatural," for to them it was not "the natural order" for the sun to rise normally. The Hebrews thought of the sun as rising each day by a direct divine act, though on this day God acted differently. This consideration, which is admittedly not very easy to grasp by the average modern mind, has an application to the modern discussion. Some critics, who have wished to expel the miraculous as far as possible from the Christian system, have argued that the theologian will not speak of "the supernatural" because this is not a biblical concept. This appears to be a most misleading, or even disingenuous plea. The idea of "the supernatural" is indeed alien to the Bible, but not at all because the idea of "miracle" is not there. In a natural order where everything is thought of as caused by God, every event is on the verge of miracle. It is impossible honestly to cite the Bible on behalf of nonmiraculous Christianity. However, in our modern thinking the well-known contrast between "the natural" and "the supernatural" provides a convenient means for discussing the miraculous element in the Christian religion.

2. THE DIFFICULTY OF THE SUPERNATURAL. Without a doubt, many people find a real element of difficulty as they approach the supernatural or miraculous element in the Bible and in the Christian Faith. The believer may have no great difficulty in arguing to himself in principle that if there is indeed a sovereign and personal God in control of the world it is reasonable to suppose that He should be able to work a miracle. Furthermore, faith may command assent to some few salient miracles, such as the incarnation and Christ's resurrection, which appear to be required by the Christian Faith. Yet the Bible contains many other stories of marvelous occurrences, such as sudden deliverances in answer to prayer, miracles of healing, visions of angels and of the divine glory, and the like. These are so outside our own experience, and contrast so strongly with the mentality inculcated by the study of natural science, that candidly it taxes the imagination to accept them, and we almost wish that they were not part of the Scripture! This is a difficulty we must try to face.

In the first place, it is not necessary for the man who prizes a thoughtful and honest mind to feel that he must come to the Scripture and to the Christian creed with strong antisupernaturalistic bias. This is not required by the scientific mentality. The advance of scientific knowledge itself, which has opened our eyes to all manner of possibilities and laws which were undreamed of a few years ago, or which were even confidently denied by the science of the time, has enforced the mystery of the universe. We dare not say that the infinite mind of God, working through the laws of nature, cannot perform marvelous actions simply because the knowledge of today is not able to comprehend them. At the same time, we need not go to the other extreme and insist as a matter of faith that every detail of every wonder-story which has come down from the past must be taken literally. Allowance must be made for the prosupernaturalistic bias of ancient times. In antiquity men loved stories of wonders as a natural support to faith, so it is not surprising that the accounts of outstanding events and of holy men should have come down to us associated with accretions which may perhaps be legendary. Yet it is an excess of skepticism to dismiss the event, or the man, as unhistorical because every detail cannot be insisted upon. Each case is to be considered on its merits.

Allowance must also be made for different modes of describing the same event. It does not follow that an ancient account of a remarkable and significant event is unreliable simply because it is framed in thought forms entirely different from those of the present day. For example, it is related that travelers through Switzerland in the Middle Ages came back with reports that it was a land of gloom and horror. The imagination of those days peopled the wild mountains with dragons, and fear closed the eye of the beholder to the beauty which we see. Nevertheless, these accounts are reliable as evidence that such a place as Switzerland was visited by certain travelers. The difference is one of psychological approach, not of fact. So likewise we have to realize that were a modern man, with the typical modern mentality, able to be present at some of the great and mysterious events of the Biblical narrative, he might well describe them in a manner very different, and much less pointedly supernatural. Yet he would still bear witness to the fact, and its wonder, and its spiritual significance.

F. Angels

Christian thought has traditionally affirmed that God's creation includes all things, "visible and invisible." The physical universe of matter and force is not all that exists. There are also thinking, feeling, and morally responsible personal beings which do not have material bodies like ours. Presumably they may have nobler powers of mind and spirit than ourselves. These are the angels, who are frequently mentioned in the Bible as the messengers of God (for example, Luke 1: 26; Hebrews 12:22). Although the spectacular ninefold Heavenly Hierarchies of "Thrones, Dominations, Princedoms, Virtues, Powers," so prominent in the thought and art of the Middle Ages, can hardly be urged in these prosaic days as a serious part of Christian doctrine, yet there is no need to retreat to the other extreme, and to dismiss the whole matter as childish fantasy. The facts of the unseen world can only be set forth in symbolical language, and the question is then raised as to what is the most adequate symbolism. At the least, the concept of angels expresses the principle that man is not the highest and noblest of God's created servants, or the center of the universe. Cynics have often falsely charged

Christian theology with teaching just this presumptuous notion. Further-more, there are many to whom this system of symbolism makes the unseen world a pressing reality, and this is all to the good. It can hardly be claimed that the existence of angels is a doctrine contrary to science, for if they have no material bodies their existence can neither be proved nor disproved by the methods of physical science. It is a question of inherent spiritual probabilities. These probabilities seem to make it quite reasonable to speak about angels, though we need not imagine them according to the conventional pictures.

Readings

a. Some other general handbooks.

Barth, K., *Dogmatics in Outline,* trans. G. T. Thompson. London: SCM Press, 1957.

Pike, J. A., and W. N. Pittinger, *The Faith of the Church.* New York: The National Council, Protestant Episcopal Church, 1951.

Quick, O. C., *Doctrines of the Creed.* London: Nisbet and Company, Ltd., 1938. (More detailed.)

Whale, J., *Christian Doctrine.* New York: The Macmillan Company; London: Cambridge University Press, 1941.

b. On the matter of Chapter I.

Temple, W., *Nature, Man, and God.* London: Macmillan & Co., Ltd.,1951.

Trueblood, D. E., *Philosophy of Religion.* New York: Harper & Row, Publishers, 1957.

Richardson, A., *Christian Apologetics.* New York: Harper & Row, Publishers, 1948. (Defense of Christian belief.)

Chapter Two

The Jesus of History

I believe in Jesus Christ, His only Son, our Lord;
who was conceived by the Holy Ghost,
born of the Virgin Mary

I. Historical Religion

In the second clause of the Apostles' Creed the Christian Faith comes down from heaven to earth. The doctrine of God, and of His relation to the world, concerns unseen realities. To set these forth, symbolism is to be used, mental pictures that it to say, framed out of man's experience in this world, to bring home fully to the mind and the imagination that which is beyond immediate experience. Furthermore, arguments to vindicate the intellectual honesty of the Christian symbolism of God are questions of abstract thought. Thus the first clause of the Creed is a matter of mental construction. However, it has traditionally been an essential characteristic of the Christian Faith to affirm that The Faith is not simply a construction of the human mind, resting for its authority upon the goodness and wisdom of those who have thought it out. In the last resort it is not a philosophy, or a set of doctrines, or a system of ethics, though all these are intimately associated with it. Rather is it an authoritative witness to events which actually happened, which are the saving acts of God performed in the course of the history of this world. And the greatest subject of debate between traditional and critical opinion within the Church concerns these two allied issues: "To what extent is the Christian Faith founded on historical fact?" and "What do we mean by 'historical' fact?"

As we turn from these questions of mental construction to the historical inquiry "Did it really happen?" we turn from that which is in general "religious," or "spiritual," to that which is specifically *Christian*. Certainly there are many sincere and good men who do not accept the recognizable Christian doctrinal tradition about Jesus. There is a long spectrum of religious conviction extending from unorthodox denominations which describe themselves as Christian, through Jews, Moslems, to the ethnic religions, great and small. It is certainly no part of the business of the Christian theologian to deny that there are elements of authentic truth in all these systems, and much genuine human goodness among the people who uphold them. There is the ground common between all those who in various ways uphold the religious or spiritual view of life. However, as we pass from the first to this second chapter, we pass definitely from this common ground to that which is specifically Christian. Many who are not Christians well know what it is to live by religious faith, but it is only specifically Christian faith if it is faith in God as He has made Himself known to man in Jesus Christ, the divine Son, incarnate, crucified, and risen. This illustrates what is meant by the statement that the center of the Christian revelation is not a doctrine, but a Person.

In what has been written in the first chapter regarding existential theology (see pp. 8–9) we have already hinted at a problem which comes fully into the open here, as we turn expressly to the Christian Faith as an historical religion. In the current discussion of this matter two issues are closely associated: "What is the relation of Christian saving faith to the Jesus of history?" and "What are we to think of the Gospel narratives as historical sources?"

Summary of Divergence : Christian Faith and the Historical Jesus

a. *Traditional Position*

i. Christianity is the religion of the Incarnation (see pp. 49–50). The act of the Incarnation is itself the supreme example of the sacramental principle (see pp. 163–65) that God, who has created the material world as an expression of Himself, uses the material for spiritual purposes. In the Incarnation of His Son, God united Himself actually and personally with His handiwork, so that He lived a genuine human life in real human conditions, in our world. Thus it is essential that the story of Christ's birth, life, teaching, wonderful works, death, and resurrection must be taken seriously as real history. However, these divine acts in history are not barely wonderful events. They are events possessing an inward spiritual meaning to be discerned by faith, which is a divine gift (see pp. 221–23). On the one hand, God acts spiritually upon the inward man of the mind, the moral will, and the heart, to make him altogether a better man. Yet the spiritual action is mediated to man through the material action. A bare knowledge of the material divine act by itself does not save man. The effect must come home to the inner man of the heart by moving the mind, will, and affections to loving trust and obedience. Yet the inward, and in a sense subjective, effect could not take place without a knowledge of the objective historic divine work. Salvation is not merely subjective, a state of feeling and willing into which man stirs himself by autosuggestion. It is a personal response to that which God has actually *done* for man, in His Son.

ii. Therefore the Scripture witness to the facts about Christ must be read as history. This history is the essential foundation of true Christian doctrine. The Scripture records the historical preparation of the world for the coming of Christ, and likewise the apostolic witness to Christ, when at length he came; His birth, life, death, and resurrection. This testimony to Christ is in fact the element in Scripture which makes it into the Church's authoritative book. The ancient Church gave large scope to allegorical exegesis, and at times seemed more concerned to discover what parables of spiritual truth could be drawn from the narrative, than to emphasise the historical character of the narrative. Traditional Protestantism, on the other hand, wishing to safeguard the primary authority of Scripture, has tended to give principal emphasis to the historical reliability of the narrative. Frequently this interest has been manifested in the form of the doctrine of the literal inerrancy of Scripture (see p. 186). Nevertheless, the difference has always been one of emphasis rather than of principle. The general Christian tradition on both sides has affirmed that the Scripture is a sufficient account of historical events, and that these historical events are of importance because they are God's expression of an inward and spiritual work.

b. A Critical Position: " Demythologizing "

i. Critical New Testament scholars and theologians have observed that in the New Testament the Christian message is framed in terms of a view of the world order very different from that which is acceptable to an educated man of today. God is spoken of as though the throne of His majesty were above the azure dome of the heavens, and that He can visit the world with the fullness of His salvation at a future point in time. There is also a vivid conception of "angels" as the messengers of God, and of mental and physical disorder as due to "demons." All this mental furniture is frankly incredible today, and must be changed and modernized. If the scientific man is to accept the Christian message, the essential of that message must be rendered into terms of the universe as we know it to be, and of human psychology as at present accepted.

ii. A word which has been prominently used in this connection, particularly by R. Bultmann and his disciples, is "demythologization." The word "myth" has been adopted from the study of anthropology and comparative religion, where the primary sense is "the narrative that belongs to a ritual which sets forth some part of man's life experience." More generally a myth may be spoken of as an imaginative story which

symbolizes a set of ideas or values.[1] Jesus thought and spoke in terms
of the myth of a descent from heaven, which is the abode of God, and
of the overthrow of Satan and his minions in this world. This clothing,
now outworn, is to be stripped off, and the essential message reclothed
in a myth, or symbolic expression, suitable to our own mental climate.
The attempt to do this is called demythologization, which is not to be
misrepresented as a mode of dismissing the Gospel narrative as unworthy
of consideration, but rather as the opposite. It is an attempt to bring
the inward meaning of the narrative to the serious consideration of the
modern man.

iii. Akin to this is the fact that the element of physical miracle, so
prominent in the Gospel narrative, is a great stumbling-block to the
modern reader (see pp. 27–28). It is not so much that the modern
believer cannot accept the idea of a wonderful divine action which
works man's salvation, but that he must view it as an action which takes
place only in the inward man of the mind, the will, and the heart. He
cannot allow it to be intimately associated with a "physical miracle,"
that is, a supposed event which would have been observable by the
methods of physical science, had there been a scientific observer present,
and yet which is alien to the scientific world view. It will make the
Gospel more likely to win the intellectual respect of the thoughtful man
if it be judiciously emptied of this element of physical miracle.

It is clear that there is a considerable degree of association between
points (ii) and (iii), because those elements in the Gospel narrative
answering to the myth which was proper to antiquity are also largely
the elements presupposing physical miracle.

iv. Relief is to be found for these obstacles to faith by considerations
arising out of what is known of the teaching processes and literary
conventions of antiquity. These were quite different from our own, and
allowance must be made for this in the interpretation of the New
Testament. This may perhaps best be illustrated from a few examples.
The ancients thought in pictures, and were not so aware as we are of
a clear distinction between that which is historically correct and that
which is symbolically expressive. Thus it was natural to them to construct an imaginative story, which to us reads like an "event," in order
vividly to symbolize an idea, and so commend it to the faith of the
hearer. So it may be argued that in writing Matthew 27:51, "the veil

---

[1] The present writer must say that he feels it to be unfortunate that so much
confusion has been introduced into the theological world by the use of the word
"myth," in connection with the Gospel, in a sense subtly and misleadingly different from that in which it is used in common intelligent parlance. To non-
professionals a myth is an unhistorical fantasy, a story which is not to be taken
seriously as a source of truth. Thus to speak of the Gospel narrative as framed in
myth almost irresistibly conveys the idea that it is a naïve story from the childhood of the race, historically unreliable, and spiritually worthless. This is not in
fact the intention. In critical writing, no necessary judgment is passed upon the
historical reliability or spiritual value of a narrative by the use of the term
"myth." Thus it is possible to affirm that the Gospel narrative contains an element
of myth, and also to affirm that this particular myth is largely historically reliable,
and spiritually most valuable. However, critical theologians have created a very
serious problem of communication here.

of the temple was rent in twain from the top to the bottom," the Evangelist was not interested in this as a visible and physical event, and conceivably did not even intend it in this sense. It is intended as a parable of the idea that in Christ's death the way of access to God, formerly symbolized as closed by the curtain which shut off the Holy of Holies in the Temple, is now laid open to all believers. Similarly, a narrative can on occasion have a touch added to it, in order to bring out more clearly the Christian claim that an Old Testament prophecy was fulfilled by Christ. Thus the curious attempt in Matthew 21:7 to represent that Jesus rode into Jerusalem on two asses is to be explained as due to a misunderstanding of the prophecy referred to in Zechariah 9:9. At least some details of the apparent "event" were in fact constructed out of the prophecy. Furthermore, a story of parabolic meaning can have its details filled out in retelling it, so as to bring out more clearly the teaching which the teller feels is implied. Thus in the parable of the great feast, as recounted by St. Luke, there is a second summons to the vagrants of the city (14:23), which clearly is intended to symbolize the great Gentile mission of the Church. On the other hand, in the more Jewish St. Matthew's Gospel nothing is said about this second invitation, but the guest who has come in without a wedding garment is expelled (22:11-12). This touch is introduced in order to indicate that some minimal degree of legally correct conduct is required of the Christian (compare Acts 15:19–20).

Again, just as an ancient Greek historian can survey the military situation before a battle by the convention of composing a speech and putting it into the mouth of the general, so the New Testament writers can symbolize the spiritual situation by constructing a scene or a sermon. Thus it may be argued that many sayings of Jesus, otherwise arranged by Luke, have been arranged by Matthew in the form of "the Sermon on the Mount" to indicate that the teaching of the Lord is the "Mountain of the Law" of the New Covenant, the Beatitudes being the equivalent of the Ten Commandments. There was no thought of pious fraud in the employment of all these methods, even though this so naturally suggests itself to our minds, accustomed as we are to entirely different literary conventions. It was just the natural and accepted method of the time, which must be understood and allowed for, not condemned.

Finally, there is an over-all consideration arising from the method of literary investigation known as "form criticism." The Gospels were not written from verbatim accounts of the life of Christ, recorded with the biographical interest of giving later generations material for compiling "Lives of Christ." Some only of the facts about Jesus and His teaching were remembered by the Church and recorded, and then not in order. These were those facts which served as the means for preaching the Gospel and winning the hearers to Christian faith. Thus the whole narrative has been filtered through the group mind of the believing community, which has gradually arranged the general presentation and order and adjusted the details of the separate narratives, the more clearly to bring out these preaching and teaching interests. The consequence is that what we meet in the Gospels is not a supposed reliably biographical "Jesus of history," but the Church's "Christ of faith."

Thus the critic can explain those mythic and miraculous elements in the Gospel narrative which are to us such a stumbling-block as going back only to the believing mind of the Church, as it expressed itself in the means natural to the time. There is no necessity to suppose that Jesus actually said all these things, or that His life was actually accompanied by all these miracles.

v. The result of all is the following general account of the historical origin of the Christian religion. Doubtless Jesus of Nazareth was a man of most commanding personality, and impressive spiritual insight as a teacher. After His death His disciples realized that personal contact with Him had brought to them a most moving and lasting sense of the presence and power of God. They had been assured of divine forgiveness, and that they were even now partakers of God's kingly rule over the world. They were possessed of a sense of loving fellowship with the God they had come to know through Christ, and they lived in a state of vivid expectancy of the completion of God's triumph. This, their "existential encounter" with God in Christ, *was* God's historic saving act, wrought out in this world. The first Church expressed this faith in its "kerygma" (Greek for "thing preached"; translated "preaching" in 1 Corinthians 1:21). The kerygma, or message, was finally recorded in writing, in the New Testament. How many of the Gospel events, pronouncements, ethical maxims, parables, and miracles (including the resurrection itself) are authentic historical reminiscences, and how far they represent the construction of the Church as it sought to symbolize and commend its faith, is a matter of uncertainty. Doubtless both elements are present in the Gospel narrative which we have received, but the character of each particular text is a matter of inherently varied scholarly judgment. Yet in the last resort this is a matter of interest only to academic scholarship, and not to religious faith, for the object of our faith is "the Christ of faith."

c. A Mediating Position

i. There are grave disadvantages both to the strictly traditional and to the extreme critical positions. In the case of the first, in order to safeguard the traditional judgment as to what is involved in the authority of the New Testament as the source of an historical faith, it is apparently necessary to reject as utterly mistaken a large number of scholarly judgments regarding the character of the Gospel narrative, even when these appear to be securely grounded, and widely accepted by cautious and moderate opinion. In the case of the second position, the Christian faith is revolutionized into something radically different from what it has always been understood to be, from the New Testament period up to the present century. If the critic still affirms that he upholds the Christian Faith as an historical religion, he is using the word "historical" in an entirely novel sense.

ii. The doctrine of the wholehearted "demythologizing" and "existential" critics is a radical departure from the historic tradition. The essential spiritual value of the traditional position that The Faith is based upon an objective act of God performed upon the plane of history, is that this is the factor which constitutes Christianity a religion of grace (see pp. 83–84) and of real divine redemption. Here is a witness to something which God in Christ actually *did* in our world, making our human situation different. To make oneself by faith one with this historic and victorious Christ is to partake of "a power *not ourselves* that makes for righteousness." However, if there is in fact no objective divine act, but only a powerful existential impression upon the minds of the first disciples, then there is no redeeming power from outside the human situation. To make onself by faith one with this "Christ of faith," a figure constructed out of the devout imagination of the Church, is in reality only an attempt to rally one's own moral will and love toward God by an exercise of psychological autosuggestion. In this case, the claim that by the agency of the Holy Spirit the Church's worship brings communion with a living and victorious Savior is a spurious claim! Christian worship is in the last resort an exercise in communal autosuggestion. The Church's autosuggestion may be unusually enlightened in moral and intellectual content, a venerable, beautiful, and disciplined system. Yet it is autosuggestion still. There is nothing *there*! This is indeed a radical departure.

iii. It would also appear that the attempt of "existential" Christianity to retreat from "physical miracle" to the inward life of the mind, the moral will, and the spirit, is an illusory relief. This position is inherently unstable. Even if a few astute academics, their minds sharpened to fine intellectual distinctions, can for a time sustain their religious faith upon it, it is only for a time. And experience shows that most people cannot so sustain their faith. The case in point is surely Christ's resurrection. It would at first sight seem attractive to some that the victory of the living Christ over the bondage of sin should be preached as an "existential" one only, wrought in the mind of the disciples, but unencumbered by the miracle of the empty tomb. However, if one presses the inquiry of why the physical miracle of the resurrection should thus be considered an encumbrance to faith, the answer surely is that "physical miracle" is forbidden by that mechanistic philosophy which cannot allow that there is a thinking mind (God) in control of nature (see pp. 27–28). And if one accepts the mechanistic philosophy, it will forbid thinking minds to the disciples, and to believers since, just as surely as it will forbid the empty tomb! The mechanistic way of looking at nature explains away the inward life of the heart and mind of man as a complicated chemical and electrical reaction, determined by physical forces. In fact, either one allows that the thinking mind of man is real, and also that there is a God who can, operating through the laws of nature, work a miracle— or else, logically, one denies both propositions.

iv. However, on the other side, it is to be admitted that these novel and critical methods of New Testament investigation possess some real measure of validity. Otherwise they would not have made their wide scholarly appeal. It can be agreed that the processes very briefly sum-marized in paragraph (b [iv]) above did take place in the formation of our Gospel narratives, and that real account must be taken of this in reliable interpretation. It is not necessary in the supposed interests of the authentic historic Faith to deny outright the findings of modern critical scholarship. All that is requisite is that these methods be not pressed to the extreme, in the manner of some of their most eminent exponents, such as the Bultmannians. Thus it should prove possible both to give a dispassionate reading to work of New Testament scholar-ship, and also to defend the dogmatic substance of the traditional and historic Christian Faith. This is a central and moderating position.

v. It is clear that there is an inherent tendency for certain critical methods of New Testament investigation to proceed to an extreme. First one minor feature of the accepted Gospel narrative is explained away as taking its origin in the interpretative and preaching interests of the mind of the early Church, and then another, and another, until the reliable historic Christ virtually vanishes. It may be asked, if the validity of these scholarly techniques be once allowed in principle, what is there to prevent this drift to extremism? An answer worthy of con-sideration is that the findings of a critical scholar are at least as much due to the philosophy of life which motivates him, and to the attitude of mind which he brings to his study, as to the character of the factual evidence.

Clearly, in the world of honest scholarship objective facts are sacred. Such facts include the existence, the contents, and the date of some manuscript or other piece of historical evidence. However, the mentality which is applied to this evidence is something *adopted* by the scholar, and which therefore can be called in question, or changed. It is never self-evident. And the orthodox Christian believer has just as much right to his philosophy and general attitude of mind as has the radical critic, or the skeptic. He has behind him the immense and impressive consensus and the long-tested endurance of the accepted Christian tradition. This is an important circumstance which must never be forgotten in reading the impressive works of learned men. One rightly respects erudition, and some learned writers of great repute are admittedly very radical in their criticisms. It must, however, always be remembered that they are not radical simply because they are deeper scholars than those somewhat more conservative. They are radical largely because of the initial sub-jective presuppositions which they have brought to the study of the objective facts.

The method of scholarly research is the comparison of biblical texts with each other, and of biblical with nonbiblical sources, to determine which may have influenced which in the evolution of the tradition. Each of these acts of comparison is a judgment which reflects the underlying philosophy or general approach of the scholar in question. Thus a learned volume of 200 pages, each with ten footnotes giving references, appears at first sight to present an irrefragable case of 2,000 separate pieces of evidence. Actually there is one piece of *determinative* evidence

—the particular mentality of the scholar who has made all the 2,000 judgments! This is why the evidence can be arranged in so many different ways.

The response of prudent Christian thought is not impatiently to reject the whole concern of critical scholarship as unreliable, irreverent, and dangerous to faith. Yet on the other hand, one certainly need not feel overawed into the abandonment of the historic Christian Faith simply because some extreme critic is a writer of great repute. More mature experience indicates that what is required is on the one hand respect for these illustrious figures, but also that they be viewed in the proper perspective from the vantage ground of the well-tried Christian tradition. In the past many stimulating schools of "modern theology" have gone all the way down one extreme track or another. After the experience of many years it has generally been shown that there was some aspect of truth in almost all, but never the whole of the truth. Those who on the one hand have candidly considered what the new school of thought has to offer in the understanding of the Christian system, but who on the other hand have treated the new school with cautious reserve, refusing to revolutionize traditional Christian theology because of it, are generally found, when the whole discussion is over, to have represented the most complete intellectual integrity and the fullest Christian wisdom.

vi. SUMMARY. If a mediating position is adopted it would appear that the New Testament account of Christ is not dispassionate biography, but an attempt so to present the facts about Christ as to win converts to Christian faith. Nevertheless, this does not imply that the account of the facts is radically unsatisfactory as historical evidence. The narrative has passed through the mind of the believing Church, which has introduced certain interpretative elements. However, these concern nonessential features. The main lines of the Gospel portrait of Christ are to be accepted as reliable, as an account of His character, teaching, death, and resurrection. They form a sufficient basis for the historic faith.

Particular leading examples of the issues discussed arise in connection with the doctrines of the Virgin Birth, Christ's resurrection, and the Second Advent.

A number of other important issues regarding the historical character of the Gospel narrative are more conveniently treated in the chapter on the Bible (see pp. 194–200).

II. Jesus Christ, His Only Son, Our Lord

The faith that in the person of Jesus God Himself had met mankind and performed His saving act in this world, came to birth in the fellowship of the disciples. The stages of the process may be traced out in the titles given to Jesus in the New Testament.

A. Jesus

This is the name given to our Lord in infancy (Luke 2:21), and speaks to us of our Lord as a man among men. The use of this human and personal name symbolizes to us the first stage of the meeting. Men first encountered Christ as one of themselves (Matthew 13:54–57). "Jesus" is the customary English rendering of the Greek name which in turn represents the Hebrew name which we read in our English Old Testament as "Joshua." Both names mean "Saviour," and our Lord was thus named after the hero who brought the tribes of Israel into the promised land (Joshua 1:1–9; compare Acts 7:45; Hebrews 4:8). There were other people with the same name (Colossians 4:11).

B. Jesus as a Prophet

1. The growing impression which Jesus made upon those who met Him was that He was a man of commanding personality, who possessed an unique grasp of spiritual things. He reminded men of the old prophets, upon whom the Spirit of the Lord descended to enable them to declare a word from God with authority. In particular, they were amazed at His power to heal, and to cast out demons. So He was hailed as a prophet (Matthew 16:13–14; Mark 6:15; Luke 7:16).

2. Answering to our Lord's human office as a prophet, is the circumstance that He received as preparation for His public ministry the typical prophetic equipment of a baptism of the Spirit of the Lord (Mark 1:9–11). Traditional Christian doctrine has decisively rejected the supposition that in this experience a certain ordinary man Jesus "became" the Christ, for this would be to make our Lord no more than an inspired man. The notion that the divine Spirit indwells all men to some extent, and Christ to the fullest extent, is not the accepted Christian doctrine of Incarnation, for such a doctrine does not represent the *union* of humanity with God. The Church teaches that the union of human and divine was complete from the first moment of Christ's conception in the Virgin's womb. We may say that He gradually became aware of His unique nature and office, and that He became aware of this through the operation of His natural human faculties. Doubtless the illumination which came at His baptismal inspiration was a decisive stage in this self-realization. Nevertheless, our Lord came to this realization on account of what He already was by nature.

C. The Christ

1. The New Testament word "Christ" is the Greek equivalent of the Hebrew word "Messiah," both words meaning "the anointed one." Anointing with oil was in Bible days the rite for consecrating a king (as in 1 Samuel 16:1–13), just as it still is in the British coronation service. Prophets and priests could also be anointed. It was a part of the Jewish faith that God had given to them the Davidic dynasty of kings as the center

of their nationhood, and had promised, in token that He would bless and protect His people through all time, that He would preserve to Israel a king of the house of David (1 Chronicles 17:9–14; 2 Chronicles 6:16). Politically speaking this hope had long and miserably failed, but their faith taught the Jews, in their subjection to pagan overlords, that God would vindicate His promise by doing with supernatural power what manifestly could not be done by political. God would set up His own "Anointed One," His king, His Messiah. Thus many of the Jewish people in the time of Christ were living in a state of expectancy for the coming of the Messiah. He could be thought of in terms of a coming prophetic, priestly, or angelic figure. However, the idea which more immediately lies behind the New Testament doctrine of our Lord is that the awaited Messiah was God's anointed king, the bringer of God's kingdom and the fulfiller of the ancient promises.

This hope took various forms. The Messiah could be thought of as a man descended from David, but equipped with the fullness of divine power (Isaiah 9:2–7, 11:1–3), or as a completely supernatural figure who had dwelt in glory with God, and who would descend to earth. His kingdom could be expected on this earth, when the creation was divinely restored (Isaiah 11.4–16), or it could bring the history of this world to an end, and exist in a new age. The hope could be given an inferior tone, largely nationalistic, and concentrated upon the victory, prosperity, and happiness of God's chosen people in that day. Yet there were men of spiritual insight whose hope for the unveiling of God's glory was by the restoration of His people to holiness and obedience to Himself, and that this restoration should be the means of divine blessing to all nations (Micah 4:1–4). This messianic hope was a most important part of the background of our Lord's ministry.

2. The first decisive stage in the growth of Christian faith among the community of our Lord's disciples occurred when first St. Peter, and then others, realized that the prophet who had so impressed them was in fact the long-expected Messiah, the Christ (Matthew 16:13–16). This involved a confession that Jesus was much more than a prophet, though it did not of itself necessarily involve the doctrine that He is divine. A Jew would quite possibly have described the expected Messiah as God's personal representative on earth, but not as divine in the later Christian sense. However, though Jesus was a very striking personality, He was very different from the military Messiah of much current expectation, and to come to this realization was a mark of very real spiritual insight, and the token that St. Peter and the others were inspired by God (Matthew 16:17). Thus the original feature of the distinctive Christian confession of faith is that Jesus is the Christ, and those who first made this confession under the leadership of St. Peter constitute in a real sense the foundation of the Church (Matthew 16:18–19).

3. THE SON OF MAN. This title was among those which could be used for the expected Jewish Messiah. It probably takes its rise from Daniel 7:13, where "a son of man," (that is, a noble *human* shape; compare Psalm 8:4)

stands for God's coming world kingdom, in the same way that the four
bestial monsters of verses one to seven stand for the four pagan world
empires of ancient times. This thought was developed in the period between
the Old and New Testaments. In particular, in the so-called Book of Enoch
(46:1–4; 62:2, 5, 9, 14), the "Son of Man" has been turned from the
personification of God's kingdom into a supernatural person, God's king.
He is destined to come from the presence of God upon the clouds of heaven
and to set up God's kingdom.

The importance of this title is that it is the one which our Lord Himself
chose regularly to refer to Himself (for example, Matthew 16:13; Mark
2:10). By this He clearly intended to claim that He was the Messiah (Mark
8:38, 14:61–62).[2] However, it seems to have been a somewhat vague title,
and a somewhat guarded claim (John 12:34). It apparently lacked the
ready-to-hand military and nationalist associations of the familiar title "Son
of David," which was the natural one to find upon the lips of the enthusiastic
crowd (Matthew 21:9). Perhaps Christ chose it as a part of His policy of
avoiding a popular messianic rebellion (John 6:15), and also used it as a
title into which He might more readily pour the notion of the nonmilitary
and spiritual deliverer. Certainly when He used it He was often speaking
of His humility and sufferings (for example, Mark 10:45, 14:41).

4. THE GOSPEL OF THE KINGDOM. This central doctrine is intimately
associated with the confession that Jesus is the Messiah because it is the
essential office of the Messiah to bring in the kingdom. Modern humani-
tarian reformers have often spoken of the kingdom of God as though it
were the ideal social order of universal human brotherhood and right,
set up by human effort in social reform. We cannot doubt that it is one
of the aims of God to stir men up to strive for social right, and so to set up
an improved social order. In a sense, then, activities for social reform may
be a mark of the kingdom. Nevertheless, this reformist doctrine can easily
obscure the fact that the New Testament kingdom of God is the action of
God and the gift of God. In the Old Testament the kingdom of God is the
sovereign power of God whereby He rules the world. It is exerted in the
world of men to rescue the distressed cause of right, and in this way to
vindicate the fact that He is king (Psalm 145:11–14; Daniel 2:44, 7:14).
The central theme of the preaching of Jesus was the gospel (that is, good
news) of the coming of this long-expected kingdom (for example, Luke
4:43). This answers exactly to the doctrine that Jesus is the Messiah, or
Christ.

This doctrine has received much attention in the modern world of New

---

[2] Radical critics would largely deny this. The tendency would be to affirm that
the quotation from Daniel was first viewed by the Church as a "prophecy of Christ,"
and then read on to the lips of our Lord to express their faith (see discussion on
pp. 36–38). Indeed, some would say that our Lord did not describe Himself as
"Son of Man," but that the title was attributed to Him by the early Church and
placed upon His lips in the narrative.

Testament studies under the title of the *eschatological* view of the mission and teaching of Jesus. Eschatology is the doctrine of "the end"; that is to say, of the end of this present Age, and of the coming of the Day of God which will bring the unveiling of God's sovereignty, the overthrow of the power of wickedness, and the redemption of God's people. Clearly, our Lord's teaching was vitally concerned throughout with the arrival of the Day of God, and the first Christians lived in vivid expectation of it (Acts 17:30–31, 24:25; Romans 13:11–14). Thus Christ's gospel of the kingdom was largely eschatological, rather than social and reformist.

In many passages our Lord appears to teach that the long-expected Day of God had now arrived. God's sovereign redeeming power was at that moment immediately available (Mark 1:14–15). Because Jesus was with men the kingdom was with men (Luke 17:21, "for in fact the kingdom of God is among you," N.E.B.). Jesus taught that His wonderful acts of healing, casting out devils, and preaching were the very tokens that God's victorious power was now at work in the world (Luke 7:19–23, 11:15–22). God's amazing gift of the kingdom was now near at hand, only waiting for men believingly to grasp it (Matthew 13:44–46).

In some other passages Jesus appears to speak of the kingdom as future. He is to come, and to come very soon, in power and glory, to bring God's judgment and redemption (Matthew 10:23; Mark 9:1, 14:62; Luke 9:26–27). The circumstance that, until they were gradually taught otherwise by experience (compare 2 Peter 3:1–9), the early Christians did largely live in a state of expectancy to see their Lord come in judgment at an early date, would on the face of it seem to confirm the impression that He actually taught something of this sort. To the Christian believer, at least, this is a matter of some perplexity, in view of the fact that Christ did not so come. A variety of views have been put forward to account for this.

The most radical critics have stated that Jesus was an enthusiastic visionary who proclaimed, sincerely enough, that the Day of God was very soon to come, possibly with Himself as judge, but that He was mistaken. However, there was much of more permanent spiritual value in the message of Jesus, which lived on in the mind of the Church, even though experience compelled the Church to reconstruct much of the Lord's original teaching. One who accepts the divine lordship of Christ can hardly accept unreservedly this view, which is apparently destructive of the doctrine that our Lord is God's very revelation of Himself, and the authoritative spiritual leader of mankind. However, it is possible to resolve the difficulty by allowing that the apparent disparity between what our Lord originally meant and what the Church later understood Him to have said arose through difference in thought forms.

It may reasonably be argued that Christ, using the imaginative language of the prophets, symbolized that which is very certain and very urgent by speaking of the event as though it were very near. However, the disciples

did not always very fully and very spiritually understand Him. Their minds
were to some extent clouded with Jewish messianic dreams (Acts 1:6), and
so in their recollection and interpretation of the teaching of their Master
they made His prophetic urgency a whole degree more visible and material
and "near in time," than He had intended. Although Jesus freely used the
eschatological language of the tradition which lay behind Him, it is also
reasonable to suppose that a person of His creative spiritual insight should
have used this stirring imagery in the most spiritual sense of which it is
capable, and not in a naïve and materialistic manner. Consistent with this
supposition is the witness in the Gospels that Christ very positively forbade
His disciples to give themselves over to curious speculations as to the exact
time of this supposed sudden event (Mark 13:32–37; Luke 17:20–21).
Attempts to calculate the "times and seasons" have always been an integral
part of the less thoughtful and more naïve and materialistic type of
eschatological expectation among both Jews and Christians. Our Lord
showed Himself fully aware of this danger, so we need hardly suppose that
He Himself was guilty of falling into it.

Possibly the best construction to be placed upon all the variety of sayings
recorded in the Gospels, interpreted in light of both the spirit of our Lord
and the experience of the Church, is that Christ taught that the kingdom is
both present and future. It was truly present and active in His presence, but
in an initial and relatively inconspicuous stage. And this authentic "seed" of
the kingdom was destined to grow and to prevail in the earth, until the whole
world order should be transformed and glorified by the full unveiling of
God's sovereign power, and the open manifestation of the fact of Christ's
presence (Matthew 13:31–32, 24:27) (see pp. 247–48). Thus the long expectation of God's people was both realized in Christ and yet remains to be
realized. That future tremendous and mysterious realization of the Christian
hope is to be awaited in solemn expectancy, yet not speculated about as
though it were sudden or soon.

5. THE CHURCH AND THE KINGDOM. Jesus also spoke many times of
"entering" the kingdom (Matthew 7:21, 21:31; Mark 9:47, 10:14–15;
Luke 16:16), or of "being in" it (Matthew 11:11; Luke 22:29–30). It has
authoritative "keys" of admission and exclusion (Matthew 16:19, 23:13).
This indicates that in addition to the primary eschatological meaning of the
kingdom as "the sovereignty of God" there is a second and derived meaning
in the mind of our Lord. The kingdom has a proper sphere of action in the
world of men. Though God rules all men, He has a special instrument for
exercising that sovereignty as it is unveiled in Christ. This is the disciplined
company of those who acknowledge Jesus as the Christ, and trust in God's
redeeming act performed in Him. Thus the Church, though not itself the
kingdom of God as some traditional theology has claimed, is the instrument
of the kingdom. It is the community of the kingdom, called into being by
the King for the extension of His rule.

D. The Lord

The developing devotion and religious thought of the New Testament Church is reflected in the use of this title for Christ, for the name "Lord" seems to carry implications going beyond that of "Messiah." The deepest conviction of the Christians was that Jesus had done for them what only God can do. In response they regarded Him as man can rightfully think only of God. In union with Christ they had been united with God, for He had conquered the guilt and power of sin and evil. Therefore they trusted Christ for salvation. They made implicit obedience to Him their rule of life. Their attitude toward Him was one of unreserved loving trust and adoration. In fact, the language of worship came instinctively to their lips as the Church gathered together to hold communion with Him. It was this experience which was the foundation for the Church's claim that Christ was higher in dignity even than the Messiah of Jewish expectation. The conviction was symbolized in the title "Lord," which indicates the object of one's religious devotion, and trust for eternal salvation. Thus, while the first primitive confession which united the Church was "Thou art the Christ," the characteristic creedal confession of the New Testament Church is "Jesus is Lord" (Acts 2:36; Philippians 2:11). This word probably has its roots in both the Jewish and the Gentile backgrounds of the Church.

1. Among other uses of the word "Lord" in Gentile religion, the pagan mystery religions commonly referred to their divinities, in whom the devotee trusted for salvation, by the title "Lord." St. Paul shows himself aware of this, and stresses both the comparison and the contrast. The one and only true "Lord" and object of devotion is Jesus, the Christ (1 Corinthians 8:5-6).

2. Furthermore, the Greek translation of the Old Testament, in common use at that time both by the Jews and by the Church, rendered the sacred name of God by the word "Lord," just as does our English Old Testament. That the Christians were able to use the same divine name for Jesus shows how far their thought had moved. It took the later Church much time and care to think out a precise theological formula by which they could say that their Lord was divine in the full sense of the word, and also safeguard the basic truth that God is one. However, we see here in the New Testament a clear witness to the fundamental convictions which made the doctrine of the Holy Trinity necessary to the Church, as a way of drawing out clearly the implications of Scripture.

E. The Divine Son

The doctrinal conviction of the New Testament Church, springing out of her profound experience of saving union with God in Christ, is supremely expressed in this title. It speaks still more exactly of the doctrine of the divinity of Christ. In calling on Jesus as Lord, that is, as the object of religious devotion and trust, the Christian had accepted an attitude to Christ

which man can only rightly adopt to God. The word "Son" crystallized their
conviction that they were correctly guided in doing this. A son has the same
equality of human nature as his father. They are of "one flesh and blood."
This is applied symbolically to Christ. Thus the doctrine of the divine
sonship of Christ symbolizes the idea of equality of divine status with God
the Father (Matthew 11:25–27; Luke 20:9–13; John 1:18, 3:16; Acts 9:20;
Hebrews 1:1–2; 1 John 4:10).

F. The Word of God

Here is an alternative way of defining the divine nature of Christ. The
Greek word for "word" (in English letters written "logos") was capable of
an interesting and subtle variety of meaning. "Logos" can mean "reason,"
the activity of the thinking mind, and also "a word." Reason is a purely
spiritual thing, whereas a word is both spiritual and material, for it is reason
expressing itself outwardly by means of a sound, and so entering another
thinking mind. This usage provides an important method of symbolizing
the relationship which exists between God the Creator and Jesus Christ. The
Creator is the intelligent thinking mind which exists behind the universe.
He is logos, reason. The creation in all its order and beauty, together with
all the noble works of the mind of man, is the outward expression in material
form of the divine reason. Thus the world is a word from God. However,
the coming of Jesus Christ into the world is the supreme example of this
general principle of the spiritual expressed through the medium of the
material. The divine reason, who is the Creator, united Himself with human
nature, so that a being lived on earth who was in a special sense both
spiritual and material, because He was both God and man. Thus Christ is
in a unique sense the Word of God. This way of thinking first comes to light
in the prologue to St. John's Gospel, a passage which has always greatly
appealed to philosophically minded theologians (John 1:1–5, 9–14).

This Greek idea of the Logos is also clearly linked with an Old Testament
one. The prologue to the Fourth Gospel, opening as it does with the words
"in the beginning," is designed to take the mind of the reader back to the
first words of the creation story in Genesis. Here God "said, Let there be
light" (Genesis 1:3; compare Psalm 33:6). The word of God, therefore,
is much more than the expression of knowledge. It is the word of a sovereign
king. It is an *executive* word, which causes something to happen. Thus to
speak of Christ as the Word of God symbolizes the doctrine that He is the
effective agent of creation (John 1:3) and also of restitution and judgment
(Revelation 19:13).

This theology of Christ as the Logos of God is of importance chiefly in that
it may be used to connect the special revelation of the work of Christ with
the general revelation which comes through the intellectual and artistic
activities of all mankind. The divine reason which has moved all true
philosophers took on human form in a unique manner in Christ. Thus all

the cultural activities of mankind lead up to Christ, and He is the focus of them all. Ancient Greece prepared the way for the gospel, just as did the Hebrew prophets. Learning, art, and science are part of the business of the Christian. However, this logos theology is not complete and self-sufficient, and needs to be balanced by the doctrine of Christ as the divine Son. Taken by itself it too easily represents Christ as simply the climax of the revelation of divine truth. Our Lord indeed is this, but still more, He is the agent of a divine redeeming historical work in the world.

III. The Incarnation

We now turn from the basic Christian convictions about our Lord, born of the experience of divine salvation, and recorded in the New Testament, to the precise theological formulae which the Church later developed in order clearly to bring out the implications of the New Testament witness. The doctrine of the divine Son as He exists in glory is more conveniently treated when we consider the doctrine of the Trinity. We now outline the Christian doctrine of the divine and human natures of the incarnate Lord.

A. The Incarnation

This word is devived from the Latin *carnis,* "flesh," and means "becoming flesh" (compare John 1:14). The Christian doctrine of the Incarnation is that the divine Son, who from all eternity is God in the same full sense that the Creator-Father and the Holy Spirit are divine, completely and permanently joined Himself to our genuine human nature, so as to form one real person who was at once both fully divine and fully human. In this way God joined Himself to the human race, His handiwork, and lived a real human life in this world (Philippians 2:5–11; Hebrews 1:1–8, 5:5–8). This doctrine is both the foundation of the whole classic Christian system and the chief cause of offense in the Christian system to naturalistic thinkers who conceive of the universe as a closed mechanistic system. The personal visit of God to His own creation is the cardinal example of a divine intervention into the affairs of men. It is the supreme miracle, which if accepted makes credible at least the possibility of other miracles. The Church originally sought to frame in systematic and unambiguous language the implications of her basic conviction that in Christ God had come to man and had done for man what only God can do. The doctrine of the Incarnation is required if Christianity is to retain its character as a religion of real historical divine redemption.

Any adequate doctrine of salvation appears to require two affirmations regarding our Lord. He must be divine, in the proper sense of the word, or His life, death, and resurrection is not the divine saving action in the world. And He must be human, in the proper sense of the word, or His saving action is not within the world of our human affairs, and has nothing

to do with us. A teacher who is prepared to regard Christianity as no more
than a philosophy of life or an ethical system can very well find himself
content with a view of Christ which represents Him as the perfectly inspired
man, and the bringer of the supreme revelation of God's will. In every age,
however, teachers who have fully appreciated the Christian religion as a
gospel of real redemption have affirmed the Incarnation. Here is "the great
divide" between the broadly spiritual and humane view of life and the
specifically *Christian* view.

By way of clarification we may outline some views of Christ which do *not*
represent the Christian doctrine of the Incarnation, and which were held
by some in the ancient world or which are current today. (The names given
to some of these in footnotes are the technical terms used in historical
theology, and are listed here for the sake of identification when they are
found in theological literature.)

1. VIEWS WHICH DO NOT DO JUSTICE TO CHRIST'S FULL DIVINITY. (a)
The Holy Spirit who inspires all true prophets descended in the fullest
possible measure upon the righteous man Jesus, so that He became the
Christ.[3] (b) There is a divine "spark" in the nature of all good men, and
particularly in the great saints of mankind, who are in this sense "incarna-
tions" of the divine. Christ was the supreme example of this general divine
indwelling.[4] (c) At the beginning God the Father created an intermediate
being who was higher in spiritual dignity than any other created soul, but
less than the supreme and uncreated God. This being became incarnate.[5]

2. VIEWS WHICH DO NOT DO JUSTICE TO CHRIST'S TRUE HUMANITY. (a)
The incarnate Son, being divine, did not have a real and material body. It
was a "spiritual" phantom which only appeared to go through the motions
of physical life (compare 1 John 4: 1–3).[6] (b) Christ's humanity consisted
only of a physical body and animating nervous system, but lacked the higher
directing faculties of reason and responsible moral will. These latter were
supplied by the indwelling divine principle.[7] (c) The humanity was swal-
lowed up in the divinity, so that it was in effect no longer itself, "like a drop
of vinegar in the ocean."[8] (d) Christ's human mental and moral experience
was radically different from our own, and was, in effect, only an appearance
put on for the purpose of acting the part of a man. Thus, being God, He
knew everything perfectly without learning, and did not share the natural
knowledge of His time. He only seemed to learn by asking questions. So also,
being God, He could not *really* be tempted by evil. It was only an appearance
put on for the sake of the disciples. Such notions reflect a naïve and unin-

3 Adoptionism.
4 Found in pantheistic systems like Theosophy.
5 Arianism, and original Unitarianism.
6 Docetism.
7 Apollinarianism.
8 Monophysitism.

structed reverence for our Lord's divine nature. The witness of the New Testament should be taken quite seriously (Luke 2:52, 4:1–13, 22:39–46; Hebrews 4:15, 5:7–8).

3. A VIEW WHICH DOES NOT DO JUSTICE TO THE UNITY OF THE HUMAN AND DIVINE. The fully human and fully divine natures went about together, in somewhat the same way as a man's shadow goes about with him. The two natures were united only in the sense that they always had the same moral will, and so acted together, almost in the manner of identical twins, who may find themselves always in perfect rapport with one another.[9]

B. _The_ Homoousios _Clause_ *of the same substance — Arius*

The newcomer to theology may well form the judgment that doctrinal formularies such as the above are extremely abstract and remote, and that the ancient fathers of the Church who disputed about them were employed in a task spiritually most unprofitable. A clearer appreciation of the process which lies behind the orthodox doctrine of the Church may be gained by a consideration of the origin of one salient clause of the Creed.

In A.D. 317 Arius, a scholarly presbyter of the church of Alexandria, in Egypt, aroused controversy by teaching which he considered gave a reasonable explanation of the person of Christ. Actually it was a doctrine of Christ adjusted to notions of the nature of God derived from a background in the secular culture of the day, rather than from the Bible. Arius taught that before the world was created, and before time began, the Father, who alone is the absolute, unmoved, and unknown God, _created_ His Son, who is far higher in spiritual rank than any other created being, and who was the agent of the creation of the rest of the world. The Son might truly be called "divine," and worshipped, but He was not divine in the same full sense as the Father is divine. This Son became incarnate by indwelling an animated human body, taking the place in it of the higher spiritual faculties. This subtle explanation was clearly an innovation, contrary to the original New Testament faith in a divine Lord and Savior; yet it proved very difficult to exclude by quoting texts, or by the established creedal formularies.

There was thus a long and obscure theological controversy, the turning point of which was the first General Council of the Church, which met at Nicea in Asia Minor in 325. Arius and those who sympathized with him were here condemned. The confession adopted to state the Church's faith was an eastern baptismal creed, into which was inserted the Greek word _homoousios,_ "of the same substance," despite the objection of some that this was a novel and nonbiblical word. This operative keyword later appeared in a fuller creed, which by long tradition is recited in the eucharistic liturgy as the "Nicene" Creed, and which goes back to the second General Council of the Church, of Constantinople, in 381. It is the word translated _"being of_

9 Nestorianism.

✝

one substance" with the Father. The intention of this word is to affirm beyond question that God the Son, who became incarnate as our Lord Jesus Christ, is divine in the fullest and most exact sense of the word, even as the Father is divine.

Since that time this Creed has won increasing prestige as a canon of orthodox Christian faith. It is today accepted as such by the Roman Catholic and the Eastern, or Orthodox, Church; by Anglicans, and other denominations descended from them, such as Methodists; by Lutherans, by Reformed or Presbyterians; and it is assented to in more general terms by many other Christian denominations. In our own time the "Nicene" Creed, with this word as its focus, has been accepted by the Ecumenical movement as the doctrinal confession which more than any other expresses the underlying unity in faith of the divided parts of the Church. It is the Creed which symbolizes the faith which is based on the Incarnation.

Looking back now, from the vantage ground of the centuries, one may affirm that the Church of the fourth century was providentially guided by the Holy Spirit in this perplexed choice. Christian existentialists argue that it is not possible to express Christian faith in abstract speculative terms drawn from Greek thought, such as "substance." However, if it is allowed that Christian faith may be expressed in these classic terms, then this authoritative Creed will be seen to express the underlying spiritual intention of the New Testament. Had the subtle doctrine of Arius been allowed, nonbiblical views of the nature of God would have been admitted to dominate Christian theology. This reduced doctrine of Christ would have perhaps sufficed to proclaim our Lord as the supreme revelation of God, and the supreme teacher. It would not have sufficed as the basis for the preaching of Christianity as a religion of real redemption from sin, by faith in a divine saving action in Jesus Christ. Christianity would have evaporated gradually into an humane but ineffectual philosophy. This is a single salient example illustrating the general process of the establishment in the ancient and undivided Church of the orthodox body of Christian doctrine.

C. Kenosis – *emptying*

In summary, the person of our Lord consists in the divine Son, who has fully, truly, and permanently united with Himself genuine human nature, like ours save that it is sinless, yet without either the divine nature ceasing to be divine, or the human nature ceasing to be human. Thus as one person, alike human and divine, God united Himself with the human race, and conquered the guilt and power of sin, as man and for man. Nothing can wholly take away from the mystery of this central proposition of distinctive Christian theology. Nevertheless, men will continue to ask, "How can this be?" Intellectual caution and reverent reserve is necessary in seeking to answer this question. Just as it is impossible fully to understand the genius of Shakespeare, so it is still more impossible fully to comprehend the inner workings of the mind of Jesus of Nazareth. And it is still more impossible fully to comprehend the nature of the divine. Nevertheless, the Christian believes that God has revealed certain things, and that they are recorded in the New Testament.

God the Son, as divine, exists in eternal and changeless bliss, and in that bright glory upon which man cannot look. His being is not material, and is unlimited to space and time. He has all power, and knows all things, past, present, and future. It is clear that these qualities cannot exist in a human being. Jesus of Nazareth was confined to one time and place, a man spiritually majestic indeed to those who knew Him, but of humble station, inconspicuous in the wider world of human affairs, and not significantly recorded by the secular historians of His time. The glory was hidden, and the power. Furthermore, the New Testament witnesses that our Lord's mind and spirit worked in a truly human way. He apparently shared the natural knowledge of the times. For example, He spoke of what we call "psychological disorder," in the manner of His time, as demon-possession (Mark 5:1–13). This was the case even with natural knowledge on subjects connected with religion, though it was combined with matchless spiritual insight. Thus He was content to echo the general traditional judgment of His times that David was the author of the Psalms (Mark 12:35–37). The divine omniscience was hidden.

Our Lord also knew what it was to have a truly human religious experience. Thus in company with other worshipers He went to the synagogue (Luke 4:16). Like other devout men, He looked up to the heavenly Father with reverence and obedience (Mark 14:36), and modestly forbade men to give undue reverence to Himself, for worship is due only to God (Matthew 19:16–17). He lived a life of trustful prayer (Luke 6:12). Though those who knew Him bore witness of the marvel of His sinlessness, yet He could on occasion face temptation, and temptation that was grim and sore (Luke 22:39–44). This would appear to involve us in the surmise that He who by virtue of His divine nature was incapable of falling to temptation (James 1:13), in His human consciousness was unaware of this invulnerability, otherwise He could not have been truly tempted. Most mysterious of all, He who was by nature perfectly united with God could on one dreadful occasion share the darkest of human experiences. Upon the Cross, and fully one there with the human race in shame and guilt, He felt separated from God (Mark 15:34). Thus even the divine spiritual serenity could be shadowed. It was impossible for Him to be genuinely human without the hiding of these bright glories.

There is, however, a divine glory which we can imagine as consistent with the genuine human experience of a perfect man. We have never encountered it, because we have never seen sinless humanity. Nevertheless, we can imagine it as in principle capable of existence. This is the divine glory of perfect love to all men, of unerring moral insight within the scope of the natural circumstances of life, and of complete moral triumph in face of temptation. This divine-human glory did fully shine forth in Christ (John 1:14; 2 Corinthians 4:6; Hebrews 1:3). Therefore the divine-human person, though limited in glory, may truly be spoken of as divine (Colossians 2:9).

This doctrine that in becoming incarnate the divine Son "emptied Himself of all but love" is called *kenosis*, that is, "emptying."[10] Clearly some form of self-emptying is necessary in any intelligible doctrine of the Incarnation, but the doctrine needs carefully to be guarded against the supposition that in order to become man the divine Son temporarily "de-goded" Himself. The two chief safeguards are, first, that this limitation of glory was not one imposed upon the divine Son by any force of necessity. It was His own sovereign action of infinite condescension (John 10:17–18). In the second place, the divine Son did not undergo any kind of alteration in His divine nature when He became incarnate. Heaven, the throne of God's majesty, is not a place, but if the metaphor be allowed, the divine Son was still as fully "in heaven" during the time of the Christ's life on earth as He was before, and has been since.

D. Communicatio Idiomatum

A further consequence of the idea of Incarnation may be shown by explaining the technical term *communicatio idiomatum,* "communication of properties." The union of human and divine into one genuine human-divine person is so intimate that that which may be said of the human, or of the divine, may truly be said of the whole person. Therefore, what is properly said of the one nature of Christ may, by application, be said of the other nature. Thus, Christ suffered and died by virtue of His human nature. The divine, considered as the divine, exists forever in bliss, and cannot suffer or die. Nevertheless, the divine-human person suffered and died, and therefore the sufferings may be called the sufferings and death of God. This is not to say that God "as He is in Himself" is invaded by suffering, but that as He exists in His Son incarnate He condescends to suffer. Here is an expression of the paradox of the Incarnation. Thus the language of Christian devotion can sing of Christ on the Cross:

> Impassive, He suffers; immortal, He dies.

The principle of the communication of properties also works the other way. We may truly say that in Christ our human nature triumphed over sin and

---

10 Compare the original Greek of the opening clause of Philippians 2:7, commonly rendered "He made himself of no reputation" (K.J.V.). This is literally "He emptied Himself."

death, in token that by divine grace we may triumph. However, the triumph of the one divine-human person was by virtue of the divinity.[11]

IV. Conceived by the Holy Ghost, Born of the Virgin Mary

A. Traditional Doctrine

The manner in which the divine and human natures in our Lord were joined at the Incarnation was that Christ was born of a human mother without the intercourse of any human father, by the special divine action of the Holy Spirit (Matthew 1:18: Luke 1:34). Thus Christ's human nature had a human mother, but no human father. From the Godhead Christ took the divine nature of the Son. From a human mother He took His real human nature.

B. Theological Significance of This Doctrine

1. The essential principle of the Incarnation is the personal union of God with His own handiwork. This is the occasion of the entry of God into His world for the purpose of breaking the fateful train of cause and effect which comes from the sinful past of the race, so as to give humanity a new redeemed beginning in a power not its own. This incarnational principle is symbolized by a birth into the human race which was both in one aspect like every other birth and in another different from every other birth. Christ wrought out the saving act of God by making Himself one with man in every sphere of human life, at the price of self-humiliation, patient endurance, and suffering; so that as man He might in every sphere of life give perfect and victorious obedience to God. His miraculous birth was a decisive act in that career of sacrificial self-identification with mankind. He who made Himself one with man in the useful toil of the workshop, the common worship of the synagogue, and the pain and disgrace of the Cross, made Himself fully one with man also in the humility of an infant birth and in the happiness of a godly home. This birth is a token of the principle of continuity with humanity, of identification. Yet the one who made Himself one with man was not just another man. He was also radically different from all men, the divine-human Man who brings from outside this world a new divine beginning for the race. Thus He was really born of a real

---

11 Another example of the communication of properties, which is a prominent part of some traditions of Christian thought, is the application to our Lord's holy Mother of the title "Theotokos" (in Greek), or "Genetrix Dei" (in the Latin Mass), which is commonly but not very adequately translated "Mother of God." The correct sense is "the God-bearer." Clearly, only the human nature of our Lord was born of the Virgin Mary, for the divine nature is eternally begotten of the Father. Nevertheless, the one divine-human person was truly born. In this sense the Virgin Mother is the "Bearer of God." The use of this title "Theotokos" is the Church's way of saying that it is not the case that a purely human baby was born, who later *became* divine. The Babe of Bethlehem was the incarnate Son from the very beginning of His human existence.

mother, and did not descend from heaven suddenly as an angel. Yet He was also born by a mysterious divine action, answering to a new divine intervention into human affairs.

2. Another theological truth symbolized by the Virgin Birth is that God performs His saving intervention through the method of human cooperation. God's entry into the race was not sudden, inexplicable, blinding in glory. He entered the human race in the normal way, working through and not suspending the natural order. We are not indeed expressly told in the Gospel record that the Virgin was given the opportunity of refusing the wonderful providence which confronted her. Yet this is to be understood, for God does not need to ask questions of this sort. The Christian believes that God chose for this incomparable destiny a woman whose response He foreknew would be the immediate impulse of self-yielding to the divine calling, in the spirit of trustful, grateful, and willing obedience (Luke 1:38). The cooperative obedience of the Virgin Mary is the essential significance of the story of the Annunciation. Here we see the supreme example of the general principle of human cooperation with God. To yield oneself up to God in loving and trustful obedience, to be used by Him with a power not one's own for the accomplishment of a mighty divine purpose, is the essential of what it means to be a Christian believer. The obedience of the Virgin is the great example of this general Christian principle, for she by her cooperation was revealed as the chosen instrument of God's mightiest action, the Incarnation itself.

Summary of Divergence: Attitudes Toward the Doctrine of the Virgin Birth

Few major doctrines of the Christian Faith have been more subjected to attack, and have found more widespread rejection in liberal theological quarters, than the belief in our Lord's Virgin Birth. In natural reaction to this, theological conservatives, in their desire to uphold a doctrine affirmed to rest upon the authority of Holy Scripture, have made a particular point in requiring acceptance of the historicity of this event. There is therefore special need for a dispassionate approach to this subject. In the first place, it has candidly to be admitted that there are some difficulties in the biblical account. In consequence, those who call the accepted belief in question are not necessarily merely trifling with the authority of the Bible. On the other hand, if we are candid we also have to allow that much of the force behind the attack upon this doctrine often comes from the antisupernaturalistic bias of many critics. We believe that the thoughtful man will avoid this bias (see pp. 28, 30–31). The tacit assumption has been widespread that the more miracles are emptied out of the Christian message, the more likely it is to prove acceptable to the thinking man of today. Yet a case can certainly be made that this assumption is in fact contrary to experience.

It has been discussed whether the Virgin Birth is an "essential" doctrine. The answer surely is that the credibility of this doctrine rests upon the fact of the Incarnation itself, not vice versa. We can in principle imagine that the Incarnation could have taken place by the divine Son uniting to Himself human nature which had a human father as well as a human mother. Indeed, many critics of the traditional doctrine argue that our Lord's true humanity is more firmly established if He had a human father, though the orthodox doctrine also has always strongly affirmed Christ's full and true humanity. In this sense the doctrine of the Virgin Birth is less "essential" than the admittedly essential doctrine of the Incarnation. The Christian system does not collapse if this particular article be denied. Nevertheless, if the greater miracle of the Incarnation be once acknowledged, it becomes possible to imagine that the lesser miracle of the Virgin Birth took place also. And the orthodox can argue with some show of reason that it is appropriate to suppose that the Man who, though truly human, was different from every other man, should be both truly born of a woman and also born in this unique and mysterious way.

a. A Critical View of the Virgin Birth

A radical criticism of the traditional doctrine, proceeding on the lines of the demythologizing exegesis of the New Testament (see pp. 35–36), is commonly made on the following lines. The Church of the first days was possessed of a deep faith that in Christ, crucified and risen, a new principle of life had been brought into the world (Romans 6: 8–11). His coming into the world was the starting point of a new human race, composed of those who were united to Him by faith (1 Corinthians 15: 22). In order vividly to express to the mind of faith this idea of a new principle of life, and a fresh human start, and effectually to preach it to the hearers, the religious consciousness of the first Church suggested the symbol of the Virgin Birth. The details of this myth were drawn from the background of the times and the common heritage of ancient religion, the chief constituent elements being mythological legends of the miraculous births of various semidivine heroes, and also the desire to find fulfillment of Old Testament prophecies (in particular, the Septuagint text of Isaiah 7: 14). If one inquires whether the framers of this preaching regarded it as historical or not, the answer is that they were not interested in this issue. The characteristic modern interest in the difference between factual history and religious symbolism passed them by. Their concern was to present their faith as vividly as possible in a striking imaginative narrative. So we may today share in the faith of the ancient Church that Christ brought a new beginning for the human race, but we need not try to defend this story as history, for this is really foreign to the intention of those who first told it. And to acknowledge that the story is unhistorical makes the Gospel more acceptable to the typical modern mind.

b. Historical Discussion of the Virgin Birth

Those who uphold the long-accepted doctrine of the Church will affirm that the above is a construction not in fact developed out of the

appropriate evidence, but read into the scriptural evidence with the
aid of a modern speculative theory which is quite alien to the mind of
the ancient Church. There is no evidence that any of the early Christians
who mentioned the Virgin Birth had any idea other than that it was
an actual historical event. We who are so far off can hardly know more
of the historical probability than they who were near. It is therefore
necessary to weigh up just what the evidence amounts to.

i. Two of the four Gospels contain clear references to the Virgin
Birth (Matthew 1:18–25; Luke 1:31–35). The other two Gospels say
nothing of the life of Jesus before the opening of His public ministry,
so it is only natural to find that this event is unmentioned. Their silence
is not definite evidence against this belief.

ii. It would seem that there were some Christians in the very early
days of the Church who either did not know of this doctrine, or who
knowing it, were nevertheless content to speak of Joseph as in some
sense the "father" of Jesus. The evidence for this is that the First and
Third Gospels, which themselves plainly intend to affirm this belief,
have incorporated in them narratives from the earlier Christian community, which employ these looser modes of expression. The editing has
not been careful to bring the earlier and later narrative to one consistent
whole. In particular, the two genealogies of Christ (Matthew 1:1–17
and Luke 3:23–38) are traced through Joseph, which only makes sense
in a Christian circle which regarded Joseph as the father of Jesus. So
also Luke 2:27 and 41 speak of the "parents" of Jesus, and our Lord's
Mother is represented as saying, "Thy father and I have sought thee
sorrowing" (Luke 2:48).

This undoubted element of confusion plainly indicates to many critics
that there was an original Christianity which did not teach this doctrine.
This shows that it was a later development, which in turn is evidence
that it is unhistorical. A possible answer is that this measure of apparent
confusion and silence is much what one would have expected. In the
first place, although such events as Christ's death and resurrection were
from the beginning integral to the Christian preaching, so that it never
spread anywhere without knowledge of them, Christ's wonderful birth
was at the very first a piece of relatively private information, known
only to a few. It therefore spread after a "time-lag," leaving some at
the first who did not know of it. That some at first did not know does
not of itself suffice to prove that the event did not take place, or serve
to overthrow the positive testimony in other passages of Scripture.

iii. It is to be admitted that there is a large degree of silence in the
New Testament regarding the Virgin Birth. Thus two of the four
Gospels are content to pass over Christ's birth and infancy, and St. Paul
says nothing unambiguous on this matter. This surely indicates to the
impartial mind that the doctrine of the Virgin Birth was not as prominent in the first days of the Church as it later became. Yet this
position does not of itself prove that the doctrine is unhistorical, particularly when one may observe an undoubted dogmatic interest in the
early Church which tended to prevent this doctrine being voiced as

readily and widely as it might otherwise have been. The essential point of the first preaching was that Jesus, though crucified, had been vindicated as the Messiah of Jewish expectation by the fact of the resurrection, supported by the argument from prophecy fulfilled (Acts 2:22–36). In light of this, there was the strongest possible incentive to represent Jesus as the descendant of David, born in Bethlehem (Matthew 2:1–6; Luke 2:1–7; Hebrews 7:14). The doctrine of the Virgin Birth was in a sense an unwelcome modification of this position, for it involved the implication that Jesus was a descendant of David only in a figurative sense. (We get a token of this adjustment in Luke 3:23.)

It is not impossible that St. Paul himself was the most illustrious theologian who found himself in this ambiguous position, which may help to explain his awkward silence. The apostle to the Gentiles to the end clung to the original Christian view that the Jewish people, children of Abraham by physical descent, retained a special place in God's plan of salvation (Romans 11:11–15, 25–32). He could emphasize that his Lord was the Messiah of Jewish expectation, "of the house of David" (Romans 1:3). He would perhaps therefore find it hard to give prominence to the doctrine of the Virgin Birth. It has very commonly been assumed that the weight of dogmatic prepossession was an influence which caused this doctrine to spread in the early Church, with the implication that its acceptance was due to "wishful thinking." Actually it can be well argued that in the very first days of the Church, at least, the weight of dogmatic prepossession was exerted in the other direction. The Christians came to accept the Virgin Birth not because they wished it to be true, but because the evidence supported the "awkward fact."

iv. It has often been argued that the doctrine of the Virgin Birth represents an infiltration of pagan thought into the Christian Church. There are two chief considerations here. First, pagan mythology contained stories of heroes or demigods coming into existence through miraculous births.[12] This idea suggested itself to Christians of Gentile background as a suitable way of expressing the divine honor due to their Lord. Second, much Gentile religious thought was strongly dualist in character, and conceived of the material as the opposite to the spiritual, and consequently of the physical body as the enemy of the higher life of the soul. With these presuppositions, sexual procreation, being passionate and bodily, was easily represented as essentially sinful. Virginity was the higher spiritual state. Therefore the doctrine of the Virgin Birth suggested itself to the Christian consciousness as a way of enhancing the doctrine of the sinlessness of Christ.

A rejoinder to this very common form of argument is that the doctrine of the Virgin Birth does not appear to have arisen principally in the background of Gentile Christianity. In the Church of later centuries

---

[12] The legends referred to in Greek mythology were of gods taking human form so as to have intercourse with women, who then gave birth to "heroes" in a manner analogous to Genesis 6:1–4. This is the idea of a divine-human birth, but not exactly of a virgin birth.

the importance of this doctrine was sometimes emphasized for reasons connected with the notion that sex is "unspiritual," and that the Virgin Birth guarantees the sinlessness of Christ. Yet this was long after the New Testament was written and long after this doctrine had become a part of regular Christian teaching for other reasons. These ascetic influences may therefore at times have enhanced the place of the doctrine, but this is a very different thing from the claim that they *originated* it. If the Virgin Birth of Christ were found to be first spoken of many years later, and in Churches of predominantly Gentile background, this would indeed be a suspicious circumstance. However, the Christians of this early pre-New Testament period, even if not all of Hebrew physical descent, were predominantly of the Jewish religion. That is, the original Church was securely based upon a Jewish religious background and framed its institutions and doctrine upon Jewish and biblical ideas. In this background there was not the slightest inclination to look on pagan mythology with anything but contempt. It would hardly be adopted into Christian doctrine. In the Old Testament, furthermore, there is no notion whatever that celibacy is a purer spiritual state than marriage. The Bible is indeed a great book of families, and a chief sign of God's blessing upon the righteous is to have a long posterity. It is very significant that the clearest New Testament reference to the Virgin Birth is the one which occurs in the most Jewish-Christian of the Gospels (Matthew 1:18–25). The circle which first treasured this story had no bias whatever in favor of virginity as a holier state than matrimony.

v. Another form of argument to explain the development of the doctrine of the Virgin Birth is that it arose out of the attempt to find a "prophecy fulfilled" in the Septuagint (traditional Greek translation) of Isaiah 7:14. This reads "Behold, a virgin shall conceive, and bear a son." If this could be applied to the birth of Christ there was supplied a wonderful mark of divine prescience in this Old Testament passage, which was taken as a proof of the inspiration of Scripture, and a vindication of Scripture's witness to Christ. Thus the Christians read the Old Testament text into the life of Christ.

It is to be accepted that the early Christians did search through the Old Testament with great care to find examples of "prophecies fulfilled." Isaiah 7:14 was in fact to them one of the most impressive examples. However, the weakness of the case here is that so far as one can judge the events were the other way around! There appears to be no particular evidence before the time of Jesus that Isaiah 7:14 was interpreted as a prophecy of the birth of the expected Messiah. Thus the event of our Lord's Virgin Birth was believed in first, and this prophecy interpreted in this way in light of it, not vice versa.

vi. SUMMARY. There are admitted obscurities in the Scripture witness to the doctrine of the Virgin Birth. Therefore it is well not to be too dogmatic. The balance of historical evidence is such that the historic character of the doctrine can be defended out of the New Testament, but not placed beyond dispute. It is incautious for the modern critic to claim to know more about it than writers who may quite possibly have known the only person who could have given direct testimony! (Compare Acts 1:14.) The argument shows how much the result of the investigation depends upon the prepossessions in the mind of the reader. One who comes with a bias against the miraculous, and an acceptance of extreme critical theories, will have no difficulty in finding grounds for objection to the traditional doctrine. On the other hand, one who starts with a reverence for the authority of Scripture as it has been transmitted to us, and for the integrity of the Church's Creed, will find equally good ground for upholding the Virgin Birth as a historical event as well as a divine sign.

C. Further Doctrine Concerning the Virgin

1. HER TITLE. Much traditional Christian devotion has expressed the reverence which is due to our Lord's holy Mother, because of her unique relationship to the divine-human person, by referring to her as the Blessed Virgin Mary. This scriptural title is derived from Luke 1:48.

2. THE IMMACULATE CONCEPTION. Much traditional Christian theology has sought to safeguard the sinlessness of our Lord's humanity by the doctrine that the Virgin, from whose human nature our Lord's humanity was derived, was herself conceived without stain of original sin (traditional proof-text: Luke 1:28, 42).

3. THE PERPETUAL VIRGINITY. Another traditional opinion which has been widely held is that the Virgin never had any sexual relations with her spouse Joseph. This makes it necessary to affirm that the "brethren" and "sisters" of Christ mentioned in the New Testament (Matthew 12:46, 13:55; Galatians 1:19) were not, as one would perhaps naturally assume from the narrative, the children born to Mary and Joseph after the birth of our Lord, but were "cousins," or possibly Joseph's children by a previous wife. The background to this doctrine is clearly an attempt to vindicate the perfect spirituality of the Virgin in terms of a conviction that virginity is a higher spiritual state than matrimony. This idea was very natural in days when monasticism and clerical celibacy so largely prevailed in the Church.

4. THE ASSUMPTION. This traditional doctrine affirms the opinion that after her apparent death, or "sleep," the body of the Virgin did not suffer normal decay, but was spiritually glorified and carried up into heaven to be united directly with her soul. Thus she is taught to be in a condition analogous to the presence of the ascended Christ in heaven (traditional proof-text: Psalm 45:9–15).

5. ROMAN CATHOLIC DOGMA. These doctrines of the Immaculate Conception, the Perpetual Virginity, and the Assumption of the Blessed Virgin Mary have been generally held as matters of pious opinion in the Catholic Church since the Middle Ages. The doctrine of the Immaculate Conception was declared by the Roman Catholic Church to be a dogma of the Faith by a papal bull in 1854, and the Assumption in 1950. A non-Roman Catholic

should understand what this step involves. It does not mean that the papal authorities exerted authority to compel Roman Catholics to believe what they previously did not believe. Roman Catholics have accepted these doctrines as a part of their system of belief for many centuries. The promulgation of these doctrines as dogmas of the Faith means that they are now to be regarded as more than accepted opinion. They are to be taught as essential doctrines of the Faith, to deny which involves a formal charge of heresy.

6. A PROTESTANT STATEMENT. As doctrine and devotional practice connected with the Virgin is one of the chief grounds for the alienation which still often exists between the Roman Catholic and the Protestant Churches, and is also sometimes a cause of reserve and misunderstanding between Eastern Orthodox and Protestants within the Ecumenical movement, this discussion may be closed with a representative statement of the Protestant position.

Honor is due to our Lord's holy Mother in view of fact that she was chosen by God for this unique connection with the miracle of the Incarnation, that she typifies to us to an eminent degree the principle of Christian discipleship, and that she is a symbol of Christian womanhood and the Christian home. Nevertheless, the Protestant feels himself bound to maintain, in all charity, that many customary marks of reverence paid to the Virgin in Roman Catholic worship are regrettably easy to be misunderstood as divine worship by untheologically-minded believers. This is indeed a matter of proportion, rather than of clear spiritual principle, and need not of itself alienate Christian brothers. One may accept the statement of competent Roman theologians that these honors are distinct from, and less than, the worship which is due only to God. Furthermore, the circumstance that a piece of religious symbolism is capable of being misunderstood does not of itself suffice to condemn it, for it is sadly true that the customs of every part of the Church are susceptible of perversion. Yet there is a matter of proportion. The thoughtful Protestant is bound to persist in his conviction that when every allowance is made for legitimate divergence of taste in religious symbolism, the Roman Catholic Church often errs in too easily tolerating, particularly among the simple-minded populations of backward countries, devotional language and practices which may obscure the fact that divine worship is to be offered only to God—the Father, Son, and Holy Spirit.

It is less often considered that there is a deeper cause of division in the Church. It will be found harder to remove because it is a matter of theological principle. One judges that the Roman theologian would defend these doctrines principally on the ground that they symbolize the high honor which is to be paid the Virgin on account of her unique connection with our Lord's humanity, and her position as the eminent type of the Christian saint. In doing this Roman theology has dangerously obscured the difference between doctrine which is symbolically true and that which is true as historical fact. Events which purport to have taken place upon the plane of history are affirmed for a symbolic reason, and affirmed without historical evidence appropriate to the case. The traditional Protestant way of stating this objection is to say that these three doctrines are unscriptural. What is at the bottom of the objection, when it is rightly understood, is legitimate fear lest the historical nature of the Christian religion be assailed. Christian speculation cannot thus take liberaties with history.

The situation has been rendered more acute, from the point of view of orthodox Protestantism at least, by the Roman Church taking action separate from the rest of Christendom to declare that the Immaculate Conception and the Assumption are essential dogmas of the faith. The circumstance that Roman Catholics hold some ideas which appear to the Protestant to be erroneous is not necessarily a barrier to spiritual recognition, if these are only matters of pious opinion which the Protestant is himself not called on to accept. However, if they are to be regarded as essential dogmas it would seem that fellowship can only be established if the Protestant will join in acknowledging them. This is what he cannot do. Here, in the Protestant view, is a regrettable and serious breach in the Church.

7. RADICAL LIBERAL VIEW. Those radical Protestants who have taken up the view of the Virgin Birth outlined in (a), page 57, and of the resurrection outlined in (a), page 103, do not to the same extent feel the force of this traditional Protestant objection to "unscriptural" Roman Catholic dogma. This is because they do not look upon the Christian Faith as a whole as "historical" in the traditional sense, and are therefore less concerned about this distinction between those articles of the Creed which affirm historical facts and those which affirm intellectual constructions. To the radical, the New Testament narratives of the Virgin Birth and the empty tomb are symbolic constructions, rather than accounts of facts, and therefore may be viewed as standing on much the same ground in this respect as the Roman Catholic dogmas of the Immaculate Conception and the Assumption. However, whether the radical liberal Protestant is really nearer to the Roman Catholic in ecumenical understanding is another matter, seeing that the Roman Church is so firmly committed to the traditional position that the Christian Faith is a historical revelation, founded upon the facts of the life of Jesus recorded in the Gospels.

Readings

Baillie, D. M., God *Was in Christ*. London: Faber & Faber, Ltd., 1948.

Boslooper, T., *The Virgin Birth*. Philadelphia: Westminster Press, 1962. (Critical.)

Bright, J., *The Kingdom of God*. Nashville: Abingdon Press, 1953.

Cullmann, O., *The Christology of the New Testament*. trans. S. C. Guthrie and C. A. M. Hall. Philadelphia: Westminster Press, 1959.

Edwards, D., *The Virgin Birth in History and Faith*. London: Faber & Faber, Ltd., 1943. (Defends the doctrine.)

Hodgson, L., *And Was Made Man*. London: Longmans, Green & Company, Ltd., 1928.

Hunter, A. M., *The Work and Words of Jesus*. London: SCM Press, 1951.

Perrin, N., *The Kingdom of God in the Teaching of Jesus*. Philadelphia: Westminster Press, 1963.

Temple, W., *Christus Veritas*. London: Macmillan & Co., Ltd., 1954.

Chapter Three

The Word of the Cross

He suffered under Pontius Pilate,
was crucified, dead, and buried;
He descended into Hell

I. The Suffering Christ

It is not for nothing that the characteristic symbol of the Christian Faith is the Cross. Many systems of religion, of philosophy, and of ethics have honored the figure of the martyr, and have shown themselves familiar with the sad truth that it often falls to good and wise men to suffer, and sometimes to suffer because they are wise and good. However, other faiths regard this suffering as the tragic accident which may overtake the prophet of righteousness. Christianity is distinguished by its insistence that the sufferings of the righteous Lord were of the very essence of what He came to do. The symbol of martyrdom is not merely the memorial of a cruel and unjust death, which took the leader away from His disciples and brought His work to an end. The history of the world is full of such sad stories. In the Christian Faith the token of martyrdom is the symbol that the Master has accomplished His work. Thus the Cross is central.

How characteristic this is of Christianity may be illustrated in a number of ways. In the first place, it was utterly unexpected. The Hebrew people were long prepared by historical experience for the coming of the Messiah. In countless ways their religious ideas and institutions and their Scriptures provide the source and background for Christianity, without which the Christian Faith and the Christian Church cannot be understood. Yet the idea that the expected Messiah should conquer, not by the unveiling of God's

65

power and glory, but by suffering, was hidden from the people. The inspired writer of Isaiah 53 may have had a passing and partial glimpse of this idea, but it was beyond his readers and passed largely uncomprehended. It was not until our Lord Himself realized that this passage was the Old Testament's clearest picture of the essential principle of His mission, and applied it to Himself (Luke 22:37; compare Isaiah 53:12; Luke 24:26–27), that the Christians were able to read in it the mysterious doctrine of a suffering Messiah (Acts 8:30–35). So it is today. The figure of Jesus of Nazareth is almost universally respected and admired among fair-minded and humane men and women of every school of thought. However, when He is respected it is commonly as a martyr, a suffering hero in the painful upward march of humanity. Yet to admire Him in this way alone is completely to miss the point of His mission in the world. It has to be admitted that the distinctive Christian doctrine of Christ as a divine sacrifice for sin is still a stumbling block to the average intellectual person (1 Corinthians 1:18–25). The "word of the Cross" is often viewed as an antiquated dogma having no contact with modern thought and conditions, and hardly worthy of notice; or else it is misrepresented in an impossibly naïve way, and then dismissed; or it is treated as utterly repulsive and degrading.

Several facts already observed set the stage for this central point of Christian doctrine. First we have seen that the argument for the goodness and wisdom of God as evidenced in the order of nature is marred by the presence of disorder within the order. In particular, there is the fact that human life is everywhere darkened by evil and woe. In the second place, the doctrine of the Incarnation is required by the circumstance that the Christian Gospel does not look upon our Lord only as the bringer of a perfect revelation and doctrine. He is the worker in this world of a divine saving act of redemption from sin. And in the third place, our Lord's making Himself one with man involved self-humilitation, endurance, pain, and disgrace. We must now draw out the implications of these facts.

II. The Mystery of Evil

A. Evil and Sin

The construction of the doctrine of a Savior requires first the consideration of what it is from which man needs to be saved. Evil is a comprehensive term, which includes everything in life which appears to be inconsistent with the good and wise plan of a God of holy love. It comprises the suffering which exists in the animal world, together with all human suffering in body and mind, due to natural calamity, disease and death, human stupidity, weakness and mismanagement, and to deliberate wrongdoing and cruelty. The concept of evil also includes the notion of sin, that is, of rebellion against the moral and spiritual order of God. Clearly, the presence of evil is the great and final mystery of life. It is to be noted, however, that this mystery, which darkens the minds and spirits of so many with frustration, bewilderment, rebellion, and unbelief, is a mystery which is created by the doctrine of the goodness and wisdom of the one sovereign God. Religious systems which teach the existence of two equal and eternal principles in conflict with one another, of good and evil, or the existence of many divinities, with wills in conflict with one another and perhaps of uncertain moral character, do not find the existence of evil so great an offense. It is simply something natural and inevitable, which has to be endured as best one can. It is a reflection of the Christian doctrine of God which causes so many to find in the manifest evil of life a temptation to religious unbelief.

Furthermore, conventional minds are chiefly perplexed at the spectacle of the suffering and woe which afflicts the bodies and minds of the race, and which makes life uncomfortable. To the Christian, however, the darkest mystery is the existence in the world of moral and spiritual evil, of sin. It is at first sight very hard to see how a God of holy love can allow continued rebellion against His own goodness, when its fruit is the degradation of the human spirit. One of the most significant aspects of Christian theology is its claim that it can in part illuminate this problem. Even if it cannot give a complete answer to every question which the mind can suggest, it can give an answer sufficient to arm man with courage for the battle of life.

Much human suffering is due to sin. This is very plain in the case of the grief and pain which arises from evil institutions such as war and oppression, from social neglect, from wrongdoing in the family circle, and from the disease which often springs from bad habits and dissipation. It is reasonable also to suppose that generations of living in defiance of God's health-giving laws has to some extent disordered or contaminated the human stock, so that many persons who are not personally "sinners" to any exceptional degree suffer from disease. Another factor is that it is sin which chiefly makes physical death into a sometimes fearsome experience. That the life of the body should come to an end, and leave room in the world for others, is in itself a good thing, and consistent with the Christian view of God. That this end should fill men with fear and grief is due to evil. The idea that the very order of nature itself, including animal as well as human life, has to some extent been disordered as a result of sin, so that the marks of God's goodness and wisdom in it are partially hidden, is an interesting speculation which often proves attractive to the religious mind (Genesis 3:16–19). St. Paul seems to have entertained some such doctrine (Romans 8:20–22).

It is an idea very natural to a simple-minded faith that a God of right who rules the world will certainly visit high-handed sin with the punishment of calamity, whereas the righteous will be rewarded with peace and prosperity in the end (Psalm 37). The Old Testament's more mature reflection upon this problem, particularly in the Book of Job, is that human life does not work out in this way. In large-scale human affairs there seems to be a power which sets a certain limit to the overflowing of human wickedness. Human systems which flourish by oppression and cruelty do seem to contain within themselves the seeds of their own decay, though perhaps only after many centuries. The Christian can rightly treat this as a mark of the divine government of the world. God will not allow His purpose for the world to be entirely frustrated by the disobedience of man. The prophetic view of history, that world powers of evil will in the end be destroyed and God's people blessed, is justified by events. Yet apparently God does not step in suddenly to take away from evil men their power to do evil. Therefore the Church, or the "righteous" nations, cannot trust that obedience to God will supernaturally protect the righteous from martyrdom, or from the calamities of defeat and adversity. The religion of the Cross, which has as its symbol the spectacle of the entirely Righteous One suffering the most unjust of all possible fates, stands as a plain rebuke to any such facile views of human destiny.

To the Christian, then, the deep problem of evil is not the problem of suffering, so much as that of sin.

B. Definitions of Sin

There is much unfortunate confusion about what is meant by "sin."

1. MORAL VIEW. This is the "common-sense" view which we have to use when we seek to frame rules of social obligation and legal justice for the community. In this view sin is an action for which a man is morally accountable, in the sense that he freely did it, knowing it to be wrong in light of the accepted standards of the community of which he is a part. This definition is legitimate for certain important purposes. If it be allowed, then "sin in ignorance" or "sin under compulsion" is a contradiction in terms, and so is sin in a child who has not come to years of moral responsibility. This standard of sin is also one which varies with every form of society.

2. RELIGIOUS VIEW. The man who discovers himself in the presence of God finds himself overcome by the sense of his own utter moral unworthiness (Isaiah 6:5). Even though he knows of no particular sinful action for which he is personally responsible, he is yet appalled at the gulf which yawns between a frail human being, dim of vision and compromised in standards, and the bright glory of the God of holy love. This gulf represents sin in the profounder sense of the word, in the religious or spiritual sense. Christian theology frequently employs the term in this way, and a common cause of misunderstanding is provided when the "common-sense" moral view of sin is taken from the general background of secular thought and read into the language of theology.

C. Sin as Pride

The average humane man, when asked what is the key to all virtue, will probably answer, "love." The Christian, will say "humility." By Christian principle the mainspring of sin is pride. At first sight this may seem to be an ignoble and unwelcome proposition, but experience illustrates what the Church has tried to say at this point. By way of example, commercial advertisers are not concerned with a theological view of human nature, but by trial and error they have discovered a practical technique of persuading people to buy goods. The standard appeal is that to possess this expensive article will make others envy one, and give status, or that to adopt some custom will make one socially acceptable, and that to decorate oneself in this way will make one the object of desire to the opposite sex. It is confidently assumed that men and women crave to live secure in their self-esteem, and to feel that those around them hold them in esteem. We instinctively yet quite irrationally live with ourselves in the center of the picture, and we trust that others will contribute to our welfare. This is what Christian theology means by pride.

Pride is to be condemned because it gives an utterly unrealistic view of life. In actual fact, the center of existence is the God of glory. Man is His microscopic creature. The least that is due to God is a life of obedient service, and any welfare which man can enjoy comes from God. Humility simply means recognizing that this is so. It is a step of spiritual realism, which is essential if life is to be restored to its proper order. Thus sex is not sinful. The desire of man for woman is in itself neither good nor bad, but natural. The self-regarding view of life, which allows a man or woman to look upon the sexual relation as a means whereby one may exploit another for one's own satisfaction is what makes the fatal difference between morally constructive marital happiness and foul lust. So also, property is not sinful. However, the attitude to life which sees oneself in the center corrodes socially constructive labor with that sordid spirit of competitive avarice which will corrupt and disintegrate any form of human society. This happens in human affairs even on the largest scale. Social wrongs continue even in the most advanced and humane societies because so many decent and well-meaning people tend unthinkingly to vote for candidates who tell them pleasing half-truths which minister to their self-esteem, in preference to those who dare to tell them the unflattering truth.

If this be so, then sin is essentially religious and spiritual. It consists in a wrong relationship to God, in a failure to acknowledge Him as the center of reverence, trust, obedience, and love. This is a conclusion against which normal human nature fights, and the reason is not far to seek. If sin is merely wrong action, or a wrong habit, then man may hope to improve himself by suitable moral effort, by superior education, and by providing a more helpful environment. This hope, which is the expectation for human improvement natural to humane and enlightened people who do not live by Christian faith, is a hope which itself ministers to man's self-esteem. But if sin is a wrong inward relationship with God, then man is crushed and helpless, unless God of His grace does something for him. Once a man realizes that God is in fact not the center of his reverence, trust, obedience, and love, he is in the condition of one who knows that he is color-blind, or has no ear for music. He is beset with a disability from which he cannot free himself.

D. The Fall

This stern and realistic doctrine about sin is set forth in the opening chapters of the Bible. The student of comparative religions will see that the stories in the early chapters of the Bible have parallels in the folklore of many primitive peoples. Originally these narratives were "tell-me-why stories," recited to set at rest the unsatisfied curiosity of men with questioning minds who found themselves in a mysterious world, and to give some sort of answer to such questions as "Why are men ashamed when caught naked?" "Why do we have to work?" "Why is the man the head of the tribe?" "Why is childbirth painful?" and so forth. Yet this undoubted similarity in form to the legends of the nations obscures to the mind of many investigators the deep spiritual significance of the biblical narrative. The Genesis story is marked as altogether superior to its parallels by the majestic sense of God which moves through the story, and by its understanding of the workings of the human heart. Built upon the foundations of ancient story there is an authentic word from God which can still help twentieth-century man toward an understanding of life. This is a good illustration of what is meant by the inspiration of the Bible.

Thus we read that man was created superior in talent to the rest of creation. In particular, he was endowed with the capacity for fellowship with God (Genesis 1:26–28). However, he wished to lift himself above his natural state of creaturely dependence (3:1–6). The spiritual result of this attempt at self-exaltation was humiliation, and shame when found in the presence of the holy God (3:7–10). A dreadful train of cause and effect was now revealed, for the first result of spiritual alienation from God is the alienation even of man from wife (3:12–13). The pair self-righteously blame one another, or the Tempter, rather than themselves. A further result is the labor, frustration, pain, and inequity of life (3:16–19). An apparently small sin leads in the next generation to a great one, and family bickering gives place to murder. The unrighteous man slays the righteous, and for the very reason that he is righteous (4:1–10). This crime deepens the curse on mankind (4:11–13). The children of the murderer increase in number, in wealth, in power, in culture, and above all in vainglory (4:16–24, 11:1–4). The final result is social wrong, which stinks to high heaven and is recompensed by overflowing calamity (6:1–13, 11:5–9). Here is the Bible's most revealing natural history of sin. We may recognize that this is the way in which sin operates in personal and social life today.

E. The Natural Man

By "the natural man" Christian theology means humanity as it is ordinarily found, but apart from God's redeeming act in Christ. Our Lord's judgment upon the human race was that it is evil, but that good is present as well (Matthew 7:11). At first sight this looks rather like the commonly accepted easy-going judgment that "Nobody is perfect," but "there is some good in everybody." However, Christian theology wishes to make it plain that the undoubted element of good which is found in all normal men, including men who are certainly not Christians, is not their own good, regarding which they can feel satisfaction in the presence of God. It is the gift of God's grace, even to those who do not recognize it for what it is. Even the decent and humane "natural man," when considered in isolation, is radically alienated from God (1 Corinthians 2:14). However, the usual Christian position has been that in fact men cannot thus be viewed in isolation, for the grace of God is operating in a preliminary way upon all who have not deliberately hardened themselves to good (John 1:9; Romans 1:20). This divine grace which *goes before,* and in a sense prepares the way for, the specific Christian operation of grace has often been called prevenient grace.[1]

F. The Bondage of the Will

Christian doctrine maintains that the will of the natural man is in a condition of bondage, so that of himself man is not able to turn to God and serve God (Romans 7:14–24; Galatians 5:17). This does not mean that Christian theology is determinist. The doctrine of the bondage of the will does not deny what is usually called "free will" and "moral responsibility." Ordinary men outside Christ have a true freedom to choose between one course and another, and between right and wrong, to such an extent that God can fittingly hold them morally responsible, looking with approval upon right, and punishing that which is wrong. All the moral exhortation of the Bible presupposes this (Deuteronomy 30:15–20; Ezekiel 33:1–19; Luke 12:47–48; Romans 3:5–8). Nor is this true freedom of choice confined only to mundane and trivial affairs of no deep moral significance. A man can, by and large, resolve to obey the law of the land in honesty and public spirit. God requires this and approves of it (Romans 13:1–7). What man cannot do of his own unaided will, apart from divine grace, is so to obey God, and so to please Him, as to accomplish his own eternal salvation (Luke 18:9–14, 25–27; Romans 7:24–25; Ephesians 2:8). He is not free to do this. However, even in this high matter man is not utterly helpless and hopeless, in the sense that there is nothing constructive which he can do. He may wait upon God in the obedience of prayer and good-doing, confident that

---

1 In old-fashioned books, "preventing grace." To *prevent* is literally "to go before." See also pages 214–15.

God will approve of him. And in God's good time He will visit him with the opportunity of receiving grace (Acts 10:1–6). There is thus no place for indiscipline and apathy in the lives of those who would find the way of salvation.

G. Entire Depravity

Christian doctrine of the Augustinian school,[2] which has sought to emphasize man's need of grace in the strongest possible terms, has naturally also spoken in the gravest terms of the sinful weakness of the race. The phrase "entire depravity" has often been used in this connection. If by this term it is intended to teach that the man who is outside Christian grace has a moral will entirely and unreservedly turned to evil, so that he can do nothing to which the holy God can give any degree of approval, most Christian theologians would hardly seek to defend this doctrine. In defense Augustinians would, however, cite such a text as Genesis 6:5. However, if the phrase "entire depravity" be taken to mean that the natural man is alienated from God in every sphere of his life, so that there is no moral action which he can perform of his own strength, however desirable or praiseworthy, which is entirely untarnished and pleasing to God, then the doctrine surely is to be defended as realistic. Taken thus it emphasizes that there is no residual area in the life even of the good and upright man which is exempt from the general impossibility that man can do something to accomplish his own salvation. It is not the case that grace merely assists frail man to come more easily and surely to a salvation to which he can by a very great effort attain in his own strength.

H. The Flesh

This term in the New Testament can express the notion of "frail humanity," in contradistinction to the glory of God (Mark 13:20, 14:38; John 6:63; Romans 3:20; 1 Corinthians 15:50; Galatians 1:16). However, the word can also often be used, particularly by St. Paul, as the opposite to the "the spirit." This may easily convey to the reader the mistaken impression that the apostle, and Christian theology following him, teaches that it is the physical constitution, with its natural and animal feelings and desires, which is the essentially sinful element in man. This carries the idea that the body is in some way the enemy of the soul, and that salvation concerns only the immaterial part of man's nature. This way of thinking is contrary to the doctrine that man's body as well as his "soul" is the handiwork of God, and is called to sanctification and destined to salvation. Actually a careful reading of what St. Paul has to say indicates that among the "works of the flesh" he enumerates purely mental and spiritual sins as well as bodily ones, and that the "works of the spirit" include the activities of the body (Galatians 5:16–26). Thus "the flesh" is human nature, and

---

2 See pages 209–12.

the whole of human nature, body or mind or spirit, insofar as it exists in alienation from God, and in rebellion against God.

I. The Universality of Sin

This doctrine is a matter of empirical observation. If there is to be found anywhere a man who professes that he is morally perfect, so that he has no need of a guilty conscience about anything which he thinks or does, those who know this man well are probably quite sure that he is suffering from a sinful delusion! Contrariwise, there is the man whose character appeals to those who know him well as that of a saint, so that they would even venture the judgment that he is uncompromised with sin. This man will be the first to confess that he has a dreadful struggle with many secret temptations. Such are the facts which show that sin is universal, so that all men and women without exception desperately require salvation (Psalm 143:2; Romans 3:9–12).

J. Original Sin

This doctrine is required as the consequence of the universality of sin. The circumstance that every child born into this world, no matter how wisely nurtured and educated, sooner or later falls into some sin, or at least is beset by temptation which can only be resisted by divine grace, seems to show that there is born into every member of the race a bias of nature. This bias makes it inevitable that he will sin, apart from grace. By way of illustration, if a coin were tossed many thousands of times, and were observed to come down "heads" just occasionally, at irregular intervals, it might be argued that the overwhelming proportion of "tails" was no more than the result of a remarkable run of chance, and that in principle it was still equally possible at every successive toss for the coin to come down "heads." However, if the coin *always* came down "tails," one would judge that there was a bias about this particular coin, which compelled it to fall in this way. In the same way, if it were observed that a few of the noblest of men succeed in turning always to the good, it might then reasonably be argued that all the remainder of the race in principle was born capable of remaining sinless also. That the majority of those who were capable of choosing good had to some extent chosen evil would just be an unfortunate circumstance. However, the observed fact that the human coin invariably comes down "tails" seems to indicate that it does so because by nature it must. There is a bias toward sin in each man, because he is a part of a sinful human stock. Thus sin is "original" to him. That is to say, it is part of his constitution from the very beginning.

This theological term can easily prove misleading because of the two usages of the word "sin" (see p. 68). Original sin is not a sinful action for which the man in question is personally responsible. Rather is it the raw material for sinful actions, and the bias which makes them inevitable in human life. Indeed, if the narrowly moral view of sin is adopted, "original sin" is a contradiction in terms. If it is "original" or inborn in one, it is not anything which one has done of free will, knowing it to be wrong. Therefore, it is not a "sin." And if it is a "sin," then it must be something one has done, and so it cannot be "original." Here is probably a chief reason why so many find such difficulty in the Christian doctrine of original sin.

However, if the religious or spiritual view of sin be allowed, then this doctrine is a profound though dreadful truth. The shameful gulf between man's murky and compromised existence and the bright glory of the God of holy love is an inborn and universal factor of human nature. The unrealistic and morally vitiating instinct to view life with one's self as the center naturally appears in its rudimentary form as soon as the growing child awakes to his first moral choices. And as the growing man and the human race in its advance of knowledge come to the awareness of greater powers, the awakening of each one brings the temptation to give way to the self-regarding attitude. Thus as men become more clever, more powerful, and richer, they do not become wiser or better or more humane. The old battle is joined again and again on new ground.

The idea of original sin answers to the conception of the solidarity of the race, rather than that of heredity. There is no particular evidence from experience to show that moral character, or weakness of character, is inherited from one's parents. Original sin is therefore best not regarded as a "thing" attached to man's physical constitution, and inherited through procreation. It would seem to be found in each one of us anew, yet found there because we are part of a race which is collectively fallen. This at least would appear to be the most reliable exposition of such a text as 1 Corinthians 15:22, "For as in Adam all die, even so in Christ shall all be made alive." Adam (the name means "the man") has been chosen by St. Paul as a *type* of the fallen human race. In Genesis 3:1–19 Adam disobeyed God, and brought ruin upon himself. This is a true picture of what the whole human race has done collectively, and each man individually as a part of the race. Thus we are "in Adam." It is noteworthy that in the other passage where Paul employs this doctrine of the human race "in Adam," he does not say that "death" (moral and physical ruin) was inherited by all men by physical generation. It comes upon all because all are members of a race which has collectively sinned (Romans 5:12). We may reject the notion which has been held in some quarters that the sexual act is in itself of the nature of sin, so that those who are born as a result of it inherit the taint of original sin. This appears to be dishonorable to man's body, which is God's handiwork, and to the method which He has established for the continuance of the human race. Nor is this a legitimate exegesis of Psalm 51:5. This text is a poetical way of confessing that man's alienation in spirit from God, which fills him with shame, is part of his constitution from his earliest days.

K. Original Guilt

Traditionally it has been taught that the stain of original sin renders man guilty in the sight of God, and worthy of punishment, quite apart from any actual sins of thought or word which he may have committed. Several alternative views are to be distinguished here.

Summary of Divergence : The Guilt of Original Sin

a. Sacramental View

Long-established Catholic tradition has held that every human being coming into the world is contaminated by the guilt of original sin. Men may only be placed in the sphere of full Christian salvation by incorporation into Christ by Holy Baptism, in which God releases man from this guilt (see pp. 168–69). It does not follow, however, that all the unbaptized inevitably go to the eternal damnation of hell.

b. Augustinian View

The characteristic emphasis of the full Augustinian theology (see pp. 209 12), for example, as notably developed in Calvinism, is that on account of its descent from sinful Adam, and its collective sinfulness, the whole human race is in the eyes of a holy God necessarily the object of just condemnation and punishment (Romans 3:5–6). Only the elect are delivered from this just punishment of universal damnation by the sovereign grace of God (see p. 211).

c. A Moderating Restatement

Much modern thought has found itself uneasy about both these traditional positions. It would be argued by some that the main reason for the development of the sacramental view has been the desire of Catholic churchmen to find a strong theological reason for upholding the dignity and necessity of the custom of infant baptism. The custom of infant baptism was first based upon natural grounds of family solidarity (see p. 171). Afterward the idea of the washing away of the guilt of original sin suggested itself as a reason of principle for the accepted custom. The Augustinian doctrine has also been criticized as a precarious speculative construction developed upon the Christian doctrine of salvation by grace (see pp. 208–9). Therefore we find that some people, both from the Catholic and Evangelical sides, have come to the judgment that the guilt of original sin is ethically a dubious notion which is perhaps best abandoned, or at least modified. The notion of guilt, in its full and proper sense, would seem to be a moral idea, and to correspond to the moral view of sin. A just God could hardly hold man guilty, in the sense of holding him liable for punishment, on account of an inborn taint of nature for which he has no personal responsibility. As man finds himself in the presence of the holy God he may rightly feel himself utterly ashamed and humiliated because of his moral infirmity, and for his membership in the sinful race. Yet this is shame rather than guilt. He is called upon to feel guilt only for those actual sins for which he knows himself to be personally responsible. However, the abandonment of the notion of original guilt in no way detracts from the doctrine that all men need salvation, for all have in fact committed actual sin.

L. The Origin Of Sin: The Fall

Christian doctrine does not profess to explain the ultimate reason why man should have sinned, and why moral evil should have its foothold in a world created and ruled by a good God. Thus, however literally the Genesis account of the Fall be taken, this does not seek to explain why there should have been a Tempter present in the garden, and why Adam and Eve should have so unaccountably fallen to his wiles. The Bible contents itself with saying that this was so. The ultimate origin of sin remains a dark mystery.

There are a few Scripture passages which have been cited in support of the doctrine that some of the angels first sinned against God in the heavenly sphere, and were cast down from the presence of God by way of punishment (Isaiah 14:12; 2 Peter 2:4; Jude 6). Most people would today feel that taken by themselves such texts provide an insecure foundation, for they are poetical figures. In justice to this idea it should be said, however, that if there are such beings as angels (see pp. 31–32), that is, morally responsible intelligent beings, belonging to a sphere of existence other than our own, it is inherently possible that some of them, being morally free, should have sinned. And a "fallen angel," an intelligent being of superhuman powers but of sinful and depraved will, would be a "devil," that is, a superior directing intelligence of evil. The natural order, which seems to display so many marks of God's goodness and wisdom, also contains mysterious tokens of disorder, or natural evil (see pp. 66–67). These are sometimes of an extraordinarily ingenious type, and almost look like the work of a satanic intelligence, corrupting the handiwork of God. Furthermore, evil in human affairs sometimes seems so pervasive and persistent that it would appear to be more than the result of the actions of individual men. It seems reasonable to believe in a corporate human evil, and perhaps in a superhuman conspiracy of evil. Possibly, then, the New Testament doctrine of superhuman satanic intelligences is as reasonable as any abstract philosophical speculation in description of the cosmic operation of evil (Ephesians 6:12). However, it is clear that to press back the origin of evil and sin into the unseen world still does not provide an ultimate reason for evil. One has explained why there should be a Tempter, but not why he should have fallen in the first place, or have succeeded in his temptations of mankind.

By the nature of things, there can never be any secure scientific evidence regarding the first mental and spiritual awakenings of the race, a change which could leave no physical evidence (see p. 78). Thus, when an evolutionary doctrine of the origin of the human race is accepted, the ultimate origin of evil is equally a mystery. The first evidence we have concerning the ideas which moved in the minds of primitive men seems to show that sin was already a dark fact of human life. Science does not know what happened upon the stage before the curtain first went up on the intellectual history of the race. The ultimate origin of evil is therefore a matter of philosophical speculation, but not the direct concern of Christian theology. However, Christian theology cannot accept those philosophical speculations which would explain away sin as not real, or as not truly sinful.

Summary of Divergence : Doctrines of the Fall

a. New Testament and Primitive Christian

The clearest New Testament doctrine is that of Adam as a "type." It was doubtless accepted in the primitive Church that the early chapters of Genesis were literal history, and that Adam and Eve were the first real parents of the race. However, the effective theological interest in the biblical narrative was as a divinely inspired symbol of spiritual principle. The story of Adam and Eve is a picture of what the race has done, and every man in the race (see pp. 85–86).

b. Traditional

Beginning with the writer Tertullian (working around A.D.200), and coming to clear expression in St. Augustine of Hippo (354–430), we find the traditional doctrine that the disobedience of the first parents of the whole race produced a physical, mental, and spiritual deterioration and contamination of human nature as originally created by God, as well as punishment by the withdrawal of the fullness of divine grace from man. This disability has been inherited in the human stock ever since, and explains why the whole human race is weak before temptation, and subject to the just judgment of God. Coupled with this is an emphasis upon the extreme heinousness of the first sin, which was such as to merit this universal punishment. This exposition is clearly linked with an emphasis that Adam and Eve were literally and historically the physical ancestors of the whole race.

The Scholastic theologians of the Middle Ages elaborated this doctrine by maintaining a difference between the "image of God" and the "likeness of God" mentioned in Genesis 1:26. The "image of God" refers to those superior powers natural to man, which make him different from and superior to the animals. Such are reason, speech, moral choice, and the power to be religious. The "likeness of God" was a supernatural gift of divine grace granted to man to lift him up to perfect communion with God, and fill him with "original righteousness." At the Fall the "image of God" was deteriorated, and the "likeness of God" entirely lost. It may be doubted whether this is correct exegesis of the original sense of the Biblical text. However, this construction does correspond to the fact that sin spiritually alienates man from

God, and also damages to some extent his natural powers of body and mind. Yet it does not completely dehumanize him.

c. Evolutionary

A number of attempts have been made to restate the doctrine of the fall in terms of an evolutionary origin of man, so as to preserve the religious values of the doctrine as a part of the Christian system, but to allow acceptance of the findings of natural science regarding the physical origins of the human race. A word of caution is necessary in the approach to this subject, the discussion of which has often generated more heat than light. Granted that man's physical frame has evolved from an animal ancestry which he holds in common with the anthropoid apes, it would appear than man's animal ancestors have been evolving on a track separate from that of the apes for a period of time enormously long compared with that period (very short by standards of geological time) during which the human race has been recognizable as "man." This long period is not so far spanned by a complete and self-evident chain of fossil "missing links." The evidence of a physical relationship to the apes is far more the indirect evidence of present structure, including that of the foetus, and of vestigial remains. There is thus a large element of mystery remaining in the physical "descent of man," and that mystery is at its greatest in that part of most interest to the Christian, namely, the awakening of man to become an intelligent and morally responsible being. Clearly by the nature of things there can be no fossil remains of this nonmaterial change. Therefore, while mystery remains, there is always the possibility that science may drastically revise her findings in ways at present unforeseeable. Nothing is easier than for those who would impugn the findings of natural science in the supposed interests of traditional religious opinions, on the one hand, or for the less thoughtful writers of "popular science," on the other, to pontificate in these matters beyond the secure evidence. The wise reader will remember that from the scientific point of view we do not altogether know how man became man, and perhaps never will. There is certainly room both to respect the secure findings of natural science, and also to accept the rise of man as a marvelous divine act.

Scientific evidence would appear to indicate that the faculty of reason, and of responsible choice, first awoke in primitive men who physically were substantially similar to modern man. Before this awakening, which the Christian may reasonably claim was a distinct creative act, man was presumably animal, neither morally good nor bad, but nonmoral. When God evoked His "image and likeness" man became human and responsible. He became a potential moral agent. At this critical stage the infant moral sense was to some extent defying the inherited current of natural instinct. Some have claimed that this would make it inevitable that the first choice to be made would be sinful. For example, an early moral crisis would occur when conscience first ruled that each member of the hunting pack should no longer scramble for his own fill when the prey was killed, but should make room for the weak and the aged. The same action which had for uncounted generations been neither morally good nor bad, but nonmoral, was now sinful. Yet it was inevitable that this sin should be committed, because it was not to be expected that infant conscience should at the first attempt entirely succeed in rebuking inborn animal instinct. This early and apparently trival sin to some extent alienated man from God, and weakened his power to resist further temptation. This opened the door to sin.

Thus we have an evolutionary hypothesis of the origin of sin, which appears to make sin an inevitable stage in the evolution of good. This is very near to the notion that sin is not really sinful, which in turn is an idea that Christian theology cannot admit. There is, however, one forgotten factor in this symbolic construction. If this first moral choice was presided over by the foreseeing providence of a God of holy love, He would surely have so supported infant but innocent man with His grace that this all-decisive moral test was an equitable one, and not foreordained to failure. It must have been possible in principle for primitive but as yet undepraved man to have chosen good, and thus to have made further good choices possible. The dark mystery of the origin of sin remains, therefore. We can reasonably argue that God had to make man free, and therefore capable of moral evil, if he was to be capable of moral good. Why man should in fact have used this divine endowment of moral responsibility to defile himself remains the final irrationality of human experience.

III. Suffered Under Pontius Pilate

A. The Occasion of Christ's Death

It seems clear that the real reason why Christ was put to death was that He too pointedly challenged the pride, position, and interests of the accepted religious teachers and ecclesiastical authorities of His day. However, the legal responsibility for the execution rests upon the Roman administration of the province of Judea (Luke 23:13–25; John 18:28–32). Thus He "suffered under Pontius Pilate." The barbarous punishment of crucifixion was not part of the more humane Jewish law, and was introduced by the Romans for the more terrifying execution of rebels and disobedient slaves. The victim normally lingered for a long time and died by slow exhaustion, so that the Roman guards were surprised and moved to superstitious awe by the circumstance that Jesus died so suddenly, and in the fullness of His strength (Mark 15:37, 39, 44). To the pious Jew the chief horror of crucifixion, however, was that it appeared to involve the curse of Deuteronomy 21:23. Thus it was not only a death in agony and disgrace. It also entailed excommunication from Israel. The reader should remember what unfortunate misunderstanding can be caused by saying unguardedly that Christ was put to death "by the Jews." Historically this was largely so. Nevertheless, the sins which crucified Christ have been seen in the life of every nation alike, and still are, so that the spiritual guilt of His death is in principle a universal guilt, and not particularly Jewish. It is much more accurately Christian to say:

> O Jesus, my hope,
> For me offered up,
> Who with clamour pursued Thee to Calvary's top.

B. The Meaning of Christ's Sufferings

1. OBEDIENCE. The first New Testament thought to be considered is that Christ's suffering and death is a sacrifice of obedience. God has made man, and therefore everything which man is and has is by right entirely at God's disposal. If man is to please God and to live in a secure relation of friendship with Him, he must obey God. Thus God graciously admits His people into a Covenant with Himself, freely pledging His word to bless and protect them. The condition of this Covenant is obedience to God's revealed Law (Exodus 24:7; Micah 6:6–8). A sacrifice may be defined as the God-appointed way in which man is to offer himself to God and come to God in fellowship.[3] Therefore the essential sacrifice is the life of moral obedience, and the ceremonial sacrifices of religious ordinance are a means to this end (Micah 6:6–8). However, the one thing which man cannot do is to obey God as He ought to be obeyed. He cannot keep his part of the Covenant, and so man is alienated from God (Jeremiah 31:32).

The essential purpose of the Incarnation was that God's Son came to do as perfect man what frail and sinful man must do, but cannot. As man, genuinely one of us, He offered to the Father in heaven the sacrifice of a life of sinless obedience (Mark 8:31, 14:36; John 4:34, 5:30, 6:38; Philippians 2:8; Hebrews 5:7–8; 1 Peter 2:23).

One of the chief significances of the Gospel record is that it shows with tragic clarity how God's Son as man met all those influences of moral compromise, and all those entrenched powers of wickedness, which have so largely governed human affairs in every age, and which daunt men from rising to a noble and morally constructive life. Our Lord encountered first the disillusioning slowness of men to respond to the call of the good (Mark 6:6). He tasted the bitterness of spiritual loneliness and of shameful betrayal (Matthew 23:37, 26:40; Luke 22:61; John 6:67). He came also into collision with the authority of religious systems which had lost their vision, and with the power of rulers who heeded policy rather than principle (Luke 6:11; John 19:12). He experienced weariness and the grim force of tempta-tion (Luke 22:39 44; Hebrews 5:7–9). This whole manner of life found its fitting climax in the awesome mystery of death, and death in torment, unmerited disgrace, and spiritual darkness (Mark 15:34; Philippians 2:8). In every successive crisis of this career Christ continued in sinless and loving

---

[3] For an explanation of the idea of "sacrifice," see pages 87–88.

obedience to the heavenly Father and in love toward man (John 4:34). Where men commonly stumble into disappointment, cynicism, and compromise, Jesus walked erect and victorious (Luke 9:51; 1 Peter 2:21–24). This is the sacrifice of sinless obedience which opens the door into the presence of the holy God (Hebrews 4:14–16, 9:14).

2. CHRIST THE VICTOR. A further basic New Testament theology of the suffering and death of Christ is that here was the victory of the power of God, the power of moral obedience and long-suffering love, against all the evil forces which tyrannize over mankind. The imaginative but concrete symbolism natural to the mind of those times depicted these forces as spiritual entities, and sometimes as demonic beings. This makes many significant texts in the New Testament somewhat obscure to the modern mind, which tends to think of man's spiritual foes in terms of abstract principles and social influences. However, if the effort is made to translate out of the idiom of one age into the idiom of another, the New Testament doctrine of *Christus Victor* becomes plain and impressive. It may be reconstructed from texts drawn from the writings of St. Paul, who gives us the fullest material. However, the same principle is found underlying the doctrine of other parts of the New Testament.

Paul teaches that sinful man is in bondage in the first place to satanic intelligences, great and small (2 Corinthians 4:4; Galatians 4:3; Ephesians 2:2, and 6:12). Christ as man put Himself into the sphere of influence of these forces, which crucified Him (1 Corinthians 2:6–8). His resurrection was the mark of victory over them. The demons were dragged off like prisoners in a Roman Triumph (Colossians 2:15).

Man was also in bondage to the curse of the Law of Moses, placed upon the disobedient (Galatians 3:10). A slavish fear of offending God could darken the spirit of the Jew. By no means all Jews felt like this about their ancestral religion, but rather rejoiced in it as their pride and strength. St. Paul, however, most significantly did so find the religion of law to be a bondage which filled him with an agony of spiritual frustration (Romans 7: 7–24). Christ was born as one of those who owed a duty of obedience to the Law (Galatians 4:4–5). He suffered the punishment marked out by the Mosaic Law as an accursed and excommunicate death (Galatians 3:13). When He rose in triumph the crucified was vindicated as the Messiah (Acts 2:23–24, 36), and the curse of the Law was shown as of no effect (Romans 7:4, 10:4; Galatians 3:13).

Another human bondage was that of sin (Romans 5:21, 8:3). Christ crucified was one with man in his most tragic lot (Romans 8:3; 2 Corinthians 5:21). Christ was tempted to the uttermost, yet did not sin, and rose in triumph, so that He can be assailed by sin no more (Romans 6:10, 8:3; 1 Corinthians 15:56–57). This was the divine victory over yet another adversary.

The last dread enemy of mankind is death (Romans 5:14; 1 Corinthians 15:26). Christ laid Himself open to the attack of this foe also, and died as men die, in torment and darkness (Philippians 2:8). The power of death was conquered by the risen Christ (Romans 6:9–10; 1 Corinthians 15:55–57).

The modern man does not typically think of his own bondage in these New Testament terms, but it is possible to see that Christ's life of obedience was a life of victory over those same social forces which visit us with frustration (compare what has been said above in paragraph 1 on Christ's obedience). His resurrection was a pledge of this victory. Thus New Testament thought can effectively be translated into modern terms.

3. DIVINE IDENTIFICATION WITH MAN. The Incarnation was the divine act of identification with man, that is, of God "making Himself one" with the human race. Identification is the essential spiritual principle by which alone one man can hope to bear the moral burden and fight the moral battle of another. This is always done at the price of self-sacrifice. Thus for example, a patriot sees his native land about to be occupied by an invading tyrant. He may be able to escape, take his professional skill with him, and earn a comfortable living in another land. Or he may voluntarily choose to remain with his fellow countrymen less fortunate than himself, so that he may use his talents to organize their resistance. By remaining with his fellow countrymen, that is, by identifying himself with them, he is able to take upon himself a major share of their common struggle, and so strengthen each one of them in his own share. This he does at the price of his own suffering, of his voluntary self-sacrifice. In one way or another every effort to lift the human race morally and spiritually has worked through the medium of identification, and has involved this price.

The Incarnation, and the human career which followed from it, is the supreme example of this action. In order that by the power of His long-suffering and holy love God might conquer as man, and for man, God's Son made Himself one with man. He shared a lowly birth and home. He humbled Himself to commonplace work among men (Mark 6:3). He graciously received social outcasts, though their ways and standards must have revolted Him, and this also cost Him His reputation (Matthew 9:10–12; Luke 7:36–50). He was glad to go with the people to their accustomed worship, though the doctrine of their teachers must always have seemed spiritually dim to His clear eyes (Luke 4:16). Here was indentification at a cost, but still more costly was His death upon the Cross. The Son of God made Himself one with humanity in its last and lowest experiences; in agony, in humiliation, in disgrace, in spiritual darkness, and in death (2 Corinthians 5:21). Furthermore, human beings are joined one to another in confidence and love by the power of sympathy, and sympathy means "suffering with" one's fellow. So God in Christ conquered the power of evil in this world by a method which unveiled His divine sympathy. That He chose this costly way is the supreme pledge of God's goodwill toward man;

of His grace, His preparedness to forgive, His love (John 3:16; Romans 8:31–39; Galatians 2:20; 1 John 4:9).

4. THE REDEEMING SUFFERINGS OF CHRIST. We may now connect what has been said about man's sinful condition, and what has been established from the New Testament regarding the sufferings and death of Christ, in order to show how God's action meets man's need. Man's moral and spiritual need is twofold. Corresponding to this need there is in the life and death of Christ a twofold work of God.

If it is asked why ordinary men do not rise above their dead selves to better things, the first answer is that they have despaired of the power of good. Primitive men continue in cruel or degrading social customs through superstitious fear of evil spirits, yet the sophisticated men of the modern world are in substantially the same bondage. They too are aware of an outward force of evil constraining them from doing the good their better natures tell them they ought to do. They fear to stand for right because of what may happen to them socially, economically, or politically. The world of human affairs therefore seems to be in the grip of social and economic forces which are malign, frustrating, vast, and impersonal, and which are so nearly irresistible that it hardly seems worth while to risk all for the cause of right. This same sense of defeat reigns in the human heart. The common experience of those who have tried to reform their own lives is so disappointing that nothing would surprise them more than suddenly to find themselves keeping their own sincere good resolutions. In face of all these powers men have said: "*It's no good.*" Here is bondage to the *power* of sin, to an objective power reigning in the world of men.

Those who have thought more deeply about life are aware that there is a problem more tragic even than the power of sin. This is the *guilt* of sin. Here is the enemy within. He who has once opened his heart and mind a little to the vision of how noble it is to follow the good, and who then candidly looks upon what he has made of his own life—the petty compromises he has knowingly allowed, his liability to mixed motives even in the most sacred of actions, the unworthy thoughts which creep unbidden into the secret imagination, and the haunting realization that even that which he sincerely accounts to be good may in God's sight be stained with evil—this man has surely said in his heart: "How God must despair of me and despise me: more even than I despise myself! Even if He could help me, I have no standing before Him to ask Him to do it. I am not clean enough within to aspire nobly after that which is noble. *Oh I'm no good!*" Here is bondage to the *guilt* of sin. This bondage answers to the spiritual or religious definition of sin, as the former bondage did to the moral.

The act of God in Christ fulfills both these needs. In the first place, Christ's life of sinless obedience is the mark that by the power of God, humanity when joined to God can conquer the power of sin. This decisive battle is a sure token that God can win the whole campaign. It is no longer necessary to say "It's no good"; for here is a proof that God can make a difference to human life, and in the human situation. In the second place, the sympathy of God, the pledge of His understanding and forgiving love, enables man, despite the past, to dare to come for God to do for him what He has offered to do. Even as the words "Oh, I'm no good" rise bitterly from the heart, man is emboldened by the spectacle of God in Christ making Himself one with man, even in man's compromise and shame. Though man is what he is, the door is open for him to come. Thus Christ crucified wipes away the barrier of guilt, as well as breaks the bondage of sin.

> Be of sin the double cure,
> Cleanse me from its guilt and power.

5. THE OBJECTIVE AND SUBJECTIVE WORK OF CHRIST. It would seem that any adequate view of the meaning of the saving act of God in Christ crucified must comprise these two sides, and keep them in balance. If man is to be redeemed he needs to be given a reasonable ground for assurance that God has actually conquered the objective power of evil, once and for all, as a matter of historical fact. It is not sufficient to see in the Cross the revelation of a doctrine, the appeal of a good example, or the psychological stimulus of warm and loving sentiment. There must be this divine *objective* "finished work," done "once and for all." Yet by itself knowledge of the objective work is orthodoxy, and not "the faith that works by love."[4] The victorious act of God in Christ needs to be brought home to the inner man of the heart, to his affections, to his moral will. It must make a *subjective* appeal. The breaking of the power of sin chiefly corresponds to the objective aspect, the wiping away of the guilt largely to the subjective, though the two are intimately connected.

6. IDENTIFICATION WITH CHRIST. It will be asked what difference a divine act performed in Galilee and Jerusalem more than nineteen hundred years ago can make to the moral and spiritual life of a man in Europe or America, living in the entirely different social circumstances of the modern age. Failure of understanding at this point is without a doubt one of the main reasons why genuine Christianity does not make a deeper and wider impact. Any explanation of the connection between the work of God in Christ then, and His work in the lives of men now, depends upon the principle of the solidarity of the race.[5] Christ made Himself one with us in order to do this thing, and by making Himself one with us He opened the door for us in turn to make ourselves one with Him. And if we make ourselves one with Him, or identify ourselves with Him, we can share in the fruit of His victory.

It is said that we live in an age of "mass humanity." In the sense that the typical modern man works in the vast ant heap of a factory or office

---

4 Galatians 5:6.
5 The work is also the operation of the Holy Spirit (see p. 116).

building, commutes to a spreading and formless suburb, watches with millions of others the same TV program, and has his habits of food and clothing dictated by mass publicity, the present is the age of "the mass man." This disguises the still more significant fact that the men and women who form these masses are frequently living in a state of extreme, and indeed often excessive and unhealthy, social isolation. A large part of the ills of modern industrial society appear to spring from this isolation. People are obsessed with the idea of "living their own lives in their own way." Their society is broken up into the smallest-sized family groups, which even then all too often do not possess the merit of enduring stability. The larger groups which in the past have normally given to men support, restraint, and guidance, such as the securely consolidated town or village community, or the traditional communal religion, have suffered a loosening of their bonds. It is important to remember that the ancient world, which is the background both of the Bible and of the development of Christian doctrine, was in contrast possessed by a very commanding sense of the natural solidarity of the race. If this principle of solidarity is forgotten, Christ's work cannot be made intelligible. Also, the chief promise of the Christian religion is that it can bring all men back to a new and rich solidarity, though at a higher spiritual and ethical level than the old.

In the broadest terms the principle of Christian salvation is this. In Christ the sovereign power and long-suffering love of God won the decisive battle over the power of sin. Because Christ did this as man, and for man, in a solidarity of suffering and triumph with the race, the door is now open for all men to make themselves one with Christ. All those who do so share in the fruit of the victory. In company with Christ each one can then conquer in the battle of life, by His power. As with the power, so it is with the guilt of sin. Christ as man offered to the Father the well-pleasing sacrifice of sinless obedience. Because He did it as man, all those who make themselves one with Him can go with Him and share in the sacrifice, and find that the deep gulf of alienation from God is banished. The barrier of guilt is thrown down, and the door is open for man to have fellowship with God. In Christ, God as man came to meet man. All those who identify themselves with Christ in a strong solidarity can therefore meet with God. Thus the effect of the initial, decisive, all-important, historical, "once-for-all" action of God in first-century Palestine is mediated to all mankind in every age and place. The way in which this happens is more fully described in the discussion of the doctrines of faith and of the Church (see pp. 155–56, 221–23).

The New Testament doctrine of "identification with Christ" may be explained by a discussion of the text, "For as in Adam all die, even so in Christ shall all be made alive," (1 Corinthians 15:22). Genesis 2:7, 19–23, describes Adam as the ancestor of the human race, the name "Adam" meaning "the man." Therefore in the thought of St. Paul, Adam is the "type" of the race. Adam is the figure whose action represents what the whole human race in its solidarity has done, and every individual man within that solidarity. Adam disobeyed, and in consequence "died," that is, brought upon himself alienation from God, moral degradation, and calamity. This is St. Paul's way of saying that the human race taken as an organic whole, and likewise every member of the race considered as an individual, has disobeyed, and dies. Each individual who disobeys makes himself one with Adam, and takes for himself his own share of the common death (Romans 5:12).

The whole race is "in Adam" not just by heredity, but by the much more profound spiritual principle of solidarity. St. Paul doubtless did believe that Adam was in fact the physical ancestor of the whole race, but his theological thought is not solely dependent upon this. This is not what he is saying here. All men are not "in Adam" in the sense that all the millions of acres of a new variety of wheat which is someday to cover the prairie are "in" the single first grain, as it lies in the hand of the plant breeder. They are "in Adam" in somewhat the sense that every citizen of the United States may be said to be "in" the President when his signature finally brings into action some new legislation. His action represents the action of the whole nation, and of every citizen within the nation, so that its effect is binding upon all in this great solidarity. In like manner, every man who by penitence, obedience, and faith, truly makes himself one with Christ in the great new Christian solidarity is "in Christ." Christ's saving action then truly and spiritually represents his own action, and each man shares in the blessing of Christ's action.

C. New Testament Words

It is necessary to explain some of the chief New Testament words used to set forth various aspects of the saving work of Christ.

1. ATONEMENT; RECONCILIATION. These two words have the same meaning in the New Testament. The word "atonement" occurs in the familiar English translation (K.J.V.) of the New Testament in Romans 5:11, but the same Greek word is translated "reconciliation" in 2 Corinthians 5:18, 19. The origin of the word "atonement" is "at-one-ment," that is, a "making at one." The verb "to atone" could in Elizabethan English be used of persons who had quarrelled, in the sense of "to reconcile" them. Thus the act of God in Christ produces the reconciliation of man to God, and is so called "the atonement." It is to be noted that the New Testament speaks of the reconciliation of man to God, not of God to man (2 Corinthians 5:19, 20).

2. PROPITIATION. This word has often been taken to imply the notion of the offering of a gift or bribe to an angry divinity, in order to appease him. This has produced a reaction in the minds of some, who have turned away from the idea of "propitiation" as unethical and unspiritual. The Greek word in question can indeed bear this sense of "appeasement" in

pagan writing, but it would appear to be established that the general sense in the Greek Old Testament, or Septuagint, which is much more determinative for the New Testament, is at an higher level. The basic biblical sense of the word rendered "to make propitiation" would seem to be "to perform an act whereby religious defilement is removed." In the earlier stages of religion this defilement was thought of chiefly in terms of ceremonial taboo, and "to make propitiation" was then to perform the customary ceremony of "spiritual disinfection." It was later realized by the Hebrews that it is *sin* in the moral and spiritual sense, and not merely breach of ceremonial taboo, which defiles man before God. The purification therefore had likewise to be a moral and spiritual one. It was seen that only God can do this, for only God can forgive sin against Himself. The verb "to make propitiation" then took on a higher usage, and came to be used of God in the sense of "to forgive," or "to provide a means by which guilt may be removed." Thus the familiar K.J.V. of Romans 3:25, "Whom God hath set forth to be a propitiation," may be rendered, "For God designed him to be the means for expiating sin" (N.E.B.). The work of Christ is the God-appointed means whereby the guilt and defilement of sin may be wiped away. Hence the Cross is a propitiation.

3. RANSOM. The original meaning of this word was that of the price paid to secure the release of a captive or the freedom of a slave. It would appear, however, that in the New Testament the word has become generalized to convey the idea of "the means of release," without necessarily being associated with the notion of "a price paid." Thus when our Lord describes His death as a ransom (Mark 10:45) we are not called upon to ask: "To whom was the price paid?" Rather does the phrase convey that Christ's death is the means whereby man is released from bondage to his spiritual adversaries.

4. SACRIFICE. This is perhaps the most profound and comprehensive word used in the New Testament to expound the saving act of God in Christ. There has been much discussion of what "sacrifice" meant in the religion of primitive men, and also in the Old Testament which is the background for the thought of the New Testament. This subject is to a certain extent a matter of surmise, because the ancient world was content to carry out its religious rites because they were customary and sacred, and has not left us critical accounts of why they did what they did. However, there would be a good deal of agreement about three general ideas regarding sacrifice.

(1) A man wishes to dedicate one of his possessions to God. He therefore offers some part of it to God as an "acted prayer" dedicating the whole. (2) A man realizes that all that he has and is belongs to God, and should be offered to Him. He therefore takes some highly significant object in his possession and sacrifices it as an "acted prayer" of his self-offering to God. (3) To share a meal together unites men in the sacred bond of host and guest, and is the means of fellowship. Man desires to have a secure bond

of goodwill with God, and to enjoy fellowship with Him. He therefore provides a sacrifice, part of which is offered to God, and part of which is eaten by the worshippers as a sacred meal of fellowship. Thus he "has a meal with God." In general, therefore, a sacrifice is the God-appointed means whereby man may offer himself to God in dedication and obedience, and hold fellowship with God. Christ in His life and death is clearly the supreme sacrifice. He is the one who actually and perfectly does what the ancient Jewish sacrifices only aspired to do.

This doctrine is particularly worked out in the Epistle to the Hebrews. The master theme here is that the Jewish sacrifices, with their approach to God in solemn ceremonial, were the preparatory earthly shadows, spiritually valid but only partial, of the entirely effective spiritual sacrifice of obedience to God which Christ on earth as man offered to God, and which He still offers in heaven. That Christ is both Himself the high priest, and His life of obedience the sacrifice which He offers, carries the implication that His saving work is essentially an act of self-sacrifice.

In the Jewish religion the high priest was a man among men, and like them frail and tempted. Therefore he was a suitable representative to appear before God of behalf of the people. In the person of the high priest the whole solidarity of the people appeared before God (Hebrews 5:1–3). On the great Day of Atonement this human high priest went with the blood of a divinely ordained ceremonial sacrifice into the Holy of Holies, which to the people symbolized the most immediate presence of God (9:1–7). This was the approach of the ancient people of God to their God in self-dedication, obedience, and communion, but enacted according to a preparatory and shadowy earthly copy which lacked the fullness of divine saving power (9:7–10, 10:1–4). Christ came and brought these old sacrifices to their proper climax by offering on earth a sacrifice which fully corresponds to the spiritual ideal of sacrifice as it exists in heaven, that is, in the mind of God. This true spiritual sacrifice brings the fullness of divine saving power.

The divine Son (1:2–3) took upon Himself human nature like ours, so that He might make Himself fully one with us (2:14, 17). Standing thus on our ground He fought our battle for us, and conquered in the wonder of a sinless life (4:15). In language which clearly points back to the scene in Gethsemane (Luke 22:39–46), the writer shows that Christ offered to the heavenly Father the sacrifice of a life of perfect obedience, even to suffering and death (5:7–8). This spiritual sacrifice, which was so much better than the ceremonial sacrifice, was in fact the sacrifice appropriate to the New Covenant of inward spiritual religion of which Jeremiah had spoken (8:6–12). Because this sacrifice was offered by one who was truly man, and who was therefore man's true representative, the effect of it can belong to all men (2:9, 18). By His endurance Christ has conquered the power of Satan for us (2:14), and has set man free from fear and death (2:15).

In the power of this victory the risen and glorified Christ ascended to heaven, to appear before the throne of the majesty of God. As the Jewish high priest went sacramentally into the earthly Holy of Holies, so Christ has gone into the true holy place. He has gone there as man, and therefore He is mankind's fitting representative before God, the true high priest of the New Covenant (4:14; 7:23–27; 8:1–2; 9:11–12, 15; 12:24). This true heavenly priesthood fittingly corresponds to the old earthly priesthood, but is of new and mysterious divine origin, and of an altogether higher spiritual dignity (5:10, 7:1–21). The heavenly high priest has offered Himself in sacrifice, and this self-sacrifice suffices to open the door for man to have true spiritual communion with the Most High God (9:24–26, 10:19–22). Thus Christ is the "captain" of our salvation (2:10, 5:9, 12:2), a word which can be rendered "leader" (N.E.B.), or perhaps "pioneer," and which can be used to describe the "founding father" of a tribe or city constitution. He is the one who at a great cost has first trodden the path which we men must tread if we are to come to God (6:20), "blazing the trail" for us. This makes it possible for us to tread the path also, if by faith we make ourselves truly one with Him in the body of His Church (10:19–25). Faith in God has ever been the guiding principle and bond of union of the true Israelites among God's ancient people. An enriched, confirmed, and more spiritual faith is the possession of the Church, which is the due spiritual heir of the ancient chosen people (11:39–12:2, 22–23). The Church is likewise the guardian of the Eucharist, which is the Christian act of sacrificial worship (13:9–10).

This noble and spacious structure of Christian thought is one of the great creative elements of New Testament writing. It demonstrates for us the potentialities of that sacrificial language regarding the death of Christ, which meets us in a scattered and less developed form in other parts of the New Testament. It has been most influential in the Church of later times, in the development of thought regarding the atonement and the Eucharist.

IV. Theologies of the Atonement

The Christian doctrine of the atonement has been expressed in various ways in different periods of the Church's life.

A. Ancient Thought

It is often said that during the first thousand years of the Church's life the ransom theory of the atonement ruled, the point of ancient controversy being whether the ransom of Christ's death was paid to God the Father or to the Devil. This gives the impression that Christian thought on this important doctrine was somewhat crude and immature. In fact, however, the Church of the Roman Empire contained many theologians who were men of deep culture and of great powers of thought. In general these follow the New Testament, and speak of the saving act of God in Christ as an actual conquest of the powers of evil which enslave men. As there was in those days a vivid sense of the existence of personal demonic powers, the conquest of Satan is naturally spoken of, and the despoiling Satan of his victims. Many vivid metaphors are used to enforce this idea, including that of ransom. A transaction is often depicted in which Christ offers His priceless soul to Satan in return for the freeing of his prisoners, after which Satan finds that he cannot hold the prize he has grasped! The theological worth of this admittedly quaint language can only be appreciated when it is realized that these metaphors are not more than the "sermon illustrations" used to expound a mature view of the work of Christ, which is dominant in the New Testament itself, and which goes back to our Lord's own view of His activity (Matthew 12:25–29). This is the doctrine of Christ as the Victor.

B. Satisfaction *theory*

In the centuries which followed the fall of the Roman Empire in the west there was a natural decay of all branches of learning, and very little constructive work in systematic theology was attempted. However, the Easter faith in Christ crucified and risen, the conqueror of Satan, sin, and death, the dread enemies of mankind, lived on in Church worship and popular piety, as it always has done. With the dawn of the Middle Ages we find the gradual rebirth of civilized social institutions, and with them a distinctive Christian culture. Naturally this was accompanied by the rise in educated circles of a more reflective form of Christian faith, and in course of time, of a vigorous theological life in the medieval universities. As a part of the medieval Scholastic theology we find the first of the great theologies of the atonement, namely, the satisfaction theory. This was pioneered by St. Anselm of Canterbury (1033–1109), and displaced the ancient ransom theory. Satisfaction ("making enough") is essentially the New Testament doctrine of Christ's death as a representative sacrifice,[6] but expressed in terms natural to those whose thought regarding the solidarity of the human race was molded by the institutions of medieval feudalism.

St. Anselm taught that sin is an affront to God's honor and to the divine order of the universe. Due satisfaction is to be made for this affront before it is seemly, or morally right, for God to forgive. Such submission of obedience must be made as will vindicate God's credit as the rightful and righteous ruler of the world. Sinful man is neither able nor worthy to offer himself to God in satisfaction for sin. He has no ground of standing before his king. A man, *and a sinless man,* must in obedience offer himself up to the glory of God before God can fittingly receive man. Therefore God Himself must become man, so that as man He may Himself do this. Moreover, the satis-

---

[6] Compare what has been written above (pp. 88–89) on the theology of the Epistle to the Hebrews.

faction for man's sin can only rightly be offered *by man:* by one who is the authentic representative of the fallen race. Therefore the divine Son fully identified Himself with mankind in its shame and woe, which is the fitting punishment for sin, and in submission freely offered Himself up to the glory of the Father. Thus by Christ's suffering and death the means was provided by God for man's forgiveness, and for his restoration to a secure status in the sight of God. The Cross was a satisfaction for sin.

This scheme, with God almost in the position of a feudal lord adjusting his differences with disobedient and disrespectful vassals, may appear to some people to be archaic. Nevertheless it has the spiritual value of giving a clear witness to the basic idea of our Lord's representative sacrifice, and to that principle of human solidarity in Him without which it is impossible to understand the atonement.[7] Satisfaction is an exposition of the Cross which to an eminent degree accords with the visible Church's sense of organic solidarity, as she joins in her sacramental worship. Thus the Eucharist, which is the earthly Church's sacrificial rite, is the means by which Christians make themselves one body with Christ, as He, the great high priest in glory, offers to the Father the one and only prevailing heavenly sacrifice.[8] Thus the medieval satisfaction theology harmonized naturally with the chief contemporary form of worship, namely, the sacrifice of the Mass.[9]

C. *Substitution*

This theology, which rose to prominence in Protestant circles at the Reformation period, in its original form states that the attitude of a holy God toward the sinner is necessarily that of wrath, which works punishment. A just God cannot forgive unless due punishment for sin is exacted, but the love of God provided the means for this by sending the incarnate Son, who as man bore upon the Cross the penalty, and suffered the curse, of the sins of the whole race. Because Christ was God as well as man, the merit of this divine suffering was so great as to suffice for the due punishment of the sins of all men. All those who by faith make themselves one with Christ, their meritorious Federal Head, share in His merit by virtue of their

---

[7] Thus it is to be observed that some of the best modern theology of the atonement is a restatement in more modern thought forms of the conception of representative sacrifice and of satisfaction.

[8] So the Consecration Prayer in the liturgy of the English Church runs: He "made there, by His one oblation of Himself once offered, a full, perfect, and sufficient sacrifice, oblation and *satisfaction,* for the sins of the whole world."

[9] The continuity in saving efficacy, yet difference in historical operation, between the "once-for-all" sacrifice of the incarnate Son on Calvary, and the constantly renewed sacrifice of the Mass has been traditionally expressed in Roman Catholic theology by calling the former the "bloody sacrifice" and the latter the "unbloody sacrifice." Some Roman Catholic theology has at times spoken of the Mass as a "repetition" of Calvary, but this dubious phrase can easily obscure the unique character of God's saving act in the incarnate Son, and would not appear to be acceptable to the most reliable Roman Catholic theologians.

solidarity with Him, and so receive forgiveness and reconciliation to God.
Thus man is saved by the transfer of the penalty of sin to Christ, and the
"imputation" of, or accounting of, the merits of Christ to man. This theology
has been traditional in orthodox Protestantism.

In the modern period this theology has been criticized under various heads.
(1) Some people feel that it appears to make the justice and the love of
God quantities opposite to one another, and thus to introduce a division into
the nature of God Himself. (2) The transfer of punishment, and of the
merit of Christ's sufferings, appears to some to be an ethically dubious
doctrine. (3) It has been observed that the New Testament "wrath of God"
is not a personal attitude of divine anger toward the sinner, but a nemesis,
or self-acting train of cause and effect, which brings retribution upon the
sinner (Romans 1:18–32). So it is the action of God to deliver from the
wrath, not to bring it upon man (1 Thessalonians 5:9). Thus the substitu-
tionary theology has been restated in the form of the so-called *governmental*
theories. These are based upon the undoubted truth that even the God of
love cannot forgive in such a way as to allow man to suppose that sin is
condoned. God's strict moral government of the world must be fully vindicated before sin can be freely pardoned. Christ indeed bore the penalty of
sin upon the Cross, but to satisfy the claims of justice before God and man,
rather than to turn away the anger of God from man.

It will be seen that this theology answers to the Christianity of individual
conversion, as satisfaction does to the religion of corporate sacramental
worship. It serves strongly to emphasize the facts of personal guilt, of
personal moral responsibility before God, and of personal liability to punishment. It gives the believer a ground for assurance that his own guilt is set
aside by God, and his own liability liquidated. Because Christian salvation
is individual as well as communal there is here an important aspect of truth,
and the preaching of substitution has been blessed by God in evangelistic
preaching. However, it will surely be agreed that the presentation of the
Cross should be such as to encourage men, united in the body of Christ,
to say "He died for *us,* and for each one as a member of that body," as well
as the individual "He died for me." The older theologies have much to
contribute here.

D. Moral Influence

This presentation of the Cross is essentially a feature of modern theology,
particularly in "liberal" circles, though it was notably advanced in the
medieval period by Abelard (1079–1142). The basis of this exposition is the
doctrine that Christ crucified is a compelling demonstration in human terms
of how sin and the sinner appear in the sight of the God of holy love. The
rejection of Christ is the supreme token of man's repulse of God's offered
love, and of the spite which the sinner does to the divine grace. This will
move the heart of man to shame and penitence. The self-sacrifice and

forgiveness of Christ is likewise the supreme token of God's forgiving love, and of His preparedness to receive the penitent sinner. This enables the penitent to return to God despite the sorry past and accept forgiveness.

It is clear that there is truth here also. Here is the atonement expounded in psychological terms, as substitution is in judicial. In fact, the moral influence theology of the atonement answers almost entirely to the *subjective* side of the atonement (see p. 84). It concerns the mental process by which the saving act of God can make an appeal to the human personality, rather than the nature and importance of the saving act itself. Taken in isolation the moral influence theology is thus in danger of representing the Cross as an appeal to sentiment, or as the revelation of a truth. It does not convey the essential Christian conception of an historic divine act in Christ, whereby the power and guilt of sin are effectually destroyed. Nevertheless, the moral influence theology helps to illuminate the manner in which the historic divine act can make an appeal to the human personality, and influence it morally and spiritually. Thus this school of thought is really an adjunct to the other systems, and a valuable adjunct, but not a sufficient doctrine on its own.

E. Summary

It is to be observed that any preaching of the Cross can be blessed by God for the salvation of souls if it can convey to man a reasonable ground for supposing that in Christ God has actually done everything which needs to be done to dispel the guilt and destroy the power of sin, and to enable man to come to God and receive forgiveness. It is therefore most unfitting to dispute around the foot of the Cross, as though one theory alone were a legitimate part of the Gospel. There are elements of value in all these approaches, or they would never have made their historic appeal. The Christian teacher should reverently seek among these elements to make his presentation of the underlying scriptural witness as profound, intelligible, and winning as possible.

V. Dead and Buried, He Descended Into Hell.

This clause of the Creed was very important in old times, but in the modern world is often the occasion of unfortunate misunderstanding. However, the desire of the Church to find a theological meaning symbolized in Christ's sojourn in the grave during the period between His crucifixion and resurrection is more than fanciful curiosity. The underlying spiritual principle of the Incarnation is the self-identification of the divine Son with mankind. He made Himself one with man in infancy, in childhood, in the labor of manhood, in the worship of His people, in temptation, in agony, in spiritual darkness, and in death. The last act of this process is that He made Himself one with the dead as they await the general resurrection. As He conquered for man in all these other phases of human experience, so He conquered in the grave.

The spiritual condition of the departed is not open to direct human experience, and therefore is not capable of description in matter-of-fact language. Christian doctrine has to be deduced from spiritual principles, and symbolized in imaginative language. The Church has inherited two traditions of symbolism, both of which are legitimate and have their own spiritual value, and are indeed complementary to one another. The form of symbolism which comes more naturally to most modern minds is derived in part from the Bible, but in part also from the philosophical thought of the Greeks. It considers the souls of the departed in Christ as now existing in the spiritual sphere, which is not a "place." They are in a state of enhanced personal awareness, spiritual blessedness, and communion with God. There is, however, alongside this a purely Hebraic and biblical system of symbolism, which speaks of the dead as awaiting the general resurrection, and the coming Day of God. Those who wait in the world of the departed are indeed not in a state of suspended animation, but their full spiritual blessedness in the presence of God awaits the Day of the Lord. The traditional doctrine which we are now to consider is framed in terms of this second and biblical system of symbolism. It is a pity that its value is concealed from the minds of some who see no further than the symbolical language of this article of the Creed, and who dismiss the matter as a piece of archaic and naïve mythology left over from the childhood of the Church.

In the familiar English Bible two quite different Greek words are translated "hell." There is *Hades,* the world of the departed, or the grave, where the dead await the resurrection, as in Luke 16:23 and Acts 2:31; and there is *Gehenna,* the place of punishment of the finally impenitent, after the Judgment, as in Matthew 5:22, 29; Mark 9:43. It is important to remember that this clause of the Creed refers to our Lord's descent into Hades, the world of the departed, not into Gehenna. This translation will seem less remarkable when it is remembered that in Tudor English, into which the Apostles' Creed was translated from the Latin, the word "hell" had a much broader meaning than it does today in our common speech. It meant simply "a covered place."[10] The Christian doctrine is, then, that our Lord spent the time before His resurrection with all the rest of the departed, however we may conceive of their mode of existence. This was the last fitting act of identification with man, which enabled Him to conquer for man in this mysterious sphere also.

Christian thought on this subject has followed the course of 1 Peter 3:19–20, which teaches that Christ "went and preached unto the spirits in prison." The Church from the beginning had a very strong sense of

---

10 Thus the old English occupational surname *Hellier* designated a man who thatched houses, and who *covered* them.

continuity with the ancient people of God. The saints and heroes of old Israel were seen as the spiritual ancestors of the Church, and therefore the Christian mind was much exercised as to the possibility of the salvation of righteous men of old time, who lived before the saving act of God in Christ was performed. The doctrinal solution was that those who because of their faithfulness were virtually "Christians before the time" would be found in the end to belong to Christ. In 1 Peter the "spirits in prison," to whom Christ went, would appear to be the unrighteous who were drowned in the Deluge, and who are here apparently given an opportunity for repentence. However, in Christian tradition they have been seen as those prisoners of Satan and the grave who were worthy to be called into Christ's kingdom. The effect is the same either way. The possibility of salvation in Christ is taken backwards in time to the beginning of God's people. Here is the theme of "The Harrowing of Hell," so prominent in medieval mystery plays and religious art. Christ the strong man, who has bound Satan (Luke 11:21–22), is depicted as descending with His angels into the world of the grave, there to spread the victory of the Cross and to release Satan's prisoners. He takes Adam and Eve by the hand, and lifts them out to salvation. Thus interpreted, this clause of the Creed speaks of the principle that Christian salvation potentially extends to every human soul who in the end will be found to have accepted Christ in penitence and faith, even though some were not apparently believers in this life. There is a real and lasting spiritual value in this belief, even though some people may not appreciate the way in which it has traditionally been expressed.

Readings

Aulén, G., *Christus Victor*. New York and Toronto: The Macmillan Company, 1945.

Brunner, H. E., *Man in Revolt,* trans. O. Wyon. New York: Charles Scribner's Sons, 1939.

Hodgson, L., *The Doctrine of the Atonement*. London: Nisbet and Co., Ltd., 1951; New York, Charles Scribner's Sons, 1951.

Newbigin, L., *Sin and Salvation*. Philadelphia: Westminster Press, 1957.

Robinson, H. W., *Redemption and Revelation in the Actuality of History*. New York and London: Harper & Row, Publishers, 1942.

Scott, C. A. A., *Christianity According to St. Paul*. London: Cambridge University Press, 1932.

Taylor, V., *Jesus and His Sacrifice*. London: Macmillan & Co., Ltd., 1937.

Chapter Four

The Power and the Wisdom

The third day He rose again from the dead,
and ascended into heaven,
and sitteth on the right hand of the Father

I. He Rose Again

The art of scratching rude words on buildings is a very ancient one. On a site belonging to the early Christian centuries there was found a rough drawing of a man kneeling before an ass's head stuck upon a pole, with the words: "Alexamenos worships his god." Alexamenos was doubtless a Christian, and those who were jesting at his expense have left a record of how the ancient world viewed the Cross. The mind of the time could worship "the genius of the emperor" and see something of true divinity in the impressive symbol of universal government. But crucifixion was not a hallowed thing to those who from time to time could actually see the grisly spectacle! It was a horrid death reserved by calculated sadism for the humiliation and torment of rebels and disobedient slaves. There was nothing of dignity there, and for the Christian to proclaim in Christ crucified and risen the act of God was so contrary to every presupposition of reasonable men that the idea was "too funny for words." In that miracle-believing age most men had no difficulty whatever in accepting the proposition that the gods could, if they wished, raise a man from the dead. Nevertheless, the gospel of the resurrection was the subject of ribald mirth (1 Corinthians 1:18, 21–24).

Long centuries of Christian culture have made the unbelieving world more polite. The figure of Jesus of Nazareth is almost universally respected, and even loved, even among those who do not believe in Him. However, the gospel of the resurrection is today just as completely "foolishness" in the eyes of the world of polite unbelief as it was when St. Paul preached in Athens, the university city of the ancient world (Acts 17:32). That Christ should have risen from the dead is contrary to every normal presupposition of the modern man. This is why the modern Christian, like the ancient martyr Church, finds himself "swimming against the tide." Secular writers will in their philosophical works or literary articles readily agree to classify Jesus with Socrates, a revered martyr in the painful upward march of truth and social right, or with St. Joan of Arc, a figure of purity perishing cruelly at the hand of ignorant and prejudiced men. Yet for them to accept the empty tomb is too great a burden. Special resistance is reserved for this doctrine.

The reason for this is not far to seek. The victory of God's power and love is a hidden victory. To the Apostle the Christian gospel is "the mystery" (Romans 16:25; 1 Corinthians 2:7; Ephesians 1:9, 3:9–10). It is a piece of divine knowledge so wonderful that the most acute human intelligence could never have discerned it, had not God willed

> To make the joyful secret known

by a special act of revelation (1 Corinthians 2:9–10). And the victory of the Cross is the central point of this mystery. That the Cross is a victory is by no means obvious. On the surface it appears exactly the opposite. The Cross looks like the most signal defeat of God's power and love. Our Lord is the one who, in His unselfish purity of intention and sympathetic friend-liness, *ought* to have won all hearts, and He has been more than decisively repulsed. If whatever is good in the human heart cannot be won by this matchless appeal, how can it ever be won? The Cross viewed as the most shameful of martyrdoms is a token of the utter unworthiness of human nature and of the black despair of mankind. To see it as a victory requires the divine gift of faith. It requires an opening of the eyes to discern that which is not in accord with the common sense of ordinary people, either in the ancient world or in the modern. Here is the place of the resurrection. It is the conquering sign wrought by God to show that the victory of the Cross *is* a victory, and that Christ's sacrifice of obedience sufficed in its high purpose. Thus traditional Christianity has always affirmed that the gospel of Christ crucified stands or falls with the resurrection (1 Corinthians 15:14, 17).

II. The Doctrine of the Resurrection

A. The Third Day

According to the usual tradition, our Lord's last supper was the Passover meal (Luke 22:1, 7, 13, 15).[1] He died before sunset on what we now call

---

[1] The Fourth Gospel places the last supper one day earlier (John 13:1).

Friday, that is, before the Jewish Sabbath commenced (Luke 23:44, 54; John 19:31, 42). It will be remembered that the Jews counted each new day as beginning at sunset (Genesis 1:5). He rose "upon the first day of the week, very early in the morning" (Luke 24:1), that is, after the Sabbath was ended. Thus Christ was in the tomb during part of two days and the full day between. According to the Jewish computation the resurrection was thus upon "the third day" (Acts 10:40; 1 Corinthians 15:4).

B. A Reversal to Death

The essential meaning of Christ's resurrection is that it was the reversal of His death. It was the abundantly triumphant "more-than-reversal" of the death of shame (Romans 6:8–9). We must speak with reserve concerning an unparalleled event of this sort. The resurrection narrative is the record of men who are seeking to describe that for which they have no adequate words. We have no right to expect common-sense coherence in every detail. Furthermore, the account was written for the purpose of proclaiming the Faith, and not in order to anticipate the detailed critical questions of a later age. Therefore we need not be surprised that there is variation as to whether one or two angels were seen (Mark 16:5; Luke 24:4), or even in the more important issue as to whether the resurrection appearances were all in Galilee, as appears to be implied by Mark 16:7; or all in Jerusalem, according to the Lukan narrative; or in both places, according to Matthew and John. We cannot know more about the resurrection than is written, and the element of mystery is bound to remain. Nevertheless, this does not necessarily hold in question the reality of the event itself.[2]

Taken at its face value the New Testament narrative appears to indicate quite decisively, on the one hand, that the resurrection was not simply an impressive vision of Christ in glory, which convinced the first disciples that their Lord was triumphant over death, even though the body lay corrupting in the grave. The tomb was empty (Mark 16:6), and the risen Christ possessed that which truly corresponded to the body which had died (Luke 24:36–43; John 20:27). We may also surmise that perhaps St. Paul was aware that there was a mysterious but important difference between the resurrection appearances to the first disciples, and his own decisive experience on the Damascus road. As he writes to the Corinthian Christians he knows that the original qualification for the office of apostle was ability to bear witness to the fact of Christ's resurrection (Acts 1:21–22). These apostles had later made their own the characteristic work of the traveling preacher and founder of churches. Paul had in fact excelled in this work, and in this sense was an "apostle" (1 Corinthians 15:10). Yet he knows full well that those who did not favor his policy of Gentile freedom from circumcision

---

2 A discussion of the general trustworthiness of the Gospel narrative recording our Lord's life and teaching will be found in the chapter dealing with the Christian doctrine of the Scriptures (pp. 197–200).

could point to the fact that he did not possess that original qualification for the work of apostleship. He had not witnessed the resurrection.[3] Hence the care with which he repeatedly rehearses the story of the Damascus road, and of the vision which had commissioned him to his preaching ministry (Acts 26:16–18). It was to him the spiritual equivalent of having seen an appearance of Christ in resurrection glory. Yet it was not more than an *equivalent*. This perhaps is the force of his curious phrase in 1 Corinthians 15:8: "And last of all He was seen of me also, as of one born out of due time." By his vision he was born into the company of the apostolic witnesses, yet he was only just born alive. He dare not claim to his Corinthian Christians that he had seen the Lord in His resurrection body, in the same way as had the original witnesses listed in 15:1–7. There was a mysterious but important difference between Christ's resurrection in a glorified body and even the most impressive of visions.

However, the Gospel narrative on the other hand indicates that the resurrection body of our Lord was a glorified body. It was not barely the body of flesh and blood which had died, now come to life again in the same condition as before. The Lord could appear and disappear, and even those who knew Him well did not always immediately recognize Him (Luke 24:15–16, 31). The resurrection body indeed corresponded to the body which had died. Christ was no disembodied ghost. Yet it corresponded at an altogether higher state of glory. Christ's resurrection body was thus a body which answered appropriately to the principle of triumphant "more-than-reversal" of death. St. Paul again struggles with the problem of expression. Writing to the Corinthians he plainly reinterprets the Jewish hope of resurrection in terms of the one resurrection which had actually taken place, and speaks of the paradox of a "spiritual body" which shall belong to the believer in the Day of God (1 Corinthians 15:35–53). The implication is that this was the manner of body in which Christ rose from the dead: no mere body of resuscitated flesh and blood, but a body answering fittingly to the body of flesh and blood, yet answering equally to the glory of the Day of the Lord. Naturally the mind is left with all manner of unsatisfied inquiries, but this is inevitable as man confronts the mystery of God's immediate and unique saving act in history.

C. A Symbolic Act

If it is asked why God should have chosen to signify in this, and in no other way, that the Cross was a victory and not a defeat, the answer is to be sought in terms of the manner in which the Jewish people thought of human nature and personality. We today usually think of human nature as a nonmaterial "soul," which is the essential man, dwelling in and expressing

---

[3] However, those who affirm that the original resurrection appearances to the Twelve were a vision only, similar to St. Paul's experience on the Damascus road, would point to 1 Corinthians 9:1 as implying a claim that he was a witness of the resurrection, in the same manner as the original apostles.

itself through a material body, which is the necessary temporary companion of the soul in this life but not the real "personality." This is a thought form learned from the Greeks, and it is important to remember that it is not biblical.[4] The ancient Hebrews did not divide man into body and soul in this way, but looked upon human nature as unitary. All that we think of as together comprised in the terms of "body and soul," or "body, mind, and spirit," were by them conceived of simply as "the man," so that it would not have been natural for them to speak of the immaterial part of human nature as "the essential man."[5] Thus to the Hebrews, for the surviving immaterial "spirit" of a man to visit this world from the world of the dead, apart from the body, would not have been seen as the triumph of that man over death. It would be the survival of a ghost, of the mere partial shadow of the man.

In terms of this way of thinking the symbol of "triumph over death" is clearly not "survival of the soul in heaven," but rather *resurrection:* that is, the raising to life of the body which has died, and its reunion with the animating "breath of life." We thus find that the Hebrew expectation of the glorious life of the Day of the Lord is framed in terms of the resurrection of the body (Daniel 12:2).[6] This expectation could be interpreted by superficial minds in a crudely materialistic way, or by the more thoughtful as the resurrection of a human body mysteriously adapted for the glories of the messianic kingdom. It was to these Hebrew people, thinking in this way, that God gave His sign. He spoke as they were able to understand. Thus Christ was raised from the dead as the due token of victory over death. God placed His stamp of approval upon the expectation of resurrection, and also confirmed a "spiritual" interpretation of resurrection, in the sense that the body which rose was not barely the body of flesh and blood physically resuscitated, but a glorified body. We have to speak with reverent reserve concerning these mysterious things, but this would appear to accord with the witness of the New Testament, if the narrative be taken at its face value.

D. The Preaching of the Resurrection

The early sermons recorded in the Acts of the Apostles are not verbatim reports. Furthermore, it was a common and quite permissible literary device in antiquity for an author to compose a speech representing his view of a given historical situation, and place it in the mouth of the character concerned. Thus many critics would argue that these early sermons are not

---

[4] This does not necessarily involve that this way of thinking is wrong or that it is not a proper part of Christian theology.

[5] We are reminded that this view of human nature is not unreasonable by the investigations of modern psychology, which have illustrated how intimately the development of the mental life and the "personality" is connected with the action of the physical nervous system.

[6] This doctrine received much development in the period of time between the composition of the Old and the New Testaments.

the very words used by the apostles on these occasions. Even so, they are something of at least equal value, for they are a valid representation to us of the way in which the Christian gospel was preached by the Church in its first days. The apostolic argument is that by His glorious resurrection Jesus had been divinely vindicated as the Christ, even though He had suffered the fate, almost unbelievably paradoxical for the Messiah, of a cursed death (Acts 2:22–24, 32–36; 3:14–15; 4:10). To this is added a second line of argument, the "argument from prophecy." The Christians, reading the Scriptures in the light of their faith, could find many passages which spoke plainly to them of the doctrine of the crucified and risen Messiah. Therefore the mysterious paradox had been foreseen by the wisdom of God, and must be reverently accepted upon the authority of Scripture as the wonderful counsel of God (Acts 2:25–31, 34–35; 3:18, 21–25; 4:11, 24–28).

E. A Sign to Faith

It is most significant for the understanding of the whole spirit of the Christian faith that our Lord in His resurrection glory did not show Himself to confound Pilate or Caiaphas, but only to His broken-hearted yet loving disciples. To our Lord His "mighty works" were full of meaning. They were marks that in His person the kingdom of God was at work among men (Matthew 11:2–5, 12:28; Luke 11:20). Yet He seems to have sought to avoid creating the impression among the crowd that He was a worker of prodigies, or was the man to bring men bread on easy terms or victory over their enemies (John 6:14–15, 26–27). Instead, He bade men so far as possible keep His works of mercy secret (Matthew 8:4; Mark 8:26). In particular, He did not work miracles to produce faith in unbelievers, but invited men to have faith before He worked the wonder (Matthew 9:27–31; Mark 5:35–36). The man to whom is granted a wonderful work is he who cries out in his distress: "Lord, I believe; help Thou mine unbelief" (Mark 9:17–27). In Christ we see that God first invites man to respond to the initiative of His grace by opening his mind and heart in trust and love. He seeks that man should respond freely for the sake of love. The man who cooperates this far with God's act can then receive a mightier act of divine goodness and power which will increase and confirm his faith.

This progression of divine initiative and of free human response is illustrated in the story of our Lord's transfiguration.[7] This impressive sign was not given until the disciples had first, and without a sign, confessed that their Master was the Messiah (Mark 8:27–29). The wonderful work cannot be performed until men have first confessed the faith solely on account of the impression which our Lord's character and teaching had freely and

---

[7] Even if the order of this narrative is due to the Evangelists, the circumstance that they placed these elements of the story in this order is a token of the way in which they understood the mind of their Lord.

thoughtfully made upon their minds. Then, and only then, is it spiritually fitting that they should receive a miraculous confirmation of faith (Mark 9:1–8). This sign is not given so that the tale can be recounted to others as a wonder-story (9:9), but because their faith is presently to be sorely tested (9:30–32). On the other hand, for men to desire a sign as the condition for faith is the mark of unbelief (Matthew 12:38–39), while the desire to constrain unbelieving men by the working of a staggering miracle is the temptation of Satan himself (Matthew 4:5–7).

The climax of this process is the resurrection itself. The resurrection appearances were granted to men and women who freely had believed, whose faith was crushed by the devastating spectacle of their Lord's accursed death, yet whose hearts still cried out to believe because they were moved by love (Luke 24:18–25, 30–32). Doubting Thomas was allowed to see the Lord's glory, not simply because he was possessed of doubt which needed to be dispersed, but because despite his doubt he did not doubt utterly, and so remained with the disciples. The Lord came to him because He knew that he was, even in his "unbelief," prepared to come to faith if he saw (John 20:24–28). Thus the resurrection was a sign of Messiahship given to faith, and this faith is not a gift merely implanted in passive man. It is *evoked* by God.

F. The Pledge of Eternal Life

It can be argued that if God is good and reasonable in His dealings with men there must be, beyond this life, an eternal life with God (see pp. 257–58). This degree of faith is confirmed by the resurrection, and raised from a reasonable supposition to a confident hope which is the comfort of man in darkness and bereavement. That God could raise Christ from the dead is the supreme "case in point" (1 Corinthians 15:20–23, 55–58).

III. The Resurrection as Fact and as Symbol

In the accepted Christian system our Lord's resurrection is an outstanding instance of the general principle that God mediates the spiritual through the material (see p. 164). On the one hand, God's pledge of Christian faith is an historical act. It is a mysterious physical miracle, in that Christ rose from the dead. On the other hand, to Christian faith the value of the resurrection is not in the outward and physical act as such, but in the inward and spiritual principle which is symbolized by the act. Perhaps many, filled with curiosity, looked into the empty tomb and simply did not know what to make of it. The factual evidence of the resurrection did not produce faith, but only bewilderment. As the early evangelists discovered by experience, demonstration of the outward fact of the resurrection does not by itself constrain men to have faith (Luke 16:31). Yet the Church has always affirmed that the inward faith could not have arisen in the first place apart from the outward and physical sign of God's saving act. And without it faith cannot be sustained today. This has been the subject of widespread modern controversy.

Summary of Divergence : the Character of the Resurrection Gospel

a. A Critical View

The following points are presupposed as the basis for discussion. One assumes what has been established regarding the literary methods of the ancient world and the manner in which the original Christian tradition could have been modified in expression by transmission through the believing group mind of the ancient Church (see pp. 36–37, 38). Furthermore, the early Christian preaching was expressed in terms of "myth" belonging to those times (see pp. 35–36). Again, if Christian faith is to be made acceptable in the modern world the element of "physical miracle" must so far as possible be eliminated, because the scientific mentality assumes the doctrine of the continuity of nature and cannot accept the notion of a miracle (see pp. 27–28). Thus in a modern presentation of the gospel the resurrection is to be expounded apart from the miracle of the empty tomb, because this would have been a physical event.

The critical case, then, is as follows. The New Testament Church became aware as a matter of immediate and incontestable experience that their Lord was present with them after His death, alive, victorious over all evil, and the mediator to them of the very presence of God.[8] This momentous experience of divine "life out of death" was in fact itself God's historic saving act, and the foundation of the gospel. The group mentality of the first circle of believers then naturally and spontaneously constructed the imaginative narrative or "myth" of the angelic messengers, the empty tomb, the visible appearances of Christ, the mark of the nails, Christ's meals with His disciples, and the like, in order to give vivid expression to their faith that the living and victorious Lord was with them. There was no element of deception in this. It was simply the natural and inevitable way in which people of that place, time, and culture clothed their thoughts so as to grasp their faith for themselves and communicate it to others. Yet today we are mistaken if we seek to take the narrative literally, so as to speak of the empty tomb as a physical fact. If it be inquired what actually happened after the burial of Christ to generate the experience of the present and living Lord, the answer has to be given that we simply do not know, and by the nature of the case cannot know, beyond the vaguest of surmise. The Gospel narrative gives the witness of the Church to its faith in Christ, but not to "facts" about the resurrection in the sense of historical or scientific facts. To press an inquiry after these is alien to the sense of the story, and obscures to our mind the nature of the Gospel witness.

---

[8] To use the current phrase, they knew this "existentially."

b. A Rejoinder

The upholder of the traditional Christian system will first emphasize that the above exposition of Christianity, now widespread in many critical circles, is not simply a reinterpretation of the Christian Faith into the language of the modern day. It is a radical transformation of the whole Christian religion into something entirely different from what it has always been. It is a denial of the basic incarnational principle, that the God who made the material world, and who indwells and works through it, uses material means for the accomplishment of His spiritual ends (see pp. 23–24, 34). This attempt to withdraw God's saving act into the invisible world of the mind, and away from the material world, is an inherently unstable and illusory way of seeking to safeguard the spiritual (see p. 39). It is likewise a move whereby the Christian message ceases to be a gospel of divine grace, for there is now no longer reliance upon an objective divine saving work, but only an invitation to spiritual autosuggestion (see p. 39). Yet the true gravamen of all these objections is that the underlying demand for a Christian preaching free from the offensive "physical miracle" of the empty tomb in fact answers to a God-denying mechanistic view of the universe. We are back in the sphere of basic assumptions about life and thought (see pp. 14–15). The upholder of Christian tradition affirms that the radical critic's extreme reconstruction does not in fact spring out of the relevant evidence. It arises from the mind which he brings to the evidence. The tacit assumption throughout is that although there may be a God who gives existence to the world, there is no Living God who can perform a miracle of grace for the salvation of man.

The exponent of historic Christianity is well content that with the miracle of the empty tomb the Christian Faith should come into open and irreconcilable conflict with materialist and mechanistic views of the universe. Here in fact is a basic choice between faith or unbelief, which has to be made one way or the other. Practical experience of Christian advocacy shows that the obscuration of this issue by the construction of a "nonmiraculous" view of Christianity does not increase one's chance of winning to Christian faith men of a scientific background. If there is a sovereign personal God in control of the world, then He could have raised Christ from the dead, even though we cannot understand the manner. In this case, the plain Gospel evidence is at least credible, even though it is not to be read uncritically. And if we live in a world in which it is possible for God to become incarnate, and within this world perform His mighty act, then clearly He can perform other providential and saving acts. The doctrine of the empty tomb stands as the uncompromising rebuke to mechanistic philosophies. The whole spiritual attitude to life is in a sense pledged for the Christian by the gospel of Christ's miraculous resurrection.

In the first days of the Church the Christian Faith was distinguished from competing pagan Mysteries and Gnostic systems by its historical character. This principle has continued to work out in the long experience of the Church, and still continues in present developments. It has often happened that Christian teachers, moved by a perfectly sincere desire to make the Christian Faith more acceptable to the general body of reasonable men, have attempted to accommodate it to some extent to secular intellectual presuppositions. The effect has always been to tone down the rugged and challenging "supernatural" element. The Christian preaching has then inevitably, though perhaps insensibly and over a long period of time, drifted into a high-minded and idealistic call to men that they revere the spirit of Christ, seek to follow His example, and attempt to live by obeying His commandments. Thus the Christianity which slips away from the miracle of the Incarnation, which regards Christ as the supremely God-inspired man, and which to match this is content to say that the resurrection is true only symbolically, ceases to be a religion of grace. High-minded idealism then gradually ebbs out into discouragement, and thence to spiritual impotence. It is not possible permanently and convincingly to preserve the resurrection faith apart from acceptance of the actual and physical symbolic resurrection fact. Revivals of vital Christianity, on the other hand, of whatever brand of churchmanship, return to the challenging religion of the "supernatural" divine act in Christ, for this alone is the religion of grace.

IV. The Evidence for the Resurrection

A. Both those who uphold the long-established Christian Faith and the advocates of modern critical theories often find it hard to approach this subject dispassionately. After all, fundamental attitudes to life and to religious faith are laid bare here. Just as the critic tends to struggle against the evidence because he is aware that to accept Christ's miraculous physical resurrection would be a painful invasion of his intellectual pride, so the orthodox believer instinctively and passionately clings to every bit of evidence because he feels that the overthrow of this belief would be to him a crushing spiritual blow. Nevertheless, the effort to be candid must be made. Christianity is an historical religion, and therefore the theologian is committed at the very center of his faith to an honest evaluation of historical evidence. The truth must be told, even if it prove painful to conventional piety.

B. The charge often made against the historical narrative of the resurrection is that it was a gradually accumulating wonder-legend, born out of the attempt of unsophisticated minds to express their unbounded reverence for their Lord. A common form of argument is that the disciples could not bring themselves to believe that one so noble could be humbled in death. When they fled back to Galilee warm sentiment and nostalgia overwhelmed them, and they became hysterical. Thus they saw visions of Christ (as so many have seen all down the centuries), which convinced them that He was victorious over death. Their courage and faith consequently revived, and in the passionate strength of sincere and high-minded delusion they went out to conquer the world. This is the general line of argument for an "explanation" of the rise of Christianity in terms of "natural causes," and some such notion commonly lies hidden under the surface in "nonmiraculous" accounts of Christian faith.

The force of this attack lies in a number of facts which have to be admitted. The mentality of the time did welcome "wonder-stories" and did construct myths and legends. People have at times seen visions, and fanatical enthusiasm, high-minded or otherwise, can unite men into a close brotherhood and inspire them to heroic morale. Religious devotion has crystallized around many figures besides Christ, and legendary accretions do gather around the great figures of history. On the other side is the circumstance that the story of the resurrection was not a gradually accumulating legend. In the narratives of the lives of such prophetic figures as the Buddha and Francis of Assisi, there is usually first the original stratum giving an account of a man very striking indeed in personality but relatively nonmiraculous. In later strata of the traditional narrative, pious imagination has been active to increase the element of wonder-legend. Christian literature, from the so-called "apocryphal Gospels" onward, bears witness to the fact that everelaborating legends did grow up around the figure of Christ, just as one could have expected.[9] However, there is no evidence in the New Testament literature of an earlier nonmiraculous stratum lying hidden beneath the present narrative and bearing witness to an original Christian preaching of a "simple human Jesus."

From the very beginning the Christian gospel centered around the proclamation of the resurrection. The fact of the resurrection itself was not a gradually accumulating legend, though legends accumulated around it later. The resurrection, furthermore, was preached not first in another city some miles away, or some few years later, by which time the factual evidence might have become a little obscured. It was preached in Jerusalem within a very short time of the crucifixion, in the presence of many who had seen Jesus on the Cross, and with Joseph's tomb around the corner. If the bitter and resourceful enemies of Christianity had at that juncture produced the corpse, the high-minded delusion would have been dispelled, the mass hysteria would have been chilled, the fanatical morale of the Christians would have been shattered, and the infant "faith" would have been stillborn. That the first Christian preaching was of this character and survived this searching ordeal indicates to many candid minds that the Easter sepulchre was in fact empty. If this argument is allowed, the narrative is to be trusted as a sufficient historical testimony to the fact of the resurrection, even though a critical scholar would not take every accompanying detail literally.

The vulgar notion that the Christians first launched their faith in sincere

---

9 Thus many cautious and relatively conservative critics would be prepared to view a narrative such as Matthew 27:51–53, or possibly John 19:34, as a beginning to this process.

delusion, and later contrived to hide the body of Jesus so as to preserve the credit of their movement and the morale of their admiring followers, is one of the miracles of unbelief. Scheming miracle-mongers have been known in the long and mixed history of the Church. There have also been well-intentioned and pious men of confused counsels, who have considered that a modicum of deception might be justified as good for the Christian cause. But men do not emerge from this shady background to become conquering heroes for Christ. It is psychologically impossible to suppose that the apostles, harboring the grisly secret of a concealed corpse, received strength to live lives of heroic devotion and to die the deaths of martyrs for a Christ whom they knew had not risen from the dead, and that no one ever betrayed the deception.

There is also the confirming argument of the Church's long experience of the new life in Christ. That the historic Church has adapted herself to ever-new environments, and has renewed herself from time to time, rising to new spiritual life from out of institutional corruption, and so has endured to the present day, is a remarkable phenomenon. This is no sufficient proof of the truth of the Christian religion. In a perverse world many errors have shown something of this strange power of self-renewal. Furthermore, the hostile critic would claim that ineluctable fate has in these better-educated days at length apparently caught up with the Church, and that it is dying out. He may be wrong, but he has sufficient superficial appearance of truth in his boast to deter the Christian from too lightly claiming that Christianity must be true because it works. Nevertheless, the Church is much more than an institution which has shown great power of self-perpetuation. Christian faith has shown itself to be the world's longest-sustained, and most wide-spread and various, spring of new life for the race. Despite the manifest sins of those who have called themselves Christians it has been history's major influence to bring spiritual renewal, intellectual emancipation, and moral and human advance.

One is aware that there are some materialists and secular humanists who will passionately deny this, and who will cite evidence to show that historic Christianity has been a source of superstition, repression, and cruelty. The failings and sins of some who have called themselves Christians are such that this case cannot lightly be dismissed. The Christian answer is that these are the failings of social groups of Christians, behaving in the manner common to social groups, but not of the faith and spirit of Christianity itself. Essential Christianity has shown itself, and does still show itself, to be this life-giving power, but the claim can be tested only by experience. To the Christian it is impossible to imagine that this beneficent wave of new life in Christ can spring from a radical and rather pathetic illusion. In a rational world an effect requires a sufficient cause, and the cause of mankind's oft-tested hope of renewal is God's victorious act. The individual believer who experiences the power of the resurrection in his own life can assure himself that he is not the victim of a beautiful but unsubstantial illusion, because he does not stand alone. His private devotional experience is declared to be valid because it echoes the experience of the great body of believers. That great historic Church Universal has been tested not by pious sentiment, but by the most searching ordeals of history.

V. He Ascended Into Heaven

A. A Symbolic Act

We read that for a period of forty days, which in the language of Scripture stands for a substantial and significant period of time, the risen Christ from time to time appeared to His disciples in the glory of His resurrection body. At the end of this period He disappeared for the last time in a special manner. He did not just vanish as before, but disappeared into the clouds of heaven (Acts 1:1–11; compare Luke 24:50–52). This was a symbolic action, and is not to be taken so literally as to involve the idea that heaven is a place above the blue sky.

The essential factor surely is that the mind of that time thought of heaven, the seat of God's majesty, as "up," though it was also taught that God did not have a body, and therefore discriminating minds even in those days would not think of God as existing in a *material* place. Indeed, we still instinctively symbolize spiritual *exaltation* as "up," saying "Lift *up* your hearts!" and the mind of that time did so even more vividly. God, as always, spoke to men as they were able to understand. Our Lord's glorious ascension was a parable acted in terms of this idea. He vanished in such a way as to impress upon the apostles that the reason they were to see Him no more on earth in His glorious resurrection body was that He had gone to be with the majesty on high, in glory. The historical redeeming act of God, which had to be performed once and for all within the limitations of time and place, was now triumphantly completed. All that remained for Christ was to reign in glory, and to distribute to His believers the fruits of His victory (1 Corinthians 15:25; Ephesians 1:20–22, 4:8–12; Philippians 2:9–11; Colossians 3:1; Revelation 5:1–10, 19:11–16).

B. "Sitteth on the Right Hand of the Father"

This phrase is symbolical and is certainly not to be taken literally, for God the Father, who does not exist in a "place," does not sit on a "throne," and has no "body" or "right hand." In an earthly court the place to the right hand of the monarch was the place of chief honor, where might sit the heir to the throne, the queen, or the chief minister. The right hand was likewise the strong hand, which held the sword. Thus "the right hand" is the due symbol of majesty, power, authority, and glory (Psalm 45:9, 98:1, 110:1). This clause of the Creed vividly expresses the universal sovereignty of Christ. By an inconceivable act of self-humiliation He made Himself man, that as man He might perform the saving act of God. Yet this historical act was temporary. We are not to think of our Lord now as humiliated, as suffering human limitation, as tempted, as the object of our compassion. He is the object of our reverence, for with the Father and the Holy Spirit He reigns over all things in eternal and coequal glory.

C. The Heavenly High-Priesthood of Christ

This doctrine has already been introduced in exposition of the Epistle to the Hebrews, regarding our Lord's death as a sacrifice (see pp. 88–89). Some implications should be noticed. It is the Christian faith that the Incarnation has not been brought to an end by Christ's ascension into glory. The union of humanity and divinity is permanent, for Christ reigns in glory in His glorified manhood (Hebrews 10:12–13). There are two points at which this doctrine needs to be guarded against misunderstanding. To say that Christ's glorified humanity is "in heaven" does not involve that heaven is a place, or that Christ's glorious body occupies space. Furthermore, the permanence of this union of human and divine does not involve any kind of change in the nature of the Godhead, for God is by definition perfect, and therefore eternally the same. The divine Son, the second person of the Trinity, who continued to be equally "in heaven" during the time of the Incarnation on earth, has united humanity to Himself, but this change does not affect His divine nature considered in its own right. Rather it is a change of the humanity. Christ's human nature is unchanged after the Incarnation. Considered in isolation it is still fully human. Nevertheless, in the Person of the incarnate Son, human nature is promoted in honor by being associated with the divine.

An important aspect of this doctrine is the doctrine of the heavenly high-priesthood of Christ. By the Incarnation, God by His infinite condescension came near to mankind in sympathy. The ascension of Christ to glory, and consequent withdrawal from the Church of the presence of Christ in His resurrection body, does not mean that this sympathy is likewise withdrawn and that God has again become distant in majesty. Rather does it mean that united to the nature of the God who reigns in glory, there is that to which frail man can with confidence make the appeal of sympathy. The humanity, which in the days of Christ's flesh was so sympathetic that social outcasts dared ask Him to be one of their company, is there still enshrined in the holy place, though now glorified. Thus the ascension has not made God distant, but has made Him for all time approachable. The high priest is there, a genuine representative of the human race, opening the door for man in Him to come to God (Hebrews 2:18; 4:14–16; 7:24–26; 8:1–2; 9:11–14, 24; 10:19–22). The ascension consequently speaks both of Christ's majesty and conquering power and of His tender and understanding sympathy, and in Christian thought unites these two qualities (Revelation 5:5–6).

Readings

Baillie, J., *And the Life Everlasting*. New York: Charles Scribner's Sons, 1933.

Filson, F. V., *Jesus Christ the Risen Lord*. New York: Abingdon Press, 1956.

Ramsey, M., *The Resurrection of Christ*. Philadelphia: The Westminster Press, 1946.

Chapter Five

The Spirit of the Lord

And I believe in the Holy Ghost

I. The Holy Ghost

A. The Name

In Tudor English the word "ghost" simply meant "spirit." Thus in the Communion exhortation of the Book of Common Prayer we have the phrase "He may receive the benefit of absolution, together with ghostly counsel and advice, to the quieting of his conscience." When the Bible and the liturgy were translated into English, the title "Holy Ghost" was naturally and freely employed, and has molded the customary language of worship ever since.

B. Definition

The Holy Spirit, the third person of the Trinity, is the personal Agent by whom God the Father and God the Son more expressly and effectually operate in the world, and in the world of men. The divine work most particularly in mind is that of man's Christian salvation, though it is not confined to this. The distinctive work of the Holy Spirit operates in the Church of every time and place, and in the personal religious experience of every believer in the Church. He mediates the sense of Christ risen and glorified, and continues in present experience the effect of the saving work accomplished once and for all in the incarnation, atonement, resurrection, and ascension of our Lord. Thus the Christian doctrine of the Holy Spirit sets forth the connection

111

between the historic work of God performed in Palestine in the first century and His practical saving operation in the world of men today. A clear doctrine of the Holy Spirit preserves the believer from confusing Christian faith with dogmatic orthodoxy or pious Christian antiquarianism, and safeguards Christian worship from degenerating into formal ceremonialism or even into magic. This doctrine is essential to vital, personal, converting, and morally active Christianity.

II. The Holy Spirit in the Old Testament

A. The phrase "the Holy Spirit" is by origin a striking Old Testament metaphor to convey the idea of "God in action in the world." Thus there is a clear and important doctrine of the Holy Spirit in the Old Testament, though distinctively Christian elements are added to it in the New. This symbolical language is a comparison from human experience. To the biblical writers "the breath" was "the life" of man. While a man breathes, he lives. When he exerts himself, his breathing is strengthened. When he breathes out for the last time, he dies. "The breath" makes the mysterious difference between a man and a corpse. This thought form is applied in the Old Testament to God. He is the Living God, and so He has "breath." When God specially exerts Himself to perform some wonder, this is "the strong breath of God," that is, "the Spirit of the Lord." It will be appreciated that "breath" and "spirit" are alternative renderings of the same word in the Hebrew Old Testament and in the Greek New Testament. We have the same usage in English, where "to inspire" medically means "to breathe in" but can also be used in a spiritual sense. "To expire" means both medically "to breathe out" and also generally "to die."

B. The act of divine creation was the work of the Spirit (Genesis 1:2; Psalm 33:6; Isaiah 40:13).

C. The Spirit called, inspired, and equipped the prophets and heroes of Israel (for example, Judges 6:34, 14:6; Isaiah 61:1; Ezekiel 11:5, among many passages).

D. It was expected that a special outpouring of the Spirit would be the equipment of the Messiah when He came (Isaiah 11:2).

E. It was expected that the day of the messianic kingdom would be accompanied by a great outpouring of the prophetic Spirit, not only upon the few, as in the past, but upon all the redeemed people of Israel (Joel 2:28–29).

F. Considered as a man, an Israelite among Israelites, our Lord Himself was the climax of the prophets. Therefore the Holy Spirit came upon Him at the opening of His public ministry to equip Him for this prophetic and teaching office (Mark 1:9–12; compare Hebrews 1:8–9).

III. The Pentecost Experience

A. The Pentecost experience (Acts 2:1–21) has often been spoken of as the birthday of the Christian Church. However, it is not to be looked upon as an isolated event. Indeed, some would argue that what we have in Acts 2 is a symbolic representation of the general state of spiritual experience and preaching activity of the Church in her very first days, in a scene which is largely constructed by St. Luke. Nevertheless, it is reasonable to suppose that the first emergence of the Church, in her triumphant experience of the risen Christ, from dubious and timid hiding to confident and courageous public witness, would be the occasion of special divine equipment. We may continue to speak of a "day of Pentecost," even though many other days witnessed a substantially similar experience, as is shown in the New Testament itself (for example, Acts 4:31). In the same way, St. Peter's famous sermon (Acts 2:14–36) is by some scholars understood, not so much as a verbatim report of what he said on this actual occasion, but as a construction to represent the mode of Christian preaching in those first decisive days. Theologically speaking this is even more valuable, for this and other early sermons in Acts do, we believe, correctly represent the experience and belief of the first Church.

It is open to discussion how far the "rushing mighty wind" and the "cloven tongues" are to be understood as phenomena which could be heard and seen physically (see pp. 29, 31). Visions undoubtedly do occur, but how they occur is a mysterious subject, and the way in which they are described depends to an unusual degree upon the customary thought forms of the beholders. Nor need the reader be unduly puzzled by the circumstance that St. Luke's account appears to read as though "the gift of tongues" consisted in utterance in a variety of foreign languages (vv. 6–8), whereas the actual description we have of this "gift" indicates quite plainly that it was ecstatic and unintelligible speech (1 Corinthians 14:1–23). Perhaps both propositions are true, the latter historically, the former symbolically. The "speaking in an unknown tongue" was perhaps not the gift of speech in a foreign language, yet the Church did speak to men of many lands, races, and languages. St. Luke sees this symbolized in the first and normative preaching of the gospel. The pilgrims of Israel from many lands, including many who were not of Jewish faith (Acts 2:10), were at the first preaching joined to the Church, which is the true Israel. This is an expressive picture of what had actually happened in the evangelistic experience of the Church.

B. We may see from the Pentecost sermon that the essential faith of the apostles was that their Lord Jesus, though crucified, was nevertheless the Messiah, the bringer of the promised kingdom. They were assured of the inconceivable paradox in the first place by the experience of the resurrection (vv. 22–24, 32–33, 36), with the compelling supporting evidence that this wonderful event could be found spoken of in sacred prophecy (vv. 25–31, 34–35). In this conviction the apostles found themselves with a certainty of the presence, the favor, and the redeeming power of God, which nothing could destroy. Men brought up upon the Old Testament recognized this experience. It was "like the old prophets again." This was a manifest outpouring of "the Spirit of the Lord." The messianic promise in Joel was fulfilled, because the prophetic Spirit rested upon every member of the new Israel of God (vv. 16–21).

C. Those who had known so well what it was to have Jesus in the company recognized the Pentecost experience in another way, which was new and even more full of meaning to them. It was "like Jesus with them again," though there was no one to see. When Jesus was at their head they felt strong for anything (John 11:16). When He was taken from them, they were crushed and beaten men (Mark 14:50; John 20:19). When they knew He was with them again in resurrection victory, their faith and courage sprang to life again (John 20:26–28). The Pentecost experience was like this, only more so, even though there was now no visible presence of the risen Christ. Therefore they naturally spoke of the Spirit of Pentecost, not only in Old Testament terms as "the Spirit of the Lord," but also in New Testament terms as "the Spirit of Jesus" or "the Spirit of Christ" (Philippians 1:19; Galatians 4:6). Indeed, "the Spirit of God" and "the Spirit of Christ" are virtually indistinguishable in usage (Acts 16:6–7; Romans 8:9).

D. Thus in Christian thought the Old Testament phrase, "the Spirit of the Lord," conveying the idea of "the manifested presence and power of God," is extended. The Holy Spirit is the agent who mediates to the Church in present experience the sense of the presence and power of God *as He is known in Jesus Christ,* and as He comes to man and performs His saving act in His incarnate Son.

IV. Aspects of the Doctrine of the Holy Spirit

A. His Person

It is Christian teaching that the Holy Spirit is a divine person, together with the Father and the Son. It is for this reason that the divine Agent is always spoken of as "He" and not as "It." This again is symbolic language, being a comparison drawn from human experience and applied to God. It is not intended to say that the Holy Spirit is masculine, but that He is a divine person, not merely an impersonal divine influence. Thus the God of creation is not the bare "creative principle" necessary to explain the existence and order of the universe. In Christian and biblical thought He is "the Living God," a personal God who has created the universe by an act of knowledge and will. When the Spirit, who is the creative "hand" or "arm" of the Lord, acts (Isaiah 48:13), there is always a sovereign person acting. It is often loosely said that there is a divine spirit in all men, and in particular in all good men. The impression may be created thereby that the Holy Spirit is simply a name for the higher faculties of the human personality. This is a confusion which is condemned by Christian theology. There are indeed these nobler faculties of human nature, which are part of man's natural existence and which are bestowed by God. Yet when the Holy

Spirit inspires prophets, saints, philosophers, and artists, there is present a divine person, quite distinct from the human personality, yet holding communion with it, who by His "personal influence" quickens the natural human faculties to their endeavors.

In particular, when the Holy Spirit mediates Christian salvation to man through the preaching of the word, and the sacraments and worship of the Church, it is not to be supposed that there is a kind of "spiritual electricity" flowing down an ecclesiastical wire. This is an example of the impoverished thought which may allow Christian rites to degenerate into formality or even into magic. God does not save man by infusing into his personality a mysterious heavenly substance which acts as a sort of spiritual preservative. It is by a powerful and transforming process of "personal influence" that He changes man in personal character, moral will, and responsible ethical action. We may conceive of this as analogous to the way in which a man of noble character may assist his friend by being constantly near to him in personal presence and personal sympathy. Thus when God in Christ visits the company of His people in the Church's ministry of word and sacraments, and brings to them their share of Christian salvation, there is always an invisible *person* there, never a mere invisible "thing." The divine agent is a person. All these important ideas are summed up in the doctrine of the personal existence of the Holy Spirit.

B. The Filioque *Clause*

The original form of the Nicene Creed declares of the Holy Spirit that He "proceedeth from the Father." This is what is still said by the Eastern, or Orthodox, Church. Following St. Augustine's teaching the Western and Latin-speaking Church sought to emphasize the strict equality of the Father and the Son by teaching that the Spirit proceeds also from the Son. This doctrine eventually crept into the Nicene Creed as it is said in the Western Church, with the result that our Creed runs: "who proceedeth from the Father and the Son," the added words being a translation of the Latin word *filioque*. It may be claimed that the doctrine represented by this addition is sound and scriptural. It helps to emphasize that it is God *in Christ* who acts for man's salvation, and that God the Son is divine in the same full sense as is God the Father. The Orthodox Church of course fully accepts both these positions. However, it is a great pity that this divergence should have appeared in the Creed, which otherwise is one of the most significant marks of the unity of the Catholic Church. The Eastern Church has much justice in her objection that this addition, though not false, is unauthorized.

C. The Paraclete

This Greek word is more commonly applied to the Holy Spirit, though it can also be used of the divine Son (1 John 2:1). It means, by derivation, "a person called to one's aid." Thus it can commonly carry the legal meaning of "the knowledgeable and influential friend one takes to court," that is, an *advocate*. This is the traditional translation used when the word is applied to Christ, as in 1 John. When applied to the Holy Spirit (John 14:16, 26; 15:26; 16:7) the traditional translation has been "Comforter." This beautiful word is, however, somewhat misleading in modern ears. In Tudor English the verb "to comfort" (from the Latin *fortis,* "strong") retained much of its original meaning of "to strengthen." Thus for a disloyal person "to comfort the king's enemies" meant "to aid and abet" them. If this sense be taken, there is not so much difference between "Comforter" and "Advocate." Thus they can be alternative translations for the same Greek word.

In light of this we see that the operative word in John 14:16, "And I will pray the Father, and He shall give you another Comforter, that He may abide with you for ever," is *another*. In the days of His flesh our Lord was the one who by His presence with His disciples, and by His personal influence, made them strong for the battle of life with a moral power which was not their own. He was the Paraclete, the Strengthener, the Comforter. However, by the nature of things, this saving activity had to come to an end. God's saving act in His incarnate Son, performed once for all as man and for men, had to take place upon the plane of history. It was done at one certain time and place, and therefore at no other. Nevertheless, God's saving activity in Christ is to be available to all men who will accept it, equally and without distinction in every time and place and circumstance. Therefore the once-for-all decisive historic act of God had come to its due end, and its place be taken by the continuing and universal act of God in Christ. The Paraclete, who is the incarnate Son, ascended to glory. And another gracious divine presence like His, that is to say, another *Paraclete,* was given "that He may abide with you for ever." Thus the Holy Spirit is the one who carries on universally and to the end of time the work of Christ in the heart.

D. The Holy Spirit and the Risen Christ

It is hardly surprising that people untutored in theology often find their minds in confusion as to the distinction between the Holy Spirit and the presence of the risen Christ invisibly with His Church. When the Church prays to her Lord:

> Present we know Thou art,
> But O Thyself reveal!

the Holy Spirit is the Agent who answers the prayer, and who works in the heart the conscious sense of communion with the Christ who is always present, whether or not man is conscious of Him. Thus devotionally speaking, there is no distinction which we can experience between the Holy Spirit and the risen Christ. Yet theologically speaking, there is a distinction *in thought.* The Son represents the saving presence of the Supreme God in the world of men, but as incarnate, and as performing the saving work once for all. The Spirit represents the same saving presence in the world, but as performing the saving work in the heart, and in the Church, invisibly, and in every time and place, on account of what was performed once for all by the incarnate Son.

V. The Work of the Holy Spirit

A. The work of the Holy Spirit is in no sense limited to the Christian salvation of men, or to the Church. Whenever and wherever the one triune God acts He acts wholly, and not in part. In a true sense the whole creation and providential government of the world is an act of God through the Spirit. So is the spiritual guidance of the hearts and minds of all men, and particularly of the spiritual leaders of mankind, whether or not they name the name of Christ. However, to the Christian the supreme example of "God in action in the world" is the work of salvation and the mediation of that salvation to men. Therefore Christian theology sees the operation of the Spirit most particularly in all the high points of the life of the Church, and at all the decisive moments in the spiritual experience of the believer.

B. The Holy Spirit, who rested upon the first apostles, called and equipped those who were later joined to the apostolic office (Acts 13:2), as well as other ministers in the Church (Acts 6:3; compare 1 Timothy 4:14). The whole New Testament Church was possessed of a vivid sense of being indwelt and guided by the Holy Spirit. He was, as it were, the atmosphere of the Church's life, so that the company of believers were "in the Spirit" (Romans 8:9–13). He bestowed upon the Church the fullness of spiritual "gifts," devotional, moral, and intellectual (1 Corinthians 12:4–14).

C. The Holy Spirit, who is the Spirit of prophecy which inspired the Old Testament (2 Peter 1:21), likewise inspired the authors of the apostolic writings and guided the Church in the selection of them to form the canon of New Testament Scripture (John 14:26). Thus the whole Bible is the gift of the Holy Spirit to the Church.

D. The Holy Spirit guides the Church, and in particular the fellowship of reverent and learned teachers within the Church, to fuller understanding of God's revelation declared in Christ and preserved in Holy Scripture (John 16:13–15). Thus as the truth of Christ is applied to the ever-changing issues of life there is accumulating in the experience of the Church through the centuries an ever-enriched body of Christian teaching. This is, however, always to be securely attached to the original historic revelation, and the tradition of the Church is therefore to be a continuous and consistent scriptural tradition. The leading points of focus of this process of the formulation of Christian doctrine are the General Councils of the ancient and undivided Church. In these councils the teaching voice of the whole Church is more expressly heard, exposing and rebutting error, and clarifying the intention of Scripture and of the existing tradition of doctrine, by the authoritative formulation of a new doctrinal statement, which is henceforth a part of the faith of the Church. It is the traditional faith of the Church that these General Councils were effectually guided by the Holy Spirit, so that their doctrinal formulations are to be accepted as fully authoritative for the Church. For a further summary of divergent views of ecclesiastical authority see pages 2–8.

E. The Holy Spirit works in the believer a renewed and righteous character of love, purity, and unselfishness (Galatians 5:16–17, 22–25). He is the guiding principle of all Christian conduct, teaching man what is right, and giving him power to do it. Thus all true Christian morality is a "work of the Spirit," and this it is which makes the Christian obligation of obedience to the divine moral law a nobler and more spiritual thing than mere legal obedience for the sake of duty, in hope of reward or fear of punishment. The Spirit enables man to obey for the sake of love.

F. The Holy Spirit guides the Church, and in particular the fellowship of authorized and responsible pastors in the Church, to an understanding of how this "spiritual law" is to be applied to the ever-changing issues of life. The moral and disciplinary standard declared by the Church is the effective standard which the conscientious man may be expected to understand and accept. Thus it is the moral standard by which God judges his actions (John 20:21–23).

G. The Holy Spirit calls men to the sacred ministry, and to other branches of Christian service. He also guides the Church in her responsible task of deciding whether those who profess this call, and who offer themselves to the Church, are indeed so qualified by divine call and by gifts and graces of character as to make it right to admit them and authorize them for their office. In principle it is essential to the rightful making of a Christian minister that he be first called by God (Hebrews 5:4), for no man is good or wise enough to be qualified as a volunteer, by his own wisdom or goodness. He can only act or speak for God if he goes as one sent by God.

H. In the consecration of bishops and the ordination of presbyters and deacons, the Holy Spirit, working through the due laying on of hands, inwardly stamps or seals the ministers of Christ to the end that their ministerial actions may be in due ecclesiastical order in the Church, and as such the objects of God's promise to give grace to believing men through the ministrations of the Church (1 Timothy 4:14).

I. The Holy Spirit gives grace to all Christ's servants, and in particular to those ordained to the sacred ministry, to enable them effectually to preach the gospel, and to give pastoral counsel in faith and morals, to the people for whom they bear responsibility. It is, we believe, a fact of experience that if Christ's servants fully open their hearts to Him in consecration the Holy Spirit can actually quicken their powers of understanding and utterance, and enable them on occasion to speak words of persuasion with a power not their own. There is, however, a deeper and more general principle expressed in the proposition that the Holy Spirit grants special grace to those ordained to the Christian ministry. The minister is deeply aware that he himself is a sinful man, in desperate need of that which he offers to others. So far as his own attainments in the Christian life are concerned he has no right to offer good advice to others, and the preacher's own words convict him of hypocrisy. Nevertheless, it is his duty to speak because God has sent him, and the Church has commissioned him with responsibility for those to whom he speaks. Thus the divine equipment alone qualifies him to say, fittingly, that which no man is fit to say. That he can exercise a useful ministry is an act of divine grace, through the operation of the Holy Spirit.

J. The Holy Spirit operates through the sacraments to make of them effectual and operative means of grace to the believing Church, and to every faithful soul (Acts 2:38, 19:5–6). (See also pp. 165, 169.)

K. The Holy Spirit prompts men to accept the gospel when it is preached to them, and moves them to faith in Christ (1 Corinthians 12:3). It is a fact of familiar experience that not all who hear of Christ believe, and that some who wish they could open their hearts to Christ in loving trust find they cannot do so, at least at that moment (see pp. 222–23). Man's will for good is in bondage, and his spiritual faculties weak, so it is idle for him to delude himself that he can turn to Christ in penitent faith as and when he will. He can only do so when God effectually calls, by the agency of the Spirit.

L. The Holy Spirit stimulates and guides man's power of prayer (Romans 8:26).

M. It is a truth particularly emphasized by some branches of evangelical Christianity that it is a work of the Holy Spirit in the heart of the believer to give to him a witness of his adoption, and of assurance of his salvation (Romans 8:14–17). (See also p. 228.)

N. The Holy Spirit operates in Confirmation, and in other rites of dedication leading to the status of communicant Church membership, to seal these vows and to enable those who have pledged their allegiance to Christ and His Church to do what they have promised (Acts 8:14–17, 19:6).

VI. Summary: The Christian Doctrine of God, the Holy Trinity

A. Now that the doctrine of the person and work of God the Father, God the Son, and God the Holy Spirit has been defined, the Christian

doctrine of God may be summarized by a treatment of the doctrine of
the Holy Trinity. The newcomer to theology often makes the objection
that this part of Christian teaching is abstract, speculative, and needlessly
hard to understand. It is first to be remembered that it is idle to expect
a *simple* doctrine of God. The world in which we live is a very wonderful
and intricate thing, and the mind of man is of limited capacity to understand
it. Therefore every branch of human study runs off into mystery at some
point. For example, only a select few have intellect sufficient to master
the most advanced branches of higher mathematics, and they only after
long and careful training. If it once be allowed that the mind of God is
the law which lies behind all the laws of nature, then the residual mystery
of mathematical law is only one single small part of the mystery of the
mind of God. God cannot be fully grasped by the human mind, and any
language framed to symbolize His nature must be such as to remind man
of this fact. That is to say, the symbol is "difficult."

Through the centuries, and today, many schools of thought have sought
to frame a "simple" doctrine of God, the general line of approach being
that He is the solitary and remote Sovereign Potentate, or perhaps even
only an impersonal first principle, who has partially revealed Himself from
time to time in the leading teachers of mankind. This is a conception of
God which makes an incarnation and a divine act of redemption inconceivable. In fact, the mystery of God has been "simplified," and the doctrine
of God made more easy to expound, by the expedient of ignoring some
of the facts about Him which the Christian is particularly anxious to affirm.
The attraction of such a "simple" doctrine of God will, we believe, be
found superficial. Many of the heresies which troubled the ancient Church
arose as the result of perfectly sincere efforts to frame Christian doctrine
in terms of a "reasonable" and "scientific" conception of God, such as
would be easy to expound as a basis for a doctrine of God and the world.
These systems of theology were found unsatisfactory because in the attempt
to make clear and simple the doctrine of God as the creator and governor
of the world they denatured the doctrine of salvation by a divine act in
Jesus Christ, God's incarnate Son. It was to safeguard the truths of salvation
that the Church, as it were, in part turned her back upon a "simple"
and "scientific" doctrine of God, and went to the world with the admittedly
mysterious doctrine of the Holy Trinity. Thus the wise student of theology
should be prepared to come to this doctrine with an open and sympathetic
mind. Its presence in the Christian system is not an intellectualist perversity,
but an attempt to safeguard the interests of the gospel.

B. The converse may be seen if the doctrine of the Trinity is approached
from the historical point of view, and the question raised concerning by
what process it came to be framed. The Church certainly did not start
with a speculative theory of the nature of God, framed for speculative
reasons. She started with the direct experience that in Christ God had

visited man and done for him what only God can do (see pp. 47–48). Thus from experience was framed the doctrine that Christ is the divine Son. The primitive Church went before the world preaching two imperative religious interests—from its Jewish background in the Scriptures, that there is but one sovereign God; and from its experience of salvation, that Jesus Christ is divine. As and when the Church developed the talent and leisure for intellectual speculation it was realized that there is a tension between these two interests. How could they both be fully safeguarded? Thus the fathers of the Church had to construct a doctrine of God which would enable them to say that their Lord was a divine Saviour, in the full and proper sense of the word, and at the same time make it plain that there is only one God. The fruit of this admittedly exacting intellectual quest is the doctrine of the Trinity.

C. The underlying issue may be stated in this way. It is the Christian conviction that God has made Himself known to man in a threefold way. There is God as He is seen in the creation and government of the universe. Our Lord taught us to call the Creator-God "our Father" (Matthew 6:9), so that the most distinctive Christian title for God is "the God and Father of our Lord Jesus Christ" (Romans 15:6; Ephesians 1:3). In the second place, there is God as He became incarnate, lived for a span of years in Galilee and Jerusalem, taught, died, and rose again. He is described as the divine Son (John 1:18; Hebrews 1:1–3). And in the third place, there is the Spirit of God, who is also the Spirit of Christ (Romans 8:9; Galatians 4:6; 1 Peter 1:11), who is the personal agent by whom the activity of the Father and the Son is applied to the lives of men and women.

The question which then faces the theologian is this: "Are we to believe that in this threefold experience the Supreme God has really visited man, and actually revealed His nature to him? Or is the threefold experience a mere concession to human ways of thought, and to human frailty; so that it is by way of an illusion, which leaves the Supreme God still out of touch with man, unknown and unknowable?" The doctrine of the Trinity is the Church's attempt to give a full and clear affirmative to the former proposition. It is a way of saying that God's showing of Himself to man as Father, Son, and Holy Spirit profoundly corresponds to the inmost nature of the Supreme God as He really exists "in Himself," from eternity to eternity. The alternative is clear, and is destructive of the whole Christian position that the Gospel is the message of a divine visit to this world, and of a divine act in this world. To deny the doctrine of the Trinity logically involves that the Supreme God is a remote God who has not come to encounter man and show Himself to man in a personal incarnation. All He has done is to give passing and partial glimpses of Himself.

It must be made plain that Christian theology does not claim that the Supreme God has made Himself *fully* known in the experience of God as the Father, the Son, and the Holy Ghost. This would not be possible, because God "as He is in Himself," being infinite, is not wholly within the grasp of limited human knowledge. There is no claim to know all there is to know about God, but only that God has made Himself known as fully and adequately as is possible in human terms, and that this knowledge is real and secure knowledge, having in it no element of illusion. It is the conviction of the Church that when in heaven believers are able to see God as He really is, they will find God's revelation of Himself to man in terms of Father, Son, and Holy Spirit to be fully vindicated and confirmed, though it will doubtless be transcended by a fuller knowledge which is inherently impossible to man in this finite life. There will be much to learn, but nothing to unlearn.

D. There is also the converse to this. The Supreme God has made Himself known in this threefold way for a reason which is fundamental to the nature of existence. It is the faith of the Church that He has come to man in the experience of this world, as Father, Son, and Holy Spirit, because His heavenly and eternal nature "as it is in itself" is like this. Thus from one point of view the doctrine of the Trinity is the last point of Christian doctrine. It is the sublimest effort of the mind of man, under divine inspiration, to climb up from the facts of immediate religious experience to speculation about the nature of God. Yet as the complement to this manward aspect there is the Godward aspect. From this point of view the doctrine of the Trinity is the first and fundamental point of Christian doctrine. The revelation in history has taken place in the way it has because this most fully corresponds to the nature of God from eternity.

E. The formula adopted by the Church as authoritative for the doctrine of the Holy Trinity is "One divine *substance,* three divine *persons.*" The sense of both these symbolical terms needs to be defined if the formula is to be expressive. In each case the word is used in a special way, somewhat different from the ordinary sense.

Substance. The modern man instinctively thinks of a "substance" as a solid body, having size and weight. Clearly this sense cannot apply to the invisible and omnipresent God. The word "substance" as used here derives from the traditional philosophy of the Church, and indicates the essential nature of a thing, the possession of which constitutes what it is. It has no material connotation. The possession of the *spiritual* "substance" of divinity constitutes a being divine. To say that there is but one divine substance is a convenient and exact way of saying that there is but one God. To say that Father, Son, and Holy Ghost each possess the divine substance means that each is in the fullest and most proper sense divine.

Person. This is admittedly one of the more difficult of theological terms for the modern mind to grasp, because one who is not grounded in systematic theology almost instinctively makes of it the equivalent of the modern term "personality." To do this is to obscure the doctrine of the Trinity and to make the idea of the "Three-One" logically impossible. The modern psychological notion of "personality" includes the ideas of self-consciousness, exclusiveness, and autonomy. A personality knows himself to be himself, and as such, distinct from all other things. By consequence, he has the sensation of a kind of mental "wall" around himself, which shuts other things out. He also has the sensation of choice. He is aware that he is not wholly passive before the force of circumstance. He has within himself certain resources of will, which can at least attempt to give direction to his activity. It is clearly an error to apply all these notions unmodified to the three persons of the Godhead. To say that God is three "personalities" would be to imagine Him as a "committee" of three separate Gods, who are only "one" in the very reduced sense that they have the same policy and action in making and governing the world. This is not the Christian doctrine of the Trinity. The three divine persons are not as separate from one another as would be three personalities, in the modern sense. Yet this is not a sign that the word "person" is here being used in a reduced, denatured, and misleading sense.

When in the ancient Church the word "person" was first adopted to designate the Three it was a legal term. It denoted a legal "party," in the sense of an individual, or group of individuals, who could possess a piece of property or be a party in a legal action. In usage it has become enriched since then, and one might say that as used in the trinitarian formula it includes the conception of self-consciousness, but not that of exclusiveness. We may symbolize the Three as "knowing" one another, but not as "shutting one another out." The divine persons are not exclusive, like human personalities, but inclusive. They "take one another in," and presuppose one another's existence, so that by the nature of existence they have but one will and action.

Here is symbolic language constructed from a comparison with human experience. A human personality comes to the experience of self-consciousness by "hitting up against" other personalities, discovering them to be there, learning that they are different and also autonomous, and by making room for them. From this experience we instinctively associate the idea of exclusiveness with personality. Yet this is a mark of the limitation of human personality, and of the fact that it has to develop. The most developed and perfect human personalities we know are not the most exclusive, those who have the toughest spiritual "wall" around themselves. They are those who have most completely transcended this limitation of growth, and who have become the most inclusive. The most completely "personal" persons we know are not the most fiercely autonomous, but those who are most completely united in mutual accord and sympathy with other persons round about them. Developed personality starts with self-consciousness, but it moves from bare self-consciousness to personal communion.

This surely is a parable of the nature of God, whose infinite, eternal, and unchanging existence is altogether superior to the necessity of *developing* a self-consciousness by contact with existence outside Himself. The three divine persons are not at all exclusive. By the law of their existence they are eternally, completely, and unchangeably inclusive. Thus the Three are more closely identified with one another than any human personalities we can imagine. Yet this does not imply that the Three are less "personal" than would be three perfectly loving human personalities. They are more fully "personal" because they are less separate than humans. Such is the highest attempt of the human mind to symbolize the nature of God. Here we may imagine the possibility of the Supreme God being both Three and One.

F. In summary, the doctrine of the Holy Trinity is the logical background in speculative thought for the devotional doctrine that God is love. It has been said that the only difficult Christian dogma is "God is love." When we think of the infinite scale of the universe, and of the dark mystery of sin and suffering in this little world, it takes a great deal of vision and courage to acknowledge that the Sovereign Potentate of all has a warm heart of love. The perhaps difficult conception of the Holy Trinity is a conception of the Godhead which makes the proposition that "God is love" at least possible to thought. There is little merit in the notion of the love of a "god" who is not the Sovereign Potentate. Some have imagined a "god" who created the universe because it brought him satisfaction and self-fulfillment to do so. He created mankind as the objects of his love because he needed them as objects of his love, that he himself might be fully blessed. This "god" is not the God of the Bible, nor of Christian theology. He is an inferior being, who because he can be improved in his mode of existence is not unchangeable in perfection. His existence inevitably presupposes the existence of a higher Supreme Being, who is the ultimate ground of existence. The wonder of the love of God is that it is the love of a mighty and self-sufficient God, who does not require the existence of anything outside Himself in order that He may be fully blessed. This is the only perfectly unselfish love which we can imagine.

The classic human example of the love which seeks only to give and to sacrifice is the tender passion of mother love. Yet even the mother loves in part because she needs to love. She cherishes her infant in part because she knows that she will be filled with grief if he sickens or dies. We cannot imagine human love which is *perfectly* unselfish. The only perfectly unselfish love of which the heart of man can conceive is the love of the self-sufficient God of sovereign majesty. It is the love of the God who when He was alone existed from eternity in unchangeable bliss. He created the universe, and man in it, as the objects of His pure beneficence, even though this love could add nothing to Himself. He set His love upon man, and in perfect foreknowledge gave to man the power to grieve His love, even though there was no necessity laid upon Him to love. This possibility is enshrined in the holy mystery of the Blessed Trinity. That happiness and self-fulfillment which man can find only in common with others God could perfectly enjoy from within the resources of His own being, when from eternity He was the solitary existence. There was love between the three perfectly inclusive self-consciousnesses, who together are one God.

This picture of God, furthermore, is the doctrine which renders conceivable the infinite condescension of the Incarnation, which act is the supreme mark of that divine love. The doctrine of the Incarnation presupposes that God the Son could in some mysterious way suspend the exercise of His bright glories, and yet continue fully to be God. This in turn presupposes a certain view of the nature of the Deity. If the Sovereign Potentate is defined only in terms of infinite and unchangeable glory, wisdom, and power, then He is the utterly remote and essentially unknowable God. He cannot, without ceasing to be what He is, give up those bright glories upon which man cannot look. The Incarnation is thus inconceivable. The conception that in the person of His Son the Highest God united Himself with His defiled handiwork, and suffered with men and for men, requires that the Sovereign Potentate be defined also in terms of perfect, eternal, unchangeable, and self-giving love. When for a season He darkened the glory the love fully shone forth, and the humiliated Son incarnate was vindicated as fully divine. To the Christian theologian the doctrine of the Blessed Trinity is the guarantee and exposition of this view of God.

Readings

Barclay, W., *The Promise of the Spirit*. London: Epworth Press, 1960.

Hodgson, L., *The Doctrine of the Trinity*. New York: Charles Scribner's Sons, 1944.

Van Dusen, H. P., *Spirit, Son, and Father*. New York: Charles Scribner's Sons, 1958.

Chapter Six

The People of God

I believe in the Holy Catholic Church

I. The Church : A Divine Plan

A. Interdependence and Community

The principle of variety is written into the very order of creation. The universe conceivably might have been created with all the stars of the same kind and size, moving upon equivalent and simple courses. Instead, there is incalculable variety and complexity. So it is in the world of organic life. There are indeed cases where the life cycle is carried on according to a very simple pattern, as when the giant panda, which eats only bamboo shoots, lives in a jungle consisting only of bamboos. Conceivably, every environment could have been peopled in this manner, but in fact such a case is remarkable on account of its singularity. The normal pattern of life is that every habitat appears to have as large as possible a variety of plants and animals packed into it, which are dependent upon one another for the means of life through a remarkably subtle and complicated system of interlocking life cycles.

The same principle holds in human affairs. Some theorists have clung to the unrealistic notion that all men are "equal." In fact, the only equality they have is one of grace, in that God chooses to love them all and value them all. They are very much the reverse of equal by natural endowments, and in the place allotted to them by divine providence in the complicated pattern of human affairs. We can see a spiritual reason behind this plan.

Were all men substantially alike in natural characteristics and abilities their "equality" would allow them to live in substantial independence one of another. They might then naturally enough be inflated with that sense of self-sufficiency which is the fundamental sin of pride. The circumstance that the human race is composed of men and women, of young and old, of natural leaders and the naturally led, of the practical and the visionary, and so forth, and that in all these partnerships the one needs the other if the business of life is to be carried on, provides the providential principle by which self-sufficiency is destroyed and mankind educated in humility. By interdependence society is cemented together as a moral discipline.

To the Christian the chief of all human affairs is man's salvation in Christ. This is the activity which illuminates the meaning of all other activities, and in which the underlying principle of all rightly-ordered human affairs is most explicitly demonstrated. Man's salvation in Christ provides the great example of that interdependence which is the cement of community. It is an important principle of theology that the Christian community, the Church, reflects a principle written into the very character of God's government of the world, and draws its existence from the eternal will of God (Ephesians 3:1–12). The Church does not take its rise from the will or convenience of man, as an expression of the principle "birds of a feather flock together." Believers do not first become Christians, and then choose to join the Church. To be incorporated into the Church is an essential part of being a Christian, and the Christian community is theologically necessary to the Christian Faith. The law of the Christian life is love, or charity. Love opens men's eyes to the fact that there are others who have rightful claims upon them, and that they themselves need others. This humbles man's natural desire for self-sufficiency, and by knitting him into the Christian community brings home to his heart and mind the spiritual principle which unites him to God.

B. Personal and Communal Religion

To speak of personal and of churchly religion as though they were in some way opposites is to obscure the character of the Christian life. On the one hand, there is a sense in which all religion is personal religion. There is no such thing as a tradition of truth or a supply of grace existing "impersonally" in the Church as such. There is only the personal action of God upon His individual children. God's method of revealing His truth to the Church is that He quickens and inspires the natural faculties of individual men to discern this truth, through their response to the experience of life and the processes of thought and imagination. New and creative apprehensions of divine truth, and new waves of spiritual endeavor in the Church, have therefore normally been associated with the lives and activities of men and women of outstanding spiritual genius, whom we may call "the prophets" and "the saints." Their influence has been mediated to the wider circles of the Church by movements of disciples who have looked to them as heroes of The Faith.

However, it does not follow from this that Christianity is essentially individualistic. The overruling principle of interdependence, which is the discipline of humility and the bond of charity, is also to be seen at work. No one man, however talented, or however completely inspired by God, can grasp all God's truth by himself. The variety of human circumstance and experience is almost infinite, and every human condition has its own lesson. Some things of the Spirit are best appreciated by the intellectualist, some by the imaginative and aesthetic temperament, and others, no less important, by the capable and common-sense man of affairs. Some lessons come in joy or success, some in adversity, sadness, or calamity. Some parts of the Christian truth are particularly the heritage of the ancient Hebrews or of the Greeks, others of the martyr Church of the early centuries, others of the ruling Church of the Middle Ages, and yet others of the age of modernity and science. Part of the discipline has been wrought out in the cloister, part in the home, and part in the workshop and the market-place. And not one of these apprehensions of Christian truth—doctrinal, devotional, or moral—is sufficient unto itself. Every man, in every condition, is in need of the discipline and fellowship of the whole body. Therefore the healthy spiritual life is communal, and the knowledge of how to think rightly about God, how best to worship Him, and how effectually to obey Him is the slowly accumulating possession of the Church. God is observed to speak to mankind most plainly, not through isolated individuals, however great, but to great individuals incorporated into the Christian community.

C. Prophetic and Institutional Religion

An important example of this principle is the relation of the "prophet" and the "saint" to the general body of the Church. If it is true that the body of ordinary believers, with their limited talents, cannot do without the vitally important leadership of the few and outstanding, it is equally true that the outstanding will commonly go astray if they are not subject to the discipline of the general body of the Church. The need of the leaders and of the led is mutual. Thus new theological truth is commonly grasped by the man of adventurous intellect, and he is often an intellectual extremist, too much in love with some brilliant theory which expresses one part only of the "manifold wisdom of God" (Ephesians 3:10). If he heedlessly goes his own way, he may easily lapse into error. If he would know the truth the Christian thinker therefore must treat the established Creed of the Church with reverence as an authoritative guide to himself. And the Church must listen to him in turn.

Much the same holds in the spheres of Christian devotion and moral obedience. The rare and splendid individual to whom the sense of the presence of God is a constant and pressing reality, who apparently finds prayer an easy joy, and who is full of spontaneous zeal for his practical duties as a Christian is himself not the self-sufficient Christian. He needs to learn many things concerning God's dealings with the human race from the experience of the multitudes of more ordinary people who often find faith and prayer hard, to whom daily affairs are a constant pressure, and who need to fall back upon the props and crutches of discipline if they are to do their duty. The spiritually able are to humble themselves gladly to bear with the less able, and to make allowances for them, for this is the very spirit of Christ's humility.

Nothing is more common in the history of the Church than the collision between prophetic and institutional religion. The established religion of the community is normally cautious and conservative, concerned with prudential rules for the discipline of frail mortals, and all too often interested in the preservation of its status and property. The awakened zealot can therefore easily write it off as hopelessly compromised, and start his own little community of like-minded zealots. This counsel of separation to form "a pure Church" is superficially attractive to many minds, but history witnesses to its eventually delusive character. With the passage of time the tempo of the new community inevitably slackens, until it also becomes an institutional religion, though an institution with less resources than the old, and of a more constricted tradition. The tension between individualist prophetic religion and institutional religion is doubtless inevitable, and to a degree even salutary. Nevertheless, the welfare of the Church is to a large degree dependent upon the avoidance of an open breach at this point, so that the new life may flow through and revivify the body of the old institution. The separation of a new denomination normally impoverishes both the old institution which is left and the new which is gradually formed. As our Lord Himself taught, there are times when a new movement of the Spirit requires new Church forms to express it (Matthew 9:17). Yet rightly understood this is not a charter for the division of the Church. It is a reminder to the institutional Church that it has a duty to be understanding with the ardent prophet, even as he has a duty to be patient with the Church.

D. Grace and the Means of Grace

The relation of personal to communal religion, and the issue between prophetic and institutional religion, is illustrated by the use of the means of grace. The means of grace are those acts of worship, and that discipline of devotion and morality, which a man is to use if he would be visited by God with His saving grace (see p. 156). It will, we judge, be agreed that man is saved by the grace of God, and that his own diligence in the means of grace does not earn salvation apart from divine grace. At the same time, if he wishes to receive God's grace he must wait upon God for it in the way which God has prescribed, that is, by expectantly using the means of grace and by trusting God's promise to honor them. Clearly, there is a balance between the due place of divine grace and of the means, and it is not always easy for the Christian to determine what this is. Some of the means of grace, such as private prayer and Bible reading, are largely individual and personal, but by and large the means of grace are communal, and correspond to the institutional side of the Christian life. Such are public worship and meetings for fellowship, the exposition of the Bible and the preaching of the Gospel, and the sacraments ordained by our Lord. These all presuppose the disciplined and ordered life of the Church. Considered in isolation, the religion of grace is inward and personal, "the walk of the soul with God." To this extent it is individual. Yet the religion of grace cannot be considered in isolation, for there are the appointed means of grace, and these are in the Church.

The doctrine which has been outlined in the preceding chapters of this book is doctrine in which the different responsible denominations of Christendom are substantially agreed. The official formularies of the great branches of the Church are recognizably at one in the doctrines of the Trinity, the creation, the Incarnation, the person of Christ, the atonement and resurrection, and the Holy Spirit. This impressive area of agreement comprises by far the larger part of essential Christian doctrine. In this sense there is truly "one body, and one Spirit...one Lord, one faith" (Ephesians 4:4, 5). Insofar as the denominations of the Church are divided by recognizable spiritual and theological interests, and not merely by social and political tradition and by aesthetic considerations, the divergence appears chiefly to occur in this matter of the due place of the means of grace. The collision between institutional and prophetic religion is closely associated with a difference in judgment regarding the doctrine of grace. Christians are substantially at one in what God has done for man in order to accomplish his salvation. They are not always at one in judgment as to the way in which the effect of this divine action is mediated to men and women in present experience.

The reason for this is, we think, not far to seek. Human temperament and human experience is inherently various, whereas God is always the same. It is fact of human experience that some souls are captivated in mind and imagination by worship which is highly institutional, traditional, and ceremonial, and largely for the reason that it is venerable, colorful, mysterious, and romantic. Others have been brought up in this atmosphere and found their hearts unmoved by any sense of God, or even repelled by the feeling that all this is empty formalism. God has met them in reaction to this, in an experience which appeared to be purely inward and individual. Some have felt their love and loyalty go out to the ancient institutional Churches because they are venerable, stable, and authoritative. Others have felt constrained in spirit by this institutional dignity, and have found liberty in a little informal group of familiar friends. Divergences of this kind clearly underlie different views which are held regarding the Church and sacraments, and different emphases in the doctrines of justification by faith, salvation by grace alone, election, and predestination. These are the issues which constitute a large part of the division between Roman Catholic and Protestant, and the division of one Protestant denomination from another.

It would seem from this that the Church has been divided by an insistence from one side or the other that a discipline of the means of grace which has proved profitable for some community ought to prove profitable for all. This method of devotion has then been claimed as of universal legitimacy and obligation. However, this discipline of devotion has not answered to the experience of some other group, which has rejected it. We therefore judge that the Church can only vindicate her unity by seeking unanimity in those doctrines which concern the nature of God and His saving action in Christ, and by allowing variety of approach and emphasis in those doctrines which concern the mediation of this saving action to man. The unity of the Church is not solely a matter of doctrinal confession, but insofar as agreement in doctrinal confession is required it is to be in those matters which are covered by the great creeds of the ancient and undivided Church. These are the Trinity, the Incarnation, the atonement, and the resurrection. On the other hand, reasonable liberty of interpretation is to be allowed in speculation as to the exact way in which the sacraments bring grace to man, or in questions of "conversion," "grace alone," election, and predestination. Attempts to secure uniformity of definition in things which are subject to the infinite variety of human apprehension will always divide the Church.

E. The Church Visible and Invisible

By the Church Visible is meant the whole number of those marked out as part of the organized body of the Church, by profession of Christian discipleship, and by Holy Baptism. By the Church Invisible is meant the whole company of those, known only to God, who are united to Christ by faith, and are heirs of Christian salvation. Ideally the two should be one, for all faithful disciples ought to be in the visible Church, and all those in the visible Church ought to be faithful disciples. This is indeed the unspoken assumption of the New Testament, where it is taken for granted that the turning of man from evil to God is necessarily both inward and outward. The inward change, that is, the gift of faith and of the Holy Spirit, and the outward change, that is, baptism in water and joining the Church are the two parts of the union of man with Christ. Thus, if one who is seeking to call upon God is baptized, he will receive the gift of the Holy Spirit (Acts 2:38, 22:16), and conversely, he who believes and has received the Holy Spirit, ought most certainly to be baptized (Acts 8:36–37, 10:47). The possibility of there being Christian believers outside the disciplined body of the Church is not considered in the New Testament, while unworthy and disorderly members of the Church are not considered as heathen outsiders, but as under the more severe judgment resting upon apostate Christians (Hebrews 6:4–6, 10:29). They are still part of the Church, though only to their own condemnation.

However, later thought and experience compelled the modification of this simple position. In the first place, St. Augustine's doctrine of election (see p. 211) required a distinction to be drawn between the whole company of the Elect, who are called to final salvation, and the Church as a society in this world, united by baptism. There is the possibility that some who have been baptized, and who are apparently members of the Church, are not in fact of the Elect, and will not persevere to salvation. There is the corresponding possibility that some of the Elect are not in fact at the moment members of the Church, though to preserve the traditional doctrine that union with the Church is requisite to salvation it is taught that before their death these elect souls will come to Christian faith and be baptized. Thus there is the company of the Elect, known only to God, which is as it were "the soul of the Church," and there is the company of the baptized, known before the world, which is only "the body of the Church." This doctrine of the invisible Church has been perforce adopted wherever the Augustinian notion of election has been taught, and it was re-emphasized in the Augustinian theology of the Reformation. It has, however, been greatly broadened in scope in the modern period by prevalent confusion as to what constitutes the Church, and as to whether or not it is necessary for a disciple of Christ to be a member of an organized Christian body. Questions are thus raised which are not answered in the New Testament.

Protestantism has witnessed a proliferation of denominations with very widely varying standards of Church membership, and the current of popular feeling in a liberal and tolerant society has frowned upon the claim of any one particular form of churchmanship to represent "the one true Church." Added to this has been the spirit of criticism of any form of "organized Christianity." Thus we have grown accustomed to the spectacle of many persons who display in their lives and characters much of the spirit of Christ, who yet are not active members of any disciplined Christian denomination. In addition, there are many organizations of Christians which certainly seem to be blessed by the activity of the Holy Spirit, yet which are difficult to bring within any intelligible and scriptural definition of the Church. For example, some Christian societies do not observe the sacraments ordained by our Lord. As so often, there is a mixture of good and evil in this familiar situation. It is good that Christians should have learned to be more tolerant and charitable toward one another than they have often been in the past, and that they should have been reminded by modern experience of the ancient position that the grace of God is not limited to those means of grace which He has ordained as the regular and promised channels of His salvation. However, it is regrettable that the majestic unity and authority of the Church should so largely be concealed by the appearance of irresponsible and even uncharitable competition, so that the thinking even of many genuinely Christlike people should be vague as to the nature of the Church and the necessity of belonging to it.

F. The Communion of Saints

In the widest sense this is the doctrine that all those who by faith are united to Christ are united to one another in a universal fellowship of mutual prayer and charity. The divisions of race, country, language, culture, and social status which separate man from man in the world are to be of no account in the Church, which is essentially one in Christ (Acts 10:34–35; Galatians 3:27–29; Colossians 3:10–11). However, the more particular theological use of this phrase, as it occurs in the Apostles' Creed, for example, is to affirm that the one Church is not divided even by death. Those in Christ who have died are not in any kind of suspended animation, nor are they excluded from fellowship with the Church on earth. The whole body of Christians as it exists in this world, living by faith and hope, compassed with infirmity, battling with evil, and growing up into Christ, is described as "the Church Militant." The whole body of Christians in heaven, living in the fuller vision of God, serving Him victoriously with ampler powers, and still growing up into Christ, is named "the Church Triumphant." The two together make up the Church, and they are in close communion with one another. Thus the Church of this world can truly feel that those who have gone before join with her in her worship and service, an invisible company having a continuing and helpful interest in the affairs of men.

It is impossible to view from a correct perspective the spiritual dignity of the Christian Church unless this doctrine of the communion of saints is fully realized. The whole world-wide company of Christians alive at the present time, with all its multiplicity of divine service, is in reality only a very small part of the Church. Most of the believers, and most of the illustrious heroes of the Faith, are in heaven. It is that wider and nobler Christian fellowship which gives meaning to ours, not vice versa. The Christian who looks only at the company on earth will be cast down by the candid reflection that the Church is an insignificant and ineffectual body, compared to those agencies which control secular society. He who has faith to look to the whole fellowship will realize that it is the existence of the Church which alone gives meaning to the entire process of world history.

Summary of Divergence: The Invocation of Saints; Prayers for the Dead

These are two devotional practices, deeply entrenched in Catholic tradition but strongly rejected by the Protestant Reformers, which express the conception of the communion of saints.

a. The Invocation of Saints

i. CATHOLIC POSITION. It is the privilege of the Church on earth to address the departed saints, who are before the presence of God in heaven, to invite them to make intercession with God on behalf of man. Of particular efficacy is the heavenly intercession of the angels, the great and illustrious saints, and above all, of the Blessed Virgin Mary, on account of the merit of their great holiness and their spiritual nearness to the throne of mercy.

ii PROTESTANT REJOINDER. It is to be agreed that it is right and helpful for the Christian to invite his fellow believers to join in prayer for him. As the Church Militant here on earth enjoys spiritual fellowship with the Church Triumphant in heaven, there is perhaps nothing inherently wrong in principle that the Church should ask departed Christians for the benefit of their prayers. However, the convinced Protestant feels that traditional Catholic devotions expressing this idea are excessive and are dangerously easy to be misunderstood by simple believers. To address the departed saints in highly reverential language is likely to be misunderstood by the simple as *worship*, such as is rightly offered only to God (Colossians 2:18). To do this before their images may admit idolatry into the Church (Exodus 20:4, 5). And even if this error is avoided, such customs may suggest that the highest God is remote and not altogether available to the unaided prayers of His humbler children. This is clearly an error, for in Christ the Mediator God has made Himself fully accessible to the believer (1 Timothy 2:5). The prayers of other Christian may be helpful, but they are not *necessary* or meritorious in purchasing divine grace. Therefore, although it is good that the fellowship of the Church Militant with the Church Triumphant should be fully and expressively symbolized in Christian worship, these traditional Catholic devotions are to be excluded from the private and public prayers of the Church, or at least allowed only with great reserve and in studied moderation.

b. Prayers for the Dead

i. CATHOLIC POSITION. Departed Christians who are in a state of grace, yet who have not performed sufficient penance to account for all their venial sins, are undergoing the balance of their discipline in the remedial punishment of purgatory (see pp. 260–61). As the Church of the unseen world is one communion and fellowship with the Church on earth, the prayers of the Church Militant can effectually assist Christian souls through purgatory, until they are accounted worthy of admission to heaven. Therefore it is the charitable duty, and the privilege, of the Church to pray for the Christian dead, and in particular to offer on their behalf the effectual and meritorious prayer of the Mass (2 Maccabees 12:41–45) (see p. 260).

ii. PROTESTANT REJOINDER. Clearly, there is no place at all for prayers for the dead in the thinking of those who accept the traditional

Protestant position that all souls go to bliss or to damnation immediately at death (Luke 16:22–26). However, some others who allow the possibility of spiritual discipline and growth in the unseen world (see p. 262) may also in principle allow the rightness of prayer for departed Christians. If intercessory prayer can help fellow believers in this life, it can also in the life beyond, because all the Church is one communion and fellowship. However, the decided Protestant will object that much traditional Catholic devotion can easily be misunderstood by simple people, and can run to excess to become the occasion of superstition. Thus, the idea that departed Christians are in a state of virtual torment in purgatory, and *require* the prayers of the Church to help them through into bliss, is felt to be an unworthy and unhealthy notion (see p. 263). The Christian need not feel that his departed loved ones and Christian friends are in some way shut out from his customary prayers simply because they are passed from sight. At the same time, they certainly need not be prayed for with anxious fear, for they are in the hands of God (Wisdom 3:1–5).

II. The Church of the Old Covenant

The conviction of the first Christians, witnessed to by the New Testament and in the writings of the early Christian centuries, was strongly to affirm the continuity of the Christian Church with Israel, the ancient chosen people of the Hebrew faith. In token of this the Jewish holy books were read in Christian worship and quoted as authoritative for Christian doctrine, as the Old Testament Scripture of the Christian Church. The spiritual heroes of old Israel were looked to with reverence as the ancestors of the Church (Hebrews 11:32–12:1). The Greek word *ecclesia* ("an assembly summoned together"), which is used of the Church in the New Testament, is the same word as used in the Septuagint, the traditional Greek translation of the Old Testament, of "the congregation of Israel," assembled in the wilderness under Moses (Acts 7:37–38). Thus in a true sense the Christian Church begins not at Pentecost, but with the patriarchs, and in particular with Abraham, the "Father of the Faithful," and founder of the Hebrew nation (Hebrews 11:1–10).

Thus it is Christian teaching that from the beginning God has declared Himself through a distinct organized community. As always, God mediated the spiritual through the natural. The natural and original bond of human community was the tribal one of physical descent. Thus we find that one tribe was selected to be the chosen people, the descendants of Abraham (Genesis 12:1–3). This Hebrew tribe started its course as one Semitic tribe among many, being essentially similar to its neighbors of the Middle East in race, speech, religion, social institutions, and so forth. Subsequent history proved it to be an altogether different nation, and particularly in the matter of religion. To this tribe was given something which distinguished it from other Semitic tribes, namely, a long series of religiously gifted and sensitive leaders, the prophets, who were able to point out to the Hebrew people the lessons which God was seeking to teach through the formative experiences of their often troubled and tragic history. The mass of the people did not learn these lessons easily or quickly, but they did nevertheless learn. Thus among all the peoples of antiquity, with the various heritages they have passed down to later civilization, the Hebrew nation was the possessor of a national religion unique for its moral and spiritual dignity and insight. The Old Testament Scripture is the story of the hammering out of this spiritual treasure upon the anvil of history, in the experience of a special tribal community enriched by the presence of the prophets.

The critic may object that every nation has to some extent felt itself to be a "chosen" people, under the immediate protection of its national gods. However, the claim of the Hebrews to have been the chosen people does not rest upon what they felt about themselves but upon the objective facts of the case. They certainly did not all show themselves always to be virtuous, but they did progressively display this unique talent for religion. Almost everything of first-rate religious value which has come down to the Christian from the ancient world has come from the Jews, and it is for this reason that their ancient books, and no others, are read today in the Christian Church. The Greeks indeed possessed a unique talent for rational argument and philosophical speculation, and provided much of the intellectual apparatus by which the Church set forth her essential faith in clearly formulated doctrine. Yet the faith which was set forth by means of this apparatus was essentially Hebrew and biblical, not Greek. Modern literary and theological criticism has abundantly vindicated the traditional proposition that the indispensable prerequisite for understanding the rise of the Christian Church and her faith is this root in Hebrew religion, enshrined alike in the books of the Old and New Testament Scriptures (John 4:22).

This proposition may be illustrated in a variety of ways. Considered in His human office as a teacher, our Lord is the climax of the prophets. He is a Jew speaking to Jews. Though our Lord's teaching shows unique comprehensiveness, balance, clarity, and beauty, the material from which it is derived is the higher and more spiritual side of traditional Jewish religion. Sometimes this derivation is expressly affirmed by Christ Himself (Mark 10:17–19); but if not, it is still there, and this long-familiar truth of traditional Christian exposition has been enforced anew by material more recently discovered, such as the Dead Sea Scrolls. In the exposition of the New Testament, it frequently happens that the correct sense is given only if the Greek words are allowed the sense they bear in the Greek Old Testament, rather than that in the pagan Greek classics. Again, the primitive Church was not uninfluenced by the pagan social environment in which it formed its institutions, yet it would appear to be an error to suppose, as some have done, that the institutions of the Church were chiefly or largely formed from pagan borrowings. The chief and formative source is to be sought in the institutions of Judaism.

The doctrine of a "chosen people" by no means presupposes the idea of divine favoritism. It is the Christian faith that God loves all men without distinction, and that of His grace He places the same value upon all human personalities. Nevertheless, it is a fact of experience that God does call some men, some communities, and some nations to distinctive tasks not open to all, and does endow them with equipment of mind and spirit suited to the task. On the one hand, these are not predetermined to be faithful and obedient. They can fall from their special calling and abuse their special gifts. On the other hand, only those with the special calling can fulfill the special task. Thus history knows of more than one nation apparently "chosen" at one time or another for a special role. So the Greeks were "chosen" to be the schoolmasters of the ancient world in philosophic argument and in art. The Romans were "chosen" to pioneer for mankind the principles of law and the administration of justice. That the Hebrews were "chosen" by God to declare the true principles of religion is the leading example of a general principle. Membership in a religiously "chosen people" was not a status of divine favor, in the sense that to be Hebrew-born made one more pleasing to God, and more certain of eternal salvation, than to be born a Gentile. The Hebrew possessed a clearer light than did the Gentile, and therefore God rightly required more of him and judged him by a more severe standard. This most uncomfortable doctrine was indeed one of the leading points of the teaching of Amos, the first great writing prophet of the Old Testament (Amos 3:1–2). To be called and equipped by God for a special and honorable spiritual office does not convey upon a man a favored position in the attainment of salvation.

III. The Church of the New Israel

A. The New Israel

The most comprehensive and fundamental definition of the Christian Church in the New Testament is that it is "the new Israel" (Galatians 3:7–9, 29; 6:16; Philippians 3:3; James 1:1; 1 Peter 2:9). The Church is the company of those who at the coming of Christ were found true and faithful "Israelites indeed" (John 1:47), and who, because they were awake to the promises of God, fulfilled the divine destiny of ancient Israel. To this nucleus was added by God the far wider fellowship of those Gentiles of many races and countries who shared the faith of the true Israelite, and confessed Jesus as Christ and Lord (Ephesians 2:11–22). Thus the Church, the community of the New Covenant, is organically continuous with ancient Israel, the community of Old Covenant. Yet she is the ancient community made new, and reconstituted upon a more completely spiritual basis.

There is a sense in which the Old Covenant was given to Abraham and to his descendants upon the basis of faith in God (Genesis 15:1-6). This higher and more spiritual side was always present in Hebrew religion, being witnessed to by many exalted passages in the prophets and psalms. However, the principle that man walks with God by faith was inevitably to some extent overlaid and compromised by the circumstance that the Covenant was given to a certain people by physical descent (though the way was open for Gentiles to become proselytes), and that the promise of God's favor was dependent upon obedience to the ceremonial and moral commandments of the Law of Moses, which was given to the people as a necessary discipline (Galatians 3:17-19). When the promised Christ came, and brought the power of the kingdom, this principle of faith, which to some extent lay concealed in the old religion, stood forth clearly. Every foretaste of spiritual good in the religion of the Old Covenant was filled to its fullness in the New, and so it could be unambiguously declared that the basis of membership in the reconstituted chosen people was faith in God through Christ. Thus membership of a particular group, and that following of communal ceremonial which was appropriate to a purely national religion, were no longer essential for membership of the people of God (Romans 3:29-31).

There is, indeed, an obligation still resting upon the Christian to observe certain outward marks of faith in Christ and of Church membership, and to follow the moral discipline of the Christian life, resting upon the ethical tradition of Judaism. Yet these outward marks and this moral discipline are such as correspond to the higher, more spiritual, and universal order of the New Covenant. Thus in the Church, with her atoning sacrifice of Christ and her spiritual ordinances of worship and morality, there was fulfilled the divine promise given through Jeremiah, that when God visited His people there would be a New Covenant of inward spiritual religion, which would bring to man a victorious power to obey the law of God spontaneously from the heart (Jeremiah 31:31-34; Hebrews 10:1-25). The Church, though soon of predominantly Gentile descent, cherished a strong sense that she was a community organically continuous with old Israel, and the legitimate heir of all divine promises made to Israel. She rejoiced in institutions corresponding to those of old Israel, but at a higher spiritual level. This is the Scriptural theology of the Church as "the New Israel."

B. The Rise of the Church

This theology of the Church corresponds to the way in which the first Church did actually take shape. St. John the Baptist, who occupies the curious but significant dual position of a Jewish prophet and a Christian saint, is the connecting link between Judaism proper and the distinctive Christian Church. The Gospels agree in regarding his preaching ministry as the mark of the beginning of the Christian movement (Mark 1:1–8). After a period of centuries during which it was apparent that prophecy had ceased in Israel, John stirred the nation with preaching which instinctively reminded all hearers of the old prophets (Mark 6:14–16). The main characteristic of his teaching was a stirring re-emphasis of the old prophetic message that mere nominal membership of the chosen people and formal participation in the religion of Israel would not suffice to put man right with God in the coming day of the Lord. It was necessary for each man born an Israelite personally to start again, and by his action in repentance and consecration to make his own the highest standards of the devotion and morality of his people (Luke 3:3–14).

This appears to be the meaning of John's baptism by water. A washing with water is a very natural rite to adopt as a sacramental "acted prayer" to symbolize turning away from the defilement of evil to good. As such it was a part of the due ceremony of making a proselyte, and the discovery of the Dead Sea Scrolls has further illustrated what importance could be attached in some Jewish circles to ceremonial religious ablutions. The significance of John's baptism apparently was that he treated as proselytes those who were Hebrews born, in accord with the principle implied by Luke 3:8. There was now within the larger community of nominal Israel, constituted by birth and formal circumcision, a smaller, awakened, and disciplined company of "Israelites indeed."

It was largely from the ranks of the disciples of John the Baptist that the nucleus of the Church was drawn. This is symbolized in John 1:35–42, where the Baptist in effect hands over some of his disciples to become our Lord's apostles. We need not suppose that when Christ called His disciples at the lake He was summoning unprepared men (Mark 1:16–20). Some or all of them had doubtless met Jesus when all went down to the Jordan together to hear the preaching of John. Jesus had made His impression upon them, and when they parted to go home He was to them their prophet and their hero. In keeping with this is the significant circumstance that the rite used by John to incorporate the unawakened Jews into the company of his disciples was continued as the initiation rite into the Christian Church. Critical scholars have much debated the question of the precise origin of the sacrament of Holy Baptism, but it remains difficult to improve upon the clear conviction of the first Christians that "the outward and visible sign" of the Church's sacrament of Holy Baptism was a washing with water which went back to the ministry of the Baptist (Luke 3:16; compare Acts 19:1–6). Thus institutionally as well as theologically the Church grew out of the awakened nucleus of the people of Israel, and was in fact the ancient people renovated.

C. Our Lord's Foundation of the Church

In the modern period some critics have claimed that our Lord did not intend to found the Church. A common argument is that as He expected to

come at an early date for the consummation of the age (Matthew 10:23),
He cannot have had an interest in the foundation of a disciplined community, because the formation of an organization implies the expectation of
a long-continued period of Christian history. Thus the eschatological view
of Christ's teaching (see pp. 45–46) seems to many to preclude an organized
Church. It is not clear that this consequence is a necessary one. However
brief the time of waiting, God's renewed chosen people were to wait in
solemn expectancy as a fully prepared people (Mark 13:32–37). That is,
there was a place for a disciplined Church. It is not claimed that in founding
the Church our Lord organized the later administrative machine.

Another form of argument, less reliable, betrays the scarcely-concealed
anti-ecclesiastical bias of many critics. It is assumed that "the spiritual" and
"the unorganized" are virtually one, so that an interest in establishing a
distinct and disciplined religious community is to be accounted largely inconsistent with the notion of our Lord as one whose care was for inward and
spiritual religion. Thus if He were a true and free prophet He "ought" to
have founded at most an informal fellowship, but not a Church with religious
rites and authoritative officers. This is decidedly to read the New Testament
through the spectacles of modern Christianity of the more "liberal" kind, and
will assuredly entrap the student into a misleading anachronism.

The traditional Christian doctrine is that our Lord founded the Church,
or perhaps better, that He refounded it, for the Church of New Testament
days was deeply aware of being old as well as new. The chief argument for
this position is the confident and unargued assumption of the first Christians
that this was so. In general, the New Testament Scriptures were composed
to meet the needs of their own time, not to answer beforehand the controversial issues of later days. Some questions regarding the Church are
extensively argued in the New Testament, particularly whether it was necessary that Gentile Christians be circumcised and adopt the national religious
customs of the Jews. This is because Christians were not all agreed. By
contrast, it is not argued whether it was the Lord's will to found the Church
and whether it was the duty of Christians to belong to it. There were no
Christians who had any other opinion, and so the matter is passed over in
silence.

The actions and words of our Lord certainly bear out the idea that He
Himself thought of the company of His disciples as "the new Israel," and as
such, a distinctive and disciplined community, even as old Israel was a community. Thus there were twelve apostles, corresponding, it would seem, with
the traditional twelve tribes of Israel (Mark 3:14). Christ described as "the
twelve tribes of Israel" those of whom the Twelve were to be the spiritual
leaders and judges (Matthew 19:28; Luke 22:30). The disciples of Christ
were "the flock of God" (Luke 12:32), which phrase is a standard Old
Testament metaphor for the people of Israel (Isaiah 40:11; Jeremiah
13:17; Ezekiel 34:3ff.; Micah 7:14). Our Lord's solemn blessing to St. Peter

as he emerges the first to make the distinctive Christian confession of faith is "upon this rock I will build my Church" (Matthew 16:18). There is both a parallel and a contrast here between the Church and the old "congregation of Israel" (Exodus 12:3), the word "congregation" in the Greek Old Testament being rendered "church" in the New Testament (compare Acts 7:38). The company founded with St. Peter as the first Christian believer, and by him led at the first public preaching of the gospel (Acts 1:15, 2:14, 3:6), is hailed by Christ as *His* congregation, His new Israel, even as old Israel was the old congregation. Finally, the distinctive Christian rite of worship which Christ ordained was a communal meal in spiritual continuation of the Jewish Passover (Luke 22:14–20), which itself was the memorial of the foundation of the chosen people as a nation, and a mark of belonging to that people.

D. New Testament Metaphors of the Church

1. THE BRIDE OF CHRIST. A frequent Old Testament figure to express the relationship of God to His chosen people was that the Lord is as a husband to His people, and Israel is the wife of Jehovah (Isaiah 62:4–5). A common variant upon this theme is that idolatry, which is the breach of the Covenant, is spoken of by the prophets as adultery (Jeremiah 3:6–10; Ezekiel 23:36–49; Hosea 2:1–5). This metaphor is naturally carried over into the New Testament, and applied to the new Israel. Thus the Church is the Bride of Christ, and the intimate union in spirit which exists between the Lord and His Church is likened to marriage (Ephesians 5:23–32; Revelation 21:2–3, 9).

2. THE BODY OF CHRIST. This doctrine is chiefly associated with the writings of St. Paul. The first stage of his argument is practical. In the passage 1 Corinthians 12:4–31, he is appealing for charity and unity in the congregation at Corinth. He points out that the Christians have a variety of spiritual gifts, some more prominent than others. However, all are necessary for the fulfilling of God's plan through the Church. The different members are like the various limbs and organs of the human body, of very different function, and some apparently more important or more dignified in use than others, yet every one necessary to the health of the body. Therefore the Christians with prominent gifts must be humble-minded, and those with only modest gifts must guard against both envy and discouragement. All must cooperate as do the organs of the body, so that the entire Church may be the healthy body of Christ.

This practical and moral line of thought is developed into a general theology of the Church in Ephesians 1:22–23, 3:6; Colossians 1:19. Here "the head," (that is, the mind) is the unifying principle of control and action for the whole human body. This holds good also of the cooperative fellowship of believers. They are united together because each one is united to Christ and directed by Him. He is therefore the head in the assembly of limbs and organs which make up the body. The final theological development displays the Church as embodying the same principle as the Incarnation. In the days of His flesh, the mind and spirit that was in Christ had a human body through which to express itself. The work of Christ is now carried on through the agency of an invisible Spirit, and it is left to the Church to make witness to the world. The Church's form and doctrine, her preaching and sacraments, her practical moral activity, and the example of fellowship which exists between her members, all visibly embody the life of the Spirit of Christ. The Church is to be Christ's lips to speak, His hands to serve. The Church's martyrs are to suffer like Christ with men and for men (Colossians 1:24). Thus the Church is the body of Christ (Ephesians 4:1–16), and is in a sense "the extension of the Incarnation."

E. The Marks of the Church: One, Holy, Catholic, Apostolic

1. ONE. Because there is but one God, who has performed the one sufficient saving act in Christ, the effect of which is mediated to mankind by the one Spirit, there can by the nature of things be only one Church. The outward disunity of the many competing denominations may disguise this essential theological unity from the superficial view, yet the unity exists in the mind of God and is the subject of the prayer and hope of faithful Christians. In token of this, believers are not baptized into the separated denomination to which they belong, but into *the Church* (Ephesians 4:4–6). Unless this principle is kept in mind it is impossible to appreciate aright either the true incentive or the aim of the ecumenical movement. Those who are discussing Church unity are not seeking to *create* the unity of the Church, as though it had to be brought into being by the amalgamation of a number of independent and self-sufficient Churches. Their task is to secure an order and practical organization of the visible Church which will express adequately the essential unity which now exists, though to do this does not require complete uniformity of worship or administration. The Church is to be made more fully the incarnation of the Spirit. And the ultimate purpose of this is not to economize human resources, nor any supposition that a large organization is more efficient or more influential than a small one. This is not necessarily so. Ecclesiastical reunion is necessary because the convincing vindication of the unity of the Church is essential if men are ever really to understand what it means to be a Christian. A divided Church is a contradiction of its own message. A divided Church, therefore, however great its zeal and devotion, cannot with full persuasiveness portray the Gospel (John 17:21).

2. HOLY. This biblical term means "separated to God, for His own use." To say that the Church is holy does not imply the claim that all its members lead very pure and upright lives, or that they are necessarily more moral than those who are not Church members. The claim of the Church is both more modest and more profound than this. It is that the Church is different from every other community because it is a society founded by God and not by

man. Its purpose is not to accomplish the will of the men who are members of it, but to fulfill the plan of God for the redemption of the race (Ephesians 3:3–6, 9–11; 1 Peter 2:9).

3. CATHOLIC. This word means *universal*. In the first place the notion of catholicity involves the doctrine that the Church as she exists in every land and place is one fellowship. Pressing closely behind this is the doctrine that the mission and fellowship of the one Church cannot be sectional. It is for "all sorts and conditions of men." He who tacitly says: "The scope of my loving sympathy, my prayers, and my evangelistic ambition, is limited to my neighborhood, or my nation, or to a particular race, or to people of culture, or to 'the workers,' or to democratic countries, and so forth," has not grasped what it means to be a Christian. He is the essential *uncatholic*.

An important secondary meaning of the word "catholic" arises from the circumstance that the guarantee of sound, balanced, and authoritative doctrine is the widest possible Spirit-guided fellowship of Christian devotion and scriptural scholarship (see pp. 3–4). The Christian message as it is apprehended only by a particular kind of temperament or human need, or by a particular nation or century with its own distinctive cultural background, is under suspicion of being possibly only a partial presentation of the gospel. The message which stands the searching test of experience from century to century, and in all manner of human circumstance, is the gospel which can be trusted as authentic, whole, and balanced. A sectional opinion within the Church may sometimes be correct, or it may be incorrect, but it is not more than a matter of opinion. The Faith of the whole, or Catholic, Church is the Catholic Faith, and the Church affirms the Catholic Faith to be the reliable doctrine, the authoritative doctrine, and the orthodox doctrine.

4. APOSTOLIC. The use of this word indicates the claim that the Church now existing is the same Church as that apostolic Church originally founded by Christ. She has maintained continuity of life and doctrine from that day to this. She rejoices in the inheritance of an enduring tradition, and repudiates the notion that one can have a "new" Church, founded by some historic Christian leader.

IV. The Doctrine of the Ministry

Many issues connected with the institutional life of the Church come to a focus in relation to the doctrine of the Christian ministry.

A. The Priesthood of All Believers

It is often assumed that this doctrine affirms either that "every man is his own priest," or alternatively, that there is in effect no such thing as priesthood in the Christian Church. Both these positions, we believe, reflect unfortunate confusion. A priest is the representative of the people. He leads their joint worship, and enables them to approach God. Having had fellowship with God he can then declare God's will to the people. Therefore the

priest is also the representative of God to the people. It is Christian doctrine
that the whole body of the Church collectively exercises this essentially
priestly function of mediation between God and the whole of mankind.

Only some within old Israel were priests, but the whole of the "new
Israel" is a "kingdom of priests" (1 Peter 2·9). Hence there is no individual
in the Church, no matter how exalted his ecclesiastical office, who is a
Christian priest by right of some influence inhering in his person and making
him, in effect, a different sort of Christian. The priest is the organ of the
whole body of the Church. Properly speaking, Christ is the Minister of
the sacraments. His Holy Spirit uses the Church as the instrument of His
sacramental action. He uses the local congregation, however small, as the
representative in that place of the whole Church, and operates through its
action that which in principle He operates through the whole. Yet in the
local representative congregation not every member of the body has the same
office. In the Eucharist one person must in fact say the Lord's words, and
break the bread, and bless the cup, standing in the place of Christ. As he
acts for all, all act in him.

The good order and the dignity of the sacrament require that this
representative member be set apart for his office in such a way as will most
fully bring out the meaning of what the Lord is doing in this ministerial
action. In particular, it should be made plain that the representative priest
is the representative and organ, not of the local congregation alone, but
of the whole body of the universal Church. Only in this way can it be
brought home to the local congregation that the sacramental action which
they are together performing in the person of their representative, they are
performing as the instruments of the one Lord as He acts through His one
Church. Hence, a fully significant celebration of the sacrament requires that
the minister of the sacrament should be in due ecclesiastical *order,* and
that this order be recognized by the wider circles of the Church as expressive
of the unity and authority of the Church. Therefore care for the ministerial
order of the minister of the word and sacraments[1] is in no way inconsistent
with the basic principle of the priesthood of the whole Church.

Thus one does not say that the conductor of an orchestra personally
produces the music. The music is produced by a common effort, in which
for a perfect rendering the part of the every player is necessary in due
proportion. The conductor is a special member of the orchestra, necessary
for the sake of *order.* So it is with ministerial order. This care for due
ministerial order does not mean that the individual believer cannot approach
God on his own. Experience proves that even the humblest believer can
in his private prayer enjoy access to God, that he can have God directly
speak to his soul through the reading of the Bible, and that he can on
occasion speak with evangelical authority to his family, friends, and neighbors

---

[1] That is, the manner in which the minister is set apart and dedicated for his office.

concerning the things of God. Yet the apparently "private" layman or laywoman is not in fact an isolated Christian individual. He does what he does as a representative organ of the whole body, representative as is the ordained minister, though he is a different organ. The mother who teaches her child to pray, and the plain man who speaks to his fellow about Christ, are not at all in the relation of "amateurs" to the official minister as a "professional." They also are the instruments of the one Lord who operates through the whole Church. If their private and "unofficial" word is with power, it is the Lord who has spoken through His Church with the highest divine authority.

B. Ministerial Order

The manner in which the representative priesthood within the Church shall be appointed is a matter of importance. Controversy over this question of ministerial order has been, and still is, one of the chief occasions of division in the Church. In the first place, any theology of order is defective and misleading which looks upon the Christian ministry as a succession of men existing apart from the body of the Church, and handing down one to another a sort of spiritual "influence" which does not flow in the Church at large. Always, the ministry is a priesthood because it is a special limb of the priestly body. At the same time, the minister should not be thought of as the mere delegate of the Church. Christ is the Minister of the gospel and the sacraments, and uses the Church as His instrument. Therefore only Christ can make a minister, and when he acts faithfully according to his calling the minister acts with the authority, not of the congregation, but of Christ. The view held by some that the congregation for its convenience deputes the minister to exercise its own powers in its own name is to be regarded as an inadequate doctrine.

Clearly, no man is proficient enough in spiritual things to acquire a personal right to instruct others and to give them good advice. Certainly no man is holy enough to be a worthy minister of the sacraments. The minister is a sinful man speaking to sinful men, and is himself fully in need of what he offers to others. His only ground for daring to go about his ministration is that Christ has of His infinite grace called him, unworthy though he be, and sent him to the work, and that he would be unfaithful to His Lord were he to shirk this duty. Therefore the first and essential stage for the appointment of a Christian minister in due order is the divine call of the Holy Spirit (Acts 13:2). There then rests upon the authorities of the Church the responsible duty of seeking to determine whether those who profess this call are sincere, of examining their natural gifts of personality and intellect, of training them, and of appointing them in due order to whatever work seems most suitable. Yet in this essential disciplinary process the Church is seeking to discover and acknowledge the call of God, and is not herself calling the minister.

Thus the Christian ministry is the Lord's "spiritual gift" to the Church (Ephesians 4:7–8, 11–12). It is a special organ in the body, created by the Lord for a special function, by which the whole body of the Church acts. By way of illustration, the tongue is not the "delegate" of the body, as though the other limbs had shared their powers with it. The tongue has a unique function bestowed upon it by Him who created the whole body, and only it can speak. Yet it is sustained by the whole body, and when it speaks it voices the thought of the mind which dwells in the whole man. Thus the tongue is a special *representative* organ. This illustrates the relationship of the ministry to the Church. The ministry is the representative organ for the most dignified and authoritative corporate actions of the priestly society, and in this sense may be described as a priesthood.

Summary of Divergence: Views Regarding Ministerial Order

We have up to this point traced the Christian doctrine of the Church and ministry in those matters which are very widely held in common by the various recognizable parts of the Church, though perhaps with minor variations of emphasis. However, the circumstance has to be faced that there are serious divergences among Christians in judgment as to what form of ministerial order does in fact most fully and fittingly express the nature of the Church. There are also differences of judgment as to how important it is that a particular form of order be kept with strict regularity. These matters are perhaps the leading occasion and mark of the division of the Church into separated denominations.

a. Catholic View

The ancient traditional Churches feel that it is a matter of the highest theological importance that the organic continuity and the authority of the Church be fully symbolized in their ministerial order of priesthood. They account it a matter of principle that their ancient continuous ministerial and sacramental order be maintained. Thus they cannot allow that any minister of the Eucharist is in due order unless he has been ordained by a bishop who is in unbroken succession of consecration, back to the first bishops of the Church. Roman Catholics would in addition claim that for this ministerial succession to be in undoubted and fully authoritative ecclesiastical order it must own obedience to the Pope, as well as be in succession to the Church of the first days. From the Catholic view, a breach of the continuous and authoritative ministerial order occasions an actual breaking off of the divinely ordained organic continuity of the life of the Church. Baptized believers who do not possess in their congregations this organically continuous sacramental priesthood, episcopally ordained, are in some sense Christians and in a reduced sense a part of the Church. However, their denominations are not more than unordered assemblies of Christ-loving people.[2] They lack one of the essential symbolic marks of organic continuity and authority. God may indeed spiritually bless them, and use their ministrations to do His work. However, the Catholic would say that these denominations are not part of the *duly ordered* and disciplined Church.

b. Evangelical View

The evangelical denominations have had their thought and feeling largely molded by a very different set of experiences. Commonly, enthusiasts for the spiritual life found themselves in unhappy collision with the accepted ecclesiastical authorities of the day. Some then felt that a break with the older organizations of the Church was necessary in order to secure a purer witness to the gospel and a freer course for the work of evangelism. The effect of this has been to work a change of emphasis as to what contitutes the due mark of the unity, continuity, and authority of the Church. Continuity of sound scriptural doctrine, and of purity of spiritual life, has been affirmed as the true succession, in preference for the ideal of "visible" continuity of ministerial and sacramental life. Furthermore, denominations possessing a ministry not in continuous succession of episcopal ordination have found themselves to be blessed by God in the ministry of word and sacraments. This experience has led them to challenge the traditional Catholic claim that the ancient continuous ministry is essential to the due order of the Church. In some cases this effect has been further reinforced by the experience of spontaneous and relatively unordered "revivals," in which men who have had no regular ecclesiastical commission of any sort have preached with spiritual power. Thus there has arisen a variety of views regarding ministerial order. Some evangelical denominations have come to regard their accustomed ministry as not more than a matter of passing organizational convenience. Others have viewed their own accepted order as a valuable spiritual discipline. Yet even so, the due and regular maintenance of it, though perhaps important, is not to them a matter of the highest theological principle. Unlike the Catholic, the Evangelical can envisage the possibility of his order being changed in changing circumstances.

c. An Interpretative Statement

There are some genuine differences of conviction regarding the Church, between Catholics and Evangelicals, and these cannot simply be smoothed over by ecclesiastical diplomacy. Nevertheless, these differences should not be viewed out of proportion. To a large extent they are differences in judgment as to what form of order most fittingly symbolizes and safeguards a right view of the Church, and these divergences in order often disguise a good deal of latent agreement about the ideal of the Church itself. It may not be easy for a staunch denominationalist to believe that spiritual values which he prizes may at times be expressed in Church forms unfamiliar and unwelcome to

---

2 "Separated brethren."

himself. Yet such is often the case, and the attempt should be made to recognize this.

Thus the instructed Congregationalist or Baptist, who has inherited the so-called Independent form of Church polity, may sincerely profess that he does indeed regard the Church as one, and his local minister as the authoritative minister of Christ, and the minister of the whole body of the Church. He can claim that his Independent institutions do symbolize these "Catholic" qualities to him, even though the Catholic may have criticized them as inadequate in this respect. So likewise Presbyterian-type Church courts may often effectually exercise those functions of authoritative government and leadership which the Catholic associates with episcopacy. Conversely, the firm exponent of Catholic institutions may not be nearly so in love with external forms as the Evangelical fears. His real interest is in the preservation by these forms of spiritual values which are widely shared. It is important for various parts of the Church not to sit in judgment upon one another defensively or self-righteously, but to look beneath the variety of forms to what is intended by them.

The upholders of Catholic institutions have often described as "invalid" sacraments administered in churches which do not have an episcopally ordained priesthood. This is increasingly recognized to be a regrettable term, because it almost suggests to the plain man that these nonepiscopal sacraments are being dismissed as "phoney" and as unblessed by God to spiritual effect. This would be a judgment alike unrealistic and uncharitable. Actually what is being asserted is that they have not been celebrated according to those rules of order which Catholic churchmen feel are necessary to symbolize the unity of the Church, though it may still be allowed that they are means of Christian grace to those who receive them. This question-begging word, "valid," should therefore be avoided in constructive Christian discussion, as being a term which invites misunderstanding. By parity of reason, the Evangelical Christian should beware of accusing the Catholic churchman that his insistence upon the continuity of the ancient episcopal order is a mark of a legalist, unspiritual, or even "magical" view of the Christian life and discipline. The traditional order is insisted on because it is felt to symbolize a spiritual quality, that is, the organic continuity and unity of the Church.

C. Historical Development of the Ministry

The history of the Christian ministry is a subject in which history and belief run together, because what different denominations think about the ministry is chiefly determined by their historical experience. Though this is not a book of Church history, and there is no room fully to go into the details of matters which have been the subject of the strongest controversy, it is necessary to say a little upon the history of the Christian ministry, in order to complete the theological argument.

It is not surprising that difficulties about Church unity arise chiefly around the ministry, and in particular around the sacramental ministry of the Church, more even than in connection with Christian belief. On the positive side this is because there is a very wide area of substantial agreement in matters of fundamental belief between the leading denominations. On the negative side this is because the ministry is more "visible," and more intimately connected with organizational discipline in the Church, than are articles of formal belief. Questions of ministerial order carry with them issues as how the Church ought to be organized, who is to be regarded as rightly in office, who is to be deferred to in honor, and who is to be obeyed if there is a dispute regarding discipline. Disputes of this kind have all too often come down to the present day associated in the popular mind with economic, social, racial, and national rivalries. All these "outward" issues present themselves vividly to the comprehension of all the members of the Church, whereas theological questions generally appeal to the few. Thus in general Christians are more likely to be in dispute with one another about the organization of the Church, the office and dignity of its ministers, and the forms of its ceremonial, than about belief. Nevertheless, though the discussion of Church unity so largely resolves in practice into the discussion of ministerial order, it must never be forgotten that the Church's ministry cannot be considered in isolation from the Church's theology and her devotion.

The original leadership and government of the Church was clearly that of the apostles, appointed and authorized by Christ Himself. The divine commission and equipment with the gift of the Holy Spirit is indeed spoken of as in a general sense given to the whole company of disciples, corresponding to the priesthood of the whole Church (John 20:19–23). Nevertheless, from the beginning the commission to bear public witness to the gospel and to lead the Church was exercised more particularly, though not exclusively, by the Twelve (Acts 1:2–8, 12–15, 21–26). They are to be regarded as the first ministry of the Church. The first extension of this ministry was the appointment of deacons, who are spoken of as administrative officials for finance and almsgiving (Acts 6:1–6), though in fact they chiefly come to view as preachers (Acts 6:8–10; 8:5–8, 26–40). However, when the office of deacon reappears in early Christian writing after the New Testament period it is as an administrative assistant for finance and almsgiving, and to assist at the Eucharist. The work characteristic of an apostle was that of traveling preacher and founder of new local churches, in view of his qualification as a witness to the resurrection. Some not of the Twelve who to a notable degree took up this work are hence also classed as "apostles" (Acts 14:14; Romans 11:13, 16:7). However, the office of personal witness to the resurrection was essentially a temporary one. The apostleship proper belonged only to the first generation of the Church.

As their representatives for the more continuous government of local congregations the apostles appointed elders, or presbyters (the two words being alternative translations of the Greek) (Acts 14:23). The ceremony for appointment and commissioning both of deacons and elders was the laying on of hands. It would appear, in the judgment of many reliable expositors, that an alternative name for these elders was bishops, or "overseers" (the two words being alternative translations). The clearest New Testament evidence for this is a comparison of Acts 20:17 with 20:28, where the same body of men are apparently referred to by both titles.[3] Further evidence, however, is derived from Christian writings of the period immediately succeeding the New Testament. It is impossible within the scope of this work to survey the complicated detailed evidence from the apostolic fathers, which has been the subject of hotly contested controversy. In general, the following points would be agreed upon by many reliable historians of various schools of thought, though it is to be admitted that those on the Catholic side would chiefly stress the element of continuity and authority within this scheme, whereas Evangelical historians would emphasize the fluid development and variety during the first period.

1. In the Church of the period immediately following the first apostles, the government of each local congregation was in the hands of a body of officials who combined in their office the functions later separated as that of the presbyter (elder) and the bishop. These primitive officials are known to Church history as "presbyter-bishops."

2. These presbyter-bishops were appointed by continuous succession of laying on of hands from the original presbyter-bishops ordained by the apostles.

3. The presbyter-bishops were assisted by deacons.

4. From the early days of the second century onwards, first of all in the more developed and numerous congregations of Asia Minor, but rapidly in other places also, one of the presbyter-bishops became by invariable usage elevated to be president of the others. There is then a single ruling bishop in each city church, supported and advised by a body of presbyters, who now hold a lower office, distinct from that of bishop. There is also the assistant body of deacons. The succession of ruling bishops in each church, and the agreement and ecclesiastical communion of these bishops together, is accepted as the operative symbol of the authority and unity of the Church. Here is the emergence of the traditional threefold order of the apostolic ministry—bishops, priests (presbyters), and deacons. The bishop is in the first place the authoritative teacher of the Church, the father-in-God who interprets Scripture aright to the faithful. He also presides

---

3 Compare also Philippians 1:1; 1 Timothy 3:1, 8.

at the Eucharist and other rites of the Church, assisted by the presbyters and deacons.

5. As Christianity spread, and the original city congregation formed associated Christian congregations in outlying communities, these were presided over by presbyters, who were then regarded as the personal representatives of the bishop.

It is almost impossible to answer intelligibly the frequent question as to whether this ancient polity was a "democracy." Representative government with popular elections was not the method of those days. The leadership and discipline of the Church was by the personal authority of a "father-in-God." However, the government of the Church was not on that account authoritarian, in the sense that the personal will of the bishop settled all disputes. He was to rule with the consent and cooperation of the presbyters, deacons, and whole company of the faithful. However, they made their counsel known not so much by voting for a proposed policy or office-holder, in the modern manner, but by continuing together in prayer until the whole body of the Church felt assured that it was being divinely guided by the Holy Spirit. There was more of the atmosphere of the traditional Quaker "taking the sense of the meeting" than of the typical modern "free vote" or "election."

D. Apostolical Succession

The traditional doctrine of ministerial order, derived from this position in the ancient Church, is commonly called "apostolical succession." This affirms that the organic continuity of the Church in every century and place is to be symbolized and safeguarded by a ministry in continuous succession of appointment, while the disciplinary and doctrinal authority of the Church is to be exercised through the allied principle that those admitted to the ministry are to be approved and commissioned by those who are already ministers. The ministerial succession is affirmed to go back without a break to the first ministry of the apostles, who were appointed by Christ. The effect of this is to deny the possibility of starting a "new" Church, or any claim of a body of believers to call into being anew their own ministry. The traditional procedure established from ancient times answering to this doctrine is that a bishop is to be consecrated by laying on of hands by three other bishops in the succession, and that ordination of a presbyter is to include the laying on of hands of a bishop in succession.

Some further definition is necessary, for the term "apostolical succession" is often used loosely, and in more than one sense. In the first place, there is the stricter doctrine, held generally by the Church from the third century onwards, and to the present day by the Roman Catholic and Orthodox (Eastern) Churches, and by some Anglo-Catholics. This affirms that the traditional threefold ministry of ruling bishops, priests, and deacons goes back in unbroken succession to the apostles themselves. This ministry is of divine ordinance and is essential to the due order of the Church.[4] There is also the more general and empirical doctrine which affirms that the historic ministry of the Church goes back in unbroken succession to the first ministry of the apostolic Church, but that within this succession of "presbyter-bishops" the distinction between ruling bishop and presbyter appeared by a process of *development,* in response to the experience of the Church and the guidance of the Spirit. This places the traditional threefold ministry upon the foundation of a kind of contingent divine ordinance, declared through the voice of Christian antiquity, rather than upon an express and invariable divine ordinance.

Those who adopt this latter view would generally allow that it is precarious to affirm as a matter of Christian faith any precise view as to how the Christian ministry developed in the first century. A positive doctrine on this point would require secure historical evidence for the complete succession of officers at a substantial number of representative churches. Actually the historical evidence is extremely fragmentary for the formative period. It suffices to make a continuous ministry going back to the apostles a very reasonable probability, but not more than this. In ecumenical discussion it is necessary, when the claims of "apostolical succession" are discussed, to have it clearly in mind in which of these two senses the term is being used, the stricter and dogmatic or the wider and empirical.

E. The Inward Intention and Outward Form of the Ministry

Confusion between the inward intention which is expressed by certain ecclesiastical forms, and the outward forms which have in point of fact been used by the historic Church to express this intention, has often made it difficult for churchmen of later periods to understand New Testament thought about the Church. The main stream of Christianity has firmly held what may be called the "Catholic" ideal of churchmanship, namely, that it is an essential part of Christian faith that the Church is one, visibly organized, disciplined, authoritative, and organically continuous in every age and place. Even at the best this ideal of continuity, unity, and authority has never been perfectly realized in practice, but this fact in no way denies that responsible Christian teaching has aspired after this as the ideal.

This Catholic ideal of churchmanship has been embodied through the centuries in the continuous episcopally ordained threefold ministry of the Church, together with the sacraments, the canon of Scripture, and the great

---

4 However, the Roman Catholic Church appears to possess no authoritative definition as to whether the bishop is a minister of an order entirely different from that of the priest, or a special member of the one priestly order who is possessed of certain distinctive ruling and ordaining powers.

creeds. It has therefore become hard for traditionally minded Christians to see that much of the inward intention and spirit of Catholic church-manship can on occasion be expressed by other forms of ministry. It is not always sufficiently realized that the qualities of disciplined unity, authority, and continuity can be embodied and safeguarded by a governing conference of presbyters, and that a denomination may possess much of the essential function of episcopacy in the absence of the traditional office of bishop. It is thus dangerous for the exponent of one system of Church polity to sit in judgment upon another, unless he makes a careful attempt to look past the outward organizational form to the life which it expresses.

This is why some find it hard to grasp the New Testament doctrine of the Church. There is in the New Testament a relative degree of absence of those outward organizational and ministerial forms which historically have been associated with the continuity and authority of the Church. There is no clearly defined ruling bishop in each church, and no hierarchy to express the unity of the bishops. This has made it too easy for some to jump to the conclusion that the first Christians were not interested in disciplined church-manship and Church unity. Actually this is a somewhat superficial reading of the New Testament. The first Christians had a living sense of the majestic unity and authority of the whole Church. In spirit they were Catholic, though this catholicity was not yet fully expressed in what have come to be called "Catholic institutions." From the beginning there was an essential spiritual quality which made inevitable, necessary, and right the development of institutions to express it.

A suggested judgment from history, bearing on current ecumenical discussions, is as follows:

1. Original and authentic New Testament Christianity is Catholic, in that it holds to the organic and visible unity, continuity, and authority of the Church and her ministry.

2. The outward operative symbol by which this quality of catholicity is ministerially expressed has from very ancient days been the continuous and authoritative episcopal ministry and sacramental system.

3. The fitting basis for the future visible unity of the Church is the preservation of this continuous and authoritative episcopal ministry, suitably reformed for modern conditions. Clearly, the only possible symbol of continuity with the historic past is the institution which existed in the historic past, and which has come down from the past to the present.

However, these propositions are to be balanced and complemented by the following:

1. It is not possible to find the institution of the single ruling bishop in the New Testament Church and in the short period immediately succeeding the New Testament. Therefore the Church can in principle exist without this institution.

2. The quality of "Catholic-type" churchmanship can be found expressed and safeguarded by authoritative forms of ministry other than the historic office of bishop. These Church polities should be treated with respect.

3. The churchman's first love must be for the inward and spiritual intention of ecclesiastical institutions, not simply for his own familiar organizational setup. In discussions of Church unity this should encourage the flexible, reasonable, and adventurous approach, rather than the doctrinaire and defensive attitude.

Readings

Flew, R. N., *Jesus and His Church*. London: The Epworth Press, 1938.

Manson, T. W., *The Church's Ministry*. Philadelphia: The Westminster Press, 1948. (Protestant view.)

Miller, D. G., *The Nature and Mission of the Church*. Richmond: John Knox Press, 1957.

Moberly, R. C., *Ministerial Priesthood*. London: John Murray, 1899. (Catholic view; Anglican.)

Newbigen, L., *The Household of God*. New York: Friendship Press, 1954.

Chapter Seven

The Means of Grace

An outward and visible sign of an inward and spiritual grace

I. Grace and the Means of Grace

A. God's Action through the Church

The theology of the Church and her ministry comes to a climax in discussion of the means of grace, because these are the means by which the general saving action of God is mediated to particular congregations and to individual believers. We move from the general theology of the Church to the actual human situation. Salvation is by divine grace (see pp. 206–7). The grace of God is, in the first place, His unmerited favor toward man. The term answers to the principle that human salvation is by divine initiative. God sets His love upon those who do not deserve to be loved, and forgives those who do not and cannot merit this forgiveness. In the second place, grace is the enabling power of God which, working in man, performs this divine good will. However, experience shows, and the Christian Faith declares, that there are certain stated, regular, and divinely promised channels through which God ordinarily bestows His grace. These are the means of grace.

Man takes his share of God's gracious saving act by faith in Christ (see pp. 221–23). Just as the life of man is both inward, of thought and will and affection, and also outward, in bodily and practical action, so also is the act of faith both inward and outward. It is both the cleaving of the heart of man to Christ in loving trust, and it is the taking of the name and sign of an open Christian disciple before the eyes of the world by loyal membership in the Church. This taking of the open signs, if done sincerely, constitutes the means of grace to the believer.

B. The Use of the Means of Grace

The Church in general holds that sinful man is helpless to save himself. His sole hope is in the grace of God, and therefore he must always await the divine initiative. His action is freely and responsibly to cooperate[1] with the divine grace. Nevertheless, there is something which man can do if he sincerely wishes God to exert His initiative and visit him with His grace. He can trustfully and obediently wait upon God at the place and in the way which God has ordained. He can do this expectantly, confident that God will fulfill His promise and make Himself known. The means of grace provide this place and method of waiting. The proper use of the means of grace is that the seeker for God is perseveringly and expectantly to use them, but he is not to trust that his diligence in the use of the means of grace will *earn* or merit his salvation. His trust is to be in the grace of God alone, not in the means. Yet he is not to think lightly of his obligation to use the means of grace, or shirk the accompanying discipline or regular and loyal church-manship and the life of private devotion, for these are the divinely appointed places of waiting.

C. Grace Not Limited to the Means

It is fundamental that God is the sovereign Lord, and is not accountable to man for His actions (Exodus 33:19; Isaiah 43:13). Therefore God's grace is not limited to the appointed means of grace. God has promised to visit with His grace, and bring to salvation, those who obediently and faithfully use the means of grace; but He can nevertheless, if He sees it to be right, save those who have not used the means. It is very precarious for overzealous upholders of the ordinances and discipline of the Church to affirm that certain classes of people who are outside the means of grace cannot be saved. This is to presume upon the prerogative of God, who alone knows who are, and are not, in a state of salvation. It is the office of the Christian witness plainly to declare God's terms of salvation to all whom he can reach, and leave all matters of judgment to God. One may ask, then, what is the advantage of the means of grace in the Church, and what the nature of the obligation to use them? The answer to this is that the means of grace carry with them a certain assurance of standing before God,

---

1 This is the usual position. The strictest Augustinians, however, wishing to affirm in the strongest terms the bondage of man's will, and salvation "by grace alone," would deny that man cooperates with the grace of God. Man is to be accounted passive in the hand of God. This is, however, an extreme position (see p. 211).

resting not upon man's merit in using the means, but upon God's faithfulness in giving His blessing in the way He has promised.[2]

By way of comparison, we do not argue that the spiritual value of home life is rigidly limited to the marriage bond. There are couples who by inadvertance have failed to comply with all the provisions of the marriage law, and some indeed who have taken to living together without any form of marriage whatever. It can happen that some of these are faithful and loving, and have rightly brought up their children. However, what is lacking is *assured status*. The union has not been bindingly pledged, in due legal form. It would appear that those who profess to love Christ and who show something of His Spirit in their lives, yet who do not use the due means of grace and who are not united with the Church, are in a condition analogous to this.

It is no business of the Christian theologian to deny that these people are sincerely good or that God's grace extends toward them or that they may finally come to eternal salvation. They may have some, or much, of Christian grace. What they lack is the *assured status* before God. They have partially or wholly neglected to take the pledges which God has ordained for those who would be marked as belonging to His people. They have not waited in the place and way which God has appointed to those who would receive His grace. This is an act of disobedience, a failure in duty toward God. Therefore, although the merciful God may in fact judge them to be in a state of salvation, they have no right whatever to count upon it. They may escape damnation, but they are not spiritually "safe," as are those who have fully united themselves to God in Christ. This is the true meaning of the traditional proposition that "there is no salvation outside the Church." This does not imply that all those who are outside the Church and her sacraments are heading for damnation, but that they have not been fully and duly admitted to the status of those who securely belong to God.

D. Grace Not Unaccountable

The divine ordinance of the means of grace shows that the action of grace is not entirely unaccountable. Grace is indeed the free action of the sovereign God, but of His own sovereign freedom God has faithfully bound Himself to visit with His grace those who wait upon Him in certain recognized ways. Therefore the searcher for God can know where he is with God. The principle of the means of grace corresponds to the reasonableness of religion. Man cannot save himself, but he never need say, "I am in the dark about God, and there seems nothing I can do about it." If he is in earnest he can

---

2 Some would say that the sacramental means of grace carry with them this assurance in a particular way, and indeed, that this is the characteristic of a sacrament (see pp. 164–65).

reasonably obey God, unite with the Church, and expectantly use the means of grace. Furthermore, the divine pledge of the means of grace answers to the general doctrine that the invitation of God's grace extends to all men[3] (John 3:16; 1 Timothy 2:4; 2 Peter 3:9) because God loves all men. All who will may use the means of grace.

II. Worship

A. The Rationale of Worship

Worship is the action of believers as they join together to express the faith and love which God has given to the Church, to the end that God may be given the praise and reverence which is His due, and the Church built up in love and faith. The principal elements of worship are therefore adoration and praise, confession of sin, profession of faith, and intercession. The media used include visual symbolism and sacred actions, as well as the word spoken and sung, so that man may use all his faculties in lifting up his soul to God. Worship is the more general term which in a sense includes all the particular means of grace, because the preaching of the word, and the sacraments, are special and decisive actions in which the principle of worship comes to its clearest expression. Worship is also in a sense the initial means of grace, because the normal way in which the growing Christian child or the convert from another religion first comes to the Christian experience of the presence and goodness of God is by joining in Christian worship in the home and in the congregation.

Worship is both individual and corporate. Many of its actions, in prayer, in meditation, and in the reading of the Bible, can be informal and domestic, and carried on without any official representative of the Church. They may even be private (Matthew 6:6). Nevertheless, the higher forms of Christian worship are corporate, being the acts of the whole Church. Yet it is a mistake to suppose that individual and corporate worship are in some way opposed one to another. Individual Christians indeed enjoy the privilege of immediate access to God, but they are not isolated individuals. When private believers and Christian families meet for worship they still do so as part of the Church, and their worship only comes to its fullest when they are aware of this, and when their prayers are offered for all men, just as when the Church meets in the public congregation.

The experience of worship is an example of the principle that God works through the natural and the human, and uses it in order to accomplish the spiritual. The underlying psychological rationale of worship is that "expression confirms impression." It is a general law of human behavior that to express the inward thought in uttered word, in meaningful sign, and in practical action, confirms and deepens the hold of the thought upon the heart. Thus to express the sense of God deepens the sense of God. If God

---

[3] Though the strictest Augustinians would virtually deny this (see p. 212).

has first given the gift of faith "as a grain of mustard seed," then to use that rudimentary faith to take part in the act of worship provides the occasion whereby faith may grow to a more adult faith. Thus worship is a means of grace.

Worship is not on this account merely the religious aspect of "auto-suggestion," or "mass suggestion." Still less is it an example of "mass hysteria." It is a fact that individual personalities powerfully affect one another, so that for men and women to feel the same feelings in company, to think the same thoughts, and to say the same words, does imprint these things upon their minds. In mysterious ways this can often happen when the people in question are not all gathered together in the same place, if they are in spiritual rapport with one another. Yet to admit all this does not explain away worship as merely a natural psychological phenomenon, though it does illuminate the natural means which God uses to accomplish spiritual effects. It is the faith of the Church that when the Church prays the Holy Spirit is there, bestowing the sense of Christ in the midst (Matthew 18:20), so that God is the dominating personality there. Worship therefore does not consist in human beings assembling to influence one another, but in the assembly of believers in the presence of the Lord. The Holy Spirit uses and works through the natural psychological process whereby expression confirms impression, so as to bring to man a power which is not his own. The weakness, in the Christian view, of some popular psychological approaches to religion, where the emphasis is made that mental adjustment can produce "peace of mind," and in some cases, physical healing, is here. The claim may be true, so far as it goes. But to go this far is not Christian worship. The objective element of God's work through the Spirit is in danger of being forgotten.

B. The Preaching of the Word

Preaching is usually the means of grace employed by the Holy Spirit to crystallize the definite conviction of personal faith. The general Christian impulse of those who have been nurtured within the Christian community, and the goodwill of dimly awakened searchers for Christ, may be brought thereby to personal experience and personal commitment. Clearly, the Church's worship is only a means of grace if the worshipping community has some degree of knowledge of who Christ is and what His discipleship means. The outward word and ceremonial is an empty form unless there is something inward to express.[4] Preaching informs and educates the worshipping Church. Some members of the worshipping community may as yet have only a very unformed degree of Christian faith. This is the case with young children, casual adherents, or confused seekers. Preaching, with its explanation of Christian life and belief and its appeal for a thoughtful

---

[4] Though simple, young, or unsophisticated believers may have religious beliefs which mean very much to them, even though they have no power to express them in the form of reasoned propositions.

response to the appeal of Christ, enables worship to result in the growth of faith.

By "preaching" we do not mean the sermon alone. The reverent reading of the Bible can itself be a "preaching of the word." The sacraments are, among other things, a most effectual "preaching of the word." Theologically adequate hymns can preach the word, and the recital of the Creed is a particularly solemn act of "preaching." The whole business of "the preaching of the word" is essentially the painting of a vivid portrait of the living Lord of Christian devotion, so that He may make His own personal and pointed challenge to men, calling them to penitent faith in Himself, to devotion and to trustful obedience.

The Word of God is Christ (John 1:1-5, 9-14), the facts of whose life are witnessed to in Holy Scripture (see pp. 195-97). Therefore the preaching of the word is based upon the Bible. Nevertheless, that preaching which is a means of grace is not the bare exposition of Scripture. Nor is it the detailing of the facts about Christ, as in an informative lecture. It is the employment of the testimony of the Church's faith, and the preacher's own testimony, to present Christ to the people. This necessarily includes some degree of instruction in the most important facts about Christ, but it goes on from this to the appeal for faith in Christ as the crucified and risen Lord, and for a life of personal devotion to Him. In true Christian preaching the preacher is careful to give central attention to Christ, rather than to his own opinions and feelings. The Holy Spirit can use this presentation of Christ the Word so that the listener hears not the voice of a man preaching, but the voice of Christ speaking through him.

It is this element of Christ-centered preaching, based upon the scriptural record of the facts, and reflecting the Church's confession of faith, which prevents Christian worship from being a mere exercise of autosuggestion or mass suggestion. Ritual which is only an emotionally impressive ceremony, and an oration which is no more than the appeal of personal magnetism to human feeling is in just this peril. It can lead men astray into uninstructed and subjective mass hysteria. It is for this reason that the liturgy must be scriptural, and not merely aesthetic. The sermon is to be out of the Bible, and not from the daily newspaper. It is worthy of note that the four Gospels are themselves examples of "the preaching of the word," preserved in writing from the ancient Church for our instruction. They represent to us the way in which the apostolic Church presented the leading facts about Christ, not merely in the spirit of informative biography, but to interested hearers for the purpose of winning them to full Christian faith (John 20:31).

C. Intercessory Prayer

This aspect of Christian worship merits attention, on account of the difficulty which many minds have found in it. It is assumed by some that it is "unscientific" to ask for God's blessing and assistance in any affairs which concern the world of nature, for example, that He will bless the handiwork of the farmer in the gift of harvest. The objector may perhaps allow that it is reasonable to ask for spiritual blessings, but his argument really amounts to the tacit assumption that this "spiritual" intercession is in fact human autosuggestion. Thus in both these cases the objector betrays the common assumption that the world in which men live is a naturalistic system of fixed laws, and that there is no God of such a character that He can "make a difference" to events either in the realm of nature, or of human personality.

This issue has already been treated of in principle in the discussion of natural law and divine providence (see p. 28). Our judgment is that the Christian theologian will affirm that while God certainly does not "break" those fixed and reliable laws of nature which are themselves an expression of His being, His intelligent mind is in control of the universe, and He can "work through" the laws of nature to accomplish His sovereign will. If it once be allowed that the Living God exists and rules the world by His providence, then it is surely reasonable to ask for His blessing in all manner of affairs, both "natural" and "spiritual," believing that He is well able to answer those prayers if to do so is in accord with His good will. And if He indeed be a God of love who is near to man in tender sympathy and compassion, it is the natural and proper impulse of His children to make all their requests known to Him (Matthew 7:7-11). A denial of the rationality and efficacy of intercessory prayer is in fact a veiled denial of the God of sovereign power and loving providence.

However, the purpose of intercessory prayer is not to remind God of human needs, as though He were in some way forgetful or unaware (Matthew 6:7-8). Nor is it necessary to stimulate His desire to do good (Luke 18:7-8). Nor do we pray in hope of bending His will, to cause Him to alter His plan for the government of the universe. It is the Christian faith that God already knows all things, past, present, and future, and that His government is already fully and entirely good for every one of His creatures. The natural and sufficient ground of Christian prayer is that this is the expression of confidence in His goodness and wisdom. We may even venture the judgment that in some things God may choose to delay the execution of His will until such time as man recollects the duty of making intercession, because it is good for man that in this discipline he should learn both dependence upon God and confidence in asking.

The ultimate purpose of prayer is that the praying Church may become the fully sensitive, obedient, and useful instrument of God for the accomplishment of His own purpose. The Christian does not presume fully to know what is God's good plan either for the nations or for the Church, or for his loved ones or for himself. He does not, therefore, in his confident intercession try to demand or to dictate. The very spirit of Christian prayer is, "If it be Thy will." This is not an "escape clause," to the effect that if the prayer is not apparently answered the intercessor may comfort himself with the pious reflection, "Well, I did not actually ask for it." Such an attitude displays complete lack of faith. The prayer "If it be Thy will" is the prayer of the believing man, whose supreme desire it is fully to be used by God according to God's will, with God's power, and to God's glory. It is prayer after the pattern of Christ Himself (Luke 22:42). If this be so, the highest act of the Church's prayer is not for health and good success, for healing from disease, or even for the peace of the world, though all these things are rightly to be prayed for. The chief prayer of faith is for increase of faith and love, for the divine equipment of the Church, and for the conversion of the world (Matthew 6:9–10).

The critic may inquire: "If man requires faith in order to pray effectually, how can sinful man, whose awareness is of his rebellion against faith, ever bring himself to pray for the gift of faith? How can he ever start? Is there not here a 'vicious circle'?" This common dilemma illustrates that the method of the divine grace is by human cooperation. Left to himself man is indeed helpless in this vicious circle of unbelief. Yet man is not left to himself, for God's grace is still calling even the man who denies the existence of God. Man can do nothing apart from the divine initiative, but that initiative is already always there. Therefore, it is a fact of human life that even careless men, and even apparently hardened men, experience under the stress of life fleeting moments of rude awakening which cause them to have dim spiritual stirrings. This is the work of prevenient grace (see pp. 214–15). In that moment it is possible for the unbelieving man, if he will, to cry out in his agony, "Lord, I believe; help Thou mine unbelief" (Mark 9:24). And this most faltering prayer is a prayer which God can bless by the gift of a greater faith. So the opening is made for the growth in grace. Yet to the end of his life the mature Christian is still praying the same prayer, and waiting to cooperate with the divine initiative of grace.

D. Religion and Magic

It is not possible here to examine the broad question of the contrast between true religion and magical superstition, either in its primitive forms or in its modern revivals. We must confine ourselves to the understanding of Christian sacramental worship. One is aware that it is possible for even the most sacred rites to deteriorate among uninstructed and superficial worshippers into magic, and even into degrading superstition. This has in fact on occasion happened in the Church. Furthermore, it is all too easy for natural strong revulsion against one error to drive some believers, and some denominations, into error of the opposite direction. Thus there are many sincere Christian believers who fail to find in the sacraments the spiritual profit and meaning which has been the traditional heritage of the Church, because they are unduly afraid of "superstition."

The betraying symptom of magic is that it is man-centered. Its basis is the notion that it is possible, by the aid of the appropriate ceremonies and incantations, to constrain the power of the gods or spirits to the will of the worshipper. It is the attempt to harness the divine power to the protection of oneself, or one's family or one's property, or to bring "good luck" to one's enterprise. If the devotee of magic does not succeed he redoubles his request, and the spirit of his prayer is to insist that he be heard on account of the persistence and correct form of his intercessions. The Christian sacraments are exactly the opposite in spirit. They are God-centered. The sole and sufficient ground for the worshipper's confident hope of divine blessing is that the sovereign God has ordained this dependable way in which to give His blessing. The blessing is an act of *grace,* bestowed as and when God will upon those who can do nothing to establish a claim upon Him. The rite, therefore, is a means of *grace,* and its efficacy depends upon the divine promise on the one hand, and the penitent and obedient receptivity of the worshippers on the other. The prayer of the sacraments is always, "Not my will, but Thine, be done."

III. The Sacramental Principle

All worship involves the use of symbolism. However severe, and even bare, the form the worshipper may choose, the words of Scripture, of the sermon, or of a hymn, are all symbols. They are the agreed outward expressions of ideas. However, the time-honored definition of a sacrament as "an outward and visible sign of an inward and spiritual grace given unto us, ordained by Christ Himself, as a means whereby we receive the same" indicates that a sacrament is a symbol which is seen and done, as well as said. It involves a proper substance and action, as well as words to be said. That the Lord should have ordained symbolic actions and visible symbols for the central acts of Christian worship is a salient example of the principle that God can work the spiritual through the material. Sacred words may on occasion be very expressive, but in general a symbol which is seen and done has more power to move the imagination of man than has the spoken word alone.

Thus there is a place for reasoned instruction in the idea of "country," "patriotism," and "public spirit." Yet if for the sake of his country a man has to take his life in his hands upon the field of battle, the season has passed for a lecture upon the principles of the Constitution! He requires a flag—a vivid visual symbol which can in a moment focus to his imagination all that he has been taught about the idea of "country." The spoken word is essential in its place, for if the flag is not understood it can make no appeal. Yet if it is understood, the symbol can have an imaginative power which goes far beyond the unaided word. Thus in a wide variety of life's experiences men resort naturally to acted and visual symbolism at moments of climax. This is eminently true of religion, and so our Lord has taken this principle into the

Christian religion. Hence the supreme symbols have "an outward and visible sign."

The use of symbolism is not a mark of lack of spirituality. Christian theology regards it as a cardinal error to suppose that the "invisible," that is, the purely mental or the spoken, is in some way more "spiritual" than is the visible and the acted. The association of material objects with the most sacred actions of Christian worship is an expression in present Christian experience of the very principle of the Incarnation itself. Christian teaching is that God created the material universe, that He filled it with spiritual meaning, that He can have contact with it, and that He can use it and work through it to accomplish spiritual purposes (see pp. 23, 34–35). The same principle which made possible the Incarnation makes possible the sacraments. Thus the sacraments bring to the worshipper the reality of the Incarnation. Christian theology has affirmed the spiritual dignity and efficacy of the sacraments by describing them as "operative symbols." An operative symbol both signifies a truth and is a symbol through which God will perform an action of grace corresponding to that truth. By way of illustration from human affairs, a marriage is a rite which embodies something of the "operative symbol." The plighting of troth, the giving and receiving of a ring, the signature upon a legal paper, and the consummation of the marriage are actions which outwardly symbolize the intention of the parties to be married. However, the symbols are much more than vivid and expressive ways by which the parties declare their true love to one another, though they are this. They actually marry the couple. They perform an action, and convey a status, which corresponds to the love which is symbolized. Thus they are more than symbols. They are *operative* symbols. The supreme example of this principle is found in the Christian sacraments. The Holy Communion is much more than a solemn dramatization of the truths seen in the Cross, as a visual alternative to a spoken sermon on the same subject, though among other things it is this. To celebrate the sacrament is the way by which the Church makes herself one with the Lord as He offers His atoning sacrifice, and by which she receives her share of what Christ accomplished in His death and resurrection. Thus the Holy Communion is not only a visual and acted symbol of Christ's sacrifice of obedience. It is an *operative* symbol of His sacrifice. God has pledged Himself to use it to bring to the Church, and to reverent and believing communicants, a due share of the merits of Christ's death and resurrection. Thus:

> The sign transmits the signified,
> The grace is by the means applied.

The sacraments are therefore to a unique degree *means* of grace. When believingly used they convey to man a secure spiritual status and assured standing before God, because the Lord has ordained that this shall be so. The secure and pledged effect of the sacraments does not depend upon the

exact mechanical performance of certain stated acts, or the exact enuncia-
tion of certain words, so much as upon a sincere and thoughtful intention
of carrying out what our Lord ordained should be done. Well-intentioned
zealots for precise ecclesiastical traditions do well to remember that in carrying out His saving work in the heart God has more regard for what is within
the heart of man than for the punctiliously observed outward sign. Nevertheless, if a Christian congregation is found careless in saying the sacred words
required by Scripture, in performing the due action, and in using the due
substances, then it is clearly deficient in intention of observing the Lord's
ordinance. This deficient rite is then doubtfully a Christian sacrament, and
the security of the divine pledge is lost. The rite, though not in proper
ecclesiastical order for a sacrament, may, however, continue to be a helpful
service of Christian worship to those who take part in it, particularly if they
err because of simplicity and ignorance.

IV. Holy Baptism

A. The Sacrament of Initiation

Holy Baptism is primarily the sacrament of incorporation into the Church
(Acts 2:37–41; 9:18; 10:47–48; 16:14–15, 33). By consequence it is the
sacrament of initiation into the Christian life, though when the person baptized is a child the initiation requires to be completed and ratified in later
years by some suitable rite involving a responsible pledge of allegiance to
Christ and His Church.

B. Baptism in the New Testament and the Ancient Church

Brief note has been made of the question of the origins of Christian Baptism (see p. 139). It would seem that Holy Baptism is a combination of John
the Baptist's washing with water, in token of the penitent preparation of
God's people for the coming of the Messiah, and of the outpouring of the
Holy Spirit which came upon the disciples of Christ to prepare and equip
them for their mission. At all events, from the time of the New Testament
it was the firm faith of the Church that Holy Baptism is the sacrament
expressly ordained by the Lord as the symbol of self-identification with
Christ, incorporation into the Church, and of the gift of the Holy Spirit
(John 3:5).

The New Testament discusses this matter in terms of the baptism of an
adult convert to the faith, involving confession of faith in Christ as Lord
and Savior (Acts 8:36–38, 16:31–33, 22:16).[5] It is possible that at first the

---

5 We are left to surmise the nature of the mysterious "baptism for the dead" mentioned in 1 Corinthians 15:29. Presumably it was an attempt to incorporate into the
Church the righteous departed, so that they might share in the coming resurrection.
This presupposes a strong sense of corporate solidarity in the Church, whereby some
members might stand proxy for others. This obscurity is a standing warning against
undue dogmatism regarding New Testament baptismal customs.

divine name which was invoked over the baptized person was the name of Jesus Christ alone. Many scholars think that this is presupposed by the authentic text of Acts 10:48 (R.V.). From a very early period, however, the universal formula became baptism "in the name of the Father, and of the Son, and of the Holy Ghost" (Matthew 28:19). "The name" is a very common Old Testament phrase for that which represents the person, character, and authority of anyone. Therefore to invoke upon a person or place the sacred name of God involved that God had claimed it for His own, placed it under His authority, and extended His protection over it (Deuteronomy 12:5, 28:58; 2 Chronicles 7:14; Psalm 20:5; Jeremiah 7:10). Hence baptism in the triune name signifies that the baptized person yields himself up to the possession and authority of the God who has made Himself known as Father, Son, and Holy Spirit. By invariable tradition throughout the Church, therefore, the essentials to Holy Baptism are the use of water and of the triune name of God.

The leading theological passage in the New Testament regarding Holy Baptism appears to imply that the washing is to be by immersion, for the imagery of Romans 6:4 seems to require that the baptized person be "buried" in the water. However, at an early date it was accounted sufficient if the candidate went into the water and had water poured over him. Indeed, it would appear that the leading interest of some circles of the primitive Church was that baptism should be in the running water of the river, presumably because the first baptisms in the Jordan were of this kind. In the early days of the Church it became the rule that the washing, by immersion or pouring, should be threefold, to correspond to the threefold name of God. The baptismal creed, in three clauses, recording the divine work of the Father, the Son, and the Holy Spirit, was learned by the catechumen, so that he might make a threefold confession of faith to correspond to the threefold washing. Later still, baptism by sprinkling was allowed, nominally as a concession in the case of a sickly infant, often, however, as the usual custom.

C. Baptism as Union with Christ

Union to Christ by faith and incorporation into the Church implies the taking up a stand as a Christian in face of a probably hostile world, and a life of service which must often entail self-discipline and self-sacrifice. In fact, the action of a Christian convert in submitting to Holy Baptism means that he "takes up the Cross" in order to be a disciple (Mark 8:34–35). Baptism involves adopting that attitude to life which Christ adopted, and which took Him finally to His death. Those who make themselves one with Christ, inwardly in the heart and outwardly in deed and fact by membership in the Church, will receive strength from their victorious living Head do this. Having by His grace persevered in the life of "Cross-bearing" they will share His gift of life triumphant over sin in this world, and over death in the next.

Such is the New Testament doctrine of what it means to be a Christian.

St. Paul saw this great principle depicted symbolically in the rite of Holy
Baptism. To go down into the water of baptism, which act is the operative
symbol incorporating the believer into Christ and His Church, was, as
it were, to go down into the grave with Christ. That is to say, it involved the
adoption of Christ's way of suffering love. To come up out of the water, now
a confessing and pledged Christian, was like rising from the dead in
company with the victorious Christ. To submit to baptism was the door into
a new life of moral triumph (Romans 6:3–6).

Thus the sacrament of Holy Baptism is a symbolic preaching of the death
and resurrection of Christ. It is a divinely appointed means by which the
faithful, identifying themselves with their Lord, may receive their promised
share in the fruits of the atonement. This, the original and most authentic
New Testament theology of baptism, shows that the two Gospel sacraments
embody a parallel principle. They are both symbols of self-identification with
the crucified and risen Christ. Baptism is the first and decisive identification;
Holy Communion is the continuing and ever-renewed identification following from this.

D. Baptismal Regeneration

This traditional theological term has been the occasion of controversy, in
part due to genuine differences of emphasis, but also through the reading
of different senses into the same word. The New Testament position is that
Holy Baptism, by water and the Spirit, is the operative symbol of conversion
to God. The turning "from the power of Satan unto God" is considered
as both inward and outward. Repentance, the act of faith, spiritual union
with Christ, the gift of the Holy Spirit, baptism, and union with the Church
are regarded as inseparable. They are so many aspects of the same thing.
The questions which have caused dispute among later Christians as to which
is more important, the inward secret union of the heart with Christ or
outward membership of the Church, and whether certain ordinances are
essential to Church membership, had not then arisen, and are therefore not
explicitly answered in the New Testament. If the New Testament position
is adopted, Holy Baptism is the mark of the beginning of the Christian
life. It is the sacrament of the new birth, or of regeneration (John 3:5).
This has been the traditional doctrine of the Church.

However, the life and discipline of no modern denomination exactly
corresponds to the New Testament position. Therefore some measure of
interpretation is necessary when New Testament doctrine is applied to the
Church of today. This is particularly the case with infant baptism. A
believer's baptism (see p. 165) is admittedly much nearer in principle to
New Testament discussions of the sacrament. Possibly the most adequate
way of viewing this matter is that the change of spiritual status which God
works in the infant in baptism is a real and significant change, yet it is
a change in promise and potentiality, rather than of immediate actuality.

Only in this way can infant baptism be vindicated as a real means of grace which accomplishes a divine work for the child, and also be guarded against the supposition that Holy Baptism, as it were, mechanically plants some sort of divine merit in the child, which is there irrespective of the later life, morals, and churchmanship of the baptized person.

By way of parallel, a child inherits, and has, as it were, implanted in him, the legal status of the nationality of his parents. This is a real status, yet one in promise. It by no means involves that he will, automatically and for the rest of his life, be a true citizen of his country. For the potentialities of citizenship to be realized requires nurture in the community and traditions of his nation, and it likewise requires a sincere response to this environment. Nevertheless, the status is real, and if the child later proves to be a rascal and a traitor he is still a citizen of his country. The only effect of this nominal citizenship is, however, that it is the law of his own nation, rather than of another, which inflicts punishment upon him. The unrealized potentiality is there, but it brings disability and blame, rather than advantage. Something similar is true of the baptism of the infant. He is permanently marked as a member of Christ and of His Church, and a real spiritual status is conferred. Nevertheless, it is a status in promise. To bring actual Christian benefit to the child the potentiality must be realized by the response of faith, consecration, and real churchmanship in the growing child.

However, the Christian child has been placed in the environment where worship is offered, Christian nurture given, and where the Holy Spirit more expressly operates. This environment effectually, though not irresistibly, helps the growing child to respond and to realize the potentiality of the status bestowed upon him. When he becomes, of his own conviction and choice, a real Christian, he has acted in accord with his baptism. And if he neglects the opportunity given to him, and fails to respond to the drawing of the Holy Spirit and the effect of the prayers of the Church offered for him, the evil-living baptized person does not become an unbaptized person. He is an apostate Christian, having a real Christian status which works judgment upon him, rather than blessing.

The baptism of a helpless infant presents the principle that salvation is by the initiative of divine grace. Before the child can do anything, good or bad, God is already there, receiving the child as His own, blessing him, and surrounding him with the influence of the Holy Spirit. The Church is likewise already there, praying for the child, and not doubting that the prayer is with power. This conception of a real, significant, and valuable spiritual status permanently imparted by God in the sacrament, yet imparted in promise, is perhaps the fitting sense in which baptismal regeneration may be attributed to the baptism of an infant.

A venerable but less satisfactory form of theology which has been widespread in some Christian traditions is that the chief function of Holy Baptism is to wash away the guilt of original sin. The power of original sin to lead men into actual sin is a fact of experience, and so is the guilt of actual sin, in which all men are found. Nevertheless, we feel that the notion of the *guilt* of original sin is a difficult and ethically dubious one. It is hard to see how the perfectly just Judge can hold men personally responsible and guilty for an inborn weakness of nature for which they are not in fact responsible. Surely He accounts personal guilt only to those evil thoughts and deeds which men have knowingly and willingly committed. The traditional doctrine of the baptismal cleansing from the guilt of original sin appears largely to be a piece of rationalization. First the rite of infant baptism appeared, upon the sufficient ground of Christian solidarity, and was accepted as a godly ordinance. Later, when the Augustinian theology introduced into the Church the notion of the guilt of original sin, the idea of the baptismal washing away of this guilt presented itself as a natural and convenient support in theological principle for the accepted practice. This has been accompanied by the transfer to infant Baptism of the doctrine of the New Testament regarding the remission of sin in a believer's baptism. It is, we feel, preferable to avoid this somewhat uncertain ground, hallowed though it is in Christian tradition, and to discuss the theology of infant baptism in terms of its original principle of incorporation into the Church, rather than of any supposed "cleansing."

Summary of Divergence: Believer's and Infant Baptism

At the time of the Reformation some of the more radical groups of Protestants emphasized, against the Catholic tradition that infant baptism is the normal usage of a Christian community, that the scriptural and only legitimate discipline of baptism is that of a believer's baptism. That is, baptism should be administered to one who is sufficiently developed in mental powers, and in particular, in spiritual experience, to be able to testify that he has already come to a personal saving faith in Christ, in token of which he desires duly to be incorporated into the Church. This emphasis has usually been associated with the claim that the only legitimate mode of baptism is by immersion, and that pouring or sprinkling of the water is an unscriptural, and therefore defective, rite. There is, however, no necessary connection between believer's baptism and total immersion. The ancient Church often practiced the immersion of infants, and the Orthodox, or Eastern, Church still does, while believer's baptism by sprinkling or pouring is also used.

The emphasis upon believer's baptism in general answers to the principle of Christian individualism. The Church is thought of, not as the Christian side of the general community life, but as a society in some sense standing apart from, and in antithesis to, the community. Church membership is to be composed entirely of personally committed Christian believers. Thus it is assumed that one becomes a member of the Church

and a Christian (in the full and proper sense of the word) by an individual, personal, and conscious conversion or act of commitment to
Christ, and not merely by incorporation into the Christian community.
On the other hand, infant baptism answers to the principle of Christian
collectivity (see pp. 217–18). It reflects the traditional confidence of the
Church that nurture from early days within the Christian community,
including the Christian home and school, as well as public worship, is
the regular, normal, and salutary (though not invariable) way by which
individual men and women become Christian believers. Clearly, these
two ideals are in some sense complementary, for there is some truth on
both sides. The two may be set out as follows.

a. The Case for Believer's Baptism

The Church is for all time to be disciplined so far as possible after
the manner of the New Testament Church. The Church of those days
was not a generalized Christian community, but a closely knit fellowship composed of those only who acknowledged a deep personal committal to Christ. Entrance to it was by a distinct and personal experience
of conversion, in token of which the believer was united to the Church
by baptism (for example Acts 9:1–18). Thus a person was not baptized
in order to make him a Christian, or even to help him to be a Christian,
but because he could profess that he was already a Christian. One has,
first, Christian individuals and then the Church, not vice versa. Baptism
by total immersion is affirmed to be the New Testament custom, and
is further to be defended in present practice because it constitutes
entrance into the Church as a challenging rite, which is only likely to
be accepted by one who is of a serious Christian purpose. It is good
for the Church and her members that there should be this clear demarcation between the Church and those who are not in the Church.
On the other hand, infant baptism takes away from the full meaning
of the sacrament. It can too easily be taken as a customary communal
ceremony by parents and friends who may be lacking in deep Christian
conviction. The child thus baptized is deprived of the later salutary
experience of challenge and committal. At its worst, infant baptism
can open the door to superstition.

b. The Case for Infant Baptism

It is to be agreed that the baptisms actually mentioned in the New
Testament in general appear to be those of adult believers. However,
this is the natural outcome of the missionary situation of the early
Church. Furthermore, some of the most notable passages referring to
Baptism contain language which answers very naturally to baptism
by immersion (see p. 166). However, the New Testament does not
give a sufficiently clear witness on these points to be determinative for
the Church of later times. Therefore we are rightly guided by the
judgment of the ancient Church, as it understood the nature of the
Christian life, rather than by the inconclusive letter of Scripture.

The custom of infant baptism began to develop from an early date in the Church, possibly even in the first Christian century. It steadily spread in the early centuries, and became the general custom as and when the Church emerged from a missionary situation into the position of the communal religion of Christian nations. In antiquity, religion was always communal and of the family. The modern notion that it is possible for a husband to be of one faith, his wife of another, and their children of yet other persuasions was an idea quite alien to the thought of the ancient world, as it is in simple tribal societies today. The early Christians did indeed discover that the new faith sometimes sadly divided the home, but this to them appeared a monstrous and unnatural thing, and one of the most painful aspects of the necessity to suffer with Christ (Matthew 10:21, 34–38).

To the mind of the times the natural event was that when the head of the household became Christian, so did the whole family, including even resident domestic slaves (Acts 11:14, 16:31–32). With this background it is plain that Christian parents would wish their children to be admitted into the new faith by baptism. This was the historical origin of infant baptism, and it is significant that the objection voiced against the custom by some in the ancient Church was not the modern one that the baptism of an infant does not mean anything, because "the baby does not know what is happening." This is the mentality of modern individualism. The objection rather was that infant baptism meant too much! It was felt to be unfair to place upon the infant the heavy Christian responsibility of living from the days of early youth a life substantially free from serious moral fault.

In a settled Christian community the normal manner in which persons become Christians is by being born into Christian homes, living in a community of at least nominal Christian standards of behavior, receiving the spiritual nurture of joining in Christian worship, and of being educated in Christian schools (1 Corinthians 7:14). The majority of believers of all denominations would place the beginning of their Christian discipleship before they can remember, in days of infancy, even though they may also be aware of moments of personal decision and consecration in later life. If effective Christian discipleship starts with infancy it is logical that the infants of the Christian community should be formally incorporated into the Church. Traditional Christianity has done this by the rite of infant baptism. The doctrine that infant baptism is an effective means of grace is in fact a token of the Church's confidence in the beneficial effect of Christian nurture.

The Christian Church is the place in which worship is offered and Christian teaching given, and where the Holy Spirit more especially carries on His work. Therefore to be incorporated into the Church is the normal first step toward becoming a Christian. This underlying philosophy of Christian solidarity has been traditionally expressed by the custom that sponsors or godparents should confess the Christian Faith, and make a promise of Christian obedience, on behalf of the child at baptism. They stand for the general body of the Church, and profess the Faith of the Church, which Faith is for the benefit of all within the solidarity of the faithful, and the infant now to be baptized in particular. Other denominations require the profession of faith and promise of Christian nurture to be made by the parents, and the congregation present, because they feel that this is a more realistic form of promise. However, the principle of this is much the same as with the traditional sponsors. It is an expression of the solidarity in Christ of the home and congregation.

V. The Holy Communion or Eucharist

A. The Name

The central act of Christian worship, in which the whole principle of the means of grace is most clearly exemplified, is the sacrament of the gospel ordained by our Lord at His Last Supper. The technical theological term which conveniently comprises this rite under all the names by which it is variously known, such as "the Lord's Supper," "the Holy Communion," "the Mass," and so forth, is "the Eucharist." This word simply means "thanksgiving," and is derived from the Greek verb *eucharistein,* "to be thankful," used in 1 Corinthians 11:24. Its use should not be understood as implying any particular theology of the sacrament.

B. The Lord's Ordinance: The New Testament Doctrine

It is not clear from the Gospels whether our Lord's Last Supper was the actual Passover meal (Matthew 26:17–19; Mark 14:12–17; Luke 22:11–16) or one of the ceremonial meals preparatory to the Passover (John 13:1). This difficult question is of historical interest rather than of importance for the understanding of the theology of the Eucharist. In either case our Lord's betrayal and death, and institution of the Eucharist, is clearly associated in the mind of the New Testament Church with the Passover. Thus if the date from the Fourth Gospel is adopted, the crucifixion took place at the time when the Passover lambs were being killed, which is doubtless what the Evangelist intends to symbolize.

At His Last Supper our Lord performed a solemn sevenfold symbolic action. He took bread, gave thanks and blessing, broke the bread, and distributed to the disciples; He took a cup of wine, gave thanks and blessing, and distributed to His disciples (Matthew 26:26–28; Mark 14:22–24; Luke 22:19–20; 1 Corinthians 11:23–26). It is clear from the narrative in 1 Corinthians 11:23–26 that St. Paul is basing himself upon a traditional formula which was always said in much the same accustomed way. He can describe it as that which was "handed on" in the Church as a recognized and authoritative tradition (v. 23). The formula he uses is apparently an attempt to weave into one all the different words and actions which the Church remembered as associated with our Lord's institution, and which are recorded in the Gospels.[6] It will be remembered, however, that the apostle does not derive his account from our written Gospels, for 1 Corinthians was written first, and is the oldest as well as the fullest written witness.

A question which has engaged the mind of some critics is whether our Lord did indeed intend at His Last Supper to found a permanent sacramental rite. It is difficult to prove unambiguously from any recorded word of Scripture that this was in His mind, though the Church has traditionally found this sanction in the phrase "this do ye, as oft as ye shall drink it" of 1 Corinthians 11:25. However, the New Testament was not written to answer modern historical or controversial questions, but to instruct the faith of believers. It is not concerned to argue the case that our Lord intended to institute the Eucharist at His Last Supper, and that this Eucharist is the permanent and distinctive Christian act of worship. This much is the working assumption of the New Testament writers, and the circumstance that the case is never argued is the clearest evidence that all the Christians were agreed on this. If acceptance of the Eucharist had been a belief which was first developed in one part of the Church, and then gradually spread to the whole, there would naturally have been in the New Testament marks of controversy over this issue. As there are none we may be assured that the Eucharist was an original part of the Christian message and institution, going back to the first apostles.

The general background of Christ's teaching on the Eucharist is that the sacrament is the new Passover appropriate to the New Israel (see p. 141). Of old times the tribes of Israel had been delivered from bondage in Egypt by the hand of the Lord at the Red Sea, and this deliverance had constituted them into a disciplined and incorporate nation. And of the Passover it was written, "And this day shall be unto you for a memorial; and ye shall keep it a feast to the Lord throughout your generations" (Exodus 12:14). It is a fundamental misunderstanding and impoverishment of Hebrew thought to suppose that a "memorial" is merely a historic memento, which by the aid of imaginative symbolism takes the worshipper back to the past in pious sentiment, and thus, as it were, "helps him to feel he was there." Rather is it that which takes the historic deliverance out of the past and brings it down with present effect to God's people of every succeeding generation. The faithful Israelite who joins in the "memorial" Passover can find that the effect of the Red Sea deliverance has come to him. Thus to partake of the feast is a mark of membership in the redeemed people.

The Eucharist, instituted by our Lord against a background of Passover thought, is the Christian parallel to this. The Messiah has come, bringing the promised kingdom. By His death and resurrection He is to deliver the

---

6 There is some trace remaining of a strain of tradition which apparently placed the blessing of the cup first (Luke 22:17).

people of God from the power of sin, a more signal deliverance than that from the tyranny of Pharaoh (1 Corinthians 5:7–8). The faithful among Israel, who accept Jesus as the suffering Messiah and who share in this deliverance, are to be reconstituted thereby into the new and true people of God, the New Israel of the Church. It is fitting, therefore, that the ancient Passover should be reconstituted as a new and perpetual "memorial" of this Christian deliverance. This thought is expressed in the words recorded by St. Paul: "This do in remembrance of Me" (1 Corinthians 11:24, 25).

The familiar words "in remembrance" often convey to the modern worshipper the notion that the Christian sacrament is simply a means to make the fact of Calvary dreadfully real to the imagination by the appeal of vivid symbolism. As one man may preach the Cross by word of mouth, and another in religious art, so the Eucharist is preaching in solemn drama. All this is plainly a part of the truth about the Church's sacramental worship, and it is an important truth. Nevertheless, this whole circle of thought does not at all do justice to what the New Testament intends by the word "remembrance," and would, indeed, hardly be recognized by the Christian writers of the early centuries as sacramental thought at all. The New Testament Eucharist is more than a symbolic appeal to the imagination. It is a sacramental *operative* symbol, which accomplishes an effect appropriate to the truth symbolized. The "remembrance" exists to take the historic delivering act of Christ crucified and risen, and also the personal presence of the Christ who performs the act, and bring them out of the past, so that they may be real in the experience of the Church in every place, and to the end of time. Those who faithfully celebrate the Eucharist are declaring and making themselves one with Christ as He performs His act, so that they may share the effect of dying with Him, in order to live with Him. The new Passover is the supreme mark of belonging to the New Israel.

It will be asked what is the meaning of Christ's solemn and mysterious words of institution, "This is My body," and "This is My blood," the due recital of which, together with the breaking of the bread and the sharing of the cup, constitutes the essential ritual of the Eucharist. It is very necessary that we come to this subject in a spirit of reverent reserve. If we cannot be sure of understanding fully the genius of a Shakespeare we must not too lightly assume that we can see into the mind of our Lord, particularly at this awesome moment. The exact meaning of Christ's words of institution has all too often been the subject of overconfident dogmatism, and at times of most unseemly controversy around the Table of the Lord. In general no sacramental doctrine which has endeared itself to the devotion of any responsible Christian denomination is to be dismissed as merely false, though some views may contain only partial truth. All schools of Christian thought are on the whole nearer to the truth in what they have positively affirmed of their own experience than in what they have denied in the doctrine of others. Christian doctrine is comprehensive and many-sided.

We therefore pass by controversial discussion as to which modern denominational viewpoint most nearly answers to our Lord's words of institution. The everyday language used by Jesus was Aramaic, and scholars of this ancient language have sought to reconstruct what phrases in it would most likely be translated into the Greek as it occurs in our New Testament. The result of this highly technical study would appear to indicate on the one hand that our Lord's sense was not "This stands for My body," and "This stands for My blood," in the sense of an imaginative reminder. Nor was it "This *is* My body," in the sense that some unseen and intangible entity which theologically may be described as Christ's body is now associated with the consecrated bread. Indeed, the original phrase on our Lord's lips probably did not contain any word representing "is." Rather, what Christ said was: "Behold, the body!" and "Behold, the blood!" The meaning of this is that in the whole eucharistic action, that is, in the recital of the Gospel word in obedience to Christ's command, in the breaking of the bread and the blessing of the cup, and in the partaking of the same, the effect of Christ's saving action by His victorious death is manifested to the Church. In particular, the personal presence of the dying Lord, now risen, is made known to the Church. We submit that among the various denominations, most thoughtful and sensitive believers would profess that something of this sort is what they are *trying* to say about the Eucharist as they use the various traditional doctrinal forms.

The Eucharist is an operative symbol, not so much of the Crucifixion, as of our Lord's sacrifice of victorious sinless obedience which lay behind the Cross. It is significant that what impressed the mind of the New Testament Church was that the Eucharist brought the "remembrance," not so much of Calvary, as of "the night in which He was betrayed" (1 Corinthians 11:23). Christian sentiment has often sought to make of the Eucharist a sacramental enactment of the destruction of Christ's body upon the Cross. The breaking of bread has been spoken of as a symbol of the tearing of His flesh, the pouring of the wine a figure of the shedding of His blood. In the last resort this comparison is not altogether appropriate and convincing. When St. Paul speaks of the sacramental bread he does not refer to it as that which is torn apart, but as that which is the union of many separate grains of wheat, a symbol of the unity of the Church in Christ (1 Corinthians 10:17). Had our Lord wished to ordain a sacramental re-enactment of the destruction of His body he could doubtless have adapted the symbolism of the slaughter of the Passover lamb. Actually what He left was a sacramental re-enactment of the Supper of the dark betrayal night in which He resolved to go to His death, and in which supremely He prayed the prayer of obedient submission to the Heavenly Father (Luke 22:39–42). Thus, if we may venture to read our Lord's mind, the Eucharist is the sacrament of His victorious sacrifice of sinless obedience. The Church cannot make herself one with the Lord as He dies, in a literal sense. The death of the incarnate Son was a mysterious and unique event. What the Church can and must do in her sacramental worship is to make herself one with her Lord as He *obeys*. In the Eucharist He comes to us, that we may go with Him as He offers His sacrifice of sinless obedience, and so have access to God.

Finally, the Bible makes it plain that both the Passover and the Eucharist look forward to God's deliverance, as well as backward. It is the paradoxical tragedy of the world that, though God has performed His historic saving act and redeemed His people, yet they are still oppressed by the power of evil. The Passover looked back to a great deliverance at the Red Sea, and proclaimed Israel to be a nation. Yet not all the people were righteous, and the nation was conquered first by one, then by another, pagan tyrant. Therefore the Hebrew people, as they observed the memorial of the Passover, were still looking for the fulfillment of the divine promise implicit in the first deliverance. They were awaiting the Messiah who would set up God's kingdom in open glory, in deed and in fact. The same is true of the Eucharist. It proclaims that the promised Messiah has come in the person of the Lord Jesus, and has brought the kingdom. Nevertheless, the kingdom, though authentically present to those who have the eye of faith to see it, is as yet only as "a grain of mustard seed" (Mark 4:30–32), containing the promise of a fuller divine deliverance. Therefore the Eucharist looks forward to the day when the kingdom shall be fully come, and the power of sin and evil entirely destroyed in the world. The Messiah will rule not as now, in the mystery of humiliated and suffering love, but in open glory as the acknowledged master of all human affairs (1 Corinthians 11:26). The persecuted "little flock" (Luke 12:32) which unites in the act of Christian worship, and as it meets finds itself "not many wise men after the flesh, not many mighty" (1 Corinthians 1:26), possesses in its Eucharist a pledge of the coming Day of God, when the Church shall embrace all the nations of the world. Indeed, that future perfected community is now possessed in reality, though in miniature, in the fellowship of the Church. Thus the Eucharist unites the end of time with the beginning, and gives a full view of what is meant by "remembrance."

C. *Theological Terms Used of the Eucharist*

Some of the chief words which have been used in connection with the Eucharist in Christian theology may now be defined.

+ 1. SACRAMENT OF THE LORD'S SUPPER. This term emphasizes the unity in thought, intention, and spiritual experience which exists between the rite ordained by our Lord and the Church's present act of worship. The name reminds us that we are doing now what He then did, and what was done in the New Testament Church. This term therefore sums up the whole body of original New Testament sacramental doctrine.

+ 2. HOLY COMMUNION. This word emphasizes the present experience of

the Church as she meets for eucharistic worship. It bears both a general
and a particular sense. In all acts of Christian worship the faithful find
the promised presence of their Lord, and in Him have fellowship one with
another. The faith and experience of the Church is that this, the distinctive
act of Christian worship, can be used by the Holy Spirit to grant this experience of communion with Christ in the most prevailing and precious of all
ways. However, and in particular, to receive in faith the consecrated bread
and wine is the due climax of the sacramental action. Thus actually to eat
of that bread and to drink of that cup, that is, to *communicate,* is for each
believer the operative symbol whereby he receives his share of that which
Christ accomplished for the Church by His atoning death (1 Corinthians
10:16). In this special manner, therefore, the Eucharist is a sharing of
Christ. It is the Holy Communion.

3. THE SACRAMENT OF UNITY. The Eucharist is the Church's act whereby
she makes herself one with her dying and risen Lord. As there is but one
Lord, all who identify themselves with Him are united in one spiritual
body (Romans 12:5; 1 Corinthians 12:12; Galatians 3:27–28; Ephesians
4:4–5). Thus the Eucharist is not only the supreme means of communion
between the faithful and their Lord; it is also the supreme means of the
communion of all the faithful, one with another. To join together in the
sacrament is the eminent mark of the unity of the Church (1 Corinthians
10:17). The unity expressed is not only the unity of the members of the
local worshipping congregation, though this is important. The congregation
which celebrates the Eucharist does so by virtue of its membership in the
universal Church, and as representing locally the universal Church. By
doing so it recollects and rejoices in its membership in the whole Church, on
earth and in heaven, and proclaims itself to be a part of the universal
Church. Thus the Eucharist is the sacrament of unity.

From this principle follow a number of important consequences. To join
in the Eucharist is a pledge of unreserved allegiance, not only to Christ,
but to His Church. Thus to be a communicant is the proper token of
pledged membership in the Church, of full status. Similarly for Christian
congregations or organizations of congregations to welcome each other's
members to their Eucharists is the token that they unreservedly regard one
another as portions of the one Church. Denominations which are thus "in
communion" with one another profess that any divergences between them of
teaching, discipline, order, and organization are in nonessentials only.
Similarly, for denominations not to be "in full communion" with one another
is the express and painful token that they feel some serious degree of
reserve about one another's Christian standing.

Thus the true aim of the ecumenical movement is not so much organizational as spiritual and sacramental. The purpose is not to achieve a "merger,"
on the dubious theory that a large organization is more efficient in the
service of God than a small one. The aim is to spread among the denomina-

tions such understanding of essential doctrine, such acceptance of essential order and discipline, and such growth of Christian charity that they may have the confidence to establish unreserved ecclesiastical communion with one another. However, this sacramental recognition is plainly not to be confined to an occasional and more or less formal ecclesiastical contact between religious organizations which in their normal and routine activity exist in a state of rivalry, or even of discord. This would be to make a mockery of the sacrament of unity! It is all too easy for diverse religious organizations which nominally are part of the same Christian communion practically to be separated by the spirit of rivalry and competition, and this is almost as great a scandal as the open and avowed ecclesiastical breach. To join in communion together must be the effective token of real goodwill in Christ, of genuine preparedness to learn from one another, and of regular, practical, brotherly cooperation in the work of the Church. This presupposes some effective degree of "organic union," visible and convincing to the world, though this is not the same as uniformity of worship or centralization of organization.

4. THE REAL PRESENCE. The traditional doctrine of the Real Presence is a strong affirmation of the experience of the Church that the universal presence of Christ is apprehended with unique power and certainty in the Eucharist. It certainly does not involve the naïve notion that Christ can be confined to a place. Our Lord in His risen and glorified humanity does not exist in space, and is always and equally "present" to every soul that calls upon Him. By the "presence" of Christ in worship is meant that at a certain time and place our Lord makes His universal presence effectually known to certain persons. It is the faith of the Church that Christ manifests His universal presence to the Church in a special manner in the Eucharist, which is thus seen to be the climax of all the means of grace.

We judge, however, that it is an error to suppose that in the Eucharist our Lord saves men in a different and superior manner than when He comes to man in the nonsacramental means of grace. The grace of God is the undeserved favor of God and the saving power of God, and whenever God loves and acts it is fully the work of grace. Grace is not a "thing," which can exist in different qualities. The special character of sacramental grace is not that it is "more saving" in effect, but that it is specially and securely pledged to man. Christ makes the very same saving presence known to the Church in praise and in prayer and in preaching, as in the Eucharist. Yet it is the profound religious conviction of traditional Christianity that in the sacrament He rises above the limitations and variability of human infirmity, and conveys His grace irrespective of the subjective conditions of religious emotion. Because the Eucharist is the special pledge of union with Him, He has pledged Himself with a unique guarantee to be there, which guarantee frail man can implicitly trust. Those who sincerely and expectantly take the sacramental pledge may on occasion not be able to "feel" anything.

Rather are they moved by conviction, by duty, and by discipline, and they may sometimes be painfully aware that at the moment they are unable to make any special response. Yet when from the viewpoint of later experience they look upon the long-continued practice of the Church's sacramental life, they find themselves unshakably aware that Christ *was* with His people, and *did* fulfill His promise. Thus it is not a special *kind* of grace, but a specially secure and *objective promise* of grace which is the virtue of the sacrament. The expression of this truth is the doctrine of the sacramental Real Presence of Christ.

5. TRANSUBSTANTIATION. This is the traditional Roman Catholic doctrine used to expound the character of the Real Presence of Christ in the Eucharist, or Mass. It is an attempt to express in the categories of the medieval Scholastic philosophy the secure and objective character of the sacramental manifestation of the presence of Christ. The medieval School-men drew a distinction between the outward "accidents" of any object (which correspond roughly to what in modern scientific terminology would be described as the chemical and physical properties of the object) and its "substance." The latter was conceived of as a subtle and invisible under-lying principle of existence which made the object what it was. The doctrine of the Roman Catholic Church is that at the consecration of the elements the invisible "substance" of the bread and wine is changed by divine power into the "substance" of the body and blood of the Lord, although the outward "accidents" remain the same. This change of substance is described as transubstantiation.

It is an error to charge Roman Catholic doctrine with teaching that there is a *material* change of bread and wine into flesh and blood, in the accepted modern sense of the word "material." The "accidents" remain the same, and the Scholastic notion of "accidents" most nearly corresponds to the idea of the material. The change is regarded as of an invisible and intangible underlying essence, which can only be described as non-material. Nor is it correct to charge this doctrine, when rightly understood at least, with teaching that the Lord is in a "place." The Roman Catholic Church shares the generally accepted Christian doctrine that the risen and ascended Christ is universally present. However, it is taught that the sacramental means by which the universal presence is most particularly and surely made known to the Church are the consecrated bread and wine as such, and these "means" *are* in a place. Therefore, while the consecrated elements remain in the church, the Lord is "present." This is a distinction from the more general doctrine of the sacramental Real Presence outlined in section (4) above, where the means of the manifestation of the presence of Christ is regarded as the sacramental action taken as a whole, but not the consecrated elements apart from the action of the worshipping con-gregation.

This doctrine has been the subject of violent controversy, which un-

Consubstantiation

happily has done much to make the sacrament of unity into a leading occasion of Christian disunity. So charged is the issue with inherited group emotion that it is sometimes hard for the parties to bring themselves to look at the matter dispassionately. This is the more reason why the effort should be made. The devout Roman Catholic, who has experienced a deep and Christian sense of the divine presence in the Mass, and who has been taught to associate this awesome experience with the doctrine of transubstantiation, finds it hard to understand that a devout Protestant can also have the sense of the divine presence, and yet deny this doctrine. He instinctively feels that the Protestant must be seriously deficient in his understanding of Christian worship, and that in his blindness he is rejecting or even assailing that which is very sacred. Equally instinctively the Protestant, who may have been taught to reject the doctrine of transubstantiation as a dangerous and materialist superstition, feels that the Roman Catholic Church has contaminated the worship of the Church with magic.

We are not arguing here that there is no effective difference between the two sides. There is a real difference of emphasis between Roman Catholic and Protestant, but it becomes a cause of ill will and spiritual reserve chiefly when each party does not understand what the other is trying to say. It is unfitting to talk lightly of "material superstition." In passing it should be noticed that the actual Canon of the Roman Mass does not itself require a belief in this doctrine, though this belief is a definite part of the doctrine of the Roman Catholic Church. Indeed, the Canon, which contents itself with reciting our Lord's words of institution, is older than the formulated doctrine of transubstantiation.

Protestant objections to the doctrine of transubstantiation are as follows: The Scholastic distinction between "substance" and "accidents" was not known in New Testament times, and therefore it can easily prove misleading to interpret the New Testament narrative in these categories. It is safer theologically, and devotionally more reverent, to be content with the New Testament doctrine as it stands, and not to seek to expound the exact manner of Christ's sacramental presence. Furthermore, in the period prior to the Protestant Reformation the idea was commonly held that, as the consecrated elements were truly the body and blood of the Lord, the sacrifice of the Mass was in some sense a repetition of Calvary, and thus added to the effect of Christ's saving work. This in turn gave rise to the doctrine that the Church could earn merit by the due saying of Masses. The Protestant Reformers strongly condemned this latter doctrine as inconsistent with the doctrine of salvation by grace, and therefore reacted also against the associated sacramental doctrine.

Other objections spring not so much from the actual doctrine itself, but from the way in which it can be, and has been, misunderstood by simple believers not competent in theology. Although the term "substance" may have meant one thing in the technical language of learned medieval theologians, it can come to mean something quite different in the common parlance of simple people. The word "substance" ordinarily conveys the notion of "the actual solid thing itself." Many Protestants therefore feel that the term "transubstantiation" invites the uninstructed to misunderstand the Roman Catholic doctrine as teaching a gross and material change in the elements. This in turn conveys the notion that the mere presence of the consecrated elements in the Church in some way brings a divine blessing to the congregation, perhaps without too much regard for their faith and morals. Therefore, the antique term "transubstantiation" should be avoided.

The informed Roman Catholic theologian will be quick to reply that these are misunderstandings of his doctrine, and that a doctrinal statement is not necessarily to be avoided because it is susceptible of misunderstanding, for this is possible with every system. It is indeed possible for a Roman Catholic to argue as follows, by way of a mediating statement. The decree of the Lateran Council of 1215, declaring the doctrine of transubstantiation to be a part of the faith of the Roman Catholic Church, is to be upheld. The Scholastic categories of "substance" and "accidents" were used at that time as the accepted means of expression, and in terms of those categories to have denied transubstantiation would have been false to the Catholic understanding of the sacramental Real Presence. Thus the Council was not in error in affirming this doctrine at that time. However, these categories of "substance" and "accidents" are not necessarily the only ones which can be used to express the essential faith of the Church. Today other and better terms might possibly be found to express to the modern mind the same fundamental devotional intention.

6. THE COMMEMORATIVE SACRIFICE. The incarnate Son as man offered up the sacrifice of sinless obedience to the Father, which enables all those who make themselves one with their great High Priest to have access to God (see pp. 80–81). The Eucharist, furthermore, is the act by which the Church makes herself one with Christ as He does this. There is, therefore, both a difference between Calvary and the Eucharist, and also a most significant parallel.

The sacrifice of the incarnate Son was a unique divine act which has transformed the situation of the whole race. There can never be anything else like it, and it is sufficient for the needs of all men. Nevertheless, both the Cross and the Eucharist express the fundamental sacrificial principle of "a God-appointed means by which man may offer himself to God in consecration and have spiritual access to God." The former is the sacrificial principle expressed once for all in the divine saving act. The latter is the sacrificial principle expressed and ever renewed in the experience of the Church, on account of that unique divine saving act. Thus the Eucharist, though not a *repetition* of Christ's atoning sacrifice, is the Church's "commemorative sacrifice." This term may perhaps be illustrated by comparison with a great piece of music. The first composition is a unique work of creative art, never to be repeated. Nevertheless, the composer has left the score behind, and to play this through again is likewise a work of creative art, though derived from the first. It is the means by which the effect of the first unique work is mediated again and yet again to later times. These succeeding renderings are "commemorations." So the commemorative sacrifice of the Eucharist is, as it were, "playing through the score again" of Christ's unique and sufficient sacrifice of the Cross. It is the means appointed by God for the realization in the Church's present experience of the effect of Christ's sacrifice.

Readings

Baillie, D. M., *The Theology of the Sacraments*. New York: Charles Scribner's Sons, 1957.

Buttrick, G., *Prayer*. New York: Abingdon Press, 1942.

Cullmann, O., and F. J. Leenhardt, *Essays on the Lord's Supper,* trans. J. G. Davies. Richmond, Va.: John Knox Press, 1958.

Dix, G., *The Shape of the Liturgy*. Westminster: Dacre Press, 1949. (Historical Study.)

Lampe, G. W. H., *The Seal of the Spirit*. London: Longmans, Green & Company, Ltd., 1951. (Baptism and Confirmation.)

Quick, O. C., *The Christian Sacraments*. New York and London: Harper & Row, Publishers, 1927.

Chapter Eight

The Written Word

The Holy Ghost—who spake by the prophets

I. The Witness to the Christ-Centered Faith

Christian worship and preaching are delivered from subjectivity and lifted above the level of mere autosuggestion and mass suggestion by the circumstance that the center of all is Christ. When Christians assemble they are not seeking to stir up their own natural powers of mind and spirit by contact with one another, but expecting that Christ will use these natural powers as the means by which He makes Himself known. Furthermore, Christ is both the Christ of history, who was born, lived, spoke, died, and rose again, and also the living Christ of continuing Christian experience. These two are one. It cannot be too strongly emphasized that the Christ of Christian faith is not a "Christ-idea," which has been framed by the mind of the Church to symbolize certain spiritual truths. He is the Christ who at a certain place and time performed a saving act, which act has brought into the world a divine power not to be explained in terms of human personality.

Acceptance of the historical facts about Christ is not of itself saving Christian faith, though it is the foundation of faith. Thus, some even who looked into the empty tomb did not believe. Those who are confronted by the living Christ in the experience of the Church and in personal experience, are they to whom are granted saving faith. In this sense, the Christ known to the Church is "the Christ of faith," and not simply "the Christ of history." Nevertheless, personal faith in "the Christ of faith" can hardly endure without acceptance of the foundation of this experience in "the Christ of history" (see pp. 38–39).

These two kindred principles, that the Christian religion is an historical religion, and that it is a Christ-centered religion, require us to consider a further special aspect of the means of grace. This is the Christian doctrine of the record which preserves for the Church both her knowledge of the facts about Christ and the portrait of the personality of Christ. This record is the Holy Scripture. Thus it is a guiding principle of all true Christian worship and preaching that it is scriptural worship and scriptural preaching.

II. The Inspiration of the Bible

It is important to understand the nature and origin of a book which occupies this central place in the life of the Church. This is the more so because the divine inspiration and the authority of the Bible have become at times the subject of misunderstanding and of controversy. Ill-advised claims on behalf of the inspiration of Scripture have sometimes produced their unfortunate reaction in a virtual denial of this truth, and in the dismissal of the conception of the authority of the Bible. Among scholars and experts the Scripture has sometimes been treated as no more than an important "source document" in the study of Christian origins. This is a radical departure from the acknowledged Christian position. The general body of believers has often been disturbed by the erroneous impression that modern science and biblical scholarship have in some way dethroned the Bible as the book of God.

We have already defined the meaning of the term "inspiration" (see pp. 24–25). It is the quickening and stimulation of man's natural powers of mind and spirit by the indwelling Holy Spirit, to enable him more fully and clearly to understand, and to declare, the revelation which God is making known. Divine inspiration does not suspend the operation of the natural human faculties, but lifts them above that spiritual infirmity which is natural to sinful man so that they may more fully act as God originally intended. The inspired man, therefore, is not a man "lifted out of himself," but the fully *human* man, the man who is fully rational, morally responsible, and intelligent in spiritual things. All great art and creative writing is to some extent the work of divine inspiration, but it is the faith of the Church that the inspiration of Holy Scripture is the supreme example of this process. Certainly many of the writers both of the Old and of the New Testament were profoundly aware that they were writing because God had in this way laid His hand upon them and given them something from Himself to declare (Isaiah 6:7–8; Jeremiah 1:4–10; Ezekiel 2:1–3, 3:4–11; Amos 7:14–15; 1 Corinthians 2:9–13; Galatians 1:11–12; Ephesians 3:1–4; Revelation 1:10–11, 19).

The authority of the Bible consists essentially in its contents, rather than in the manner of its writing. The manner in which the book was composed under the guidance of the Spirit is of interest to the Church, but it is the actual message from God which is of importance. The special place of the Bible in the Church lies in the fact that it gives the essential, the sole, and the sufficient witness to the facts about Christ. In the Old Testament there is the story of the historical preparation of the people to whom Christ came, and the account therefore of the religious and moral thought forms of the people among whom He moved.

The New Testament is still more directly a witness to Christ, for it is the sole and sufficient account of the essential facts about Christ—His birth, His personality and character, His acts, His teaching, His death, resurrection, and ascension. In this sense Christ, who is the Word of God and the central subject of Christian preaching, is "contained in the Scripture of the Old and New Testaments." The New Testament also gives the record of the creative witness to the meaning of these facts for Christian faith. This is a witness of faith which, because it is the first in time and made by those who, historically speaking, knew Christ in a way no others ever can, is determinative for the witness of faith in all succeeding Christian generations. It is this unique content of witness to Christ which to the Church makes the Bible entirely different from all other works of Christian devotion or theology, no matter how true and divinely inspired they may be.

Summary of Divergence: Doctrines of Scriptural Inspiration

a. *Allegorical*

This is the view characteristic of the ancient Church, though to some extent it still lives on in traditional Christian circles alongside later views. It is assumed that the inspired writers were guided by the Holy Spirit as to the very form, wording, and literary character of their composition, so that it is possible to argue theological truth from these forms. Furthermore, the writers were so lifted above normal human faculty that they were able to utter oracles containing forecasts, often mysterious and veiled, of events in the life of Christ, though this was far in the future. However, the emphasis in ancient exegesis was not upon the significance of historical detail in the narrative, though this was not denied. The Scripture was read, by the method of allegory, as a series of symbolically appropriate pictures of Christian truth. A particular example of this approach was the finding of "types of Christ" in the Old Testament. Thus it is affirmed that the inward and "spiritual" meaning of Scripture is of a higher order than the merely literal and factual.

This method comes to its fullest development in the traditional doctrine that corresponding to the threefold nature of man—body, mind, and spirit—there is an ascending threefold sense of Scripture. The lowest, and, as it were, "bodily" sense of Scripture is the literal and historical. So we may read Genesis 22:1–14 as a narrative, that Abraham was prepared to offer Isaac in sacrifice. Next there is the moral sense, corresponding to the mind in man. Thus this passage displays an example of obedience to God which ought to be followed. Yet the really Christian and most precious sense, which alone lights up the meaning of the Scripture, is the "spiritual." This story is "a type of Christ." On this mount of sacrifice the Temple later stood, the place of the Old Testament sacrifices. It was the place also of the Lord's death, when the full meaning is seen of Abraham's prophetic oracle: "My son, God will provide Himself a lamb." This example is typical of ancient exegesis, which was fertile in reading the Scripture as a source of Christian doctrine and edification, but at the price of the danger of fanciful subjectivity.

b. Literal

This school of thought, though not unknown in antiquity, has chiefly been characteristic of orthodox and conservative Protestantism. The motive has been to emphasize as strongly as possible the clear, self-sufficient, and objective authority of Scripture against any school of thought which would give undue weight to the authority of ecclesiastical interpretation in the approach to Scripture. The tendency has been to emphasize the spiritual value of the literal and factual accuracy of the text of Scripture. This principle can be applied in various degrees. Some of this school can allow considerable room in the composition of Scripture for the play of human personality and the mental background of the times, so long as its self-sufficient objective authority is affirmed. The strictest doctrine is that of complete verbal inspiration, by which it is affirmed that the Holy Spirit so completely guided every word of the Biblical writers that the Scripture is virtually the inerrant dictation of God.

c. Historico-Critical

This view is concerned to determine so far as possible the sense which was in the mind of the biblical writers as they wrote. This alone is considered the legitimate meaning of Scripture. Applied Christian allegorical interpretations are rejected as unscientific. The widest play is allowed for the free human personality and idiosyncrasy of the writers, and that they must all be understood to speak in terms of the thought forms of their own day and culture. Some critics go so far as to treat the text of Scripture simply as one source document among many others, so that the traditional sense of the authority of canonical Scripture is virtually lost. To the devout scholar of this method, however, it is evident that many of the biblical writers possessed faculties of creative genius of the highest order. Nevertheless, these vary in kind and in degree from chapter to chapter. Nor are these creative faculties different in kind from those which have gone to the composition of other great but nonbiblical literary works. Furthermore, some biblical writers are more spiritually sensitive and mature, more obediently led by the influence of the Holy Spirit, than others. This spiritual leading, furthermore, is not different in kind from that which has gone to the composition of nonbiblical Christian works.

Thus, when the manner of composition is considered, the Bible is one venerable book among others, to the Christian supreme in its class, no doubt, but not different in kind. In this sense of the word its "inspiration" may be compared to that of other books of wisdom or devotion. It is different only in degree and manner. The difference in the Bible, whereby Scripture stands apart from other books, is in its contents. For the Scripture to be fully authoritative in its content, as a witness to Christ the Word of God, does not require that its writers be lifted to a superhuman inerrancy in their composition. It only requires that their human faculties were sufficiently guided by the Holy Spirit that they were substantially reliable witnesses.

Thus, by way of comparison, the radio transmission of an SOS message upon which the lives of men depend may be marred to some extent by interference or static. Yet provided the medium of transmission is clear enough to convey the message, the message comes with full urgency, which is not increased even if the transmission happens to be technically perfect. A reliable medium is required, but the authority is in the content of the message, not the medium. So it is with the Bible. The true task of Christian scholarship in relation to the religious authority of the Bible is not the fruitless effort to prove that it was written in a "different" and superhuman way. It is to vindicate its *content*.

III.   The Canon of Scripture

The Greek word "canon" means a rule, or measuring rod. The canon of Scripture is the list of books recognized by the Church as authoritative Scripture, and as such set apart from all other books. The mark of canonical Scripture is that it may be read in Church as a regular part of Christian worship and quoted in proof of doctrine. Clearly, any doctrine of the authority of Scripture must include an exposition of the authority of the canon, for a decision must be made and justified as to which books are authoritative. This is best illustrated by the historical process by which certain writings have become regarded as canonical Scripture in Judaism and in the Church.

In general, the doctrine of an authoritative canon is a salient example of the belief that the Holy Spirit effectually guides the Church. Those who composed the biblical narratives (very often originally in the form of oral tradition, before it was recorded in writing) were aware that the Holy Spirit was moving them to set down what they felt was of high religious importance. Yet as they wrote they would hardly have looked upon it as different from other and "human" religious composition. Nevertheless, the passage of centuries showed that these writings could meet the searching test of long-continued experience. Many books of religious worth made a partial appeal to the community. They were valued perhaps by a section, and for a time. Nevertheless, they never rose beyond the status of religious literature. Other books made a more significant appeal. They increased in repute until they were accepted by the whole, or virtually the whole, of the community, as of the highest degree of religious value.

The long passage of time saw this estimate endure, and be confirmed by the experience of succeeding generations, until respect deepened into a characteristic traditional veneration. By the force of traditional judgment certain books were thus set apart from others, until the appeal could be made that a certain text is authoritative because it occurs in the sacred collection. The original sanction of the repute of the writer, or of the immediate appeal which the book made, is now superseded by this traditional sanction. The final stage is when the verdict of the whole community is officially ratified by ecclesiastical authority. In Judaism a group of rabbis, in the ancient Christian Church a council of bishops, pronounced that certain books were by long, universal, and established consent regarded as canonical Scripture.

This final stage is not to be regarded as an external and artificial process of "censorship," whereby ecclesiastical authority suppresses some books and adds its authority to others. The history of the canon shows a much more profound and spiritual process. The books were set apart by the place which they established for themselves, and authority then ratified the verdict. As we, from the vantage-point of time, look back and compare the books which were accepted as canonical with those which were set aside, we may have confidence that the early Church was guided by the Holy Spirit in the choice which was actually made. Again we see that God granted the spiritual through the natural. The process took place through a human medium, and was not inerrant. There were some "borderline cases" of choice. Some books were accepted as canonical more readily than others, and in the case of some of the minor books both of the Old and New Testaments it is possible for the critic to dispute whether there are not some other noncanonical books of equal intrinsic merit. Nevertheless, the general and substantial judgment of the Church is to be upheld as an authoritative act of guidance by the Holy Spirit.

A glance at the actual historical process illustrates the general principle that the venerable is the canonical. The classification of Luke 24:44 sets forth the threefold division of the Jewish Scriptures, as reckoned by the rabbis. The five books of the Law (Genesis–Deuteronomy) were, and still are, regarded by Judaism as canonical Scripture to the most eminent degree. They were accepted as a body of canonical Scripture by about 400 B.C. The secondary division called "the prophets," which in Judaism includes

Joshua, 1 and 2 Samuel, and 1 and 2 Kings (as Christians count them), as well as the greater and the minor prophets (apart from Daniel), was canonized later, about 200 B.C. The "sacred writings," comprising the remaining books of the Old Testament proper, became regarded in the succeeding period as in some sense Scripture, largely because of the use made of them in the Jewish worship and festivals. However, in the period when the Jews of the Dispersion increasingly came to speak and write in Greek, the accumulation of religious books still continued. Consequently the Septuagint, or ancient Greek translation of the Old Testament, contains more books than does the Hebrew canon. The traditionally minded rabbis maintained a certain reserve about these more recent books. This is the part of the Bible commonly known to us as the Apocrypha. It is noteworthy that among the Dead Sea Scrolls Hebrew originals have been found to some of these books of the Apocrypha, which traditionally have only circulated in the Church in Greek or Latin translation.

The Church of the early centuries commonly used the Septuagint, and is found to quote the Apocrypha as "Scripture," in the same way as the books of the Hebrew Old Testament. However, some of the more learned Christian fathers, and in particular St. Jerome (A.D. 347–419), the translator of the Hebrew Old Testament and Greek New Testament into the Latin Vulgate, were aware of this distinction of canonicity between the ancient Hebrew Bible and the newer Greek Apocrypha. Nevertheless, the Latin Vulgate, containing as it does the Apocrypha, was used as authoritative Scripture by the Western Church down to the Reformation, as it still is by the Roman Catholic Church. The Protestants were in general glad to revive the ancient distinction between the older and fully authoritative Hebrew Old Testament and the later Greek Apocrypha, largely because the leading traditional "proof texts" for prayers for the dead, and so forth, occurred in this latter part. The Church of England, however, as in some other things, established a compromise. Passages from the Apocrypha were continued in the lectionary to be read in public worship, but the books of the Apocrypha are not to be used for the establishment of doctrine.

The same process by which the venerable graduates upwards into the canonical may be seen to take place in relation to the New Testament writings. Where in the New Testament itself "the Scriptures" are referred to, the Jewish Scriptures are intended. In the first Christian writings after the New Testament this usage is continued, and the Old Testament is alone quoted expressly as "Scripture." However, the words of our Lord are also cited as a ruling authority, and the writings of the apostles likewise as an authority. Nevertheless, this apostolic authority is not yet that of a traditional canonical book, but a personal authority. The New Testament writings are of authority in this early period because they are the substitute for the personal presence of an apostle, who is the primary witness to the gospel. Hence is derived the traditional Christian doctrine that the New Testament canon is constituted out of "apostolic writings," that is, the writings of apostles, or of the immediate disciples of apostles, who are to be regarded as virtually their amanuenses. The leading books of the New Testament rapidly gained place during the second century as a distinct body of authoritative writings, which might be read in Christian worship alongside the ancient Scripture. By the fourth century our present New Testament canon was virtually fixed and accepted, and in the Council of A.D. 692 was expressly ratified.

IV. The Old Testament Scripture

A. Historical and Linguistic Value

The unique value of the Old Testament as Christian Scripture is that it is the story of the historical preparation of the ancient people of God for the coming of Christ. Here is the principle that Christianity is a religion embedded in history. The Christian Faith carries with it a system of thought and of ethics, but essentially it is a religion of redemption, founded upon the saving acts which God has performed in history. These acts form a long historical series, leading one from another up to the climax in the Incarnation, death, and resurrection of Christ, and proceeding down from that climax, since that time, in the acts of the Holy Spirit in the Church. It is impossible fully to understand the Christian climax without a view of the whole process. Therefore to the Church the Old Testament is Scripture speaking of Christ. The essential element in the Old Testament is that it is the story of God's choice of the chosen people at the beginning; of their deliverance from bondage, which constituted them into a nation; of the formation of their national and religious institutions; and of the subsequent long and often painful process of their education, through historical experience, in understanding of the nature and ways of God.

In this account we again see that God gives the spiritual through the natural. Most impartial scholars would allow that the history, considered as history, is not inerrant as to fact. It is history composed according to the mentality and methods of antiquity, and not according to modern critical and scientific methods. Scholars of the Old Testament have to make allowance for this. Nevertheless, the historical narrative is such that it bears effective witness to the divine process in history. Thus the deliverance at the Red Sea is certainly not described as it would be by a modern secular historian, but an authentic witness is preserved that a deliverance did take place, and in particular, an interpretation is given of the religious meaning of this event. Furthermore, it is easy to regard too lightly the value of the Old Testament narrative as a historical source in the modern sense of the word. Many critics have made haste to dismiss this or that narrative as "unreliable," or "legendary," only to discover that later historical and archaeological research has wholly or partially vindicated the biblical record.

An important aspect of this value of the Old Testament is the linguistic. Our Lord spoke to the people of the Old Testament, using their thought forms. The first apostles, who interpreted the meaning of Christ, employed the same Old Testament thought forms. Therefore the meaning of phrases and words in the New Testament cannot be fully and accurately grasped without an understanding of what these words mean in the Jewish background of Christianity. There are some elements in the New Testament which are perhaps to be interpreted, at least in part, by reference to the Gentile background of the ancient Church. By and large, however, the New Testament is to be understood in light of the Old. Thus many leading words in the Greek New Testament, such as "the righteousness of God," "the wrath of God," "propitiation," and so forth, will be misunderstood if they are given the meaning they would normally carry in pagan Greek literature. The Greek Old Testament gives the correct sense.

B. Progressive Revelation

If the Old Testament is the record of a process of historical education and discipline, some lessons will be found more advanced than others. The point of departure for the process of education was the religious outlook natural to antiquity. The Hebrew people started their history as one Semitic tribe among many in the Middle East, having a tribal religion similar to that of other kindred peoples (Joshua 24:2). By the end of the process they revealed themselves to be the people of the prophets, a nation with a unique genius for religion. However, there are many passages in the Old Testament which represent the partial process of growth and education, where the primitive background and the new lesson are mingled. Thus in some Old Testament narratives there are displayed conceptions of God and of His will which are not to be defended as fully Christian.

On the other hand, it is not to be assumed that narratives later in time are necessarily more advanced in spiritual understanding. Spiritual religion does not simply "develop" in an evolutionary manner. The disciples of great prophetic leaders can painfully lag behind, so that religious movements may deteriorate and fall into corruption, as well as advance, with the passage of time. Therefore, the Old Testament as a whole is to be interpreted both in the light of the finest things in it, and in light of the New Testament, with its clearer standards declared by Christ. The Bible, in fact, is not a collection of "proof texts" to be quoted in isolation from one another. It is to be read as a religious whole, as an historical "progressive revelation" in many stages, though all coming from one and the same God.

C. Devotional Value

Pressing close behind the essential historical revelation in value is the devotional treasure of the Old Testament. When it is stated that the ancient Hebrews possessed a unique genius for religion it is not intended that they were all virtuous. The Old Testament itself is full of rebukes for the sins of the people. What they had was a very vivid sense that God is real and important, so that religion is a matter of immense concern. God is sovereign, majestic, active, near. Even if a Hebrew disobeyed God he had a great sense that he was sinning, not merely against tribal taboo or conventional morality, but against a mighty God. This "sense of God" is a leading characteristic of the Biblical narrative, and is the surest mark of its divine inspiration.

For example, compare the Genesis stories symbolizing the creation of the world and the origin of the human race with the parallel stories in pagan mythology. Certain general similarities are to be observed, and one highly significant difference. This is the portrait of God which appears in the biblical narrative. Greek mythology may tellingly symbolize certain truths, and do so with great artistry. Yet the Greek gods, with their infirmities, their faults, and their quarrels, are not such as to command the reverence of the thoughtful and intelligent man. In the biblical narratives there may be found a prescientific and a nonphilosophical view of God, but there is a spiritually adult view of God. He is a great God, of right and truth, who commands the reverence of men. So it is when we come to the story of a military hero like Gideon. This is not told, as are the hero-stories of the Gentiles, to display from what great men the nation is descended, but "to justify the ways of God to men." The Lord is the most important character in the story, and it is told to His glory. This "sense of God" runs through the whole of the Old Testament, and comes to its climax in the splendid devotional poetry of the Psalms and prophets.

An artist looks at an apparently commonplace face or landscape and beholds in it a beauty which less sensitive eyes cannot see. As he paints he enables us to see something of what he can see, so that we come to look upon the object itself to some extent with an artist's eye. In the same way, the Bible looks on every part of life from the point of view of a man to whom God is the most pressing reality of existence. As we follow his meditations, and read his narrative, we begin in his company to look at life from that point of view. We see life no longer from the commonplace point of view, but as it exists under the eye of God. This is the first and indispensable lesson of religion. There are many humane and educated men today who have a much more developed view of the nature of God than did most of the ancient Hebrews. However, He is to them a part of the academic theory of life. They can argue about God to a nicety, but have little comprehension of what it means when one reads: "And the Lord spake unto Moses face to face, as a man speaketh unto his friend" (Exodus 33:11). This is where the Church of all ages, and of today, can learn from the Old Testament. Even narratives which express a less than perfectly Christian view of God are full of the sense of God, and so can teach the sense of God. Thus it is not necessary to vindicate at every point the morality of the stories of the patriarchs, the judges, or even of the prophets. They still make a contribution to Christian devotions.

A leading example of this principle is the use of Scripture in Church service. When the Bible is read in public worship it is read not so much informatively as *liturgically*. Rendered into magnificent, dignified, and poetic English the elevated chapters of the Scripture are read and preached from, and hymns and prayers framed in the thought forms and language of the Bible are used, in order to help the worshipping congregation to *feel* in a certain way. Having caught the sense of solemn awe men begin to exclaim, "Surely the Lord is in this place," and "How dreadful is this place!" (Genesis 28:16, 17). They have then learned the first essential lesson of religion, and can go on to instruction in Christian faith and morals. Herein is the devotional value of the Bible, and not least, of the Old Testament.

D. Prophecy of Christ

The Christian position is that the Scriptures of the Old and New Testaments together form one series, so that each part is to be understood in the light of the other. This doctrine has in Christian tradition been expressed in a particular way, which requires some measure of judicious restatement and modification if it is to be usefully preserved in the modern Church. One of the first great issues which faced the growing Gentile Church of the early centuries was whether it should preserve its living link with its Judaic past. The symbol of this dispute was naturally the position of the venerable Hebrew Scriptures in the Church as Christian Scripture. One of the chief spiritual considerations which guided the Church to keep the Old Testament was the desire to preserve the "argument from prophecy."

From the beginning it was realized that large numbers of passages in the Old Testament, hundreds of years old, could with a little ingenuity and selection be read as forecasts of all sorts of details of the life of Christ, and sometimes most unexpected and mysterious details. This gift of apparently divine prescience was treated as a sure token of the divine inspiration of the Bible, and so of its authority. By way of salient example, the accepted Septuagint text of Isaiah 7:14 read like a forecast of the Virgin Birth of Christ, an event so remarkable that no human mind could have foreseen it. To the ancient Church this demonstrated the divine origin of the prophecy, and the prophecy, thus vindicated as of divine authority, could in turn be used in proof of the Christian doctrine.

Although on the one hand many conservatively minded Christians still feel much of the force of this venerable mode of argument, and it is expressed freely in the liturgy of the Church, it must be admitted that this method of presenting the spiritual continuity of the Old and New Testaments, though immensely convincing to Christian antiquity, is much less so today. The great growth of historical and linguistic knowledge, and of the principles of scientific criticism of ancient narratives, has brought to the Church a much clearer knowledge than she has ever had of the original and historical meaning of all manner of biblical texts, which were previously often most mysterious. This process has in general demonstrated that these traditional Christian "prophetic" meanings are often not what was in the mind of the biblical writers when they composed their narratives. They are secondary meanings which have been read into the text by later Christian faith. To the scientific scholar the Old Testament is no longer a book packed with mysterious forecasts of Christian doctrine, and of details of the life of Christ. It looks as though the validity of the venerable "argument from prophecy" is overthrown.

However, reconsideration indicates that the vital Christian doctrinal interest is to vindicate the spiritual continuity of the historical process by which the religion of the Old Covenant prepared the way for Christ. Christian faith wishes to see the foreseeing wisdom of God at work in history, revealing Himself. The traditional method of stating this interest can be modified or even abandoned, if the interest itself may be preserved.

In the first place, prophecy does speak of the expectation of the Messiah, in general terms, and our Lord did claim to fulfill that expectation. The basis of the Christian faith is that this claim is true. In the second place, our Lord molded much of His teaching and activity in terms of Old Testament messianic prophecy, even to the point on occasion of literally enacting events spoken of in prophetic oracles. Thus in the most notable instance, Zechariah 9:9 had symbolized the nonmilitary character of the expected Messiah by writing of Him as "lowly, and riding upon an ass." As a sign to the people of what manner of Messiah He was, Christ literally rode into Jerusalem upon this unwarlike animal. Thus the idea of the fulfillment of detailed events is not wholly to be excluded. In the third place, however, there is another way in which our Lord "fulfilled" Old Testament prophecy, which to many thoughtful believers may well appear more spiritually satisfying. In the great passages of the Old Testament there are authentic though partial glimpses of great spiritual principles which are perfectly set forth in the person, teaching, and saving work of our Lord. Our Lord fulfilled the Old Testament prophecy in the sense that He filled it to the full. He realized the potentiality of what had been dreamed of by visionaries.

The great example of this, which serves to illuminate others, is our Lord's treatment of the great passage Isaiah 52:13–53:12. From the first days of the Church (Acts 8:30–35) the "Song of the Suffering Servant" has been the key example of "Old Testament prophecy fulfilled." We remember that our Lord Himself gave precedent for the traditional exposition whereby today we cannot read this chapter without thinking of Christ and His atonement.[1] There is thus the highest sanction for the proposition that it may be

---

[1] The Jewish exegetes did not read this passage as referring to a *suffering* Messiah.

devotionally fitting to read a secondary and Christian application into an Old Testament Scripture.

There has been much dispute as to what the original writer meant by "the Servant of the Lord." The usual construction is that he is a personification of Israel, or of the righteous nucleus of Israel, or perhaps of the ideal Israel. In drawing the figure, some actual martyred individual may also be in mind. In this passage the judgment of conventional piety is dismissed, that the overwhelming and repulsive sufferings of God's people are simply the punishment for sin. Rather are God's relatively righteous people suffering to work the blessing of the unrighteous pagans, who behold in amazement this mysterious divine plan. Here in this piece of prophetic insight is a passing glimpse of the principle which the sacrificial sufferings of Christ perfectly exemplified. As He read this passage He saw in it a picture of what He knew His own destiny to be, and so on at least one most significant occasion He expressly applied it to Himself, and to His mission of suffering (Isaiah 53:12 in Luke 22:37).[2] It is doubtless also the chief among the passages referred to in Luke 24:25–27. Thus there is a continuity of spiritual type from Isaiah 53 to our Lord's own view of His messianic death. The same God can be seen at work in both, in the first preparing the way by a partial vision, in the second "fulfilling." This remains the case even if the supposition of detailed forecasts of events in the life of Christ is abandoned.

V. The New Testament Scripture

A. The Apostolic Witness

The supreme treasure in Scripture, which gives the Bible its special place in Christian doctrine and devotion, is that it gives the historic witness to Christ. It is the indispensable, the sole, and the sufficient witness. The essential office of an apostle was to be a witness to the facts about Christ—His life, His teaching, His deeds, His death, and supremely, the fact of His resurrection (Acts 1:21–22). This was the testimony to the saving act of God in Christ, upon which Christian faith rests. As the apostles were taken from the Church by death their unique office as immediate personal witnesses came to an end. As a substitute for, and as a sufficient continuation of, their witness the Church treasured the apostolic writings. This historic witness is the heart of the New Testament.

The interest of the Evangelists in composing the Gospels is not biographical, in the accepted modern sense of the word. They are not recording

---

2 It is only fair to note that those radical critics who do not accept the general historical character of the Gospel narratives would treat this as an example of an incident constructed by the Church to symbolize its devotion. It would be claimed that the words have been placed on the lips of Jesus so as to create a "prophecy fulfilled." This would apply also to Zechariah 9:9 (p. 194).

data for the purpose of providing raw materials for the authorship of "Lives of Jesus." A modern-style biography of our Lord would give a dispassionate treatment of every part equally of Christ's life and activity, and a clear outline of the order of events, and of the places where things happened. It is well known that the Gospels do not give this. For example, our Lord's early life in Nazareth is passed over in almost complete silence A third of St. Mark's Gospel is devoted to recording the circumstances of Christ's death, which is a curious proportion for a biography. A comparison of the Gospels will show that His teaching is recorded in a variable order, which is plainly due to the Evangelists more than to the course of events. The purpose of the Gospel writers is evangelical rather than biographical. They are recounting such of the facts about Christ as were remembered in the Church because they were important for Christian faith and discipleship, and recounting them in such a way as to bring the reader to Christian faith (John 20:30–31).

It must be clearly kept in mind, however, that this does not of itself serve to hold in question the authenticity and value, as biographical evidence, of the facts recorded. It only means that there is no secure evidence for a *complete* and orderly biography. The Evangelists were well aware that theirs was an historical faith, the advancement and preservation of which depended on the recording of facts (Luke 1:1–4). Unless some other evidence is brought forward to impugn their accuracy, the mere fact that their interest is evangelical rather than biographical does not of itself assail the historicity of the Gospels.

Another important circumstance which is at times rather overlooked in current discussion of the New Testament is that the ethical teaching of our Lord is an integral part of the Gospel message. It is the case that the essential and uniquely Christian element of the Gospel is the message about the saving act of God in Christ, in His Incarnation, death, resurrection, and ascension.[3] However, our Lord is also the master of disciples who follow Him. His teaching is their authoritative rule for ethical conduct in the new life in Christ and for the government of the Church (Acts 20:35; Romans 12:20; 1 Corinthians 7:10, cf. v. 25; 1 Corinthians 9:14, 11:23; Ephesians 5:31; James 2:8, 5:12; 1 Peter 2:21–23). The ethical teaching of our Lord is not absolutely different in kind from that of other prophetic teachers. Indeed a great part of it is reproduced from the Old Testament, being selected from the loftiest and most spiritual strain of prophetic Judaism. So also there are many parallels to be found between the teaching of Jesus and current rabbinical maxims. Furthermore, many noble principles enunciated in the teachings of non-Christian religious leaders, moralists, and philosophers show parallels in the words of Christ. However, it has never been part of the essential Christian position to affirm that our Lord's

---

[3] This essential message of the saving act of God in Christ is the so-called primitive Christian *kerygma,* "thing preached" (1 Corinthians 1:21).

unique position depends upon the character of His moral teaching. It rests upon His divine saving work.

Nevertheless, the Christian will claim that our Lord's teaching is the focus of all that is good, and that He excels all other masters in grace and balance, and in freedom from the partiality and prejudice of a particular time or race or circumstance of life. And the proclamation of this teaching as the rule of life to be obeyed by the Church has been from the beginning a part of the essential Christian message. Indeed, a leading reason why particular sayings and parables were remembered by the Church in the period of oral tradition, and so found their way into the written Gospels, was that they were of interest to the Church to provide "a word from the Lord" in guidance upon some point of Christian conduct or ecclesiastical discipline.

B. The Authenticity of the Witness

This is almost certainly the most important present-day issue of New Testament scholarship. We have seen on the one hand the manner in which Christian faith, as an historical religion of God's gracious saving act in Jesus Christ, depends upon the facts concerning Christ. On the other hand, the substantially historical character of the Gospel record has in the modern period been assailed as never before by many radical critics possessed of great academic learning. This matter has already been referred to in what has been written above on the theme of Christian faith and the historical Jesus (see pp. 35–38). A discussion of the authenticity of the Gospel portrait of Jesus must now be taken further. Those who are convinced that loyalty to traditional Christian faith compels them to adopt the literal view of Biblical inspiration will naturally reject this whole discussion as erroneous, or even impious. On the other hand, those who acknowledge that the methods of critical analysis and historical investigation developed by modern New Testament scholarship are to be accepted as technically sound within their own field are faced with a far-reaching issue of judgment.

This issue is: How far are the methods of this admitted technique to be pressed? Is it the case that the portrait of Christ, His life, character, and teaching, recorded in the Gospels is substantially reliable history, though with a few minor interpretative touches added as the narrative was transmitted through the believing consciousness of the Church? Or is the interpretative element considerable? Or has most of the Gospel portrait of Christ actually been constructed out of the believing mind of the Church, as the Christians sought imaginatively to symbolize their faith—with the consequence that we know little for certain about historic Christ? This issue, we affirm, is one of interpretative attitude brought to the New Testament, rather than of secure objective evidence contained in the New Testament narrative itself. We have stated that a mediating judgment is to be preferred, which does not seek to deny the techniques of modern New Testament scholarship, but which insists that the scholar can speak honestly and meaningfully of an authentic historic Christ (see pp. 38–41). It is now necessary to consider some reasons in support of this judgment.

The canons of interpretation to be suggested are three: (1) the consistency of the Gospel portrait of Christ, (2) the spiritual majesty of the Gospel portrait of Christ, (3) the continuity of type in Christian thought.

1. THE CONSISTENCY OF THE GOSPELS. One of the most significant facts about the four Gospels is that although they belong to different traditions there is an underlying unity of treatment. There are differences of attitude toward the Christian life between the Jewish-Christian First Gospel and the Pauline Third Gospel, and this affects to some extent the representation of Christ Himself. Yet the Christ portrayed by the two is recognizably the same figure. There is a greater divergence between the Synoptic Gospels and the Fourth Gospel, for there is a more developed element of doctrinal interpretation in the latter, and along a very definite line. Nevertheless, there would appear to be an underlying unity of doctrine between the Synoptics and St. John. A very large part of the striking superficial difference of treatment is that doctrinal implications in the earlier Gospels have been made explicit in the later. Thus in St. John the "divine claims" of our Lord are made in distinctly formulated statements from His lips, but they do not in fact claim more in substance than the *implications* of what Christ says about Himself in the synoptic narrative.

So also, when we turn to doctrinal interpretations of Christ, there are various lines of development represented in the literature of the New Testament, such as the Pauline, the Johannine, the Epistle to the Hebrews, and the Revelation of St. John. There are striking differences of treatment, yet these are not contrary one to another. Thus in the Fourth Gospel the original eschatology is greatly modified, while in the Revelation it is displayed in vivid Jewish clothing. Yet in St. John the eschatology is *modified* and restated, not merely eliminated, whereas the eschatology of the Revelation is *Christian* eschatology, not merely Jewish eschatology in disguise. Even across the widest of New Testament divergences there is a similarity of type. There are two contrasting aspects of the same Christian faith, not two faiths. In general the distinctive elements of the various schools of New Testament thought are interpretations of the same object of faith, and are complementary to one another in a full understanding of our Lord.

If it were indeed the case that the greater part of the New Testament representation of the person and teaching of Jesus Christ was the imaginative construction of the Church, it is almost inconceivable that the New Testament could present this unity. The ecclesiastical and dogmatic interests of the different groups of Christians would have had nothing to check them in their free development. There would have been no original central tradition within which local variations could arise. The "variations" would have constituted virtually the whole of Christianity. The New Testament, if by chance it had ever come together into one canon, would have contained a number of entirely divergent portraits of Christ, and a number of doctrinal interpretations having no real contact with one another beyond the bare name of Christ.

This is plainly not the case. The various interpretations must have taken their origin from an historical figure sufficient to account for the many and leading elements found in common in all the various traditions. This involves that the general picture of our Lord painted in the Gospels may be accepted as substantially trustworthy as a record of fact, and that the interpretative element due to the dogmatic interests of the Church is not more than a minor factor. It may be well argued that the minor variations in tradition confirm rather than impugn the value of the historical evidence. If there were almost complete literal and dogmatic consistency in the New Testament one would suspect that later ecclesiastical authority had been at work, carefully and artificially reducing all to order. As there is so much of freedom and variety in the New Testament writings, the independence of the various witnesses is vouched for, and the substantial underlying unity made all the more impressive.

2. THE MAJESTY OF THE GOSPELS. The portrait presented by the Gospels of Jesus of Nazareth, His person, His character, His deeds, and His words, is one of the imperishable spiritual and imaginative figures of humanity. It has won the admiration and reverence even of those who refuse to believe in Him with Christian faith. It is not to be supposed that the group mind of the primitive Church possessed the sheer genius necessary for the construction of this spiritual miracle. The Evangelists strike us as faithful but rather ordinary men, who excelled themselves in what they wrote simply because they were not constructing out of their own talent, but copying what had been remembered from the life.

We have various pointers as to the level of creative genius and spiritual insight of the primitive Church, and they all point the same way. There are the so-called Apocryphal Gospels. These are ancient works purporting to be lives of Christ, and so forth, which were not accepted as reliable or authentic by the Church. They are valuable evidence as to the sort of work which was in fact produced by the group mind when it allowed itself freedom to construct imaginative stories about Christ. These constructions betray themselves as spurious by the altogether lower level of good sense and spiritual understanding displayed, when comparison is made with the canonical Gospels. If the New Testament itself had been constructed out of the same resources it would be of the same inferior character. This effect is borne out by the character of the most ancient Christian writings following the New Testament, and which were accepted by the Church as reliable and orthodox Christian work. These are the works of the so-called apostolic fathers. They are in the main at a much higher level of good sense than the Apocryphal Gospels, but they do not compare in creative spiritual genius with the books of the New Testament. The apostolic fathers are to be venerated as outstanding figures of the heroic age of the martyr Church. They served Christ faithfully in building up the discipline of the infant Church. Yet they certainly had not the genius and insight to *create* the figure of the Christ of the Gospels.

Without disrespect it may be said that the same is true even of the New Testament writers themselves. Possibly the greatest and most formative spiritual leader of the Church in the first generation was the apostle Paul. We have examples of his work. They contain passages which display the highest degree of spiritual genius. His writings are reverenced by the Church as canonical Scripture, and are some of the most creative and influential books of religion the world has ever seen. It is harder to give higher praise than this. Nevertheless, as we read even St. Paul we find passages where we candidly say: "This is not altogether the great apostle of the Gentiles, the first great doctor of the Church! In this text we have some echo of Saul of Tarsus, the intelligent and educated first-century Jew, speaking to his day from the standpoint and conventions of his day" (for example, 1 Corinthians 11:1-15; Galatians 4:21-31). The genius even of Paul, though magnificent, is variable and beset by human limitation. He does not rise uniformly to the level of His master. Paul is not above criticism, but when men criticize Jesus it is only because He is too sublime for us!

Paul, then, did not have it in him to create the portrait of Christ, as a novelist of genius might create a character of prophetic genius. Nor could St. John. And it is impossible to believe that within the circle of those early disciples there were other men of profounder spiritual genius than these, now entirely lost to historical memory, who so fertilized the group mind that the first generation created the Gospels. This is to suppose that the effect can rise above the cause. As faithful Mark depicts the stark scene of Calvary we do not have the impression that he was a man of admirable talents. He was a good but commonplace man, and we suspect that he himself did not always have the most perfect insight into what he was writing about. How then did he come to write in this commanding way? It was simply that Peter had seen and heard, and could not forget, and that Mark had so often heard St. Peter that he could not forget either. The only reasonable explanation of the majesty of the Gospel portrait is that it was copied from the life.

3. THE CONTINUITY OF CHRISTIAN THOUGHT. It is impossible for the Christian scholar to come to the reading of the New Testament without mental prepossessions of some sort. The question is therefore raised as to what are in fact the most rational principles to bring to the study. We would affirm that experience plainly teaches the value of the principle of continuity. The Church has seen a good deal of the rise and fall of schools of theological thought, by the following process. Some stimulating writer advances a new

theological understanding. He gains repute as an intellectual leader in the world of Christian scholarship, and founds a "school of thought." He may seem for a time to dominate the theological horizon, and many hail him as the authority for Christian understanding. However, hardly have his influential books had time to accumulate a little dust than a new lead is given, in quite a different direction. A new authoritative school of thought arises, with "assured results" contradicting the old. After many years it is realized that each school of thought owed its strength to the circumstance that it was emphasizing, or rediscovering, some segment of Christian truth. The weakness of each lay in the fact that it was unbalanced in its overconfident and extreme emphasis upon this one element, and in its lack of appreciation for the many other segments of truth. The rise and passing of the new movement is found, however, to have added some small offering to the great and permanent store of Christian understanding.

Through all these disputes and discoveries there has been in the Church a principle of cautious stability in face of "new theologies," and of reverence for the heritage of the past in face of brilliant individualist innovation. The prudent Christian scholar will always be the honest reader of new researches, but he will never feel constrained radically to reconstruct the whole of the Christian religion on account of some much-discussed "new theology." This is the guiding principle of the continuity of type in Christian thought.

A valuable canon of interpretation to be used in deciding how far one may reasonably go in following the new critical techniques for the reading of the Bible is that they may be accepted insofar as they yield a greater understanding of the historic Christian Faith. Yet the historic Faith itself is not open for radical change, as though the Church did not already know the truth. Scholarly theories, no matter how brilliant, are not to be followed to the point of revolutionizing Christianity. This will be done if it is once allowed that the New Testament witnesses only to a subjective "Christ of faith," and virtually not at all to a real historical Christ.

The principle of the continuity of type makes it reasonable to suppose that the cohesion of Christian thought, which has held firm through all the long centuries covered by theological history, holds also during that all-important, formative, yet unrecorded gap which exists between our Lord Himself and the formation of our written Gospel tradition. The wise theologian will make the interpretative assumption that the New Testament Christians substantially understood their Lord, or at least, that they understood Him better than we are likely to do at this distance of time if we seek to judge apart from their witness. The skeptical assumption that they radically misunderstood their Lord, and do not reliably witness to what He really and historically said and did, is therefore to be rejected. A thoughtful reverence for the continuous historic tradition of Christianity is the rational canon of interpretation to bring to the New Testament. It is a more realistic and reliable canon than the critical assumption that the Gospel must be approximated to the prepossessions of the latest passing phase of secular thought.

C. The Apostolic Faith

The unique and indispensable treasure in the New Testament is the witness to the facts about Christ. A further element of great value is that the New Testament is the witness to the first formative ventures in theological interpretation of these facts. It is the faith of the Church that all through her history the Holy Spirit has been guiding the consensus of devout Christian scholars to a fuller understanding of the meaning of Christ and His teaching, and teaching them how to apply the fixed principles of Christian faith to the ever-changing circumstances of successive centuries (John 16:13–14). Thus the life of the Church has been marked by a series of doctrinal decisions, which, when they are found indeed to be decisions of the whole of the Church, are fully authoritative decisions for the whole Church.

In consequence, any new doctrinal decision must be built upon the foundation of the past, and must be taken within the limits of that which has been already authoritatively decided. It is not allowable to abolish the fully authoritative decisions of the past, but they can be clarified in light of new doctrinal issues arising out of new circumstances. What is acceptable to the Church is a fuller understanding of, and a clearer formulation of, the original faith (Jude 3). Superficially, so far as the wording of doctrinal formularies is concerned, the progress of Christian doctrine may look like an evolutionary process, moving further and further away from the beginning. In spiritual and intellectual substance, however, it is a conservative process, for the reformation of doctrine always consists in a recapture of its original principles.

Clearly, the criterion of this whole process is the place of the New Testament itself. If each authoritative doctrinal decision of the Church is determinative of the bounds within which later decisions may be made, the earlier the decisions the more determinative they are for the Church. The very first decisions laid down the basic structure of all later teaching. "As the sapling is bent, so is the great tree." The New Testament contains the witness to these most momentous of all doctrinal decisions. The process of doctrinal discussion, interpretation, and decision as it is seen in the New Testament must not be separated from the same process as it is observed in the Church of later times. In principle it is the same. Nevertheless, the initial stage of the process had results more significant than those of any later time. The New Testament contains the witness to these first basic decisions of the Church, which make natural and necessary the later formulations of the doctrine of the Trinity, the Incarnation, the Atonement, and so forth.

Readings

Dodd, C. H., *The Bible Today*. London: Cambridge University Press; New York: The Macmillan Company, 1947.

Kelly, B. H., ed., *Layman's Bible Commentary:* Vol. I: *Introduction to the Bible*. Richmond, Va.: John Knox Press, 1959.

Peake, A. S., *The Bible: Its Origin, Its Significance, and Its Abiding Worth*. New York: Doran, 1913.

Bultmann, R., et al., *Kerygma and Myth*, ed. H. W. Bartsch, trans. R. H. Fuller. London: S.P.C.K., 1953. (Discussion of the "demythologizing" exegesis, with a rejoinder.)

Chapter Nine

The Double Cure

I believe in the forgiveness of sins

I. Personal Religion

It has been emphasized that Christianity is the religion of an objective divine saving act performed in history. With this is connected the other fundamental, that Christianity is the religion of divine grace. The Christian Faith is the message of that which God did in His incarnate Son, and which He now does through the operation of the Holy Spirit. Therefore the Christian religion is a *gospel*. It is not the call to man that he accept a revelation, a doctrine, or an ethic, and attempt to summon up all his powers to live in accord with it. It is a gracious summons that he put his sole hope for life in what God has done for him, and will do in him.

However, answering to this historic and objective side of Christian faith there is a personal and subjective aspect. What God has done can only make an actual difference to real human beings if it makes an appeal to their minds and wills and affections, and if it produces a response from the human personality. Here is an important example of the principle that a right understanding of Christian faith is largely a matter of preserving a due balance between apparently opposite propositions, which are in fact truths complementary one to another. If one comes down too heavily upon the historical and objective side, the Faith becomes antiquarian and academic. It is then seen as a call to men to accept a set of doctrines. Such religion seems to have little contact with the practical life of ordinary men. On the other hand, if the presentation of Christianity discounts the historical and objective and becomes too purely subjective and personal, one is left with a religion of sentiments and emotions. At the best this will offend the thoughtful man, because it seems to be basing its claim for acceptance as true upon the circumstance that its devotees "feel" it to be true. At the worst it can degenerate into uncontrolled emotionalism. The due balance between historic Christianity and personal religion is a matter of no small importance.

Another aspect of this balance is that God carries on His present work of the Holy Spirit chiefly, though not exclusively, through the means of grace in the Church. However, the classic plan of personal religion, and of "the Christian experience," has been hammered out chiefly from the actual personal experience of certain outstanding Christian individuals. It also naturally turns our thoughts to the way in which the Holy Spirit works in the heart of the individual believer. Inevitably, therefore, the theology of personal religion tends to be individualist theology. Here again is a due balance to be kept between apparent opposites which are in fact complementary.

A presentation of Christian faith which is too exclusively thought out in terms of the Church may become simply communal, formal, and external, and lapse into a sterile ecclesiasticism. An understanding of faith which is too purely individual may become individualistic, introverted, undisciplined, subjective, and even eccentric. It will lack the sustaining discipline and the broad views which come of a great and ruling sense of the Church. In turning, therefore, to the theology of "the Christian experience," it is necessary to keep clearly in mind that the individual believer we are here discussing is not an isolated individual. Normally and ideally he is an integral part of the closely knit fellowship of the Church.

Although God is always the same, human nature is inherently various. Consequently the ways of divine grace in dealing with sinful men are various. It is hardly surprising to find, therefore, that the Church is not as united in the doctrines which reflect the personal religious experience as she is in the doctrines which expound the nature of God and His saving act in Christ. Indeed, there are some issues which are so much a matter of human temperament that it would appear spiritually improper for the Church to attempt to make universal doctrinal decisions upon them. They are matters of religious opinion, where the wise rule is toleration. Various denominations in the Church have on occasion made separate dogmatic decisions on some of these points, and in doing so have regrettably divided the Church. The Church can rightly insist that there is one true doctrine of God and of His divine act in Christ. Here the faithful ought to be united. Yet the ways in which souls are led to God on account of that saving act are various, and it is wrong for a section to seek to insist that the way it finds most helpful is the only correct way. It is necessary, not only to define the words which different Christian denominations use, but also to under-

stand the spiritual intention they seek to convey by them. The divisions of
the Church with regard to salvation by grace are in part due to genuine
differences of spiritual apprehension. Yet divergences are also largely due
to the use of words in different senses. By tradition one denomination has
become accustomed to use a term in one sense, and perhaps a bad sense.
Another has used the same word in another and a good sense. They may
therefore be much nearer in real intention than their doctrinal formularies
superficially indicate. To understand these issues is a service to the peace
and unity of the Church, and through this, to its fuller understanding of
the gospel.

To this study of personal religion there are two parts. In the first place,
there is the doctrine of grace. This is the attempt to give a clear exposition
of the way in which God exerts His initiative in the salvation of man.
Then there is the doctrine of the life of Christian grace. This is the
systematic account of how the heart of man may respond to this divine
initiative.

II. The Doctrine of Grace

A. Grace

Two ideas are commonly united in the term *grace*. The root idea is that
grace is the undeserved favor of God. The word indicates that God has
set His favor upon His people not at all because they merit it, but simply
because according to the mysterious counsel of His love He wills so to do
(Deuteronomy 7:7–8). He forgives man, not because man can do anything
to deserve forgiveness, but because He is a God of love (Exodus 33:19;
Psalm 51:1; Romans 9:15–16). God does not regard man according to
what he has done, but according to His own universal goodness (Matthew
20:1–16). A second idea, derived from the first, is that grace is the action
which God takes to effect His gracious will. Grace is the saving and enabling
power of God, indwelling man, which comes to the assistance of man's
infirmity, to do for him what he cannot do for himself (Acts 4:33, 18:27;
Romans 12:3, 6; 2 Corinthians 12:9; Philippians 1:7; Hebrews 13:9).
Thus the believing man is in "a state of grace" (Galatians 5:4).

B. Salvation by Grace

The Christian religion is a *gospel* ("good news") of grace. That is to
say, it is not God's call to man that he obey God's law by his own strength,
and thus fit himself to receive God's favor. Sinful man is not able to do
this (see p. 72). The gospel is God's offer to man, in his desperate infirmity,
that He will give to him a strength not his own which alone will enable
man to obey the law of God and so please his Maker (Ephesians 2:8). Man
can turn to God only when God exerts His initiative and calls him (Isaiah
55:6–7). Man can give himself to God's service only as God summons

him and equips him (John 15:16; Romans 10:14–15). Man can give to God only that which God first gave to him (1 Corinthians 4:7). In all things even the holiest and wisest of men remains completely dependent upon God, his Creator and Master.

Summary of Divergence: Catholic and Reformation Doctrines of Salvation by Grace

a. Catholic Doctrine

Catholic teaching does not exclude the conception, which has been so formative in Reformation doctrine, that God's initiative of grace in man's salvation is a personal confrontation in power and love, which moves man consciously to repentance and faith, occasioning the experience of "conversion." However, in practice this conversion experience has been thought of as characteristic of the lives of certain outstanding saints and devotees. Formative in Catholic doctrine has been the supposition that the normal Christian grows up, and is nurtured as such, in the Christian Church and community. Thus God's initial gift of grace has been thought of sacramentally and ecclesiastically. By the regeneration of Holy Baptism (see pp. 167–69), the person baptized, normally the child of Christian parents, is placed in "a state of grace." Those who in this state faithfully use the means of grace will grow in grace, and come to Christian virtues and character. To these Christian "good works" God is of His grace pleased to attribute merit. Thus man "works out his own salvation" (Philippians 2:12, 13) by cooperation with the divine grace which works in him, and having attained a Christian character and good deeds, comes to his eternal reward (Revelation 14:13). Final salvation, therefore, is by "divine grace, and the merit of good works" (Matthew 7:21–23, 25:31–46; James 1:25; 1 John 2:17; Revelation 20:13). It is by grace, for at every stage God must exert His initiative first, or man is helpless. Yet at every stage man must freely cooperate with the initiative of grace, within the discipline of the Church.

b. Reformation Doctrine

Reformation doctrine has characteristically shown a distinctly different proportion of emphasis, often associated with the Reformation formula "salvation by grace alone." The traditional Catholic idea of the initial spiritual blessing bestowed through baptismal incorporation into the Church has not necessarily been denied, and has indeed sometimes been cherished in Protestant circles. Nevertheless, the leading influence has been the theology of the personal, conscious, and individual "conversion experience." There is clearly a significant difference of Christian apprehension here. However, it should be remembered that it is a difference of proportion and emphasis, rather than of inherent principle. Pre-Reformation Catholicism did indeed assent to the principle of salvation by divine grace, but it would be widely admitted on both sides that in much popular Catholic devotion this principle had been practically overlaid by "the merit of good works," and in particular such "works" as attendance upon ceremonial Masses, ascetic practices, reverence for relics, pilgrimages to shrines, indulgences, and so forth. The Reformers characteristically were moved by a strong revulsion against all this, for they felt that the foundation principle of grace was almost completely obscured by the doctrine that man can and must *earn* his own salvation by his diligent churchmanship. Thus the Reformers wished carefully to exclude the conception of "the merit of good works." Characteristically they embraced the Augustinian theology of grace (see pp. 209–12), and in particular emphasized the formulae "justification by faith alone" and "salvation by grace alone."

This may be illustrated by the formative experience and example of Martin Luther (1483–1546).

In his young days as an exceptionally conscientious monk, Luther strove with all his powers in the customary devotional discipline to attain to the experience which he knew he ought to have, of being so filled with the love of God that he would be able to obey God spontaneously from the heart, and not merely as a stern duty. He found instead a deep frustration of spirit, until God brought him to a profound evangelical experience, in which he clearly realized that the principle of Christian salvation is loving and obedient trust in the saving love and power of God declared in Christ. In strong reaction against his background of "merit earning" he, and those who followed him, emphasized the doctrine of salvation "by grace alone." The purpose of this is clearly to safeguard the position that sinful man can of himself do nothing to accomplish his own salvation, and cannot hope to establish his own status before God. The whole saving action is of God's grace, and all the glory belongs to God.

c. An Interpretative Statement

Some would argue that the classic Protestant formula "salvation by grace alone" is acceptable as a maxim of Christian devotion, but is not by itself a sufficient principle of systematic theological thought. It belongs properly to the realm of Christian experience. The man who, having wandered far and struggled hard, suddenly comes to a profound experience of God's saving power and love in Jesus Christ finds that the instinctive cry of his heart is: "God did it all! I was not faithfully listening for Him, but He called me. I was not obeying Him. Though I did not realize it, I was wandering further and further from Him, until He chose me, visited me, overcame me by His power, and set up His throne in my heart. And as for the service I have since rendered Him—it is not at all to my credit. It is the result of His power working through me. *God did it all,* and all the glory is His!"

This experience is one of the fundamental facts of the Christian life, and no sound theology of salvation can be constructed without taking the most serious account of it (pp. 71, 220–21). We observe this form of experience is by no means limited to the Protestant or evangelical tradition. Believers of every age and place have shared something of this apprehension of the grace of God, though they have not always expressed themselves in the manner natural to a disciple of Luther. Out of the heart's cry "God did it all" is fashioned the theological maxim, "salvation by grace alone." Nevertheless, the critic would urge that if the believer wishes to advance from devotional experience to the construction of a systematic theology expounding the relation of God to all human souls, it is precarious to make the basic assumption that "salvation by grace alone" is virtually a sufficient foundation for all.[1] There are a number of other principles equally to be taken into serious consideration, such as, the love of God to all men, His reasonable dealings with mankind, human moral responsibility, and the duty of devotional discipline in the means of grace. There is a case that the Catholic position more fully answers to these considerations, in its greater degree of emphasis upon free and responsible cooperation with grace.

C. Augustinian Theology

The theology of "sovereign grace" has come to its most developed exposition in relation to the thought of St. Augustine of Hippo. The theological thought of this, possibly the most influential teacher of the Church since New Testament times, is proverbially difficult to expound on account of its diversity. When he discusses the doctrines of the Church, ministry, and sacraments, Augustine clearly displays himself as belonging to the Catholic tradition. His theology was, indeed, one of the formative influences of medieval Christianity. When, however, he turns to the theology of divine grace, the conversion of souls, the experience of personal religion, and the hope of salvation, he is the originator of that system of Christian thought commonly known as Augustinianism. It is not easy completely to reconcile the two sides of the great master's doctrine.

Significantly, St. Augustine's theology of grace was molded chiefly by his own early personal experience of conversion. His moral and spiritual bondage was much more sore than that of Luther, the upright but frustrated monk, for Augustine had tasted years of humiliation during which he unavailingly struggled with lust and unbelief. Furthermore, when he came to the gift of faith, and to an experience of spiritual release and moral purification, he continued to be a man of boldly aspiring speculative interests, who significantly did attempt to construct an intellectual system out of the theology of grace. This Augustinian doctrine places the whole responsibility for man's final salvation with the initiative of God's grace, and makes man virtually the instrument of God's action. From the time of

---

[1] As some would put it, "grace alone" is true existentially, but not wholly true as a matter of systematic doctrine.

Augustine on there was within the pre-Reformation Western Church a continuing minority tradition of Augustinian theology, or of theology verging upon Augustinianism, though it has never captured the general judgment of the whole Church.

The most influential movement of Augustinianism, however, was seen in the classic Reformation theology, which for reasons natural to evangelical Christians wished to give the strongest emphasis to the doctrine of grace. Protestant Augustinianism was most clearly and systematically formulated in the thought of John Calvin (1509–1564), with the result that fully developed Augustinian thought is now often described as "Calvinism." However, there are those who have adopted the Augustinian standpoint who are not Calvinists. "Barthianism" is a leading modern school of Augustinian thought.

The Augustinian would naturally affirm that he has adopted this doctrine essentially because he believes it to be required by Scripture, and would quote the texts which speak of man's entire depravity, divine election, and so forth. However, this leaves outstanding the question why others interpret the Scripture differently. The determinative influence appears to be the manner of religious experience by which different classes of believers have come to spiritual liberty and moral power in believing. Those whose experience has prompted the heart to cry "God did it all" have been inclined to give a leading emphasis to some texts, and to interpret others in light of them, and to find thereby the support for Augustinian doctrine. Others, with a different form of devotional discipline or religious experience behind them, have read the Scriptures in a different way.

One side of Augustinian theology has already been outlined. Its doctrine of man and of sin naturally lays a strong and distinctive emphasis upon entire depravity, the bondage of the will, and the guilt of original sin, whereby the whole human race justly merits eternal damnation because of the Fall (see pp. 70, 75). We may turn, then, to the other side, and consider Augustinian positions with regard to saving grace.

1. ELECTION. In addition to the characteristic Augustinian position there is a general doctrine of election, or of divine choice, in the Bible. The interest of this is to affirm that God is the foreseeing master of the human situation. His saving action is no mere expedient forced upon Him by man's perversity. It is the outcome of an eternal and wise plan, which will in the end fully vindicate His goodness and glory, even through the sorry processes of human disobedience (Romans 11:25–36). In this connection it is to be remembered that the Hebrew writers do not express themselves in terms of "indirect causation" (see pp. 29–30), with the result that an evil which has been *permitted* in God's world, and which has taken place under the divine order, is spoken of almost as though God had positively willed it. Thus in the passage referred to above, the proper sense of verse 32 is that the unbelieving Jews "*became* shut up in unbelief."

A second interest of the general doctrine of election is to show that according to His mysterious but all-wise counsel God chooses some persons, and some nations, to play a particular role in history. That this must be so is the conviction of one who believes that the world is overruled by the providence of God, for it is a plain fact of experience that some persons and some nations are more endowed with natural gifts than others, and are endowed in various ways, and that nations and persons are placed in historical circumstances which give differing degrees of opportunity for the exercise of their gifts. Thus the Hebrews, and no other nation, were "elected" as the chosen people. So in the passage introducing the one already referred to (Romans 9:1–13), Jacob and Esau, the traditional founders of the tribes of Israel and of Edom respectively, figure in St. Paul's theology as the "representative heads" of the two nations. The divine election, which "loved" the one and "hated" the other, was the choice which made the Israelites, and not the closely kindred nation of the Edomites, into the chosen people. However, it by no means follows from this that all Israelites, merely by the circumstance of birth into that nation, were thereby faithful to their destiny, or more righteous and more sure of eternal salvation than other men (see p. 137).

The Augustinian system, however, proceeds from this to a *particular* election. It teaches that God has chosen certain individual souls out of the mass of those destined for perdition, and appointed them to be the heirs of salvation. These are the Elect. This demonstrates God's unaccountable mercy, whereas His leaving the rest to go to the perdition which all alike deserve vindicates His justice, and hatred of sin. The leading Scripture passage cited in support of this doctrine is Romans 9, interpreted on the basis that the figures of "Jacob" and "Esau" are individual, personal patriarchs. The chapter is then viewed as a discussion of the divine destiny of individual souls, to heaven or to hell. It is clear that the doctrine of particular election is the logical outcome of the proposition "God did it all." If this is the whole of the matter, it then follows that some souls are converted simply because God has chosen that they shall be converted, and others fail to receive the gift of faith, and to be converted, simply because God's grace has chosen to pass them over.

2. PREDESTINATION. It is fundamental to the doctrine of God that His will is always the same, and that He foreknows the future. Therefore the Elect are chosen not at the time of conversion, or at birth, but from the beginning of God's dealings with the human race. Thus the Elect are called according to an eternal decree of election. This is the doctrine of predestination (Romans 8:29–30).[2]

3. IRRESISTIBLE GRACE. If those souls who are of the Elect are predestined to receive the gift of faith, and to be converted, it follows that God's grace

---

2 A nonpredestinarian exegesis of this and similar texts would be given on the lines of the opening of the section above on election (p. 210).

is "sovereign" toward them in the sense that it is a matter of necessity that it must have its way with them. Thus it is a part of the Augustinian system that converting grace is irresistible. This does not mean that the unbelieving sinner is purely passive before it, and cannot resist. St. Augustine's own experience was that of a long and stubborn fight against grace. The doctrine of irresistible grace affirms that although a man may resist, God's purpose is bound to have its way with him. Even the most obstinate sinner, if he be of the company of the Elect, will of necessity capitulate to grace in the end, and then the grace of God carries all before it in his heart, turning his will from evil to good (Romans 9:19).

4. FINAL PERSEVERANCE. The Augustinian position is that those who are of the Elect, who receive the gift of faith, and who are in consequence in a state of grace, must necessarily continue in this state so as to arrive at a believing death, and so be confirmed to eternal glory (John 10:28, 29). Though those who have been truly converted may *seem* at times to fall into sin they will surely repent and return to faith in the end, under the influence of irresistible grace (Proverbs 24:16). And those who may seem at one time to have been in a state of grace, yet who die in a state of apostasy, have never been truly the subjects of God's saving grace, even though they may for a time have sincerely believed themselves to have been converted. The measure of divine grace granted to them may have sufficed to keep them from some degree of wickedness, but it was not *effectual, saving* grace.

5. REPROBATION. This is the culmination in logic of the whole system. The most strict Augustinians have held that God did not merely leave the non-Elect to go in their own way to the damnation which all alike deserve. He positively sentenced them to this punishment. This is the decree of reprobation.

6. EVALUATION. The Augustinian system of scriptural interpretation clearly enshrines important spiritual values, otherwise it would not have made its appeal to some of the greatest figures in the history of Christian thought. Nevertheless, its austere principles have never appealed in an unmodified form to more than a minority tradition. This would appear to indicate that taken in isolation it is not a complete apprehension of the Christian truth. The more general mind of the historic Church is that of a mediating position, namely, that the positive spiritual values of Augustinianism are to be accepted, but that the system requires judiciously to be modified by taking into account other spiritual considerations. It is good for man thus to be solemnly reminded that the Christian God of love is not a benign heavenly "buddy," upon whose goodwill man can safely presume. He is the glorious sovereign Potentate of the universe, who from eternity rules all worlds with a wisdom man cannot presume to scan. Indeed, that His love toward sinful man is the love of so great and holy a God is the very

thing which makes the love of God the unspeakable wonder that it is. The doctrine which at first sight appears so forbidding, that the aim of the work of salvation is the full vindication of the sole glory of God, as holy, just, and good, stands as a most necessary rebuke to the constant easy-going human tendency to look upon communal religion as the oil for the wheels of society, the purpose of which is to make this world a respectable, prosperous, and comfortable place in which to live.

Furthermore, the doctrine of particular election does seek to take account of the great mystery that some people appear to be born with so much more spiritual talent than others, or in circumstances of so much greater spiritual privilege, and that some respond to their spiritual opportunities and are converted, whereas others, with apparently equal opportunities, so unaccountably turn away from Christ. We cannot understand this, but have to trust that a good God overrules all for the best, in this world and the next. Finally, this forbidding Augustinian portrait of God preserves to the religion of grace the element of stern duty, and if rightly apprehended can nurture Christians who are men of iron.

However, we believe that the doctrine of "grace alone" is more safely understood as a truth of the devotional life, and as a maxim of spiritual experience, than as a speculative principle. Aspiring speculation can all too easily turn into arid speculation, which represents the God and Father of our Lord Jesus Christ as an utterly remote monarch of arbitrary might.

This limitation of predestinarian speculation is surely in accord with the spirit and intention of the Scripture. The texts traditionally quoted by Augustinians are the heart's cry of men upon their knees before the God of glory, not the musings of academics in their proverbial "ivory towers," and they must be treated as such. A judicious attempt at theological interpretation is provided, albeit in somewhat quaint and antique language, by the celebrated Anglican Article XVII, *Of Predestination and Election*. This is the work of cautious and astute men, whose care is to preserve an even balance between extremes, and to safeguard the peace and unity of a Church torn by theological factions. The opening paragraph of the Article is a statement of the positive side of the Augustinian position, and affirms that according to an eternal and mysterious purpose God has decreed the salvation by grace of those who are saved. Most significantly, however, it does not introduce the phrase "grace *alone*," nor say that divine grace is irresistible. In particular, it is silent regarding the negative side, the doctrine of reprobation.

The second paragraph turns to the devotional experience, and away from predestinarian speculation. The practical value of the Augustinian position is observed to be in the humble assurance and confidence which it brings to those whose sole hope in life is that they are the objects of God's sufficient grace. Thus the doctrine "is full of sweet, pleasant, and unspeakable comfort to godly persons, and such as feel in themselves the working of the Spirit of Christ." This is the profound truth of the lines:

> Let me no more my comfort draw
> From my frail grasp of Thee:
> In this alone rejoice with awe;
> Thy mighty grasp of me.

However, "for curious [that is, *speculative*] and carnal persons, lacking the Spirit of Christ, to have continually before their eyes the sentence of God's Predestination, is a most dangerous downfall." Thus John Milton, the Calvinist poet of Puritanism, can write of the devils in hell:

> Others apart sat on a hill retired,
> In thoughts more elevate, and reasoned high
> Of providence, foreknowledge, will, and fate,
> Fixed fate, free will, foreknowledge absolute,
> And found no end, in wandering mazes lost.[3]

Finally, "we must receive God's promises in such wise, as they be generally set forth to us in Holy Scripture." This is a reminder that the doctrine of the Bible is many-sided. As well as passages which speak of election, and of God's sovereign power, there are also gracious promises of God's love to the whole world (John 3:16), and of His will that all men should be saved (1 Timothy 2:4; 2 Peter 3:9). Thus these high matters are not to be settled by the facile quotation of a few isolated "proof texts" in controversy. They require a unified, ordered, learned, and reverent exposition of the whole of Scripture.

D. Prevenient Grace

Prevenient grace is literally the grace which "comes before." That is, it is the action of divine grace which precedes any conscious personal experience of the life of grace. Some degree of moral and spiritual good is almost universally diffused among mankind, quite apart from whether men are definite Christian believers. The doctrine of prevenient grace safeguards the position that this good is not man's natural possession, but is a gift of divine grace (see p. 71). Associated with this is a second aspect. The notion of salvation by grace answers to the idea of the divine initiative in salvation. At every stage of the Christian experience man can only answer the call of God because God has already called him. This process of divine initiative has started long before the awakened soul is found seriously reflecting about sin, repentance, and conversion.

Psychological investigation has found itself in agreement with the traditional Christian position that the human personality can be powerfully influenced for good in the early days and years of life. Certainly the growing child in the Christian community, who is not yet old enough to have any

---

3 *Paradise Lost*, Book II, ll. 557–61.

reflections upon sin or salvation, can have a sincere love of Jesus, and a sense of the presence of God in worship. The activity of prevenient grace is to be seen here. The proverbial careless person who, thinking nothing of religion, goes to church to accompany a friend or to get out of the cold, and is there surprisingly convicted by the truth, is likewise the object of God's prevenient grace. The spiritual choice before him when he went was a very dim and unformed one. Yet he might well have chosen differently, and that he acted as he did was a response to a preliminary leading of the Spirit of grace.

Furthermore, there are sincere seekers after truth who, on account of some unfortunate disability due to the deeply entrenched prejudice of upbringing, or to some past regrettable experience, cannot bring themselves to see the truth of the Christian position. However, if they are indeed sincere seekers it is not to be doubted that these are the objects of the leading of God's prevenient grace, even though some of them may profess to be atheists and the enemies of religion. In fact, the life of grace is not to be limited to the little company of those who seem to be very religious. The Spirit of Christ is already striving in the hearts of all men everywhere to lead them to that which is good, and ultimately to Christian faith (John 1:9). It is not for man lightly to draw any limit to the preliminary and unconscious operation of Christian grace, and to write off any abandoned creature as virtually lost to its influence.

E. Universal Grace

The majority tradition of the Church has affirmed that the grace of God is in principle universal. The chief reason for maintaining this position is that it appears to be the consequence of the fundamental doctrine that God is love (1 John 4:8). It would seem that if God loves all men He must will the salvation of all (Psalm 145:8, 9; Isaiah 49:6; Jonah 4:9–11; Matthew 5:43–48; Luke 13:29; John 3:16; 1 Timothy 2:4; 2 Peter 3:9).

A contributory reason for upholding the doctrine of universal grace is the Church's regard for God's promise of grace in the means of grace. It is true that a man cannot by his much desiring make himself believe in God or love God. To do this is the gift of grace. Nevertheless he can, if he will, use the means of grace. He can listen with a teachable mind to the reading of the Scripture and the preaching of the Gospel, and if he expectantly persists in this long enough God will honor the means of grace, and give to the seeker the gift of faith and love. The penitent and awakened seeker, who is painfully aware of the poverty of his spiritual experience, cannot make himself grow in grace. Nevertheless, he can, if he will, devoutly receive the sacraments, and God will faithfully fulfill His promise in them. Therefore honor for the means of grace appears to involve an offer of effectual grace to all sincere comers.

A number of important consequences follow from the doctrine of universal grace. In the first place, it involves the idea that the sovereignty of God's grace is a self-limited sovereignty. God allows men, if they will, to defy Him. If grace is both irresistible and universal, all men would be bound to be saved (see p. 268). In the second place, the doctrine involves that the ultimate responsibility for whether a man is saved rests finally upon man, not upon God. This is an important limitation of the notion of the bondage of the will. Left to himself, sinful man's will is indeed in bondage, and apart from the grace of God he cannot turn to God. Yet when his will is assisted by grace he is then truly free either to make or to mar himself forever.

It will be appreciated that the doctrine of universal grace holds genuine difficulties, even as does the opposed notion of particular election. The only way to Christian salvation is through faith in Christ (Acts 4:12). Yet it is not clear precisely in what way all men receive the opportunity to come to faith in Christ. In this life some, and perhaps the vast majority of the human race, never hear of Him at all. Many others, even in nominally Christian communities, never fully and intelligently hear the Christian message, so as genuinely to be confronted with the decision of Christian discipleship. There are also some who are apparently armored against the Christian appeal by a psychological "blind spot" implanted by past unhappy experience (the so-called "invincible ignorance"). Thus it is hard to defend the proposition that saving grace in Christ extends to all men without logically being led to extend the operation of grace beyond the life of man in this world (see pp. 262–63). This again may ensnare the theologian in precarious speculations and attempts to know that which man cannot know, or perhaps to affirm doctrine beyond the warrant of Scripture.

Thus, whether saving grace is affirmed to be particular or universal, God's good and wise dealings with all His creatures remain shrouded in an air of mystery, and we cannot afford to be too dogmatic. All that can be presumed is that all those who in this world have lived according to the limited light which was granted to them will find, when they awake in the life to come, that they belong to Christ, even though in this life they were not apparently Christians. This is an illustration of the general principle that it is the business of the Christian witness to declare God's terms of salvation, namely, faith in Christ, but to leave to God all judgment as to who are, and who are not, in a state of salvation.

F. Arminianism

This term is the name which has often been given to the continuance within Protestantism of the prevailing Catholic doctrine of universal grace, in opposition to particular election and reprobation. It indicates a central or mediating position.

This school of thought takes its name from the Dutch theologian Jacobus Arminius (1560–1609). He was a teacher of humanist and liberal views who, although accepting the Reformed theology prevalent in Holland, repudiated the Calvinist doctrine of reprobation. Thus in course of time the word "Arminian" came to be used in England as a term of reproach, applied by their Calvinist opponents to the non-Calvinist "Laudian" High Church divines, to indicate that these were not wholehearted Protestants, and were unsound on the doctrine of grace. The term was later adopted for himself as a title of honor by John Wesley (1703–1791) to designate his "central" or synthesizing school of non-Calvinist evangelicalism, which on the one hand strongly emphasized salvation by grace and justification by faith, but on the other hand firmly repudiated particular election, predestination, and reprobation. This judicious and moderating "Arminian Evangelicalism," which is now so largely characteristic of Anglo-Saxon Protestantism, is perhaps the most enduring and important contribution of the Methodist movement to theological understanding in the Church.

III.   The Life of Grace

A. Nurture and Conversion

We now systematically consider the response of the human soul to the initiative of divine grace, and follow through the classic outline of "the personal religious experience." It is to be remembered that this outline is a *classic* outline. It is based upon the unusually distinct and formative religious experience of certain outstanding leaders of Christian devotion, and in particular, upon the teaching of the so-called "evangelical succession" of St. Paul, St. Augustine of Hippo, Martin Luther, and John Wesley. It does not follow, however, that the religious experience of more ordinary believers corresponds at every point. In the classic outline the facts of religious experience are brought out in black and white, in more order and clarity, than they often are in the more pedestrian devotional discipline of the Church.

This issue is presented in the contrast between Christian nurture within the Church and "conversion" as paths to Christian saving faith. Most Christians are such chiefly because they were born into the Christian community of the home and the Church, and were educated in Christian worship, morals, and belief. The prevailing attitude of the great institutional branches of the Church naturally corresponds to this. They lay great store by infant baptism, family prayers, Christian education in day-school and in Church school, regular habits of worship, reverence for the liturgy and the Church calendar, the status of communicant, and so forth. This devotional discipline, it is believed, will if used with sincerity and regularity bring men and women to a living faith in Christ. The great majority of believers through the centuries have lived their Christian lives substantially after this method. In this sense, the way of communal Christian nurture in the Church is the "normal" way to faith. Theologians who speak from this background instinctively lay more emphasis upon the value of man's free and responsible response to grace in works of devotional discipline and charity, and in consequence less proportional emphasis upon the mysterious action of divine grace. They speak of divine grace, but not perhaps, of "grace alone." They are not happy with the notion that those who are brought up as Christians need to be "converted," for to them "conversion" is a change from another religion, or from open unbelief, to Christianity.

It is necessary, however, also to do justice to the theology which reflects the religious experience of those outstanding individuals who have come to the apprehension of grace in an eminent degree. The importance of their witness is not to be measured by their relative paucity in number. They are men who have been led by experience to a deep conviction that God calls His children to something much more profound than a busy preoccupation with churchgoing and conventional morality, and indeed, that this preoccupation, however well intentioned, may easily become the delusive substitute for real religion. Normally such men have come to a deep frustration of spirit in the religion of ecclesiastical discipline, and then, despairing of all else, have been granted a great sense of spiritual and moral release through trust in the saving act of God in Christ. Experience has made them into "theologians of grace." Very often this experience of release has been described as a "conversion," though some would question whether this designation is entirely appropriate in the case of those who for years have been sincere churchmen. Perhaps "evangelical experience" is a better phrase to use.

In times when vital spiritual religion is reviving anew, perhaps from a background of formal churchmanship, these outstanding leaders often are joined by numbers of followers, who also share the distinctive evangelical experience. Thus a new denomination may be formed, which naturally comes to regard a "personal decision" as the normal and expected way into Christian faith, and which may even seek to repudiate the Christianity of incorporation into and education within the Church. However, as these new groups establish themselves into the settled ways of Christian communities they normally begin to discover the necessity for the traditional discipline also. It is a great pity that the inevitable tension between the Christianity of incorporation and education and the Christianity of conversion has so often generated mutual distrust for the spiritual bona-fides of the other party, and division in the Church.

Clearly, the two approaches are not opposites, but complements one to the other. The normal path into a great releasing experience of divine grace is through Christian nurture and discipline. By parity of reason, the pastors of settled and disciplined Christian communities should certainly teach their people that mature believers ought to expect to rise above formal churchmanship to a deep personal experience of God. In many ways the two forms of Christian devotion belong to one another as partners, and can enrich one another. There is certainly a great need for the exponents of both sides to see that this is so, and to understand one another. We are now to consider the classic outline of the Christian "personal experience," as it has been traced by its outstanding and formative leaders.

B. "Preaching the Law"

By *legal* religion, or the religion of law, is meant that religion which is based on the recognition of man's absolute duty to obey the declared will of God, and thus to please God (Romans 10:5). The gospel of free forgiveness and saving grace cannot profitably be declared to men unless they first appreciate the strict ethical character of God, the gravity and guilt of sin in His sight, and the unsparing necessity of obedience to Him. Otherwise they will presume upon His mercy, and the gospel of grace will lead to moral laxity (Romans 3:5–8). Therefore the preaching of the religion of law is the due preliminary to the preaching of the religion of grace. This was true historically. The idea of God's free forgiving grace was certainly not unknown in the Old Testament (Psalm 103:8–14; Hosea 11:7–9). However, in effect it is the minor theme. For the more part, the religion of the Old Testament is the religion of law. Moral and ceremonial commandments are given, under fear of punishment for disobedience, and with hope of blessing and reward for obedience. This was the necessary preliminary discipline, until the Jewish people were thoroughly established in the religion of ethical monotheism. Then, and only then, could they appreciate the gospel of Christ (Galatians 3:23–24).

The first Christian preachers in the Gentile world well understood this principle. In Acts, when an apostle addresses Jews or proselytes, who accepted the Mosaic Law, he speaks of Jesus as the crucified and risen Messiah (Acts 2:22–36, 13:14–41). However, when we find St. Paul addressing pagans, whether they are naïve rural idolaters or more sophisticated unbelievers, he speaks chiefly as a Jew might to Gentiles, out of the Law. The distinctive Christian element is kept largely in reserve (Acts 14:12–18, 17:16–31, 24:24–25). This was typical of the evangelistic method of the ancient Church. So it is today. The necessary background to the preaching of the gospel of grace is the declaration of the sanctity of the moral law of God, and the absolute duty of man to obey it.

There is also a sense in which the common Christianity of the Church is partly *legal* still. In ideal and principle the Christian believer has advanced beyond the level of the religion of law, and no longer needs the discipline of commandments, rewards, and punishments (Romans 10:4; Galatians 3:2, 3, 25). His sufficient rule of life is guidance into all manner of loving conduct by the indwelling Spirit of Christ, and this is the Christian's "law of liberty" (Romans 13:8–10; 1 Corinthians 8:1–13; 2 Corinthians 3:17; Galatians 5:16; James 1:25, 2:12). Nevertheless, most Christian disciples are not adult enough in faith to rise wholly to this level. They find it still spiritually profitable, even with their Christian liberty, to have some fixed guiding rules, moral and spiritual, ready to hand, and a measure of firm ecclesiastical discipline to remind them to keep those rules (Acts 15:22–29; Romans 13:1–5; 1 Corinthians 5:1–13; 2 Thessalonians 3:10).

C. Conviction of Sin

As our Lord Himself said, "They that are whole have no need of a physician, but they that are sick" (Mark 2:17). Men will not seek the gift of grace unless they first come to see their unspeakable need of it. To the Christian, therefore, the door into faith, and into all the virtues of love, is humility (Philippians 2:3–8; 1 Peter 5:5–6). That salutary and realistic judgment of himself as he stands before God, which makes a man at last prepared to accept from God that which he can never hope to repay, and which will leave him forever at the disposal of God, is worked in the heart chiefly by the realization that he has sinned, and sinned deeply and inexcusably, so that he can never deserve forgiveness (Luke 15:18–19, 18:13). The purpose of "the preaching of the law" is therefore to bring to man this conviction of sin (Romans 3:19–20, 7:9–13; 2 Corinthians 7:10). Here is the first stage of the Christian experience, and it is worthy of note that the deeply troubled and humiliated conscience is a work of divine grace (Hebrews 4:12).

"The preaching of the law" does not consist in the denunciation of the gross sins of the people who are not in Church, congenial task though this may be to the preacher and his hearers. Men and women are not brought to humble penitence before God by deploring the wrongs of the times, denouncing the wickedness of communism, warning of the peril of the hydrogen bomb, lamenting the tragedy of the divorce rate, and scarifying the puerilities of popular television! All these considerations, though true enough in their way, too easily encourage the hearers to say to themselves, "God, I thank thee, that I am not as other men are" (Luke 18:11). This confirms well-intentioned and morally decent men in that self-regarding self-righteousness which is the condition natural to man. It separates them still further from God. The effectual "preaching of the law" is the enforcement to the sincere and moral man of the spotless purity and inflexible justice of the God of holy love, the absolute requirement of obedience from the heart to Him in all things, the grievousness of slighting His offered love, and the lamentable spiritual consequences, here and hereafter, of alienation from God by pride, selfishness, and moral compromise.

D. Repentance

When the serious-minded man is confronted with the majesty of the moral and spiritual law of God, with the dreadful consequences of disobedience, and with the blessedness promised to those who obey God, the Spirit of grace can then work in him the response of penitence. Humble penitence is the indispensable condition for the forgiveness of sins (Luke

7:44–48, 15:7, 18–24, 18:13–14; Acts 8:22, 11:18). Christian repentance
is not merely remorse for sin, for the apostate Judas felt remorse, though
he did not, like penitent Peter, return in humility to Christ to seek forgiveness. Certainly repentance is not merely regret that one is not a better and
purer man, for any candid mind can feel this sentiment, even as it cherishes
its self-righteousness in comparing itself with others who have done worse.
Repentance involves a completely sincere purpose to turn away from evil
to good, and from self-pleasing to God (Isaiah 1:16–20; Luke 19:8–9).
However, the tragedy of human nature is that even the man who sincerely
repents discovers that he cannot turn away from evil to good, for his
moral will is in bondage. Secretly in the heart, and to some extent even
openly, he continues to commit the sins which he now loathes. Thus human
repentance is not fully effectual to work an actual change of life. Its chief
fruit is a deepened sense of conviction of sin (Romans 7:14–24). The
paradox is that the thoroughly awakened soul, which has come nearest to
sincere penitence, and which is now striving with all its might to obey and
please God, is the one which has the clearest realization that apart from
the grace of God man cannot even truly repent. Repentance is the gift of
God (Acts 5:31, 11:18; 2 Timothy 2:25).

E. Faith

The initiative of divine grace toward the sincerely penitent sinner is the
offer of the gift of saving faith. It is important to appreciate what is meant
by Christian saving faith, for the word "faith" is often used in reduced and
variable senses, and there is much confusion. There is a distinction between
"The Faith," that is, the body of reliable doctrine preserved in the Church,
and "faith," which is union with God in Christ, in loving personal trust
(see pp. 1–2). From the point of view of systematic theological thought
"The Faith" is the foundation of "faith," though from the point of view
of the actual devotional experience it is often and largely the other way
about. A man first embarks upon God in personal trust and faith, and then
goes on to think out the implications of this in the acceptance of a body
of belief. However, in principle a man must have some reasonable ground
for supposing that there is a God, and a God who has in Christ performed
the saving act of power and love, before he can give himself to that God
in worship, trust, and obedience (Hebrews 11:6).

This is an important point of devotional discipline, as well as of theology.
Faith is not merely subjective. It is not a state of human feelings, which
is "true for me because I feel it to be true." Christian saving faith is a
response to the objective facts, and to the reasoned truth (Romans 10:17).
However, it is equally important that Christian saving faith is not merely
orthodoxy, or the candid acceptance of correct doctrinal views. It is a
personal response to a personal God, who comes to meet man in Jesus
Christ. If there is no personal response of loving trust and obedience to-

ward the God who is admitted to exist, there is no saving faith (James 2:19).

If the foundation of faith is acceptance of revealed Christian truth a second element in faith is what may be called *fidelity*. This is the proverbial "betting one's bottom dollar on God," and in response to what one believes about His power and goodness, committing one's whole way of life to Him in trust and obedience. This may be described as "the faith of Abraham" (Genesis 15:6), who in obedience to the call of God "went out, not knowing whither he went" (Hebrews 11:8). This faith, or steadfast fidelity, is the faith which is chiefly spoken of in the Old Testament (Hebrews 11:1–39). This is the authentic spiritual precursor of the fuller Christian faith of the New Testament (Romans 4:1–25).

However, fidelity does not comprise everything which the Christian means by full, saving, Christian faith (Hebrews 11:40). The essentially *Christian* element in saving faith is trust in the love and power of God as it is fully declared to man in the atoning death and glorious resurrection of His incarnate Son. And the climax of this is a personal faith in a personal Savior. Saving faith takes up into fellowship with Christ the whole personality of man, the affections of his heart as well as the convictions of his mind and the resolve of his moral will (Romans 10:9, 10). It is "faith which worketh by love" (Galatians 5:6). Therefore the essence of faith is a personal "faith-union" with Christ (Galatians 2:20). The most comprehensive New Testament term to express this idea is that the believer is "in Christ." The personal presence of Christ in the Spirit is the dominating and uniting principle, and the very "atmosphere" of the whole Church, of which the believer is a living member (Romans 16:7; 2 Corinthians 1:21, 5:17; Galatians 1:22; Colossians 1:2).

Saving Christian faith is the gift of God. A sincere inquirer may to some extent seek to convince himself of Christian truth, and seek to obey God on account of what he accepts. However, this alone will not take him very far upon the path to God. He cannot by desiring and striving constrain his heart to be filled with loving obedient personal trust in his Savior. Attainment of this "personal experience" is the work of the Holy Spirit (1 Corinthians 12:3). The Augustinian position in relation to this is that at the appointed time God implants the work of saving faith in His Elect, and so converts them. The more general theological position is that there is human cooperation at this point. Indeed, this is the crucial point of all human cooperation with God, for in the moment of decision man is free to choose whether or not he will open his heart to that offered gift which alone makes possible further divine-obedience.

It is precarious overconfidently to dogmatize about this mystery of the human heart. Clearly, man has to wait upon the initiative of grace. He may heartily *wish* that he were converted, and may sincerely pray for the experience, but he cannot say to himself, "Go to now, I *will* be converted!"

Before he can say "Yes" to God he must await the time when God shall choose to call. Yet it is the general confidence of the Church that those who do sincerely and expectantly wait upon God in the means of grace will in due season, sooner or later, certainly be called, and brought to the place of decision where they may receive the gift of faith. For a man of troubled spirit, under conviction of sin, to be found thus clinging to God in the use of the means of grace is on the one hand evidence that he has not yet been granted the gift of full, saving, Christian faith. Nevertheless, it is also a mark that he has faith of a sort, a dim and unformed faith, a faith informed by hope or by duty or by fear, rather than by love. If man will not use this "faith as a grain of mustard seed" for what it is worth, and watch for God in prayer, God will not lift him any further. Yet if he uses his will to make a faithful choice, God can answer the seeker's prayer of "Lord, I believe; help Thou mine unbelief" (Mark 9:24), and bring him to the point when he can, if he will, receive the gift of full Christian faith.

F. Justification

The action which God in grace takes toward those who by loving, trustful, obedient, and penitent faith unite themselves to Christ is described by evangelical theology as *justification*.

1. DEFINITION. The Biblical word "to justify" means "to bring in a verdict of 'not guilty' "—"*to acquit.*" Our Lord taught that the loving Father freely forgives the truly penitent sinner. This fundamental doctrine of grace is in the writings of St. Paul rendered into the language of the law court. The only way in which free forgiveness of the penitent sinner can be so rendered into legal phraseology is by the use of the rather startling paradox that God "acquits the guilty," or to use the more conventional translation, that He "justifies the ungodly" (Romans 4:5). Thus "justification" is forgiveness, and acceptance with God.

2. NEW TESTAMENT DISCUSSION. The reason for this important change in phraseology is seen in the circumstances of controversy within the early Church. Rabbinical Judaism, which was the background of so much of Christianity, was largely a religion of law. Its working assumption was that due obedience to all the commandments of the Mosaic Law is the ground of man's acceptance, as he appears before the tribunal of God the Judge. Man's great question as he appears before God is always: "What is the verdict?" His hope of acquittal, or "justification," is in the works of the Law. The first major decision which faced the infant Church was whether it was necessary for Gentile believers to become Jewish proselytes, and to be circumcised and observe the whole Law of Moses. The unity of the Church was maintained by a measure of judicious compromise, and by a decision that Gentile Christians need not keep the whole Law (Acts 15:1–29). St. Paul has his place as the chief protagonist of the "freedom

party," who was against the enforcement of circumcision, and he expressed his view in the formula "justification by faith, and not by the works of the Law" (Galatians 2:16). By this he meant that Christianity was not a revived and purified form of rabbinical Judaism, but a religion of salvation by grace. Man could not hope to earn a status of acceptance before God the Judge by his merit in fulfilling the Commandments. He had by penitent faith to accept free forgiveness in Christ. Thus the notion of "free forgiveness" came to be rendered into legal phraseology.

Summary of Divergence: Roman Catholic and Protestant Doctrines of Justification

a. Reformation Doctrine

Martin Luther and those who followed him felt that popular Roman Catholic devotional practice, and also much of the medieval Scholastic theology, overlaid the fundamental gospel of salvation by divine grace with the doctrine of "the merit of good works" (see p. 207). This issue presented itself to Luther in the following way. He felt that the Christianity of "merit earning" embodied the same principle as rabbinical and pharisaic Judaism. It was the religion of law creeping in to obscure and contaminate the gospel of grace. In opposition to this he took up St. Paul's formula, "justification by faith, and not by the works of the Law" (Galatians 2:16), and extended it into a general theological principle, applying it thereby to the controversial issues of his own time. Thus the practical and specific Pauline maxim "justification by faith" (Romans 1:17, 5:1; Galatians 3:24, and so forth) is expounded as the general doctrine of "justification by faith *alone*." To the evangelical theologian, following Luther, "justification by faith alone" is a strong and necessary affirmation of the proposition that sinful man's acceptance with God cannot be earned or merited by any human performance, no matter how virtuous. Man must humbly recognize that if he is ever to be forgiven it must be a *free* forgiveness, offered by God solely for the sake of His unmerited favor to those who accept the atoning work of Christ.

b. Roman Catholic Doctrine

The Roman Catholic Church has continued to speak of the merit of good works as contributing to justification. The Roman response to the challenge of Luther's doctrine is crystallized in the authoritative canons of the Council of Trent (1547). The following propositions are there condemned as in error: "That the impious is justified by faith alone—if this means that nothing else is required by way of cooperation in the acquisition of the grace of justification, and that it is in no way necessary for a man to be prepared and disposed by the motion of his own will"; and "That justification once received is not preserved and even increased in the sight of God through good works, but that these same works are only fruits and signs of justification, not causes of its increase." It will be seen that the purpose of these condemnations is to reaffirm the traditional Catholic position that man must freely cooperate with divine grace if he is to be finally saved. The canon is directed primarily against what Roman Catholic theologians felt would be the misunderstanding into which the people would be led by the formula "justification by faith alone"—namely, the notion that it is not essential for the saved to show a changed character and conduct, and that in salvation God does not take account of a virtuous character and conduct.

c. An Interpretative Statement

There is apparently a great gulf fixed between the rival formulae "justification by faith alone" and "justification by faith and the merit of good works." Both sides have often felt that the other is guilty of a radical corruption of Christian faith. In arguing that this divergence is not so great as it looks it is well not to overstate the case. Between the two sides there is some degree of genuine difference of apprehension of the Christian religion. As we have seen (pp. 217–18), Catholic tradition has been chiefly molded by the Christianity of nurture within the Church, and of discipline within the means of grace, whereas Evangelical tradition has been more influenced by the Christianity of the personal "conversion experience." Nevertheless, the divergence is not so great as appears. A difference of emphasis or proportion has been elevated into an apparent difference of essential principle by confusion of terms and mutual misunderstanding.

It will be seen that the authoritative condemnations framed for the Roman Catholic Church at Trent are directed against what were felt to be the dangerous implication of Protestant doctrine, particularly when misunderstood by simple people, rather than against the Lutheran formula itself. Catholics have been afraid of "antinomianism" (this word means "against the [moral]·law"), that is, any understanding of "salvation by faith" which would impair the link between faith and strict morality, including fidelity to the Church and her institutions. And "justification by faith alone" has seemed to many to involve just this. The purpose behind the affirmation of "the merit of good works" has been to safeguard the claims of morality and devotional discipline within the Church, and to enforce that God both strictly requires these things of man, and graciously approves of them in him. Yet Evangelicals would be just as firm in maintaining that their doctrine is not "antinomian." Only when man is changed by the converting grace of God into the good tree can he even begin to bring forth the good fruit of a righteous life, and when he is so changed he will inevitably do so.

The difference of terminology centers around what is meant by the word "justification." Roman Catholic doctrine has defined justification to be not alone God's initial verdict of acquittal pronounced upon the penitent sinner, but as including also His final verdict upon the believer,

at the Last Judgment (Matthew 12:36–37). Clearly, if this is justification, then the maxim "justification by faith alone" does appear to imply
that man is to be admitted to heaven on account of his "spiritual experience," rather than on account of his actual character of righteousness
and love. Such a notion allows Christian faith to sit lightly upon
Christian morals, and is contrary to our Lord's own teaching (Matthew
25:31–46; Luke 6:46). Thus Roman Catholic theology has preferred to
say that man is justified by faith and the merit of good works.

However, if justification is man's *initial* acceptance with God, the
Protestant position is to be upheld, because sinful man, apart from the
grace of God, certainly cannot earn his forgiveness.[4] Every good thing
which he possesses is already the gift of God, and any service which
he can hope to render in the future is only that which it is his duty
to do to the Giver of all (Luke 17:10). Thus he can never make amends
for the past, and so be "justified by works." The Protestant would
affirm that "justification" is St. Paul's characteristic word, and that
therefore it is only rightly used in his sense, which corresponds to the
Protestant exegesis of the New Testament. It would appear that the
apostle's general usage is that justification is forgiveness, or man's
initial acceptance by God. However, the usage is apparently not absolutely invariable (1 Corinthians 6:11).

In stating the evangelical doctrine it is necessary to avoid the
suggestion that justification is only a matter of form, a bare change
of legal status before God. Still less does it imply that by a legal fiction
God treats the sinner as other than he really is. The God who freely
forgives the sinner who does not deserve to be forgiven indeed treats him
as other than he is, but this is no legal fiction. In relation to the doctrine
of the atonement we have seen that man requires "a double cure" (see
pp. 83–84). He needs an assurance that the saving power of God can
make a real difference to sinful man in his condition of bondage, and he
needs also an assurance that the saving mercy of God will actually
receive him, despite the guilty past, if he goes to God to claim this
saving power. These two parts of "the double cure" are connected. The
load of a guilty conscience, and of the tragic frustration of self-despis-
ings in the presence of God, is the chief factor which prevents the
prodigal from rising to go to his Father, to find what He will do for him.
If this be so, then release from the burden of a guilty conscience, and the
assurance that the God of love has accepted him as a reconciled child, is
the chief factor which releases in the heart of man a new constructive
wave of moral power. To be justified, therefore, is the first and all-
important stage in a renewed manner of life, actually changed for the
better in mind and heart, in will and action. Justification, that is,
assurance of acceptance before God, is indeed only the *initial* stage

---

4 And a Roman Catholic theologian would agree with this, for the "good
works" to which God attributes "merit" are those done in "a state of Christian
grace." However, this initial divine grace is interpreted normally as baptismal
regeneration.

of the changed life. It is the change worked in promise, and in this sense is a change chiefly of status. Yet it is a real promise, and a real beginning.

G. Regeneration

This is an alternative word for the initial step in the life of saving faith in Christ. The legal term "justification" has in mind this step chiefly from the aspect of man's standing before God, and of acceptance with Him. The broader and more "organic" term "regeneration," or "the new birth," has the same initial step in mind, but considered chiefly as the beginning of a new course of morally changed life. Those who in Christ are accepted by God as His reconciled children are indwelt by the personal presence of the Spirit of Christ, and enabled by His power, so that they are changed in heart and mind and will and action, and enjoy a power not their own which enables them to live a life well-pleasing to God. Thus they are regenerate, or born again by the Spirit (John 3:5, 7; 1 Peter 1:23).

So it has been said that justification is that which God does *for* us, regeneration that which God does *in* us.

H. Adoption

This Pauline word is yet another metaphor used to describe the new life of those who are united to Christ in faith. They are, as it were, taken into the spiritual family of God, so as in some sense to share Christ's filial privilege of confident access to the Father. Thus the word chiefly has reference to the believer's sense, in Christ, of a confident standing before God (Romans 8:15; Galatians 4:5, 6).

I. Assurance

The use of this word raises the issue of whether, and in what way, the believer may be "sure" of his salvation. Several different answers have been given in the Church.

Summary of Divergence: the Assurance of Salvation

a. Catholic Doctrine

The position traditional to Catholic doctrine has been, and is, that while the faithful Christian need not live in a state of anxious apprehension as to his state of salvation, he cannot be "sure" of it until he arrives at a godly and believing death. He should not doubt either the goodness of God or the security of His promises to bestow grace in the means of grace. However, no man can presume beforehand that he will not fall from the discipline of the Christian life, and from the way of salvation, until death takes him beyond the power of temptation. Thus "there are no saved Christians but dead Christians." This is a common-sense though somewhat prudential view of the matter.

b. Calvinist Doctrine

The Calvinist doctrine of assurance has been based chiefly upon the doctrine of the final perseverence of the saints (see p. 212). The decree of election is fixed, and therefore if a man once knows himself to be the object of God's irresistible grace he is assured that he will persevere through life to a state of salvation. Though he stumble into temptation at times, he cannot finally fall from grace.

c. Wesleyan Doctrine

The preaching of John Wesley (1703–1791) gave much prominence to the doctrine that it is possible for the believer to enjoy the spiritual privilege of a full assurance of salvation. As in some other matters, Wesley's teaching was a mediating synthesis, and a doctrine of practical piety rather than of speculative theology. The leading text, Romans 8:16, "The Spirit Himself beareth witness with our spirit, that we are the children of God," had already been used by the Calvinist divines to establish the idea of an inward witness of the Holy Spirit, but Wesley made a fuller exegesis to substantiate his distinctive doctrine of assurance. He observed that St. Paul speaks of two "witnesses." There is first "the witness of one's own spirit." According to Wesley this is the believer's common-sense argument that since his conversion he has experienced such a distinct change of inward moral will, and of outward practical discipline, that it is impossible for him to doubt that he is the object of God's saving grace (compare 1 John 2:3, 5, 29; 3:14, 24; 4:13). This was the essential foundation of assurance, to be looked for in all who claimed the privilege.

The full and sincere believer, however, might expect that God would add to this the additional privilege of "the witness of the Spirit of God." This Wesley describes as "an inward impression on the soul, whereby the Spirit of God directly witnesses to my spirit, that I am a child of God." From what he writes one may judge that as the former "witness" is the activity of the Holy Spirit in the moral life of the believer, so this "witness" is the imprint of the Spirit upon the emotional life, though it is certainly not necessarily a matter of exuberant or ecstatic emotion. It is, in fact, the abiding mark left by the experience of "the heart strangely warmed." When the two "witnesses" are conjoined in the Christian experience, then the believer rejoices in a full assurance that he is in a present state of salvation. However, Wesley teaches that this assurance is the *privilege* of the believer. It is to be prayed for and expected, but the circumstance that one does not possess it does not indicate that one is not in a state of salvation. Furthermore, he strongly affirms that it is the moral witness which is the essential element. To claim assurance on account of a state of emotion, but in absence of the profound moral change, is rebuked as a sure symptom of most dangerous fanaticism. Furthermore, Wesley teaches that this full assurance does not entitle the believer to presume that he is bound finally to be saved. If he does not carefully watch himself in the moral and devotional discipline of the Christian life the believer may fall from grace, and lose both his assurance and his salvation.

J. Sanctification

This is the name given to the growth in Christian grace which starts with regeneration, and which is to continue progressively all the days of the believer's life (Romans 5:3–5, 6:13–14; 1 Corinthians 6:9–20, 9:24–27; Ephesians 4:20–32; Colossians 3:1–17; 1 Thessalonians 4:3). A fundamental point is that this continuing spiritual and moral improvement of inward character and outward conduct is not a self-improvement imposed by discipline. It is the fruit of the effectual operation of the indwelling Spirit of grace (Romans 8:1–13; Galatians 5:22–26). Thus all his days the Christian continues to be dependent upon God's saving grace, no matter how confirmed in good habits he may become. However, the process of morally responsible cooperation with grace continues also (Philippians 2:12–13). It is at this point that Christian theology opens out into the whole field of Christian morality, the guiding rule of which is the "law of liberty" under the guidance of the Holy Spirit (1 Corinthians 8:1–9; James 1:25), as applied to ever-changing practical circumstances of life by the authoritative pastoral guidance of the Church (John 20:23).

K. Holiness

All who seek to follow a high ideal are bound to live in a certain state of tension between that ideal and what is practicable in real life, in view of the limitations and frailty of human nature, and the fallen state of the world. The Christian has espoused the noblest ideal of all, and therefore he is more than others aware of this tension. It is not surprising, therefore, that there should be in the Church many and sharply contrasting views as to what is the realistic ideal of Christian living in this world.

Summary of Divergence: Doctrines of Holiness

a. Catholic Doctrine

The traditional Catholic doctrine of the saintly life has been, and is, that of a double Christian calling. As this has been expressed in Roman Catholic teaching, all the faithful are called by God to follow the "evangelical precepts," while the few are called to the higher standard of the "counsels of perfection." The chief scriptural warrant for this doctrine has been found in the word of our Lord to the rich young ruler, that if he would be "perfect" he should forsake all his property, and take up the austere life of a wandering disciple (Matthew 19:21).

The background of this doctrine of a double standard is the assumption that the whole of the baptized community of the "Christian" city or nation is in some sense called to Christian discipleship, even though the majority are frail and compromised human beings who can only follow the Lord from afar off. However, there are within the community a number of self-denying and devoted souls, who are called by God to a life entirely given to the service of Christ, and who are equipped with the special grace necessary to follow this calling.

Thus in the matter of property: ever since the Fall contaminated this world, the lower spiritual order of private property, with the social divisions which follow from it, has been necessary as a matter of discipline. The evangelical precept binding on all in relation to this private property is to be law-abiding, just, honest, diligent, and charitable to the poor. The corresponding counsel of perfection is that those who are called to a life of entire Christian devotion should seek the higher spiritual condition of religious poverty, in the brotherly life of communal property. In the matter of the relation of the sexes, likewise, the standard suitable to most Christian men and women is that marriage and the procreation of children is ordained by God, in order that the race be continued and vice restrained (Genesis 1:27–28, 3:16; 1 Corinthians 7:1, 2, 8, 9, 27, 28). The evangelical precept is that each man should live honorably with his wife in the sanctity of the marriage bond, and bring up Christian children (Matthew 19:1–9). However, those who are called to the higher devotion of the counsels of perfection are to remain celibate in the service of Christ (Matthew 19:10–12; 1 Corinthians 7:29–35).

This may be described as a "realistic" doctrine. It takes serious account of the admitted circumstance that it is impossible to discipline the entire nominal Christian community to live *en masse* according to the highest Christian ideals. Any attempt to constrain men to live beyond the grace granted to them will defeat its own end. It is to the spiritual advantage of most ordinary men that they discipline themselves according to a more moderate and prudential standard. However, there are a few to whom is granted an outstanding zeal for religion, and they have a calling from God to render outstanding service. For these it is good to attempt a stricter discipline. And each branch of Christian discipline has its own due place in God's plan.

The effect of this doctrine is to make Christian "perfection" virtually synonymous with the conventual life of a religious Order, under the canonical vows of poverty, chastity, and obedience. A danger in the system is that it may suggest to the general Christian community that the most which can be expected of them is a second-rate standard of discipleship, and that serious religion is the business of the separated clergy and the monastic Orders.

b. Reformation Doctrine

The Protestant Reformers strongly reacted against the medieval doctrine of the counsels of perfection, because to them it seemed to answer to the notion of "the merit of good works," and to be inconsistent with the doctrine of salvation by grace. Thus classic Reformation doctrine frowned upon the mention of "perfection" as inconsistent with an adequate view of human depravity, and of mankind as absolutely dependent upon grace. The emphasis here is that even the converted man is bound to continue all his life as a helpless sinner, though "a sinner saved by grace." Thus until he arrives in heaven the Christian is "both justified, and a sinner."

This latter maxim of Reformation theology is not intended to permit moral laxity or antinomianism, for the man who is in a state of grace ought to be living the life of the Spirit, and growing up to a thorough spiritual and moral change. However, this doctrine can display a weakness, for it may suggest the "world-despairing" attitude which regards the manifest moral ills of ordinary human society as in principle beyond repair. The conclusion is then close to hand that the most which the Christian man can do is to live the life of grace within the sphere of Church worship and private devotion and allow the social, economic, and political conventions of the community to be regulated by social, economic, and political influences. Thus the division which in the Catholic system appeared between the "secular life" and the "religious life" here reappears between the devotional life and the civic life.

c. Wesleyan Doctrine

The doctrine of holiness is another matter in which the preaching of John Wesley significantly attempted a mediating synthesis in the form of a strong evangelical doctrine of grace, which yet called the earnest believer to the hope of perfection. This system of thought, often modified in various ways, and sometimes deteriorated, has since Wesley's time been influential among Methodists, and also with other groups of Evangelicals whose tradition goes back to the revival of the eighteenth century, rather than to classic Protestantism.

The background of Wesley's teaching is not that of an evangelical Church which ministers to a whole community, but that of a closely knit society of religious devotees within the Church, banded together by unsparing discipline for the purpose of reviving the general body of the Church. Thus the appeal is avowedly made, as in the Catholic system, to the minority who are called by God to a life of outstanding devotion and service. Wesley indeed held out the ideal of holiness to all men, but his guiding interest is not prudentially to legislate for what is practicable in the general body of the "Christian" community. He is holding up an ideal to ardent devotees. However, this disciplined group is not, as in general Catholic practice, to pursue a course of monastic life more or less separate from the secular community. The expectancy of the highest standard of Christian discipleship is confidently to be held out to ordinary men and women who are surrounded by the cares of home and family, and who have a living to earn in the world.

The group seeking holiness is to be marked off from the rest of the world by its strict devotional discipline, by its austere life of diligence, frugality, and charity, and by its plain-spoken zeal in reminding men of the claims of real religion and in rebuking the sins, follies, vanities, and compromises of conventional society. Thus it is to possess something of the office and spirit of monasticism, but it is a "monasticism" to be lived out in the home, the market, and the workshop. Wesley assures ordinary men and women that if they have genuine and wholehearted faith no limit is to be set to the power of Christ completely to transform the human personality. No known and willing compromise is to be accepted as inevitable. Nevertheless, the tension between the ideal and the generally practicable inevitably reappears, though in another form. There is tension between the group seeking holiness, who are to be accounted "Christians" in the full sense of the word, and the rest of the community, who are but nominal Christians. The spiritual danger here is manifestly that the society of the zealous may slip into self-righteousness, and into alienation from the main body of the Church.

Wesley's doctrine is that Christian perfection, or holiness,[5] is to be defined as the divine gift of "perfect love." This is not "sinless perfection." The believer cannot expect to be lifted in this life beyond all human limitations. He who has the gift of holiness will still be tempted, and may sincerely misjudge other people, inadvertently doing them wrong. He may be entrapped into a fault through ignorance or inexperience, or by being taken by surprise in unforeseen circumstances. He will still be beset by his natural human limitations of temperament and mental equipment, so that he may not be able to render God all the service which man ideally ought. However, when he recognizes temptation he will turn from it with a ready instinct of loathing. When he finds himself in a fault he will not dally with sin and defile himself, but will straightway repent, and will beware of that fault again. In fact, holiness in the gift of a heart which entirely goes out in love toward God. Man cannot arrive in this life at sinless perfection, but perfect love can grant entire victory over all known and willful sin.

This condition, according to Wesley, is Christian perfection, and is the fulfillment of our Lord's promise and command, "Be ye therefore perfect, even as your Father which is in heaven is perfect" (Matthew 5:48). Those who uphold this as the due ideal of the Christian life affirm that to deny this standard is to allow that willful compromise with known sin is inevitable in the Christian life, no matter how sincere be the faith of the disciple. This is to deny the power of Christ to save to the uttermost, and in practice cuts the nerve of Christian endeavor.

A prudent judgment is, however, that the divine gift of perfect love is something to be believed in, prayed for, preached, and expected, rather than to be claimed for oneself. This Wesley himself never claimed that he had attained. The reason for this limitation is that modesty is a part of human goodness. Our sinless Lord Himself did not go about making claims for His sanctity, and He plainly did not like being praised for His goodness (Luke 18:18–19). His followers are to walk in the

---

[5] Also called "entire sanctification."

same way. We can imagine a believer of exceptional experience and discipline refusing to deny his inward conviction that God had indeed performed this wonderful thing for him, though he would certainly speak in fear and trembling. Yet for anyone easily and lightly to claim it for himself, and particularly to claim it upon the basis of a sudden emotional upheaval, is surely a mark of a crude lack of spiritual sensitivity, possibly verging upon fanaticism.

It was Wesley's belief that the divine gift of perfect love was given in a moment of time. This idea is an inherently reasonable one. Profound psychological experiences of all sorts commonly work up to a sudden climax, and so it is natural to expect that if some believer were to come to an unusually enhanced spiritual illumination the experience would be granted in a flash of insight. Thus some have thought of "entire sanctification" as an instantaneous experience, parallel to "conversion," and this has given rise to the name for it of "the second blessing."

L. Mysticism

The discussion of the work of grace in the heart may be brought to a close by a brief evaluation of the mystical experience. In the wider sense a mystic is one who comes to an experience of immediate union with, or communion with, God. Thus everyone who has any experience of religion which is inward and spiritual must have at least a little of the mystic about him. If mystical communion is totally lacking, the worshipper can get no further than a conventional attendance at church service, and the bare pursuit of moral duty. However, there are some few souls possessed of exceptionally active and sensitive spiritual faculties, who are able to follow the experiences of inward and spiritual religion to an enhanced degree. These are called, in the proper sense of the word, the *mystics*.

The normal mark of a mystic is first, that the sense of spiritual unworthiness before the holy God, which in the normal believer is to be described in terms of "conviction of sin," is to the mystic deepened into a profound and agonizing sense of utter separation from God. This has been written of in the meditations of the mystics in such terms as "the dark night of the soul," during which man has to walk by "naked faith," that is to say, by faith in God utterly unsupported by any sense of joy or peace. This descent to the depths will then be followed by the other normal mark of the mystic, namely, a height of spiritual rapture which is beyond words to express. That which in the normal believer is described as joy and peace in God, and perhaps as the full assurance of salvation, is by the mystic spoken of in such terms as "the marriage of the soul with God." The witness of the mystic is that he has been granted a precious experience of complete union with the divine, such as he cannot utter (2 Corinthians 12:2–4).

First it may be said that the psychological mechanism of the mystical experience is natural, though unusual. Thus there have been true mystics in religions other than the Christian. The factor of importance, therefore, to the faith of the Church is not whether a certain man or woman has a genuine mystical experience, but whether or not he is a true *Christian* mystic. The mark of distinctively Christian mysticism is its secure attachment to the historic Christian faith, and to the historic Christian Church. The Christian Faith and Church may be likened to the filament in an electric lamp, and the intense spiritual experience of the mystic to the powerful electric current which makes the filament glow. The true calling of the mystic is to infuse a strong sense of the inward and spiritual into the familiar apparatus of worship and doctrine. Thus, when the mystic remains in the Faith, and in the Church, he can shed a clear and guiding light. However, if he yields to the temptation to isolate himself from the historic Faith and Church, as from religion at an inferior and "unspiritual" level, he may be found in serious error. The mark of delusion in the mystic is to seek to enjoy the heavenly light apart from the objective and common-sense "filament."

One or two symptoms of this error may be noted. In the first place, it has been defined above that a mystic comes to an experience of immediate union with, or communion with, God. There is an important distinction between "union" and "communion." Some mystics have spoken of "union" with the divine as though in the moment of spiritual rapture the personal distinction between God and the human soul were erased. This reflects the pantheistic doctrine that the soul of man is a "drop of divinity," that God is "the ocean of divinity," and that the destiny of man is for the drop to be lost again in the ocean. This is a notion inconsistent with the fundamental Christian doctrine of a sovereign personal God. True Christian mysticism speaks rather of the closest intimacy of personal *communion* with God, the personal distinction between God and man being carefully preserved.

Furthermore, some mystics have looked to the immediate inward and individual communion of the soul with God as an authority for new revelations of doctrine. This is a lapse into subjectivism. The true and Christian purpose of the mystical "inner light" is not to transcend historic doctrine, or to supersede reason, but to illuminate the rational and historic faith with passionate personal devotion. Clearly, also, the mystic is characteristically somewhat of a religious individualist. The most spiritually profitable Christian mystics have lived their lives of devotion within the regular institutions of the Church, even though in a sense they have sometimes been "in the Church, but not altogether of it."[6] Thus their activity has kept alive within the institutional Church the sense of inward and spiritual

---

6 Many Roman Catholic mystics have been of this type.

religion. Other mystics have yielded to the natural temptation to write off the established ecclesiastical machine as hopelessly formal, external, and "unspiritual," and have formed private circles of their own disciples.[7] These have then gradually institutionalized themselves into new denominations, usually of a highly individualistic character, and sometimes also of an unorthodox and deviationist doctrine.[8] This is, we feel, a loss to the cause of Christian faith.

Readings

Barclay, W., *Turning to God*. Philadelphia: Westminster Press, 1964.

Hodgson, L., *The Grace of God in Faith and Philosophy*. London: Longmans, Green & Company, Ltd., 1936.

Flew, R. N., *The Idea of Perfection in Christian Theology*. London: Oxford University Press, 1934.

Watson, P. S., *Let God be God!* London: The Epworth Press, 1954. (Historical study of Luther's doctrine of grace.)

Yates, A. S., *The Doctrine of Assurance*. London: The Epworth Press, 1952.

---

[7] For example, George Fox.
[8] For example, Jacob Böhme.

Chapter Ten

The Hope of Glory

He shall come to judge the quick and the dead.
—The Resurrection of the body,
And the life everlasting

I. The Christian Hope

One of the clearest marks of authentic Christianity is that it is the religion of a reasoned and a triumphant hope—a hope for the future life of the individual, and a hope for the future of the world. This note rings out clear and plain throughout the New Testament (Romans 5:4, 5; 1 Corinthians 13:13; Ephesians 4:4; Colossians 1:27; Hebrews 6:19; 1 Peter 1:3, 3:15). This was one of the chief factors which gave early Christianity its "cutting edge" in the pagan world which was its mission field. The mythological religions of antiquity had been discredited, and the people were left with no secure religious view of life on which to lay hold. The few and educated tried to comfort themselves as best they could with the somewhat rarified consolations of philosophy, and the ignorant walked in dread of magic. There was a hope of immortality among the Gentiles, but it was the wistful hope that a reduced echo of man's present personal existence might continue for a while in the unseen world. As for the world order, the golden age was thought of in terms of the remote past, and if there was hope for a better day in the future it was conceived of in the frustrating doctrine that history is a cyclical process. Throughout all time the wheel of good and bad fortune went round and round.

What deeply impressed the pagan world about the Christians was the spectacle of men with hope. There was a hope for the world. Human history, under the hand of a mighty God, was actually going somewhere worthwhile. Therefore life was not "a tale told by an idiot, full of sound and fury, signifying nothing." And the Christians were so sure of a personal and blessed life with God, as a part of this world-hope, that they were not afraid to die, and to die the dreadful death of the arena. That proud Regulus, fortified by considerations of birth and public honor, should summon up his courage to face a patriot's death by torment was known among the Romans, and held in high regard. A doctrine which could put this heroic spirit into the lower classes, into weak women, and even into cringing slaves, was new and strange, and strangely impressive!

What was true in the ancient world is eminently true also in the modern. One of the leading symptoms of a denatured popular Christianity is a pulpit which is vague and sentimental about heaven. It is sentimental, in its implied suggestion that all tolerably decent people will surely go to heaven, and quite apart from living faith in Christ and moral obedience to Him. It is vague, in that it leaves the impression that this sentiment is no more than a sentiment, for which the Christian preacher has no more substantial support than that he wishes to say something comforting and kindly to the mourners at a funeral. He does not speak as though the Christian hope were a matter of secure knowledge.

Clearly, also, for the same reason, comfortable people surrounded by a score of pleasant luxuries in their homes are in a state of morbid excitement about the world situation. Though they profess, sincerely enough, to believe in God, they cannot bring themselves to believe in a God who is actually in control of the world. The assumption natural to "the modern man" is that human affairs are a current of events driven along by the desire to earn a living, and to win an improved standard of living. This is a view which interprets life as a process without any deep and satisfying meaning. All too often it passes unnoticed that the factor which sometimes gives a tiny Communist minority its fatal secret of iron morale in time of crisis, and which lends to it the power to browbeat the helpless driven herd of "economic men," is the very characteristic which belongs to the authentic Christian! Communists have persuaded themselves that there is a ruling process in world history, and that in their restless political activity they are the instruments of an irresistible force. This is a factor of which conventional statesmen can take no adequate measure, for it is outside their accustomed categories of practicability and sectional interest. Here is the element of hope, stolen from the Christian system! Therefore in many ways the Christian doctrine of the Christian hope, personal and historical, is the very climax of the whole conception of the life of Christian grace.

There was a spring of hope in the ancient world, and significantly it rose from among the Jews, a nation which had greatly suffered. The faith of the Jews was fixed upon one personal and sovereign God, who rules the world in justice. The history of the world, therefore, is no mere cyclical process, but a train of events flowing from the hand of a mighty God. It has a meaning, and will end in a manner worthy of God. The power of evil indeed appears to rule in this world, but in His chosen time God will show Himself to be king by visiting the world with His power. He will overthrow the might of evil, and advance His chosen righteous ones to power and glory, and this sovereignty He will exert in the person of His Messiah.

However, the mainspring of this hope was not the natural desire of the people to be free of the pagan yoke. It was a craving to see God's ways justified to men. This deeper spring of hope it was which gave to the suffering Jewish people their obstinacy of expectation. In a sad and difficult world those who are hoping for some good thing for themselves will in the end lose hope. Those whose eyes are fixed upon the sole glory of God Almighty will count it worthwhile, if necessary, to be martyrs, for they have an assurance that though they perish their sufferings are not in vain. And this preparedness to be a martyr is the sure secret of that heightened morale which can sustain the distressed cause of right in the day of adversity, and rise to opportunity in the day of opportunity. Therefore it is no accident that the theology of the Christian hope is the most Jewish-Christian part of the Faith. This Hebraic character is both the source of its strength, and the reason why it is so hard for the average modern mind to appreciate it aright.

The inquiring mind will next ask how it is possible to have a theology of hope, for hope concerns the future, and the future is unknown. It is for this reason that it is so widely assumed that when the Christian speaks of the hope of heaven he is doing no more than voicing his own private speculations, which have no more authority than his own limited wisdom. The suspicion is then close to hand that the power of wishful thinking is at work. The skeptic advances his theory that it is comforting for man to believe that he will see his loved ones again, and in a happier place, and that therefore the subconscious mind suggests the natural and sincere delusion that there is such a better life. So it is also with the Christian hope for the world order. When this is treated by the serious theologian it is often sadly the case that no part of Christian doctrine is more securely wrapped in incomprehensible jargon! And if it be treated plainly, for the plain man, it is all too often made the peculiar preserve of "Adventist cranks," who revenge themselves upon a Church which has often failed to speak plainly of the Christian hope by preaching a variant of Christianity which consists of virtually nothing but this doctrine.

In all these ways the impression has been spread abroad that the doctrine of the Christian hope is not a matter of reliable knowledge. This has gone far to subdue the spiritual expectation and relax the moral tension of our accustomed Christianity, and so to cut the nerve of heroism and confident hope. If the answer is made that the ground of Christian knowledge of the future hope is simply and sufficiently the doctrine of the Bible, the issue is still not settled. When it was commonly assumed that God inspired the Scripture by implanting mysterious knowledge on the passive minds of the writers, it could be supposed that these writers could foresee the future. However, if it is accepted that God revealed His truth through the working of the human minds of the biblical writers, then it still remains to be asked how they could be inspired to speak of the future.

As science depends so largely in her methods upon an act of faith in the *continuity of nature,* so does the Christian doctrine of the future destiny of the soul, and of the world order, depend in the last resort upon an act of faith in *the continuity of the spiritual order.* The scientist who pronounces that the sun is at a distance of 93 million miles, and is of such and such a mass and temperature, has not "been up to see." He has perfected the laws of measurement in this world of immediate experience, where his theories can be verified by practical experiment. He then makes the assumption, which the findings of science indicate to be a reasonable assumption, that these laws apply also to spheres of existence of which he can have no immediate experience. Therefore, having made his observations of the effects of the sun in this world of immediate experience, he climbs the ladder of mathematical calculation to knowledge of the distant substance of the sun.

So also, the biblical writers, and the theologians who reason from the Bible, have not "been up to visit heaven." They have, however, made the basic assumption that life is a spiritual and moral order. It proceeds under constant laws which are the expression of the will of a God who is always the same, and who can be depended upon to deal with His children in a reliable manner. If spiritual laws are to be observed in this life, it may be assumed that God's government of men will proceed according to analogous laws in the life to come. If the present spiritual and moral process, which is inevitably broken off by the dark mystery of death, appears to be leading toward some goal, then it is a rational act of faith that that goal will be reached, and that destiny fulfilled in the future. A good God, who is reasonable in his dealings with His children, will not raise hopes only to disappoint them—universally, inevitably, and completely![1]

A leading example of this process may be seen from the manner in which this hope originally arose among the Jews. The earlier Hebrew conception of the destiny of the departed was similar to that of many primitive peoples, and was of the kind which is naturally evoked by mysterious and uncanny psychical experiences such as "familiar spirits" and "haunting," and also by dreams about persons who have died. It was supposed that the spirits of the dead survived in a dim underground world called Sheol (Job 11:8), a word which is customarily though not very happily translated as "hell"

---

[1] Thus the Christian belief in immortality has traditionally been accounted a part of natural religion (see p. 24).

(Psalm 16:10).[2] Their existence there was but a reduced and disjointed continuation of the life of this world, a kind of dying echo (Isaiah 14:9–17), because "the spirit of life" had been taken from them (Job 34:14–15). In particular, the dead in Sheol had no effective communion with God, who was the God only of the living (Psalm 6:5, 115:17; Isaiah 38:18). However, God's sovereignty extended there (Job 26:6; Psalm 139:8; Amos 9:2).

Among the more spiritually sensitive Hebrews the impact of religious persecution upon this ancient system of belief was very profound. Faith suggested that in His Day God would destroy the power of evil in the world, and set up His kingdom. However, it would seem that the departed righteous would be excluded in Sheol from this promised day of divine vindication. The problem to faith was particularly acute in the case of the martyrs, who would apparently be shut out from the satisfaction of that day by the very death which was the crown of their religious merit. From this background was developed the doctrine that the righteous would rise from Sheol at the Day of the Lord. Their bodies would be reunited with "the spirit of life," so that they might live to take part in God's triumph, (Isaiah 26:19; Daniel 12:2). This doctrine of resurrection was naturally complemented by the conception of the resurrection of the wicked to judgment. It will be seen that the basis of the doctrine of resurrection was *an act of faith in the justice of God.*

As we consider the Christian hope, and the doctrine of the Last Things,[3] we face a number of propositions which *"must"* be true if God is fully sovereign, just, good, and reasonable in His dealings with men and women. As with the Jews in their hope, the ultimate ground of these beliefs is an

---

2 Gehenna, the place of punishment of the finally impenitent (Mark 9:47), is also translated as "hell." However, the two terms are quite different.

3 *Eschatology, apocalyptic.* We may here explain these two technical terms, for they are common in theological writing. *Eschatology* (from the Greek *eschatos,* "the extreme, the last") is the doctrine of the final destiny of the human soul, and of the world order. In the general sense it can include the conception of a far-off destiny, but it generally carries the connotation, particularly in much modern theological writing, that God's final act of history is at the present time or in the immediate future. Thus the eschatological expectation brings the sense that man is living at the crisis of the ages.

Apocalyptic (Greek "unveiling") is a distinctive form of biblical eschatological writing, in which the rise of the power of evil in the world order, and its final overthrow at the Day of the Lord, are traced out in a kind of drama of superhuman personifications and symbolical events. The vivid, and commonly even bizarre, coloring of the imagery answers to the heightened psychological tension of men who are fighting to retain their faith and hope in the most desperate of situations. Those who are summoning up their courage to die the death of martyrs cannot be content with a placid or level-headed presentation of faith. The apocalyptic writings speak out of the situation of persecution, and therefore appeal to the Church primarily in times of persecution and insecurity. The most developed example of this type of writing in the Bible is the Revelation, or Apocalypse, of St. John. Daniel 7–12 and Zechariah are also of this character, and there are many noncanonical apocalyptic books, Jewish and Christian.

act of faith in the spiritual constancy of God. Even within the confines of a life hemmed in by inevitable frustrations and limitations man has been confronted by God in Christ, and granted the gift of life in fellowship with God. Faith teaches that what God has once initiated He will bring to due fulfillment, for He is an unchanging God whose purpose none can ultimately resist. Therefore the present saving act in Christ carries implicit within it the promise of an unlimited and unfrustrated confrontation by Christ, in a world not darkened by sin.

The skeptic's charge is that this hope is a subjective delusion conjured up by wishful thinking from the subconscious. This common charge can indeed come home with devastating force to the widespread, easy-going, and sentimental delusion that in the unseen world everything will be automatically serene and happy for all tolerably decent folk, because the God with whom we have to do is an indulgent God who is bound easily and lightly to forgive. And it is well that this false hope should be deflated, even though the loss may bring pain to some. The God whom all men have to confront is a God of holy love, and the just judge of all the earth, whose love requires holy love in return. An eternal destiny of life with Him is certainly not the hope which wishful thinking will suggest as attractive to the mind of the natural man (Hebrews 10:31). The true Christian hope is an austere hope, which only those can dare to contemplate whose trust reposes in the saving work of Christ. The Christian hope, therefore, is not the illusory man-centered hope of those who are seeking comfort for themselves, but the secure and God-centered hope of those whose concern it is to see the holy love of God fully vindicated (Matthew 5:6).

The Christian doctrine of the Last Things is set forth in the Bible in imagery and symbolism. This is a necessity of thought and expression, for these doctrines concern matters which are not part of immediate human experience in this world. Therefore they cannot be described in matter-of-fact language drawn from human experience, and which can be taken literally. However, it by no means follows that this part of Christian doctrine is vague, unsubstantial, fanciful, unimportant, and not to be taken seriously as a branch of spiritual knowledge (see pp. 12–13). Provided the symbolism is properly understood, the eschatological and apocalyptic parts of the Bible contain truths of spiritual value. However, these truths do not consist so much of factual information about future events, as a sense of heightened yet solemn expectancy which is to pervade the whole of the Christian system of life and thought. This part of the Christian creed is a battle cry to be shouted, and an ode of victory to be sung, rather than a set of propositions to be reflected upon!

We do not say that our Lord's second advent, the general resurrection, and the last judgment are not events, though they are not in the ordinary sense of the word *historical* events, for they will take place when God has brought to an end the present course of history. However, the spiritual and theological importance of these events does not consist in what we factually know about them, so much as in what we *feel* about them. A vivid expectation of our Lord's victorious second advent, and a strong sense that the judgment is even now upon us, is one of the leading elements which lifts Christianity above the level of a placid and good-natured system of reasonable doctrine, customary worship, and admonitory ethics, and makes of it a fighting creed which can move men to stern endeavor, and for which they are even prepared to die. This element of Christian hope fills the New Testament, and the stories of the martyrs. It is an integral part of balanced and healthy Christianity. If this nervous tension is relaxed, one of the principle sinews of faith is severed. Nevertheless, it is also a fact that overcurious and overinsistent pressing of such questions as, "When will it happen?" "Will it happen visibly and suddenly?" "How far are we to take the Biblical symbolism *literally* and *pictorially?*" is contrary to the intention and genius of the Bible itself. It is an asking of the wrong questions, which can all too easily take the mind away from the important biblical answers. To wish for *matter-of-fact* knowledge of these future events is to desire to know the unknowable, and to find in the Bible that which is not there.

Some writers have assumed that an urgent advent hope and a care for ecclesiastical and moral discipline are interests in some way contrary one to another, because those who are daily awaiting the end of the Age will not be interested in the organization of the Church or the right ordering of human society. It is asserted that this was the case with the first Church. This surely is a mistake. A belief that the time remaining before the end is short will affect the Christian judgment as to what is appropriate moral conduct. Thus St. Paul's teaching to the Corinthians regarding marriage and slavery clearly reflects this influence (1 Corinthians 7:18–35). However, a vivid sense that the Church is living at the crisis of the ages, when every action counts because divine judgment is at the door, is generally found to be one of the most powerful of all influences to nerve the Christian community to strenuous moral endeavor and strict discipline. Those who are waiting are to be on the alert (Mark 13:34–37).

II.   Hebrew and Greek Symbolism

The background of our Lord's teaching and ministry was the Jewish messianic hope (see pp. 45–46). He apparently announced that the expected kingdom had come, and spoke of Himself, at least guardedly, as the Messiah of divine promise. This message was thus framed in the thought forms of the Hebrew prophets, and to some extent, at least, in the imagery of apocalyptic. It is fundamental to an understanding of our Lord's teaching to realize that it was eschatological, though we believe that it is an error to assume, as some critics do, that it was naïvely or crudely eschatological, or

that Jesus was virtually a deluded messianic dreamer (see pp. 245–46).
Nevertheless, the fact remains that the symbolism which is largely used in
the New Testament to express the Christian hope and the doctrine of the
Last Things is radically Hebraic.

This Hebraic symbolism views the history of this world as a succession
of divine acts performed under the sovereign hand of God. During the
present evil Age Satan and his forces are permitted by God to exercise a
certain amount of sway over the sinful human race. At the end of the
Age will come God's last and most significant act. He will invade the world
with the power of His sovereign kingdom, destroy the power of evil, judge
all men, redeem His people, and thus, in bringing to an end the present
history of the world, will show Himself to be God indeed. The dividing
line between this evil world and the supremacy of the things of God is,
as it were, a vertical wall, a demarcation in the future. One order will
suddenly pass away, and another take its place. In terms of this scheme
God's gift to man of triumph over death is the resurrection of the dead,
and divine judgment is the future last judgment.

However, this is not the only system of symbolism which is used to express
these truths. Thought forms which go back in the main ultimately to the
more philosophical and scientific mentality of the Greeks provided the chief
intellectual apparatus of the ancient Church, once it had grown away from
its Jewish-Christian origins. These Greek thought forms are a main constituent of secular thought in the Western world of today. Here is another and
contrasting form of symbolism for expressing the relationship between this
world, and the supremacy of the things of God. A lower and material
sphere of being, of less intellectual and spiritual worth now exists, and also
the higher and essentially nonmaterial sphere of reason and of spiritual
values. There is, as it were, a presently existent horizontal wall between
them. The course of events in this lower world is regarded as a self-acting
process under natural law, presided over by superior reason. When religious
faith wishes to affirm the supremacy of the things of God in terms of this
system of thought one arrives at the familiar proposition that human personality and eternal spiritual values are more important than "the material."
God's gift to man of triumph over death is the promise that the invisible
soul, which is "the real man," survives the death of the body, and lives
in communion with God in a blessed immortality. Divine judgment is God's
present attitude to the thoughts, feelings, and acts of man, and is a continuous process.

These two systems of symbolism for the Christian hope, the Hebraic, or
biblical, and the Greek, are not mutually exclusive. Though superficially
very different they are in fact complementary, for each has its own theological value. One cannot say that one or the other is "right" or "wrong." If a
surveyor and an artist were both sent to visit a beautiful city, and to
bring back a true representation, their work would be very different in

superficial appearance. This would be due to the difference in medium of expression. Nevertheless, both the town plan and the landscape would be valid in its own medium, and useful for its own proper purpose. So it is with the Greek and Hebraic types of symbolism. Superficially they are very different, and some have pronounced them to be inconsistent. Some have affirmed that the original Jewish-Christian eschatological presentation of the Christian hope is naïve and crude, and that it was right and good that it should have been displaced in the Church by later and more philosophical conceptions. Others have seen the same change as the Hellenizing corruption of early and authentic Christianity. A more considered judgment is that both these views are partial and erroneous.

The underlying spiritual intention of both the Hebraic and the Greek forms of doctrine is to express the triumph of the things of God, and to assure the believer of the fulfillment of his life with God. The concrete and nonspeculative Hebrew system is primarily of devotional value. It serves to preserve in the Church that heightened expectancy of hope which nerves the believer to seriousness and courage. The more philosophical and scientific Greek scheme is of value in systematic theology. It fits in the Christian hope with the rest of the system of Christian doctrine. For example, the believer's triumph over death when considered in terms of the divine gift to the soul of immortality harmonizes with the doctrine of the communion of saints (see pp. 133–35). The Greek system of symbolism also harmonizes with systems of Christian philosophy. In the doctrine of the Christian hope there is therefore within the Church a twofold tradition. To keep the two sides together, and to keep them in balance, is not always easy, but the Church affirms that both are necessary to the sound body of doctrine.

It is no accident that the doctrines of the second advent, the resurrection of the body, the millennial kingdom, and the Last Judgment, which are perhaps the most distinctively Hebraic parts of the whole Christian system, have often proved some of the hardest to understand. This is on account of the immense contrast between this mode of thought and that which is customarily employed in ordinary modern secular thought. Yet the Church should not neglect to understand these doctrines, for there are important spiritual values to be preserved. The gradual reinterpretation of the Christian hope into the more philosophic terms of Greek thought was made necessary as the Church rapidly became a predominantly Gentile body, and had to make herself understood in the Gentile world which had not been nurtured upon the Old Testament.

The incipient change of emphasis is seen within the New Testament itself. Thus the twofold doctrine can be regarded as scriptural. St. Paul's original vivid Jewish eschatology was apparently misunderstood at Gentile Thessalonica, and he had to write to tell his converts that they must not live in daily and agitated expectation of the second advent, so as to give up earning a living (2 Thessalonians 2:1–8, 3:6–10). Later on he had personally to face the possibility that he might die before the coming of Christ (2 Timothy 4: 6–8). Later still, some in the Church were perplexed at the prolonged delay, and had to revise their Scripture exegesis and calculations (2 Peter 3:3–9).

In particular, we are faced with the problem of the virtual evaporation in the Fourth Gospel of the original urgent Jewish eschatology. To some expositors John 20:17 appears to imply that Christ's ascension to glory took place immediately after His resurrection, while John 14:15–18 almost seems to indicate that the promise of Christ's return after His ascension was fulfilled in the gift of the Holy Spirit. A glorious presence of Christ with His Church in current experience has virtually taken the place of the anticipated future advent in glory. In line with this, God's judgment upon man through Christ is a present and continuing process (John 3:17–18). However, although the general resurrection is immediately present in Christ (John 11:25), our Lord is still also the Son of Man (the Messiah), who is to come bringing a future resurrection and judgment (John 5:25–29). Not everything is plain in this profound and various book, but the Church is clearly feeling her way toward the later double tradition. In the Fourth Gospel there is the Greek as well as something of the Hebraic Christian hope.

The Gentile Church of later tradition did not always find it easy to keep a just balance between its original Hebraic and biblical Christian hope, and the Greek thought forms which it had to employ in order to interpret Christian faith to the Gentile world. The Greek mentality was rarely altogether at ease with the vivid and concrete imagery of the Jewish and Jewish-Christian apocalyptic literature, which is so largely associated with the doctrine of the Christian hope. This was because, unlike the Hebraic mind, it was systematic and pictorial. It would hardly have occurred to the Jewish apocalyptists to try to draw pictures of the heavenly or infernal visitants of which they wrote. Indeed, their religion forbade them to portray the human form, as in the picture of an angel. Thus when an apocalyptist speaks of an "angel" he does not think of a figure with white robes and wings, after the manner of later Christian art. He is symbolizing a concrete and embodied message.

Nor was it their interest to arrange the apocalyptic visions successively into a chronology, as though history were a process. The "half-hour" or "thousand years" of the Revelation of St. John are not measured on a clock. They are symbols of spiritual quantities. When the Greek-minded reader came to such books, if he wished to take them quite seriously he instinctively understood them in a much more pictorial and chronological manner than was justified by the original intention of the writer. The result of this was the naïve and at times crudely material millenarianism of some of the Church fathers. In the same tradition are the stirring but fantastic pictures of the last judgment found in medieval Churches, and the endless series of attempts to calculate the date of the supposed "end of the world."

And if the more philosophic and sophisticated Greek-minded Christian turned away from this, as some eventually did, he just as naturally took Jewish apocalyptic much less seriously than its due. This part of the Scripture was spiritualized away into obscure parables of speculative theology. Thus one arrived at a Christianity which was academic, philosophical, and almost entirely noneschatological. Here was a serious loss of Christian spiritual values, in the relaxation of the Christian hope. Time then took its vengeance on the Church in the rise of an opposing and equally unbalanced emphasis upon the coming of the millennial kingdom.

As we approach the details of the doctrine of the Christian hope we may therefore expect to find a comprehensive double tradition, with a strongly Hebraic eschatology subtly balanced against a more philosophic system. The main lines of the compromise which has generally commended itself to the Church are prefigured in the doctrine of St. Augustine of Hippo (354–430), who taught that the world order of his time, that is, the partnership of the Christian Roman Empire and the Christian Church, was itself the thousand-year rule of the saints (Revelation 20:4). The effect of this was to affirm that there would indeed be a momentous second advent of Christ in glory, but to place this event in the uncertain future, and quite possibly in the very distant future. Thus the Christian eschatology is preserved, but its primitive day-to-day immediacy of expectation is in the light of the long experience of the Church resolved into a less intense expectation, solemn indeed, but generalized.

This is clearly a far-reaching modification of the original Jewish-Christian hope, and yet it can be vindicated as a legitimate interpretation of the spirit and general intention of our Lord's own teaching. On the one hand, Christ did frame His message within the thought forms of eschatology, and the apocalyptist's typical urgency breathes through His teaching. Yet on the other hand, He solemnly warned His disciples against fruitless and delusive speculation as to the date of the end (Mark 13:1–7, 32–33; Acts 1:6, 7). Those parables of the kingdom which call Christ's disciples to watch in ready expectancy, also plainly carry the implication that the time of waiting may well be so long that some will be tempted to lose the sense of expectancy and settle down to spiritual slumber (Matthew 24:48–50, 25:5, 6, 19, 37–39; Mark 13:34–37). Christ's own modified advent expectation indicates for us the wise attitude to take toward the Christian hope. We are neither virtually to dismiss these high matters from serious practical consideration, nor to plunge into the less balanced type of "adventism." The judicious Christian will prudently legislate for the century-long discipline of the Church and the community, yet day by day he will remind himself that all these affairs take place under the hand of a sovereign God who disposes, however wisely man may propose. We cannot foresee the future, or know how long a time we have.

III. The Second Advent

A. The Parousia

This word (*parousia*) in the Greek New Testament is usually translated "coming," or "advent" (Matthew 24:3, 27; 1 Corinthians 15:23; 1 Thessalonians 2:19, 4:15; James 5:7; 2 Peter 3:4). The one objection to the familiar word "coming" is that it suggests the idea of movement from one place to another. Clearly, a spiritual being like the divine Son does not exist in a place, nor does the Son incarnate, in His risen, ascended, and glorified humanity (see p. 99). The idea which is symbolized in the familiar phrase that Christ "comes" is that He who at all times and in all places is immediately present, at a certain time and place makes that universal presence known to His people. It is well expressed in the lines:

> Present we know Thou art.
> But O Thyself reveal!

The New Testament word *parousia* conveys something of this conception, for by derivation it means "a being present." Among other usages, it can most significantly mean "the royal Presence" (as in the phrase "the Presence Chamber" of a royal palace). The sovereignty of a monarch extends at all times throughout his dominions, but on occasion he will visit his subjects, and grant to them, in his royal progress, the presence of his sovereignty in a personal way. They are then admitted to "the royal Presence." This is a picture of what we mean by our Lord's advent, or coming. He is truly present with all men at all times, even when they are not aware of Him. He can, however, personally manifest His presence, so as to make the fact of His sovereignty impressively real.

B. The Advent in Glory

When the divine Son united Himself with our humanity, and was born as the Babe of Bethlehem, the universal divine presence was made known to man in a special way. This was the first *parousia,* the first advent, and it was a coming in great humility (2 Corinthians 8:9; Philippians 2:8). In order to effect His presence, our Lord suffered labor, misunderstanding, rejection, contempt, torment, and death. His presence brought the kingdom of God and accomplished the saving act of divine sovereignty (see pp. 44–45). Nevertheless, the ruling power of the kingdom was then only manifested "as a grain of mustard seed" (Mark 4:30–32). The number who had faith to see the suffering Messiah for what He was, and to accept the offered hidden treasure of the kingdom, were but few (Matthew 7:14). Therefore the Church, the community of the kingdom, found herself to be a contemptible minority in the world (1 Corinthians 1:26–28),

> ...humble and unknown,
> Loved and prized by God alone.

The great ones of this world, though in point of fact they exercise their power under the providence of God (John 19:11; Romans 13:1), commonly did not recognize this fact. Therefore they snapped their fingers at Christ, His law, and His Church, and so the natural and expected calling of the people of God in this world is labor, hardship, contumely, and martyrdom (Mark 8:34; Luke 6:22–23; Acts 5:41; 1 Corinthians 4:9–13; 1 Peter 2:20–21, 3:14–17). By and large, this has been the condition of human society ever since, though the apparent outward prosperity of the Church has at times concealed this from the superficial view. It is indeed true that the power of Satan is destroyed (Luke 10:18), but this does not appear to be so (Luke 4:5–6). Christ's presence is with His world, but in great humility.

However, the Christian act of faith in the goodness, power, and constancy of God is that *"history will end in a manner worthy of God."* This is the very essence of the advent hope. It is something which "must" be if God fulfills the promise implicit in what He has already done, and can be trusted not to disappoint the hopes which He has Himself raised. The mark of this end of history will be a manifestation of the presence of Christ no longer in humility, but in glory. This is the promised Second Advent. He who is now with us will then manifest His presence in a way which will transcend in glory even the gracious and awesome presence which was seen in the Man of Galilee and the risen Christ. He will then be revealed as the rightful and undisputed Master of the whole human situation, and of all the affairs of the world (Matthew 25:31–32; Mark 8:38; Luke 17:24, 22:29; 1 Corinthians 15:24–25; Philippians 2:9–11; Revelation 5:1–7, 19:11–16). Those who in the days of His humility have loved Christ, witnessed to Him, and hoped in His despised cause, will then see the joy and desire of their hearts realized, and be filled with unspeakable bliss (Matthew 25:21; Romans 8:17–18; 2 Corinthians 4:8–18). Supremely, this is the promised reward of the persecuted, and the martyrs (Luke 6:21–23; 1 Peter 4:12–14; Revelation 6:9–11, 7:9–17). The servants of Christ will in that day be clothed with authority over men, such as answers to their divine calling (Matthew 19:27–30). Those who have neglected or refused to open their eyes to the presence of Christ will then be compelled to do so, however reluctantly, and those who have rejected Him and done Him despite will be confounded at last (Matthew 25:44–45, Mark 8:38;

Revelation 1:7). All this is comprised in the Second Advent of Christ, in glory.

C. The Visible Return of Christ

The certainty of the triumphant manifestation in this world of the royal presence of Christ is a cardinal element of Christian faith. The precise manner of it raises a number of perplexing issues. The traditional doctrine of the Church has been that at the Second Advent Christ will visibly return to the earth in glory (Revelation 1:7). However, this expectation has been widely questioned in the modern period. It is not altogether explicit what is the motive of the critics, but in general it would seem to arise chiefly from the desire to approximate Christian doctrine to the presuppositions of current secular thought, and to present Christianity as a nonmiraculous and smoothly evolutionary system. The typical secular thinker does not find it easy to accept the notion that there might in the future be a sudden and revolutionary change in world conditions, such as is presupposed by the traditional doctrine. Clearly, to the Christian this does not entirely dispose of the matter. The discussion is of events which are not part of the course of history, and which are outside the ambit of ordinary human experience. The presuppositions of current secular thought do not necessarily apply to such conditions.

A more substantial rejoinder to the traditional doctrine of a visible Second Advent is the argument that possibly this is not in keeping with the real intention of the Bible itself. A common inclination of the Greek mind in the Church was to take the imagery of Jewish apocalyptic more pictorially and chronologically than the intention of the original writers justifies (see p. 245). Without a doubt the feeling has been widespread in the Church that if the passages which speak of our Lord's Second Advent are to be taken seriously they ought to be taken literally, as of a visible descent from the heavens. Thus it is argued that the phrase, He "shall so come in like manner" of Acts 1:11 must be understood as teaching that the process by which the glorious presence of Christ will be revealed is to be thought of in terms of the ascension in reverse. It does not follow, however, that this is St. Luke's real intention. It can be maintained that a sense of the presence of Christ with His Church, discerned by the eye of interior faith as we "see" Him now, but of immeasurably greater majesty and clarity, is quite in accord with the real mind of Scripture.

Nevertheless, there is on the other side the powerful consideration that the God-given mark of Christ's risen presence, victorious over sin and death, was a *visible* presence, and in a real sense, a bodily presence, though of a glorious body. There is weight in the plea that if this experience, which was the climax of our Lord's advent in *humility*, was as impressively objective as this, Christ's Second Advent in *glory* can hardly be less than "visible." Clearly, for Christ's glorified humanity to appear in a visible and bodily form does not require that this body be a material one, in the ordinary sense of the word. This is indeed a mysterious subject, and we are warned against trying to take symbolical doctrine in a matter-of-fact sense. A certain degree of reverent reserve is fitting when we discuss whether the Scripture requires us to expect Christ's Second Advent as a visible return to earth. It is incautious either to affirm or to deny this dogmatically.

IV. The Millennial Kingdom

Lo! He comes with clouds descending,
Once for favoured sinners slain;
Thousand thousand saints attending,
Swell the triumph of His train:
Hallelujah!
God appears on earth to reign.

The Jewish expectation was that when the advent of the Messiah brought the inflowing of God's kingdom to this world the power of evil in the world order would be finally destroyed. God's chosen people, restored to righteousness of life and national integrity, would then live in holiness and happiness upon earth, to the glory of God (Daniel 7:9–18, 27–28). This hope was taken over and adapted into Jewish-Christian apocalyptic, with the Church, the new Israel, in the position of the restored and glorious people of the messianic kingdom. Our Lord Himself used the prophetic imagery of the messianic banquet (Luke 22:16; Compare Isaiah 25:6–8; Luke 14:15). He spoke of His apostles as reigning in glory in that day (Matthew 19:28), and St. Paul echoes the same idea (1 Corinthians 6:3).

However, the passage which has been by far the most influential in Christian thought on this subject is Revelation 20:1–6, which describes how Satan will first be chained, then the martyrs will rise from the dead in "the first resurrection," and reign with Christ upon the earth for "a thousand years." After this Satan will be released for his last effort in wickedness, and final overthrow, which will be followed by the general resurrection, and the last judgment of all men (vv. 7–13). It is this passage which is chiefly responsible for the doctrine, which is found in many of the ancient fathers of the Church, and which has continued to some extent in the Church ever since, that at the end of the Age, but before the final bliss of heaven, there will be the thousand-year "rule of the saints" upon earth, or millennial kingdom ("millennium," a period of a thousand years).[4]

---

[4] It will be appreciated that in detail this is a most complicated issue. There were in circulation in the early Christian centuries many noncanonical Jewish and Jewish-Christian Apocalypses, containing all manner of variants of the apocalyptic scheme. These books continued to be read and revered, particularly in the less philosophical sections of the Church, and are responsible for some of the details of the doctrine of the Christian hope found in various ancient writers.

There is here raised a perplexed theological issue which has often been the subject of unreasoning controversy. A judgment between the conflicting spiritual interests is both necessary, and not easy to come by. Here the divergence of spirituality between the Hebraic and Greek elements in the twofold tradition of the Christian hope most clearly comes to view. The insistence of some that Revelation 20, and allied Scriptures interpreted from it, must be taken literally, provides the point at which the Jewish-Christian and apocalyptic variant of the Christian hope comes to its most vivid expression. It also provides the point at which this form of the Christian hope presents the maximum of offense to the more sophisticated and philosophical mind. The position as it has stood in the history of the Church is that philosophical, cultural, and ecclesiastical schools of Christianity have generally turned away from the doctrine of the millennial kingdom. It has either been treated as an unimportant matter of vague speculation, or repudiated as naïve, crude, fanatical, and repulsive. The Scripture passages in question have been treated as of minor importance, and it has been affirmed that they must be interpreted in a symbolic sense only.

There is justice in the latter part of this plea. It has been a general tendency of the non-Jewish mind in the Church, when moved by a desire to take apocalyptic *seriously*, to interpret this Hebraic writing more chronologically and pictorially, and in this sense, more "literally," than is justified by the original intention (see p. 245). This is the leading case in point. The greatest degree of reverence for the authority of Scripture does not expressly require "the thousand years" to be taken as referring to a period of historical time as we know it. Nor is it either necessary or possible to fit all the details of all the relevant Scripture passages into one consistent chronology, as the course of biblical controversy abundantly indicates. At the same time, it is necessary to do justice to the long tradition of "adventism" in the Church, which is the testimony of history to an essential element in Christian faith.

The school of thought which has insisted upon the literal interpretation of these passages, and in consequence upon the doctrine of the *earthly* millennial kingdom, has characteristically lived in the hope that these tremendous and mysterious events would happen in the near future. This in general has not been more than an unpopular minority view within the Church. The official exponents of Christianity have normally looked upon its claims with disfavor, and at times this form of the advent hope has been treated virtually as a heresy. Nevertheless, it has shown the power of vitality and persistence. Again and again these views have appeared in the Church, despite all forms of official discouragement, and those who have adopted them have often found in their distinctive theology the secret of the strongest Christian hope and resolution. This historical phenomenon is not merely an accident to be explained away in terms of the gullibility of the ignorant.

By and large the Christian circles which have entertained the millennial advent hope have either been the socially unprivileged or culturally deprived, or else rebels, social, cultural, or political, who were standing against "the powers that be" in church or state. Times which have witnessed the shaking of established institutions and securities, of warfare, invasion, and political insecurity, or of revolutionary social changes, have also commonly seen the increased appeal of "adventism." In fact, those who find life grim, cruel, or dangerous experience the need of a heightened nervous tension such as will enable them to renew their hope when prospects are black and human hopes dead. These are they who turn with ready instinct to the Hebraic scheme of the Christian hope. The confident assurance that the Almighty is even now breaking into history to rescue the distressed cause of the right, symbolized by the vivid apocalyptic imagery—this it is which lifts up the hearts of God's people, and which strengthens their arms for the conflict. The books which came out of persecution speak in every age to the persecuted, and to those who are in a spiritual condition analogous to persecution.

There is enough of embattled wrong, of tragedy, and of uncertainty in life to make this an important part of the Christian gospel. Nevertheless, uncertainty, tragedy, and embattled wrong are not the whole of human life. Not all Christians are all the time so engaged to face the persecutor or oppressor that they have no leisure to consider wider human affairs. Indeed, there comes a day when there exists a university of "Christian" learning, a communal or national "Christian" religion, and even a "Christian" civil government. There is therefore a legitimate place for that more reflective Christianity which seeks to present Christian truth as an integral part of the whole intellectual and cultural activity of men. There is the place likewise for the churchmanship of prudential pastoral discipline, even though this is but a crutch to assist unheroic Christians in the performance of routine spiritual duties. And there is a place for the religion which seeks to be preservative of law and order in the community at large, the cement of the conventional morality of decent society.

This communal, prudential, reflective Christianity is not the faith of men who are contemplating the end of the Age. It is the religion of those who are legislating for the welfare of their grandchildren. It is "low tension" Christianity. Yet it answers to a part of life. The Christianity of the relaxed eschatological tension instinctively moves into the Greek scheme of presentation for the Christian hope as being more humane, reflective, and philosophical. The apocalyptic chapters of the Bible are then interpreted in a symbolic, and not a literal sense. Our Lord's Second Advent is affirmed indeed in principle, but contemplated as though it were likely to take place only in the remote future.

We may ask, "What is the just balance between these two legitimate Christian interests? What is the ground of common understanding which will suffice to hold together these two traditions, the majority and ecclesiastical, and the minority and "adventist," both of which have in their own way vindicated themselves upon the stage of history?" Surely true Christianity is the religion of divine intervention, but not of an utterly unaccountable divine intervention. It is also an evolutionary religion, but certainly not a merely evolutionary religion. It is faith in a process of reasonable and providential development, set within the background of divine intervention.

The expectation of the millennial kingdom vividly symbolizes the cardinal truth that Christianity is not a world-despairing religion. It is a world-subduing faith. This answers to the principle displayed in the incarnation and the sacraments, that the material creation is the handiwork of God, created in order to signify a spiritual purpose, and visited and used by God for the accomplishment of spiritual ends. The fitting climax of this principle is the doctrine that the ultimate destiny of this material world is not to be "cast as rubbish to the void." The whole world order is to be radically redeemed (Romans 8:19–22). The ideal of the Christian is not, therefore, to flee as a hermit to the wilderness, or to wait for a reward in a heavenly sphere, while the nations of the world go to the devil in their own way. Christ's final and complete triumph is to be vindicated in this very world which rejected Him and put Him to an open shame (Philippians 2:10–11). The whole life of nations is to be radiantly transformed under the mastership of Christ so that the glory of God may be fully revealed therein (Revelation 11:15).

It follows that there is implicit within Christianity a world-affirming and active spirit, and even, in its due place, a socially idealistic, reforming, and "progressive" spirit. The New Testament teaches that the civil government, though not "Christian" in the fullest sense of the word, yet exists under the providence of God, and by its legal rewards and punishments can do something to uphold human morality and minister to the will of God (Romans 13:1–5). It is therefore very much the business of the Christian to practice civic virtue in every way open to him (Mark 12:17; Acts 25:10–12; Romans 12:9–21, 13:6–10; 1 Peter 2:11–22). Furthermore, experience shows that wise and humane political constitutions and social conventions, improved educational and cultural standards, and better conditions of housing and hygiene, will often help ordinary men and women to live a decent and dignified life. These good things do not indeed bring Christian salvation, but they may avoid human degradation, and this is no light matter. Thus Christian history indicates that the civic virtues of Christian men and women have often, as a kind of by-product to their service of God, decisively helped in the upbuilding of helpful cultural, educational, social, and political institutions. Christianity therefore by no means despairs of the social, economic, and political order, but cherishes the ambition to conquer it all for Christ. The "rule of the saints" is the promise of God.

Nevertheless, the attitude of the Christian to "the kingdoms of this world" is not one of evolutionary utopianism. The Christian citizen wishes to help his fellow citizens to better citizenship, and accounts this an important part of the service of God. Yet he does not rest his hope for the reconstruction of the world order upon anything so insecure as this. Associated with the Christian doctrine of the Second Advent in glory and the millennial kingdom there is the conception that as history proceeds to its close there will be a greater and greater overflowing of human wickedness, bringing world strife and unparalleled persecution of God's people (Mark 13:3–13; Revelation 6:1–17, 8:6–9:21). Indeed, this consummation of wickedness is in apocalyptic passages personified as *Antichrist,* who will appear at the head of the forces of evil, only to be overthrown and judged to make room for the final triumph of right (2 Thessalonians 2:1–10; 1 John 2:18; Revelation 9:11, 20:7–10). There can hardly be any doctrine more repugnant than this to the presuppositions of ordinary secular thought on social subjects. It is the tacit working assumption of well-intentioned humanist thinkers that as history proceeds and human society develops, human righteousness ought generally to advance, and culture and happiness to increase. If the course of sad events disappoints this hope, we see evidenced the spread of disillusionment and bitterness, and the rise of "angry young men" who spend their days and talents in cynical criticism because the human race has so signally failed to take their good advice!

Christian doctrine takes a more realistic and more balanced view. The intention of the Bible in speaking of Antichrist is not so much to declare that the world is actually and positively becoming more wicked as time goes on, but to teach that both good and evil are showing themselves ever more plainly to be what they are. Human affairs are a mixture of right and wrong, and as human institutions develop both the right and the wrong develop together (Matthew 13:24–30). That right and wrong reach their climax together is symbolized in the conception of the appearance of Antichrist, and of the Messiah. We have already indicated that active Christian service in the world can prevail to some extent. Nevertheless, the somber fact of human life remains that human nature is infirm and human institutions even at best are painfully mixed in character. Therefore spiritual, moral, cultural, and social advance is limited and variable, and its triumphs inherently insecure.

Thus the ancient Hebrews excelled at religion, but not at art; the Greeks at art, but certainly not at religion. The social structure of the Middle Ages gave man a secure place in society at the expense of freedom, the society of today freedom at the expense of contentment and security. The Renaissance produced magnificent works of art, literature, and architecture from a society stained with cruelty and corruption. The modern Western world is much more humane and kindly, and this has contributed greatly to the sum of human happiness, yet one's heart sinks as the tawdriness and vulgarity apparently inseparable from the machine age goes all around the world. And so examples might be multiplied, in personal life as well as in communal. It is not that human striving achieves nothing, for the spirit of man has accomplished wonderful things. Yet as he moves forward in one activity he slips back in another. There is a principle of limitation and frustration woven into the very fabric of human affairs.

Nor are the feats of man secure. Long centuries can build up great civilizations, but civilizations can also decline through loss of political nerve, through social corruption, through invasion, or merely from the effect of soil erosion. As the Christian looks upon this world process his heart does not fail. The moral of all is not that God repudiates social endeavor, or that social endeavor is not worthwhile. It is simply that man is not to put his trust for the final and secure salvation of the world order in human endeavor toward educational, cultural, social, and political advancement. The ideal society is to be set up by the power of God.

It is fruitless to argue whether the dropping of the atom bomb was a greater or a lesser crime than the sack of Magdeburg. There is no way of comparing either the human suffering or the human guilt. It is simply that the age of science and mechanical production can work both human welfare and human destruction on an unparalleled scale. We are assured by some men of science that it is now technically possible to extinguish the human race. The Christian does not pretend to more wisdom in these matters than other men, and it is difficult to know the truth. We suspect that when publicists declare "war would be the end of civilization" they really mean "war would be the end of comfortable urban civilization, replete with automobiles, washing-machines, and television." The Christian is not so easily shaken in his faith. On the one hand, he does not argue, "This is too horrible to think of. It cannot happen here!" In a world which crucified the Lord of glory crimes sufficient to consume civilizations both can happen, and have happened. Historical experience shows that God does not suddenly step in to prevent man reaping the recompense of human pride and folly. The real but horrible possibility that the climax of man's knowledge and power should indeed be used to accomplish the most universal of all crimes is exactly what the Bible symbolizes when it speaks of the revealing of Antichrist.

Yet the Christian, who takes this most severe and realistic view as to the possibility of all manner of evil in a sinful world, also has a spring of hope not known to other men. The natural process of human affairs is that one sin makes another easier, one wrong provides the incentive for another. If this were all, final ruin would be inevitable. However, if this were all, final ruin would have taken place long ago! The Christian holds that if human affairs had been left to the natural process of development, sin would have in past centuries produced sin to such effect that the world today would be nothing but a squalid and brutal shambles. That this is not so indicates that there is "a power not ourselves that makes for righteousness."

God providentially overrules the sins, crimes, and follies of humanity so as either to rescue man from the utmost consequences of his own actions, or else to work his moral discipline through those worst consequences. Therefore by divine intervention the world order holds together. This is why the Christian, alone of all realistic thinkers, can look upon the future even in this perilous day with a sober measure of hope. Discreet statesmanship, moved by fear of awful consequences, may skirt around one international confrontation, and another, and another. Yet some fool is bound to press the button in the end! This is the most that the worldly-wise can rationally hope for—because he forgets the sovereignty of God.

The processes of human development take place within the overriding context of divine intervention. As man matures in power his wickedness flowers, but the purposes of God bear fruit as well. The ideal society is therefore not to be built by the power of man alone. It is the work of the majestic power of God. This is what is symbolized in the doctrine of the millennial kingdom. The biblical doctrine is to be taken seriously as reputable theology. It describes a real divine act. Nevertheless, it must not be forgotten that the biblical doctrine is a symbolic one, and as such is to be understood.

V. Human Destiny

A. Eternal Life

> Thy love I soon expect to find,
> In all its depth and height;
> To comprehend the Eternal Mind,
> And grasp the Infinite.

As we turn from the Christian hope for the world order to the Christian hope for the child of God we take up again the theology of the life of grace, and continue it through the gates of death. The broadest term for the gift of God to man is eternal life (John 10:28, 17:2; Romans 6:23; 1 John 5:11). It is unfortunate that this phrase is so often misunderstood. Eternal life is not simply the survival of death, to an existence of endless duration. This would be a very mixed blessing, even though the human mind shrinks naturally from the thought of passing out of existence. Eternal life is the life of the heavenly sphere, or to put the matter in a more distinctively Christian and personal manner, it is life in fellowship with God (John 17:3; 1 John 1:2).

Eternal life is a present possession. It is something which man now has, if by faith in Christ he is joined to God, not something which he hopes to possess only after death (John 3:16, 18, 6:54, 10:28; 1 John 1:2, 5:11,

13). Thus in a true sense the Christian believer is already in possession of heaven and the gifts of the age to come (Luke 10:20; Philippians 4:20; Hebrews 6:5). The central point of Christ's original gospel of the kingdom was that the blessing which had been so long expected was in Him now granted (see pp. 44–46). Yet paradoxically, what He has already granted is but the first installment, and token of good faith, of the fullness of God's gift in the day of the Lord (Romans 8:23–25; 2 Corinthians 1:22, 5:5; Ephesians 1:13, 14).

Here again is an example of the master principle of the continuity of the spiritual order. The ultimate ground for the biblical and Christian hope of a personal life of blessedness with God beyond the grave is the same as that which prompted the faith of the Hebrews to evoke the hope of resurrection. It is an act of faith in the goodness of God. By way of comparison, let it be imagined that an artist is at work. He lavishes all his genius upon a piece of great creative art, and then, before the paint is dry, he thrusts it into the fire and starts to paint again. Every picture is thus destroyed; not the rough sketch only, not the imperfect attempt, but the perfect work— and for thousands and thousands of times. One would say, "This artist is no true artist. He has a divided personality, for he destroys that which it is his very nature to create. He is a maniac!" If what the Christian believes about God be true, it is impossible to imagine that He can be like that. It would be a denial of His own rational constancy for God to call into being His sublimest work, and then, before the work was finished, to annihilate it.

Yet man is not God's creative art. He is God's created child. Suppose a couple were to say to one another, "It is a nuisance to have this child about the house. Had we not desired; he need never have been born. Therefore he is at our disposal, to do with what we will. We will put him in an orphanage, so we can enjoy our liberty." Such would be a profoundly immoral act, because freely to procreate a living personality which can be loved, and which requires love for his happiness and welfare, brings upon the parents a binding moral obligation to bestow that love.

So God need not have made us, and we are at His absolute disposal. Nevertheless He has made us, and made us capable of knowing and loving Him, and made us so that we have no true blessedness apart from fellowship with Him. Therefore, it would seem that the sovereign God, who has created us men and redeemed us in Christ, has freely taken upon Himself a binding moral obligation, if He indeed be good, to give that blessedness of which His children are capable. To raise the hope of fellowship with Himself by the Christian experience of this life, and then inevitably, universally, and utterly to disappoint this hope by annihilating man at death would be inconsistent with what God has shown Himself to be in Christ. The affirmation of Christian faith is that the constancy of the spiritual order requires that the gift of life with God in this world shall continue to its proper and rational fulfillment. Eternal life, therefore, is life of such a quality now that it will continue beyond the grave. As the poet puts it:

> Thou wilt not leave us in the dust:
> Thou madest man, he knows not why;
> He thinks he was not made to die;
> And Thou hast made him: Thou art just!

It will be noticed that the conception of eternal life largely answers to the Greek presentation of the Christian hope. It reflects the idea that the higher side of the life of man, in which his faculties of mind and spirit are taken up in fellowship with God, is a present possession of an imperishable character. Therefore it is not surprising that this doctrine is particularly prominent in the Johannine literature. However, the doctrine of eternal life is not inconsistent with the Hebraic conception of resurrection. That future act of God can be regarded as the fulfillment of the present possession (John 6:54).

B. Immortality and Resurrection

The personal Christian hope as presented in Greek terms is also well expressed by the use of the word "immortality." This speaks of the imperishable character of the spiritual personality of man, which continues its sentient and moral life after the death and decay of the material body. This doctrine has been accounted a legitimate part of Christian theology, even though it is not altogether the biblical way of expression. It has several advantages. It accords with the conviction, which to most thoughtful people appears a reasonable one, that the mental and spiritual aspects of man's life are of a nobler order, and more significant for the evaluation of his personality, than are the bodily and material. Furthermore, it harmonizes with the doctrine of the communion of saints. The faith that departed Christians are at this moment alive to nobler powers, and in a blessed existence of communion with God, excludes the erroneous notion that they are in a state of suspended animation, awaiting the resurrection, as well as the inadequate idea that they are in a frustrated and limited Sheol-like existence (Luke 23:43; Philippians 1:23; Revelation 7:13–17). The doctrine of immortality makes it possible to affirm in an unqualified manner that the departed saints are in spiritual fellowship with the Church Militant (see p. 133).

However, justice must also be done to the other side of the Christian tradition, and to the spiritual values preserved in the biblical doctrine of the resurrection of the body and the general resurrection, even though it requires a certain degree of mental effort if the modern man is to carry himself back into the categories of thought employed. The guiding principle is that the ancient Hebrews did not look upon man as twofold, composed of a nonmaterial "soul" or "spirit" dwelling in a material body. Still less would they have found it natural to say that the nonmaterial "soul" was "the real man." To the Hebrew, man was a unitary organism. That which we so naturally separate in thought as "body" and "soul" was not separated. Just as the body of a man without "the breath of life" was not a man, but a corpse, so by parity of reason, a disembodied spirit was not "the real man," but the shadow of a man, a mere ghost.

Once this background of ancient thought is granted, it is natural for the triumph of man over death to be spoken of as "resurrection." Thus the Jewish hope was that at the Day of the Lord the spirits of the departed would be released from their dim existence in Sheol and reunited with their risen bodies. They would again be fully and entirely alive. In the time of our Lord the more conservative Sadducee priests rejected this relatively late development of doctrine, but otherwise it was generally accepted among the Jews (Mark 12:18–23; John 11:24; Acts 23:6–9). Thus the intention of the biblical doctrine of resurrection is strongly to affirm that the man who will be alive at the day of God's triumph is not to be thought of as a pale ghostly copy of the man who lives now. Christian doctrine knows nothing of the "spiritualist" expectation of mere "survival," and the survival of a somewhat disordered or reduced echo of the personality. "The resurrection of the body" symbolizes the conception of "the whole man alive again," complete in every vital faculty. The implication is that the Christian believer need not fear that the life of heaven will be a somewhat rarified and chilly existence, "all passion spent." We will be more fully alive then than now.

However, in order to symbolize this truth it is not necessary to insist that the resurrection of the body must be interpreted as the mysterious reconstitution of the actual material and physical frame in which man has lived. In his great chapter St. Paul wrestles with this very point, and apparently seeks to restate the traditional Jewish doctrine of resurrection in light of the one resurrection which had actually taken place. In raising Christ from the dead God had set His seal upon the general idea of resurrection as triumph over death, and also had modified and spiritualized the expectation (see pp. 98–99). Christ's resurrection body was a "glorified" body which truly corresponded to the purely physical body which had died, and which yet transcended it. St. Paul affirms that this will be the case also with the human body at the general resurrection, though to express himself he has to employ the somewhat paradoxical phrase "a spiritual body" (1 Corinthians 15:35–54).

The two sides of this Christian tradition, the belief in immortality and in resurrection, are to be reconciled by the doctrine of a future life which is not purely static. It is the Christian faith that the departed are fully alive, and that the dead in Christ even now rejoice before Him, and serve Him with nobler powers. However, it can hardly be the case that at the moment of death the development of the soul is suddenly arrested. We may believe that there is still room for man, in ever fuller response to the grace of God, to be changed "from glory to glory" (2 Corinthians 3:18). We must be cautious in speculation, and not seek to know the unknowable. We cannot affirm positive doctrine beyond Scripture, and it is to be remembered always that the scriptural teaching is symbolic. However, general Christian tradition does allow the position that the life beyond the grave is not static. The dead in Christ are already in a state of spiritual well-being, and useful in God's service, and yet there is the mysterious prospect of bliss still greater, and service more noble, when God brings to its final culmination His good purpose for the whole creation. This idea is symbolized in Christian theology by the doctrine of a present paradise, and also of the general resurrection at the last day. Thus the symbols of present immortality and future resurrection are complementary one to another.

Summary of Divergence: Doctrines of Human Destiny

a. Ancient and Eastern

In the Jewish background of the Church the idea was known that the departed might have to undergo discipline on account of past sins, and that the prayers of the faithful might help them in this (2 Maccabees 12:42–45). It is not surprising, therefore, that this same idea is voiced by some of the ancient fathers of the Church. The Eastern, or Orthodox, Church has continued conservatively, remaining more or less on this ground. It teaches that the souls of the faithful departed, who may not have had occasion fully to bring forth the fruits of repentance in this life, will continue in discipline and spiritual growth in the unseen world. The prayers of the Church, particularly at the Eucharist, can assist them in this. Philosophically minded Orthodox theologians have guarded against the notion that this purgatory is in a "place," or that the purging "fire" is a physical flame.

b. Roman Catholic

The Roman Catholic Church has developed from the above simple teaching to a much more elaborated doctrine of purgatory. The basic principle is that those who are in a state of Christian grace must demonstrate penitence for their sins by the due performance of penance, or disciplinary punishment. This leads to divine forgiveness. Those who are not able in this life to perform sufficient penance to secure the discharge of all their sins must make up the balance by undergoing the remedial punishment of purgatory before they are admitted finally to heaven. In this discipline they can be assisted by the prayers of the Church, particularly at the Mass. It is to be noted that this is not a doctrine of a "second chance" for those who have died in wickedness or unbelief. Those who die in the *mortal* sins which separate the soul from God, such as pride and unbelief, are irrevocably lost. It is only those departed in a state of grace, and who are on the sure road to final salvation, who are admitted to purgatory to make amends for their lesser, or *venial,* sins.

This doctrine clearly provides a wide scope for spiritual discipline and development in the unseen world (Matthew 12:32; 1 Peter 4:6). The general assumption of Roman Catholic teaching is that some period in purgatory is the destiny of the general body of believers. The great and illustrious saints, however, who have died full of the good works produced by grace, may go straight to heaven. Infants dying unbaptized cannot be admitted to heaven in the fullest sense, but exist in a state of relative happiness. Traditional Roman Catholic teaching has often spoken of purgatory as though it were a "place" of purging "fire," and its remedial discipline as occupying a period of "time." This language of popular piety is, however, more authoritatively and reliably regarded as symbolic.

c. Protestant

Classic Protestantism reacted strongly against the Roman Catholic doctrine of purgatory, and has in general affirmed that at death all souls go immediately either to heaven or to hell (Luke 16:26; Hebrews 9:27). The basic theological reason for this is that the Roman Catholic doctrine of purgatory answers naturally to the conception of "salvation by grace and the merit of good works." The opposed Protestant principles of "salvation by grace alone," and "justification by faith alone" would appear to exclude the principle of meritorious remedial suffering, and therefore the notion of purgatory. Some would maintain, however, that what is excluded by these Protestant principles is not so much the idea as such of remedial discipline and spiritual growth in the life beyond, as the notion that the merit of remedial discipline can atone for the unresolved guilt of venial sins. The latter idea is clearly denied by Protestant principles.

However, it can hardly be doubted that the wider popular Protestant abhorrence of the very idea of purgatory was due to its association with Masses for the dead, and indulgences for the benefit of souls in purgatory. These practices undoubtedly became the occasion of widespread abuse, both devotional and financial, in the period leading up to the Reformation. Protestant feeling reacted very strongly against these abuses and tended to shun everything apparently associated with them, even indirectly. It is not surprising, therefore, that Protestantism abandoned the traditional belief in purgatory.

d. A Constructive Statement

It is necessary to approach the doctrine of human destiny in the unseen world with a measure of reverent reserve. Our knowledge is derived in part from general spiritual probabilities, which are not more than probabilities, but still more from Scripture. Yet is it not always clear how far the Scripture in question is to be interpreted literally, and how far symbolically, as a parable of truth.

Those who do not accept the doctrine of purgatory, either in its simple form, or in its developed and Roman Catholic form, still have to admit that there may be some difficulties attendant upon the total abolition of the conception of remedial discipline and growth in the unseen world. The abandonment of the doctrine of purgatory appears to consign to eternal damnation all those who are not saintly enough to go immediately with rejoicing into the presence of God. A thorough-going Augustinian is indeed prepared to accept this stern result. Just as popular Roman Catholicism has worked upon the general presumption that the destiny of most ordinary people in the nominally Christian community is the pains of purgatory, and afterward Heaven, so the assumption of some schools of evangelical teaching has been that all those who are not "soundly converted" are lost. This implies the damnation of the great majority of the human race (Matthew 7:13–14). This in turn is a conclusion so fearsome that the mind of the average humane person refuses to take it altogether seriously. The reaction has been the spread of that prevalent, sentimental, and delusively comforting notion that all tolerably decent folk go straight to heaven, and quite apart from any genuinely devout Christian discipleship. This is to short-circuit the whole Christian faith, and to produce that "modern man who is not worrying about his sins."

It is not easy to strike a judicious balance in this matter. There is little explicit direction from Scripture, which perhaps indicates that this is a matter of speculation in which it ill becomes the Christian teacher to be too exclusively dogmatic. The parable of Dives and Lazarus (Luke 16:19–31) perhaps gives us a glimpse into the mind of our Lord. Christ both speaks most seriously of "a great gulf fixed" between the morally careless and the hope of salvation, and also significantly places the torment of Dives in Hades, the abode of the departed awaiting the resurrection, and not in Gehenna, the place of the finally lost (v. 23). Already there seems to be some stirring of compunction in his formerly hardened heart, and some thought for the welfare of others (v. 28). All this, moreover, is the imagery of a parable. It is not systematic theology, nor even the raw materials for systematic theology, but a guide to practical devotion. We suggest that the Christian teacher who follows the doctrine and spirit of Christ will warn men that there is a most dreadful judgment awaiting the morally and spiritually careless, but he will also allow himself to hope that the very rude awakening of the unseen world may quite possibly be the occasion of an awakening of many to penitence, faith, and righteousness. This is not the doctrine of "a second chance." There appears to be no basis for this hope either in Scripture or in logic. There is no ground for supposing that those who have deliberately turned away from Christ in this life will be able to turn to Him in the next (see p. 264). Yet this is not really the problem.

The number of those is small who, like Judas, have clearly faced Christ, and then unaccountably turned from Him in deliberate apostasy. The burden upon Christian thought is the vast company of those who have apparently passed through life without ever making a clear decision, for Christ or against. Many of these are perhaps Church members and Church attenders of a sort, through social habit or a vague instinct that this is "right." They are the multitudes of kindly, decent folk, who have sincerely intended to stand for the right, yet who by preoccupation, confusion, or apathy have failed effectually so to do. Here is the real moral and spiritual problem of the world, for most of the human race is in this condition.

When these souls pass into the clearer vision of the life beyond, there will be stripped from them all those preoccupations which have enabled them so easily to shuffle through their days on earth without ever making a decision. Then there will surely be a rude awakening indeed, and pangs of remorse! And it is by no means inconceivable that many of these will then discover, in that remorse, that passing gleams of Christian truth which they had before accepted, and faint kindlings of Christian resolve which they had entertained, will have some degree of hold upon them. This may very well be the beginning of spiritual discipline and of spiritual development. It would seem that this may be a reasonable view of the destiny of most ordinary folk after death. Perhaps their immediate lot is neither that highest bliss which will be the reward of those who on earth have made it their joy to love and serve Christ, nor the pains of everlasting damnation, but a state of growth. Yet this does not necessarily involve the Roman Catholic doctrine of purgatorial suffering as penance.

One proviso is, however, to be made in this doctrine. It should not be presented as though one would terrify men and women into good ways. Here was in fact the abuse which destroyed the spiritual repute of the common medieval doctrine of purgatory. In the end men came to feel that their ignorant fears had been unfairly exploited, and they rebelled. One of the mysteries of Christian experience is that in Christ the goodness and the severity of God are eternally conjoined (Romans 11:22). As the serious-minded Christian turns his mind to the God of holy love who has come to him in Christ, he is bound to feel that his moments of religious realization bring to him life's most searching pain. He can probably assure himself that he has played his part not too discreditably as a citizen, a businessman, a Churchmember, as a husband and father, considering always the limitations of human nature. But what of his standing as a child of God? What man dare seriously consider the wealth of the offered love of God, and the utter poverty of his own response? This is a thought to chill the spine with apprehension! Yet by a strange alchemy, that moment of serious contemplation also brings into the believer's life the joy which in all human joys is the very spirit of joy: "That unsparing Judge loves *me,* and in Christ suffered for me, and has freely forgiven me! Therefore I must fear— and yet I need not fear." If this be so now, it will surely be more so in the life beyond. Men must be seriously warned that the pain of realization will be greater. Yet they may be comforted that to those who have sought to love Christ, the conjoined bliss will be the greater too. Therefore discipline and growth beyond the grave are to be taken seriously, but not dreaded, for man's hope of standing boldly in the presence of God rests ultimately in divine grace, and not in human performance.

C. *Judgment*

The Bible teaches that judgment is both present (John 3:18–21, 12:31), and future (Matthew 12:41; Romans 14:10; Hebrews 9:27, 10:27). There is no true inconsistency between the two sides of the Christian tradition, for here is another example of the principle of the continuity of the spiritual order. It is a dreadful fact of experience that to see the good and deliberately to turn from it makes it for the future harder to see what is good, and to do it when it is seen (1 Timothy 4:2). On the other hand, to respond to grace and to go through the open door into the good, opens the door into a higher good choice and makes it easier to go. In the present spiritual order both good and bad choices tend to confirm themselves. The conclusion of this is plain. If this process of choice continues in a consistent and rational manner there is inherent the dreadful possibility that those who continue long enough to resist the drawing of grace will finally confirm themselves in evil. They will then no longer be able to see the good as good when it is presented to them, but will account it to be evil (Mark 3:28–30). And even if they could see the good, they would no longer have any desire to turn to it. By parity of reason there is inherent in the process the possibility also that those who continue fully to open their hearts to grace will arrive at a condition when they will be able fully to see the good, and fully to love it when they see it, and to do the good with a will no longer in the slightest divided. They will then be confirmed in good. God will have given them the power to live sinlessly. Thus the process of present choice leads to a climax in a final and all-decisive choice. Present judgment leads to the last judgment.

Divine judgment is not an act of arbitrary power. The sovereign Lord certainly has the right to punish breaches of His holy law (Romans 3:5, 6). However, it must be understood that the God of universal love punishes for man's own ultimate good, and not just to vindicate the divine dignity or to compel man to acknowledge the divine sovereignty (Hebrews 12:5–10). Therefore God's judgment upon sinners is not an external penalty of suffering which God of His sovereign will attaches to man, but which, if He willed, He could quite rightly forego. The punishment for sin is something which man's free choice of evil makes inevitable, because the world is God's moral order. The final judgment upon the impenitent sinner is not, then, a last act of divine vengeance, but a culmination of the principle of the continuity of the moral order.

This is seen in the New Testament usage of the phrase "the wrath of God." "The wrath" is thought of as a spiritual entity existing in the world, as it has been created by the holy God. It represents the principle that out of self-centered and rebellious pride, which is idolatry, and its fruits in sinful action, come the inevitable effects of moral degradation and final

utter ruin (Romans 1:18–32). Thus it is "the wrath of God," for it exists
in God's world, and He is responsible for it (Ephesians 5:6). Nevertheless,
the New Testament avoids making the verb active, and saying "God is
angry," because in the last resort "the wrath" is not something which God
does. It is something which *happens,* and God's positive action in the
matter is to rescue from it those who will be rescued. It is not the case
that after a certain limit of forbearance God will not accept repentance.
When man has finally hardened himself he cannot repent, even though
God call him with all His grace.

The climax of the Last Judgment differs from the present process of
judgment in two important ways. In the first place, the present judgment
is a secret judgment, known with certainty only to God. The men of this
world judge right and wrong largely by the standards of outward conventional morality, and by canons derived in the main from prudential considerations of the preservation of human society. This is a dim and shifting
standard. Therefore the world goes on its way substantially ignoring the
judgment of Christ upon its affairs, and putting Him to an open shame.
Also, the Christian understands that he has no right to judge his neighbor,
for he cannot know how clear light his neighbor has, and what is the
strength of his temptations. Only God, who can see into the heart, can
decide who is the righteous and the unrighteous man, and who is in a state
of salvation (Matthew 7:1; Romans 14:13; 1 Corinthians 4:5). The Last
Judgment, however, will be an open judgment, of which all men, however
unwillingly, will be compelled fully to take account (Matthew 25:31–32;
Romans 2:5–10, 14:10; 1 Corinthians 3:13; Revelation 20:11–13). In the
second place, the present judgment is a provisional judgment. Even the
obstinate sinner, if he repent, can yet find mercy (Ezekiel 33:10–11; 1
Timothy 1:12–15). And it is possible for believers to fall away if they do
not keep themselves in the means and discipline of grace (1 Corinthians
9:27, 10:12). The judgment of the last day, however, is a final judgment,
and seals man's fate forever (Matthew 25:46; Revelation 22:11).

God's action of judgment is taken according to man's attitude to Christ.
Thus Christ is the mediator of judgment (John 5:22; Romans 14:10;
Revelation 22:12). This is true of the present judgment. Men are now
being judged according as they accept or reject Christ (John 3:17–21).
This process will come to its due climax of open and final judgment when
Christ appears in glory (Matthew 25:34–36, 42–43; Mark 8:38; Revelation
14:14–16, 20:4).

The question has been discussed whether man's final acceptance with
God at the Last Judgment depends on faith in Christ or on "good works."
This chiefly depends on what is meant by these terms. Clearly, the moral
character and Christian service even of the holiest of men cannot of themselves win acceptance with the holy God, for the utmost man can do is

only that which is his duty, and none has done this (Luke 17:10). In this sense, man's sole hope for an unashamed appearance before God at the judgment is divine grace, made known to those who are in Christ (Romans 8:1). Nevertheless, men are judged at the end not according to the profession of faith they have made (Matthew 7:21–23), or even by the "experience" they have enjoyed, but according to the constructive response they have made to the offer of grace. God judges men as they really are in character, and life, and deeds (Matthew 25:31–46; Revelation 14:13, 20:13). In this sense, although man's initial acceptance with God, or justification, is by faith alone (see pp. 225–26), his final acceptance is by the works of love which faith brings forth (1 John 4:17–19). The two errors to be avoided are that man can and must earn his final salvation by his own merits, apart from grace, and that he can be vindicated at the Last Judgment apart from a thoroughly changed life and character.

1. HELL.

> Every eye shall now behold Him
>   Robed in dreadful majesty;
> Those who set at nought and sold Him,
>   Pierced and nailed him to the tree,
>   Deeply wailing,
>   Shall the true Messiah see.

In Jewish eschatology Gehenna was the name given to the place of punishment of the finally lost.[5] This vivid and somber symbol was, like so much of current imagery, adopted by our Lord (Matthew 5:29; Mark 9:43–48). Traditional Christian theology has therefore drawn the tragic logical consequence from the fact of a final and irrevocable divine judgment. This consequence is the doctrine of hell, the everlasting perdition of the finally impenitent.

Clearly, this is a doctrine of almost inconceivable dreadfulness, which is almost impossible for the thoughtful mind to accept, were it not that the difficulties implicit in rejecting it are so great. Christianity can be made to appear repulsive, and even ludicrous, to sensitive minds through an incautious zeal in stating the doctrine of hell. It should therefore never be spoken of "unadvisedly, lightly, or wantonly," but with every care taken to avoid misunderstanding. In the first place, like all doctrines of the unseen world, this teaching is framed in symbolic language which, though it expresses an important fact, is not to be taken materially. Nor is it needful to suppose that our Lord, in using on occasion the vivid symbolism of Jewish

---

[5] The name "Gehenna" comes from the Vale of Hinnom, outside Jerusalem, where in times of idolatrous backsliding obscene and barbarous human sacrifice had been offered. Ever afterwards it was regarded as a place of ill omen, and the name was adopted in Jewish apocryphal literature for the place of punishment of the wicked. It is not the same as Sheol, Hades, the abode of the departed who await judgment.

eschatology, took it in a crude and material sense. Thus hell is not a "place," nor a place of "fire."

Second, we should follow our Lord in stating the doctrine with great reserve. Christ spoke as one who believed in the dreadful possibility of the endless loss of the finally impenitent, but He was decidedly not a "hell-fire preacher." In the background of our Lord's mind there plainly lurked a grim and shuddering foreboding of an inconceivable fate awaiting those who finally rejected Him (Luke 17:1–2). Yet it was not His central point of appeal. The chief appeal which Christ made in summoning men to repent and turn to the good was always the goodness of God, and the blessedness of responding to this goodness (Matthew 5:43–48). This is the rightful proportion for Christian teaching and preaching. It is most significant that although the general framework of our Lord's gospel of the kingdom was eschatological, He avoided that note of strong denunciation of God's fiery judgment against sinners, which was so usual and natural an element in the apocalyptic scheme. In nothing does He more clearly rise above the limitation of the thought forms of His background.

Three leading difficulties arise in connection with the doctrine of ever lasting damnation. First it is asked how heaven can be a condition of bliss if the righteous know that some of their loved ones, or indeed, any sentient creatures, are suffering eternal loss. The traditional answer to this difficulty is that the final judgment, and the sentence of damnation, includes the loosing of the ties of nature, so that the former loved ones are no longer loved. The righteous are loosed from the duty of feeling pity for them, and think of them no more. This grim doctrine at least brings home to the mind the horror of sin.

Next it has been objected that the notion of final loss is inconsistent with God's sovereignty. If some souls eternally resist His saving purpose, His plan for the universe remains forever partially marred, and this would be inconsistent with the perfection of His glory. In answer it may be said that this objection depends upon an assumption regarding the divine perfection and sovereign glory, which is not necessarily a valid one. It is assumed that for God to be fully God every creature must submit to His will. The Christian conception is that God's highest glory consists in the loving and willing obedience of all His creatures, and not merely in their obedience. It would not contribute to His glory to compel the finally impenitent to submit, and it is not inconsistent with His sovereignty to permit them forever to continue in the way they have chosen.

The fundamental difficulty is that everlasting punishment would appear to be purposeless because, if there is no hope of it ending, there is no hope for it to prove remedial. It is felt that only remedial punishment is consistent with the conception of the love of God, everlasting punishment being purposeless torture. Here is one of the last dark mysteries of human thought, and no entirely satisfactory answer is possible. One solution which has been suggested is that God will ultimately annihilate the finally impenitent, so as to bring their useless sufferings to an end. Surely this is a matter of speculation, and it is precarious either to assert definitely that this will be so, or that it is absolutely impossible.

There is a certain speculative difficulty to the doctrine of annihilation. The only ground upon which it appears possible to reconcile the goodness of God with the continued existence of man after his fall, in view of the untold wrong, degradation, misery, and cruelty which have flowed from sin, is that the continuance of sin is a tragic necessity if God is to respect and preserve the moral freedom which He has Himself given to man. And this freedom is in turn a necessity if man is to obey God freely and lovingly, as a child and not as a slave. Therefore God's universal love and perfect goodness is more fully vindicated in the creation of the higher order of moral freedom, even at the price of the possibility of moral tragedy, than it would have been in the creation of a lower order of mechanical obedience to His laws, though orderly and painless. If God has once decreed this order as the highest and best, it is so to eternity, and He will not alter it because some have proved impenitent. Or to put the matter the other way around, if it is required by God's perfect goodness and universal love that ultimately He annihilate obstinate sinners, we may with all reverence say He ought to have done it long ago!

In so uncertain a realm of speculation it would appear to be safer to abide by the simple word of Scripture, which knows nothing of the ultimate annihilation of the wicked. Nevertheless, we are reminded that the passages which speak so plainly of the endless punishment of the wicked (for example, Matthew 25:46) are symbolic, and we may have some reserve in insisting that these *must* be interpreted literally. The guiding principle is that in the last resort the Scripture is not a book of cosmological speculation, written to answer abstract questions about ultimate human destiny. It is rather a practical book of guidance, spiritual, devotional, and ethical, addressed to man's actual situation. In this situation a doctrine of the unlimited tragic consequence of unrepented sin is more salutary for the soul of man than are more easy-going doctrines, even though the traditional doctrine of hell is accompanied by some speculative difficulties. In the last resort Christian doctrine is not molded by speculative interests, but by care for the devotional and moral life of man. Man does not know all. Life is mysterious. A doctrine is not false because it leaves the mind of man with unfathomable difficulties. Yet this austere scriptural doctrine of the possibility of eternal damnation for the finally impenitent is for man's practical good. And the Christian believes that in the end all God's purposes will be vindicated as good.

2. HEAVEN.

> The dear tokens of His passion
> Still His dazzling body bears;
> Cause of endless exultation
> To His ransomed worshippers;
> With what rapture
> Gaze we on those glorious scars!

The process whereby the free response to grace brings a more effectual drawing of grace, and the choice of good confirms man in the power to choose good, logically culminates in a final and decisive choice for good, which yields up the soul wholly to the sovereignty of grace. This is Heaven, for the final great reward of good is good. In classic phrase St. Augustine struggles for words to express this conception of the final confirmation of the saints in the love of good and of God. "It does not follow that they will not have free choice because sins will have no power to attract them. Nay rather, it will be more truly free, when set free from the delight of sinning to enjoy the steadfast delight of not sinning. For the first freedom of choice, which was given to man when he was created upright, gave the ability not to sin, but also the ability to sin. This new freedom will be the more powerful just because it will not have power to sin; and this, not by its unaided ability, but by the gift of God."[6]

This is the counterpart to the inability of the finally hardened to see the good and to repent. The Last Judgment upon the righteous is freely to be lifted by grace forever above the battle with sin. This is no mere reward of pleasure, however "spiritual," arbitrarily bestowed on the righteous by God. It is the fitting, natural, and inevitable reward for good, in a world which is a continuous and rational moral order. The reward of good is to be made into the man who can fully delight in good, which is to delight in God.

The Christian doctrine is that this created universe is not eternal in existence. The eternity of creation would appear to make the creation necessary in some way to the fullness of the Deity, which would be to infringe upon the absolute sovereignty of God (see p. 25). Therefore it is taught that when the material creation has fully served its purpose as the expression of the goodness and wisdom of God, and when it has been completely restored in the millennial kingdom, it will then pass away. The notion of an end to the present material creation is expressed in typical apocalyptic imagery by the doctrine of the "conflagration" of 2 Peter 3:9–13. However, in this passage this is expected apparently at the Second Advent, and therefore presumably before the millennial kingdom. The obscurity reminds us of the error of seeking to take apocalyptic imagery chronologically.

---

6 *De civitate Dei*, XXII. 30.

More notably, the Revelation of St. John expresses the idea by saying that after the millennial kingdom there is to be "a new heaven and a new earth: for the first heaven and the first earth were passed away" (Revelation 21:1). There is then a description of a permanent and more glorious, and apparently nonmaterial order. However, the essential of the Christian hope is clear. The final blessedness of the perfected is to see God face to face, and forever to join in His worship (Revelation 22:3, 4). Thus the Summum Bonum is the Vision of God. When Christian theology, which is the greatest and most august system of thought which has ever entered into the heart of man to conceive, comes to the limit of its aspiration, and all things go out in mystery, the whole purpose of creation is fulfilled in the gracious promise of our Lord: "Blessed are the pure in heart: for they shall see God."

Readings

Baillie, J., *And the Life Everlasting*. London: Oxford University Press, 1934.
Cullmann, O., *Immortality of the Soul or Resurrection of the Dead?* London: The Epworth Press, 1958.

Indices

Index of Names and Subjects

Index of Scripture References[1]

---

[1] Numbers referring to Bible chapters and verses are printed in roman type; page numbers are in italic type.